Cases on Effective Universal Design for Learning Implementation Across Schools

Frederic Fovet
Thompson Rivers University, Canada

A volume in the Advances in
Educational Technologies and
Instructional Design (AETID)
Book Series

Published in the United States of America by
    IGI Global
    Information Science Reference (an imprint of IGI Global)
    701 E. Chocolate Avenue
    Hershey PA, USA 17033
    Tel: 717-533-8845
    Fax: 717-533-8661
    E-mail: cust@igi-global.com
    Web site: http://www.igi-global.com

Copyright © 2024 by IGI Global. All rights reserved. No part of this publication may be reproduced, stored or distributed in any form or by any means, electronic or mechanical, including photocopying, without written permission from the publisher.
Product or company names used in this set are for identification purposes only. Inclusion of the names of the products or companies does not indicate a claim of ownership by IGI Global of the trademark or registered trademark.

Library of Congress Cataloging-in-Publication Data

Names: Fovet, Frederic, 1966- editor.
Title: Cases on effective universal design for learning implementation
  across schools / Frederic Fovet, editor.
Description: Hershey PA : Information Science Reference, [2024] | Includes
  bibliographical references and index. | Summary: "This book showcases
  Universal Design for Learning (UDL) efforts in both the primary and
  secondary sectors and acknowledges the impact the COVID pandemic and the
  online pivot has had on this reflection and these highlights efforts
  through case studies in both the public and private environments"--
  Provided by publisher.
Identifiers: LCCN 2022024501 (print) | LCCN 2022024502 (ebook) | ISBN
  9781668447505 (hardcover) | ISBN 9781668447543 (paperback) | ISBN
  9781668447512 (ebook)
Subjects: LCSH: Instructional systems--Design--Case studies. | Inclusive
  education--Case studies. | Classroom environment--Case studies. |
  Universal design--Case studies.
Classification: LCC LB1028.38 .C386 2023 (print) | LCC LB1028.38 (ebook)
  | DDC 371.9/046--dc23/eng/20220707
LC record available at https://lccn.loc.gov/2022024501
LC ebook record available at https://lccn.loc.gov/2022024502

British Cataloguing in Publication Data
A Cataloguing in Publication record for this book is available from the British Library.

All work contributed to this book is new, previously-unpublished material.
The views expressed in this book are those of the authors, but not necessarily of the publisher.

For electronic access to this publication, please contact: eresources@igi-global.com.

Advances in Educational Technologies and Instructional Design (AETID) Book Series

Lawrence A. Tomei
Robert Morris University, USA

ISSN:2326-8905
EISSN:2326-8913

MISSION

Education has undergone, and continues to undergo, immense changes in the way it is enacted and distributed to both child and adult learners. In modern education, the traditional classroom learning experience has evolved to include technological resources and to provide online classroom opportunities to students of all ages regardless of their geographical locations. From distance education, Massive-Open-Online-Courses (MOOCs), and electronic tablets in the classroom, technology is now an integral part of learning and is also affecting the way educators communicate information to students.

The **Advances in Educational Technologies & Instructional Design (AETID) Book Series** explores new research and theories for facilitating learning and improving educational performance utilizing technological processes and resources. The series examines technologies that can be integrated into K-12 classrooms to improve skills and learning abilities in all subjects including STEM education and language learning.

Coverage
- Bring-Your-Own-Device
- Classroom Response Systems
- Curriculum Development
- Digital Divide in Education
- Educational Telecommunications
- Hybrid Learning
- K-12 Educational Technologies
- Virtual School Environments

IGI Global is currently accepting manuscripts for publication within this series. To submit a proposal for a volume in this series, please contact our Acquisition Editors at Acquisitions@igi-global.com or visit: http://www.igi-global.com/publish/.

The (ISSN) is published by IGI Global, 701 E. Chocolate Avenue, Hershey, PA 17033-1240, USA, www.igi-global. com. This series is composed of titles available for purchase individually; each title is edited to be contextually exclusive from any other title within the series. For pricing and ordering information please visit http://www.igi-global.com/book-series/advances-educational-technologies-instructional-design/73678. Postmaster: Send all address changes to above address. Copyright © IGI Global. All rights, including translation in other languages reserved by the publisher. No part of this series may be reproduced or used in any form or by any means – graphics, electronic, or mechanical, including photocopying, recording, taping, or information and retrieval systems – without written permission from the publisher, except for non commercial, educational use, including classroom teaching purposes. The views expressed in this series are those of the authors, but not necessarily of IGI Global.

Titles in this Series

For a list of additional titles in this series, please visit: www.igi-global.com/book-series

Best Practices for Behavior Intervention in Special Education
C. Roch Turner (University of Montana, USA)
Information Science Reference • copyright 2024 • 307pp • H/C (ISBN: 9798369305836)
• US $175.00 (our price)

Augmented Reality and the Future of Education Technology
Rashmi Aggarwal (Chitkara Business School, Chitkara University, India) Prachi Gupta (Chitkara Business School, Chitkara University, India) Satinder Singh (Chitkara Business School, Chitkara University, India) and Rajni Bala (Chitkara Business School, Chitkara University, India)
Information Science Reference • copyright 2024 • 297pp • H/C (ISBN: 9798369330159)
• US $175.00 (our price)

Integrating Generative AI in Education to Achieve Sustainable Development Goals
Ruchi Doshi (Universidad Azteca, Mexico) Manish Dadhich (Sir Padampat Singhania University, India) Sandeep Poddar (Lincoln University College, Malaysia) and Kamal Kant Hiran (Sir Padampat Singhania University, India & Lincoln University College, Malaysia)
Information Science Reference • copyright 2024 • 532pp • H/C (ISBN: 9798369324400)
• US $295.00 (our price)

Considerations and Techniques for Applied Linguistics and Language Education Research
Hung Phu Bui (University of Economics, Ho Chi Minh City, Vietnam)
Information Science Reference • copyright 2024 • 241pp • H/C (ISBN: 9798369364826)
• US $245.00 (our price)

Comprehensive Sexuality Education for Gender-Based Violence Prevention
Mariana Buenestado-Fernández (University of Cantabria, Spain) Azahara Jiménez-Millán (University of Córdoba, Spain) and Francisco Javier Palacios-Hidalgo (University of Córdoba, Spain)
Information Science Reference • copyright 2024 • 342pp • H/C (ISBN: 9798369320532)
• US $245.00 (our price)

701 East Chocolate Avenue, Hershey, PA 17033, USA
Tel: 717-533-8845 x100 • Fax: 717-533-8661
E-Mail: cust@igi-global.com • www.igi-global.com

Table of Contents

Foreword xv

Preface xvii

Acknowledgment xix

Section 1
Introduction and Context

Chapter 1
Universal Design for Learning Across Schools in the Global Context: Current
Complex State of Play 1
Frederic Fovet, Thompson Rivers University, Canada

Section 2
Case Studies

Chapter 2
How Universal Design for Learning Transformed My Teaching: An
Elementary Educator's Journey of Implementation 29
*Jana Nicol, New Brunswick Department of Education and Early
Childhood Development, Canada*

Chapter 3
The Enactment of the Principles of UDL in Practice in an Irish Post-Primary
English Classroom: A Snapshot 53
*Margaret Flood, Education Department, Maynooth University, Ireland
Louise O'Reilly, National Council for Curriculum and Assessment,
Ireland
Elish Walsh, Kingswood Community College, Ireland
Sarah Dunne, Kingswood Community College, Ireland*

Chapter 4
A Case Study Examining One School's Trek Towards More Inclusive Practice 80
*K. Alisa Lowrey, University of Southern Mississippi, USA
Kathy Howery, University of Alberta, Canada
Leonard Troughton, University of Southern Mississippi, USA*

Chapter 5
Incorporation of Virtual Tour Guides Into Tourism Class as an Online
Engagement and Retention Strategy 107
  Haley Whitelaw, Fanshawe College, Canada
  Frederic Fovet, Thompson Rivers University, Canada

Chapter 6
Perspectives From an In-Service Teacher UDL Action Research Project 130
  Lauren Tucker, Southern Connecticut State University, USA

Section 3
Wider Conceptual Considerations

Chapter 7
Achieving Genuinely Inclusive Bilingual K-12 Education: Using UDL
to Shift the Bilingual Classroom Irretrievably Away From Deficit Model
Practices 160
  Frederic Fovet, Thompson Rivers University, Canada

Chapter 8
Beyond COVID-19: Innovative UDL Implementation in Early Childhood
Education 188
  Liton Furukawa, Royal Roads University, Canada

Chapter 9
The Shifting Landscape of Digital Accessibility for Students With Visual
Impairments in K-12 Schools: Inclusion, Diversity, Equity, and Accessibility. 219
  Natalina Martiniello, School of Optometry, Université de Montréal,
    Canada

Chapter 10
Navigating the Gap Between Theory and Practice in UDL Implementation
Within the K-12 Sector: Understanding an Ongoing Tension 253
  Pamela Gurney, Thompson Rivers University, Canada
  Frederic Fovet, Thompson Rivers University, Canada

Chapter 11
Aligning Teacher Competencies and Professional Standards to the UDL
Framework Across Two Initial Teacher Training Contexts on the Island of
Ireland 284
> *Tracy Galvin, Ulster University, Belfast, UK*
> *Karen Buckley, Dublin City University, Ireland*
> *Jennifer Roberts, Queen's University Belfast, UK*

Compilation of References 323

About the Contributors 373

Index 376

Detailed Table of Contents

Foreword xv

Preface xvii

Acknowledgment xix

Section 1
Introduction and Context

Chapter 1
Universal Design for Learning Across Schools in the Global Context: Current
Complex State of Play 1
Frederic Fovet, Thompson Rivers University, Canada

This chapter serves as an introduction to the volume. It sets out key information about Universal Design for Learning (UDL) in order to support the reader as they navigate the various narratives of field practitioners and implementers who analyze their journey with UDL in the K-12 sector. The chapter also examines the current landscape in relation to UDL implementation and offers some broad ecological observations as regards the contemporary state of play. It broadens the discussion to the global scale and discusses geo-political divergences that will support the international reader as they connect the material to their own regional context. The chapter highlights certain themes that appear as either facilitators or stressors in teachers' journeys with UDL, themes that will be echoed by the various chapters, and analyzes in more depth within them.

Section 2
Case Studies

Chapter 2

How Universal Design for Learning Transformed My Teaching: An
Elementary Educator's Journey of Implementation.. 29
*Jana Nicol, New Brunswick Department of Education and Early
Childhood Development, Canada*

The purpose of this chapter is to provide a summary of research and recommendations
for implementing Universal Design for Learning (UDL) in the elementary school
setting through a review of the literature (2016 – 2021), one teacher's account
of UDL implementation with elementary school-aged students (K-5) in a fully
inclusive public education system in New Brunswick, Canada, and the findings
of action research undertaken through a partnership between the New Brunswick
Department of Education & Early Childhood Development (EECD) and University
of New Brunswick (2013 – 2015). The goal of the action research was to determine
what tools will help facilitate the implementation of UDL in elementary school
classrooms to improve student engagement. Implementing UDL in the elementary
school setting results in observable gains in inclusion, student engagement, and
academic achievement. Teachers can take a personalized and incremental approach
to UDL implementation guided by CAST's UDL Guidelines.

Chapter 3

The Enactment of the Principles of UDL in Practice in an Irish Post-Primary
English Classroom: A Snapshot.. 53
Margaret Flood, Education Department, Maynooth University, Ireland
*Louise O'Reilly, National Council for Curriculum and Assessment,
Ireland*
Elish Walsh, Kingswood Community College, Ireland
Sarah Dunne, Kingswood Community College, Ireland

Due to the relative newness of Universal Design for Learning (UDL) in post-primary
education in Ireland, there is a lack of examples that show teachers how the principles
of UDL work in practice. This chapter addresses this gap through providing snapshots
of learning, teaching, and assessment through the lens of representation, engagement,
and action and expression. These snapshots take place in two junior cycle English
classrooms. The teachers describe the goal and tasks of the lessons, take the reader
through their UDL planning and actions, and finally reflect—and invite—student
reflection on the lessons.

Chapter 4
A Case Study Examining One School's Trek Towards More Inclusive Practice 80
K. Alisa Lowrey, University of Southern Mississippi, USA
Kathy Howery, University of Alberta, Canada
Leonard Troughton, University of Southern Mississippi, USA

The purpose of this chapter is to discuss an in-depth case study involving one school's mission to increase inclusive practices through the utilization of Universal Design for Learning paired with evidence-based practices. Specifically, a K-9 private school in Canada approached a research team about utilizing a measurement tool to measure the inclusion of students with autism spectrum disorders in inclusive classrooms. After much discussion, the researchers and team agreed upon a year-long course of action to improve services for all students within the school, including those with ASD. A course of intervention was outlined that included pieces such as a needs assessment, training coaches, multiple observation assessments, intermittent coaching, and scheduled professional development. The purpose of this chapter will be to discuss the overall plan designed as well as lessons learned along the way.

Chapter 5
Incorporation of Virtual Tour Guides Into Tourism Class as an Online
Engagement and Retention Strategy 107
Haley Whitelaw, Fanshawe College, Canada
Frederic Fovet, Thompson Rivers University, Canada

Universal Design for Learning (UDL) has been evidenced as a powerful framework for the inclusion of diverse learners in the K-12 sector. Little attention has been paid, however, to the sectors of further education, adult education, vocational training, and all other alternate forms secondary education can take beyond the mainstream or conventionally delivered grades 11 and 12. Yet, it is clear that UDL may have a greater impact in these alternate paths within which learner diversity is significant. This chapter examines the use of UDL within a vocational end of secondary alternate pathway program. It explores specific UDL strategies within a tourism course. The chapter discusses the implications of this case study within the wider global discourse on UDL integration in the classroom. It showcases a reflection around UDL in vocational secondary settings which is growing but still poorly documented in the literature.

Chapter 6
Perspectives From an In-Service Teacher UDL Action Research Project 130
Lauren Tucker, Southern Connecticut State University, USA

Including universal design for learning in graduate programs for in-service teachers is crucial to increasing the application of the framework in practice. This chapter will introduce an action research assignment within an American UDL graduate course and its impact on teacher practice and student learning. Eight case studies across disciplines and levels will be shared. During this process, teachers identified a classroom challenge, developed a UDL intervention, analyzed student data, and shared implications. In-service teacher reflections will be shared on the continued use of a UDL approach beyond their course work and its impact on their teaching practice. The chapter will begin with an introduction to the context of the implementation, investigation questions, methodology, case study presentation, discussion, and conclusion.

Section 3
Wider Conceptual Considerations

Chapter 7
Achieving Genuinely Inclusive Bilingual K-12 Education: Using UDL
to Shift the Bilingual Classroom Irretrievably Away From Deficit Model
Practices 160
Frederic Fovet, Thompson Rivers University, Canada

This chapter examines the pervasive and perpetuated deficit model perspective which informs much of the second language instruction which occurs, in relation to diverse learners—particularly learners with disabilities—in the Canadian K-12 sector. The chapter argues that Universal Design for Learning (UDL) has a key role to play in shifting language teachers away from deficit model views in this context and has the potential to revolutionize the bilingual classroom. The chapter also demonstrates the extent to which UDL aligns seamlessly with communicative method approaches in second language instruction. The chapter explores and analyses phenomenological data drawn from the author's lived experience as a second language teacher over a decade. The chapter considers the repercussions of this reflection on pre-service teacher training, in-service professional development, and leadership practices for inclusion.

Chapter 8
Beyond COVID-19: Innovative UDL Implementation in Early Childhood
Education 188
Liton Furukawa, Royal Roads University, Canada

The pandemic impacts children's physical and mental health, and children are now experiencing increased mental health and physical challenges as a result of COVID-19. This chapter presents Universal Design for Learning as a framework for curriculum reform that will improve children's learning experiences and enable more effective planning towards a more inclusive and interactive education method in early childhood education settings. This chapter focuses on a pilot study employing a mixed-methods design that explored how an innovative UDL model—interactive multi-sensory physical movements (IMPM)—was implemented in a kindergarten in Canada. This research is an evidence-based ongoing interdisciplinary study that highlights this new model with the aim of incurring long term benefits for children, parents, and ECE professionals. This research will also benefit the international ECE industry, scholars, researchers, and informed policy makers.

Chapter 9
The Shifting Landscape of Digital Accessibility for Students With Visual
Impairments in K-12 Schools: Inclusion, Diversity, Equity, and Accessibility. 219
*Natalina Martiniello, School of Optometry, Université de Montréal,
Canada*

Technologies based on universal design foster greater inclusion and proactively embed accessibility for all learners. Today, the digital workflow of students with visual impairments incorporates universally accessible tools used alone or alongside specialized assistive technologies. At the same time, opportunities remain to address persisting gaps in inclusion, diversity, equity, and accessibility within the K-12 landscape. Among these priorities, there is a need to empower educators and administrators with the tools to ensure accessibility in classroom content, embed disability allyship in change management efforts, consider access equity within change measurement outcomes, and contemplate the empowering ways that accessible digital tools can be used to deepen student engagement and diversify the curriculum. This chapter traces the shift from traditional to mainstream digital accessibility for students with visual impairments, outlining how broader issues of inclusion, diversity, equity, and accessibility can inform and advance inclusive learning and UDL implementation efforts.

Chapter 10

Navigating the Gap Between Theory and Practice in UDL Implementation
Within the K-12 Sector: Understanding an Ongoing Tension 253
Pamela Gurney, Thompson Rivers University, Canada
Frederic Fovet, Thompson Rivers University, Canada

This chapter examines the gap which exists between theory and practice in the
K-12 Canadian school system in relation to Universal Design for Learning (UDL)
implementation. It blends the voices of two academics, one examining UDL adoption
from a theoretical and conceptual point of view, and one presenting observations
from the field. The chapter argues that the current academic discourse related to
UDL integration in schools is misleadingly optimistic, when the reality of on terrain
integration is radically grimmer. The chapter argues that this glossy perception of
progress must be unpacked and re-examined as it otherwise is at risk of creating
and perpetuating a false narrative regarding the efforts that remain to be applied in
the area of inclusive design and UDL adoption. The chapter's recommendations
include a more pragmatic and realistic assessment of the work that remains to be
achieved in the field before UDL can be considered in the process of becoming a
reality for teachers and students.

Chapter 11
Aligning Teacher Competencies and Professional Standards to the UDL
Framework Across Two Initial Teacher Training Contexts on the Island of
Ireland 284
>   *Tracy Galvin, Ulster University, Belfast, UK*
>   *Karen Buckley, Dublin City University, Ireland*
>   *Jennifer Roberts, Queen's University Belfast, UK*

Teacher training programs take many forms and vary in duration if it is an
undergraduate or postgraduate option. In addition, there is variation in terms of
the cost involved and the placement opportunities within a school setting and
type. There is also an increase in the debate around inclusion globally, which has
long been included as a core part of the lexicon of educational establishments and
policymakers. A more intentional UDL approach is discussed to a lesser degree,
which does not divert away from a strategy of inclusion, but more intentionally
provides a shared language across providers. In this chapter, the potential of UDL
in initial teacher education is explored across the island of Ireland, which consists
of both the Republic of Ireland and Northern Ireland, by mapping the UDL to both
professional standards and teacher competency frameworks. It highlights how pre-
service teacher training providers can embed UDL into their programs and practice
and support student teachers in an ever-changing learning environment.

Compilation of References 323

About the Contributors 373

Index 376

Foreword

In today's rapidly evolving educational landscape, the development of inclusive education has become a cornerstone of progressive societies. The focus on providing equitable education for every learner, regardless of their diverse skills, talents and needs has gained significant momentum. The adoption of Universal Design for Learning (UDL) in K-12 schools is at the forefront of this inclusive education agenda. UDL is a pedagogical approach that aims to remove barriers to learning by leveraging the principles of flexibility, accessibility, and engagement. Its foundational concept is rooted in the belief that a one-size-fits-all model of education does not effectively meet the needs of every learner. By applying UDL principles, educators can create learning environments that cater to learners' diverse learning styles, preferences, and capabilities.

One of the significant aspects of UDL is its universality, transcending geographical boundaries and becoming an influential force in educational systems worldwide. This, I believe, is due to the generality of the core concepts of UDL, variability is the norm, learning and teaching is contextual, and UDL is goal-orientated.

Written for an international audience, this book, while exploring all the UDL concepts, places an emphasis on the importance of context in the design and implementation of UDL. Each region around the world designs and delivers their curriculum based on their own political, social, and cultural context. And this context matters. It matters in how contextual variables can influence the success of UDL in different cultures. More importantly, in terms of moving away from deficits in the learner to deficits in the environment, the concept of context in UDL allows for educational systems to use the UDL Guidelines.

For example, North American schools have witnessed a significant shift towards UDL implementation due to legislation and policy changes. The United States, in particular, has seen notable progress with the adoption of UDL principles in federal legislation, such as the Individuals with Disabilities Education Act (IDEA) and the Every Student Succeeds Act (ESSA). In New Brunswick, Canada their inclusive education policy is underpinned by the principle of UDL. Across the Atlantic in

European schools, UDL is gaining recognition and prominence through initiatives such as the European Agency for Special Needs and Inclusive Education. The agency has played a pivotal role in disseminating UDL practices and supporting policy development. In response to the United Nations Convention on the Rights of Persons with Disabilities (UNCRPD) many European countries have embraced UDL as a means to address the diverse strengths, talents and needs of their learner populations, foster social inclusion, and prepare learners for active participation in a global society. For example in Ireland further and higher education institutions are collaborating to develop a Universal Design for Education Charter for Tertiary Education while government agencies have been exploring the potential of UDL in K-12 schools for several years. However, even with common overarching goals individual states, schools and educators will bring their own knowledge, attitudes and skills to the implementation process.

To appreciate the impact of UDL, it is crucial to examine its development and implementation in the context of various regions. Thus this book, dedicated to exploring UDL in K-12 schools internationally, is a timely and invaluable resource for educators, administrators, policymakers, and researchers seeking to understand and implement this innovative framework.

As the journey towards inclusive education continues, this book serves as a guiding light, illuminating the path to successful UDL implementation in K-12 schools. Through an exploration of international experiences, readers will gain insights into the challenges, successes, and best practices associated with adopting UDL principles. The lessons learned from these contexts will provide educators and stakeholders with examples of practice, policy approaches, and courses of action in different contexts to cultivate inclusive learning environments that empower all learners to reach their full potential.

May this book inspire and ignite transformative change in K-12 schools internationally and foster a future where every learner, regardless of their unique strengths, talents, and needs can thrive and succeed.

Margaret Flood

Maynooth University, Ireland

Preface

Universal Design for Learning (UDL) has been hailed for over a decade as a revolutionary lens that allows schools to shift their efforts to create inclusive environments, from a medical model lens to a social model approach. In recent years, UDL has gone beyond disability and impairment and is now considered an effective tool to create inclusive classroom provisions for Indigenous students and more widely for culturally diverse learners. There is now a sizable body of literature that details the benefits of implementing UDL in the K-12 sector. There is, however, a paucity of studies and papers examining the strategic challenges of developing UDL across schools and school boards. While the initial concern has been to evidence the pedagogical benefits of introducing UDL to the classroom, the challenges discussed at this current stage by classroom practitioners and school leaders are of a different nature: they are strategic in nature and focus specifically on the organizational hurdles of scaling up these initial efforts and exploratory pilot projects. It is time for the UDL implementation drive in the K-12 sector to go beyond curiosity and to explore sustainable growth and development.

Cases on Effective Universal Design for Learning Implementation Across Schools fills the gap that exists in the UDL literature at present. It offers case studies and practical examples of the reflection which accompanies the systemic implementation of UDL on a wider scale across schools and schoolboards. It examines the full spectrum of ecological implications of this growth in momentum. Covering topics such as deficit model practices, bilingual K-12 education, and UDL implementation, this case book is a dynamic resource for educators and administrators of K-12 education, instructional designers, curriculum developers, pre-service teachers, teacher educators, community leaders, government officials, researchers, and academicians. It also represents a unique example of teacher and practitioner voices being recognized as a groundbreaking beacon for a conceptual reflection on UDL growth and strategic planning. These field experiences represent a rich body of evidence of the practices that make a difference and allow for systemic adoption of UDL across K-12 schools. The process of sharing these experiences constitutes, for the K-12 authors in question, a participatory process which is also, in itself, innovative and precedent setting.

Frederic Fovet
Thompson Rivers University, Canada

Acknowledgment

This volume would not have been possible without the precious contributions of our reviewers from the field. These colleagues lent their expertise, support, and knowledge to assist the editor in reviewing chapters, providing feedback to authors, and giving the volume the pragmatic flavour it has attained. IGI Publishing and the editor are extremely grateful for the time and commitment these reviewers have invested in this project.

Reviewers for this volume included:

Brian Gay, Royal Roads University

Cora-Lee Baker, North Okanagan-Shuswap School District

James Hardiman, New Connaught College of Further Education

Mandy Bonisteel, George Brown College

Richelle Greathouse, University of Prince Edward Island

Robert Wielgoz, Thompson Rivers University

Wendy Kraglund-Gauthier, Yorkville University

Section 1
Introduction and Context

Chapter 1
Universal Design for Learning Across Schools in the Global Context:
Current Complex State of Play

Frederic Fovet
https://orcid.org/0000-0003-1051-4163
Thompson Rivers University, Canada

EXECUTIVE SUMMARY

This chapter serves as an introduction to the volume. It sets out key information about Universal Design for Learning (UDL) in order to support the reader as they navigate the various narratives of field practitioners and implementers who analyze their journey with UDL in the K-12 sector. The chapter also examines the current landscape in relation to UDL implementation and offers some broad ecological observations as regards the contemporary state of play. It broadens the discussion to the global scale and discusses geo-political divergences that will support the international reader as they connect the material to their own regional context. The chapter highlights certain themes that appear as either facilitators or stressors in teachers' journeys with UDL, themes that will be echoed by the various chapters, and analyzes in more depth within them.

INTRODUCTION AND CONTEXT

This chapter serves as an introduction to the volume. It sets out key information about Universal Design for Learning (UDL), in order to support the reader as they navigate the various narratives of field practitioners and implementers who analyze

DOI: 10.4018/978-1-6684-4750-5.ch001

Copyright © 2024, IGI Global. Copying or distributing in print or electronic forms without written permission of IGI Global is prohibited.

their journey with UDL in the K-12 sector. The literature and scholarship on UDL have grown to such an extent that it can be daunting for the novice reader or practitioner. This can be counter-productive in the sense that UDL is all about offering educators a simple, user-friendly, and clear framework with which to streamline their creation of inclusive provisions in the classroom. The chapter will therefore serve as reminder of the core objectives of UDL, of its key characteristics, and of its most urgent implications.

The chapter also examines the current landscape of UDL implementation and offers some broad ecological observations regarding the contemporary state of play. The literature on UDL has grown considerably over the last decade, but most of its content and focus have been centered on evidencing the pedagogical soundness of UDL or its impact on teaching and learning (Capp, 2017). There has been limited writing exploring the strategic implications of UDL as a process of change in educational institutions, or across the K-12 landscape. There is little evidence of best practices in terms of leadership, management of change, administrative support for educators, or sustainable growth. The reason for this is that much of the literature on UDL has been framed within educational theoretical paradigms (constructivism, social constructivism, social model of disability, experiential learning, and critical pedagogy) (Fovet, 2021), rather than within theoretical frameworks that might account for organizational pressures and institutional realities. Instead, this chapter applies to UDL an ecological paradigm which acknowledges the scope of UDL implementation as a process, the breadth and variety of educational stakeholders that it involves, and its complexity as a process of change. Ecological theory records and evidence phenomena from a systems perspective (Vargas-Hernandez et al., 2023). It explores the interactions between these systems, and their influence on actors in the landscape. An accurate assessment of the weight or impact of the multiple actors that are involved in the UDL implementation process on the specific stakeholder or unit that leads the drive for UDL growth will be of key importance in offering a realistic and complete road map for UDL integration.

The chapter, as a result, highlights certain themes that appear as either facilitators or stressors in teachers' journeys with UDL, themes that will be echoed by the various chapters and analyzed in more depth within each. There has been much literature focusing on instructor perspectives in relation to UDL integration, but the literature reflecting and amplifying the voice of K-12 teachers in this area has been limited. There has been scholarly reflection produced by researchers about the realities faced by K-12 school practitioners in relation to UDL adoption, but far less literature emerging from these teachers themselves.

The reasons for this are immediately apparent: teachers, when they engage with UDL, often have limited time and resources to record this experimentation. They may also lack the confidence, familiarity, or support to tackle the process of aca-

Universal Design for Learning Across Schools in the Global Context

demic publication. There is evidence that the academic field ironically frequently discards practitioner perspectives in the field of education, and prioritizes instead conceptual and theoretical reflection, creating a dichotomy between discourse and practice (Resch et al, 2022). There has, historically, indeed been a wide range of UDL initiatives and projects carried out sporadically across the field and across jurisdictions. Little evidence remains, however, of the processes adopted in these projects or of their outcomes. This represents a vast body of practitioner oral history around UDL that unfortunately has never become part of formal scholarship. Yet, much of this work was originally framed and carried out as part of action research and would have rich contributions to make to the literature. There is existing evidence of the wider challenges faced by educators adopting action-research in successfully completing the process of publications of findings and outcomes. As a result, it would be fair to assert that the K-12 teacher voice has thus far been missing from this area of scholarship. This volume has the specific objective of addressing this gap and of recording these narratives.

The chapter also broadens the discussion to the global scale and discusses geo-political divergences that will support the international reader as they connect the material to their own regional context. There is still great disparity in the geo-political spread of UDL scholarship. Global power dynamics mean that practitioner voices on UDL from the Global South are still under-represented (Fovet, 2020). Although there is clear synchronicity between UDL and the objectives of Indigenous education – or even more specifically the Calls for Action of the Truth and Reconciliation Commission Report (TRCC, 2023) -, there is very little literature acknowledging this overlap, or discussing UDL implementation within Indigenous contexts (Vasilez, 2023). More widely, there is also disparity in the involvement in UDL research, in the Global North, between certain contexts: remote communities, areas of low socio-economic development, culturally and ethically diverse communities, and areas of high immigration remain absent from the scholarship that map out the growth of UDL in K-12 communities. It is time to diversify the portrait that the literature offers of UDL implementation contexts, and this volume addresses this need, to some extent, by highlighting local and regional experiences., rather than just overly homogeneous, middle class, urban, and mainstream narratives.

LITERATURE OVERVIEW

This section of the chapter will examine key elements of the literature which should be examined and acknowledged as a background to the reflection carried out within it.

What is Universal Design for Learning?

UDL is a framework that encourages educators to consider the inclusion of diverse learners from a radically different stance than the deficit or bio-medical models prioritized until recently. Much of the professional development literature on inclusion, or resources for teachers, has focused on including diverse learners by focusing on their exceptionality, and by providing individual targeted provisions. The central notions are those of 'special needs' and 'adaptations' (Winzer, 2007). These views, practices, and stances are not just reflected in teacher resources; they are also embedded in policy, funding, and legislative provisions (Tefera et al., 2019). UDL, instead, encourages educators to consider learner diversity as a given and to prepare for this diversity proactively at all stages of the planning (class planning, assessment design, choices of resources, etc.) (Lambert et al, 2023). It can therefore be less daunting for educators than traditional models for inclusion in the sense that it shifts the focus from live, just-in-time, daily individual interventions in class – often cumbersome and resource intensive -, to proactive and planned reflections that happen throughout the year and right along the career of an educator (Ok et al., 2017). UDL, as a practitioner reflection, is indeed proactive, whereas most traditional inclusion models are reactive. They usually involve a form or retrofitting, which is the modification of mainstream provisions (instruction, assessment, or access to resources) after the fact, as an afterthought, when realization occurs that the original choices or the design does not fit the expectations or preferences of all learners (Dumont & Ready, 2023). It is acknowledged currently that retrofitting is much more costly, challenging, stigmatizing, and burdensome than was originally thought in the field (Haft et al., 2023). As a result, there are growing concerns about the sustainability of retrofitting as a format of inclusion in schools.

Social Model Practices Versus Deficit Model Approaches

UDL translates the social model of disability into classroom practices, and it is therefore essential to make readers comfortable with the social model when developing visibility around UDL (Fovet, 2014). The social model of disability positions disability as a construct, and not as an inherent individual characteristic (Lawson & Beckett, 2021). It argues that disability and impairment are different, and that disability is in fact the result of a friction, or lack of fit, between personal embodiments and the way spaces, experiences and products are designed. The social model of disability is a very powerful concept in the classroom, as it immediately shifts the focus away from learner diversity, which is seen as a given, towards the responsibility of the educator as designer. A teacher can design inclusively or not, and thereby include or disable diverse learners in their class (Rose, 1999; Rao et

Universal Design for Learning Across Schools in the Global Context

al., 2014). UDL translates the social model of disability into classroom practices, as it moves away from considering exceptionality as a personal characteristic, and instead sees it as a simple friction between individual embodiments and the traditional and historical design of learning experiences (Piccolo, 2022). It places the onus on educators to design with diversity in mind, in order to create learning experiences that are less likely to clash with learner expectations and preferences (Rose & Meyer, 2002).

Deficit model approaches on the other hand have been pervasive in traditional educational settings. They tend to see learner exceptionality as a personal and inherent characteristic; this may be acknowledged or simply implied within certain assumptions made about the diverse learner. The deficit model sees the exceptional learner as fundamentally lacking abilities or competencies that the traditional learner possesses. It designs instruction and assessment for a textbook, mainstream, or traditional learner and will then seek to identify learners who do not fit this profile and require specific attention. Adaptations or modifications are then made to the traditional classroom experience to address any discrimination diverse learners might experience in this traditional setting. This is often described as a process of 'teaching to the curve' and then subsequently addressing the needs of learners 'on the margins' (Sims & Jerrim, 2022). Deficit model thinking is pervasive in current K-12 settings, first because it is embedded in legislative provisions, but also because it frames funding processes, is predominant in pre-service teacher training, and still very much dominates mindsets in school communities (Dudley-Marling & Paugh, 2010; Valencia, 2010). Evidence of the limitations of the bio-medical model in the field of inclusion is, nevertheless, growing, and practitioners are usually aware of its limitations when it comes to achieving what it seeks to produce: the authentic and seamless inclusion of all learners in K-12 experiences (Jenson, 2018).

What Might it Look Like in the K-12 Sector?

The chapter has thus far discussed UDL in the K-12 classroom in fairly abstract terms. While it is important for practitioners to understand the theoretical grounding of UDL and its conceptual objectives, it will also be important for the reader to fully grasp what UDL might look like pragmatically in the field. There is a breakdown, within the UDL framework, of the inclusive design mindset it encourages educators to adopt into three different dimensions of this design work. This breakdown is immediately useful to practitioners, as many teachers will readily admit they have neither experience with the design process, or training in this area. The notion of inclusive design can therefore seem daunting and complex to K-12 teachers, and it is important to make it palatable, user-friendly, simple, and easy to approach.

The UDL literature argues that there are essentially three dimensions to learning. It argues that inclusive design is about injecting as much flexibility within each of these dimensions, so that the learner can always have the option to work from a strength-based position, using strategies which are their own (Vostal et al., 2023). The inclusive design reflection therefore centers on offering the learner optimal flexibility in terms of (i) how teachers offer information (multiple means of representation), (ii) how learners are encouraged to, in turn, produce content and present information (multiple means of action and expression), and (iii) how the learner is expected to demonstrate engagement (multiple means of engagement).

The educator is encouraged to identify barriers that might be present in their teaching, using a common sense approach to hypothesize about challenges many diverse learners might face. They then identify which UDL principle comes into play with regards to the possible barrier to learning they have spotted. They use the UDL principle in question to integrate optimal flexibility to this dimension of their teaching, in what becomes essentially a lay person's process of redesign. The design solution is then implemented into practice over time, and the educator ideally has the opportunity to carry out some form of learner-check to see whether the design solution has addressed the issue and removed the barrier to learning which had been identified. The breakdown of the process of redesign into distinct steps also normally encourages teachers to focus, in turn, either on instruction or on assessment as a first step. This process is constantly repeated, every time an opportunity arises, in the teacher's year or career, for a return to the design stage (Lohmann et al., 2023). It is understood this is not an overnight process; it is a career long journey of reflection. It should be seen as the consistent application of a reflective lens on practice throughout one's engagement with teaching and learning. The redesign is progressive, but the design solutions become sustainably integrated into the practitioner's toolbox.

Recent Developments of UDL Implementation in Schools

Much of the original reflection around UDL in the K-12 sector has originated out of CAST and is therefore US specific (CAST, 2023). It has taken some time for more targeted scholarship to emergence in Canada, and later in other Global North jurisdictions (Griful-Freixenet et al., 2020). In this sense, it can still be seen as an emerging scholarship or body of practice (Almeqdad et al., 2023; Karisa, 2023). The chapter has already acknowledged that the UDL literature is also significantly ignoring the realities of Global South and Indigenous contexts (McKenzie et al., 2021). The historical origins of the framework can represent a hurdle in its adoption

Universal Design for Learning Across Schools in the Global Context

by teachers, or in terms of the receptiveness of scholars worldwide, as it can still be seen as too focused on US realities and overly context specific. This is changing slowly, however, and there is now an encouraging acknowledgement of more diverse regional realities globally. This volume, in particularly, evidences the diversity of emerging UDL voices across provincial Canadian contexts, as well as in the Irish setting.

Much of the original literature has focused on the pedagogical benefits of UDL for the inclusion of leaners with disabilities. This was a historical focus, as many of the original advocates for UDL have been accessibility specialists (AlRawi & AlKahtani, 2021). It likely that this strong footprint from the accessibility field will continue for some time, and disability remains a central focus of much of the UDL scholarship, but there is emerging work focusing on the use of UDL with international and second language learners (Fovet, 2019). The overlaps between UDL and culturally responsive pedagogy are becoming more apparent (Kieran & Anderson, 2019). There is also some effort to consider the potential of UDL within anti-racism education (Griggs & Moore, 2023). There is also growing interest for UDL within Indigenous contexts, or in relation to the process of decolonization of the curriculum or of classroom practices (Vasilez, 2023). Some dimensions of UDL are nonetheless still ignored by the literature, notably the use of UDL with LGBTQ2S+ learners, and its potential in the inclusion of first-generation learners. It is also apparent that the UDL discourse to date has not adequately addressed the extent to which students facing socio-economic challenges also encounter barriers in the K-12 design.

In terms of specific settings where UDL literature has emerged, it would be fair to assert that much of the early scholarship has focused on the teaching of high school level social sciences, STEM, or English/ literacy (Bray et al., 2023). This is changing and there is growing interest for UDL in middle schools (Ewe & Galvin, 2023), as well as in early education (Brillante & Nemeth, 2022). There was to date an explicit concern among educators in the field that the UDL model might not be suitable for early years, as it was sometimes assumed that young learners might not have the capacity or self reflection required to determine their preferences, have the autonomous strategies necessary to make informed choices, or possess the capacity to become 'expert learners' (CAST, 2022). This view has changed, and the evidence confirms that this approach to learner autonomy is in fact well suited to all ages and grade levels (Rose & Meyer, 2006; OK et al., 2017). The scope of subjects and disciplines which are experimenting with UDL is also widening, and case studies and papers are appearing that discuss UDL in physical education, second language acquisition, art education, and trades-based courses; two of these settings are brought up in chapters in this volume. As a result, the array of learning spaces where UDL is being considered is also widening in terms of range, and this reflection is no longer limited to the mainstream classroom; it now includes science labs, outdoor experiences, art studios, and trades workshops (Kelly et al., 2022).

Resources and Training

The number of resources and training sources available that are related to UDL have grown significantly. This is a welcomed development, but it also gives rise to concerns. There can be some theoretical and conceptual haziness as to what is presented as UDL training material (Capp, 2017; Griful-Freixenet et al., 2020). The COVID pandemic, in particular, has led to increased interest in UDL as a support framework for teachers to redesign their instruction and assessment overnight during the online pivot (Basham et al., 2020). This level of interest has been beneficial to anchor UDL in the collective psyche of teachers, but it has also allowed for the proliferation of material that is not actually authentically UDL in content and flavour. This creates a strategic struggle when it comes to distinguishing between credible and conceptually sound sources and material that is misleading, for teachers who are not yet familiar with the model. This may also be problematic in the sense that it gives ammunition to practitioners who may be resistant to change and who may be reluctant to adopt UDL; the conceptual confusion feeds the level of suspicion sometimes encountered in the field.

There are, however, also encouraging example of more formal training avenues now being offered to practitioners. Some courses on UDL now exist in the post-secondary sector, directed at in-service teachers (QUFE, 2023). Some online courses do exist, but they tend at present to be targeting post-secondary instructors rather than K-12 teachers (AHEAD, 2023; ATU, 2023). Though the emergence of these courses and programs is encouraging, these training resources still appear as insufficient in proportion to the vast number of candidates who may eventually be seeking training or resources. The amount of exposure to UDL in pre-service teacher training remains low, although the importance of early exposure to the UDL principles for pre-service candidates is evidenced as being crucial (Kazmi et al., 2023; Woodcock et al., 2023).

In-service professional development (PD) for classroom practitioners is generally problematic across the field. There is evidence that its provision is poor at best, and generally seen as endemically faulty. PD opportunities are generally too infrequent across the K-12 field; they can also frequently be under-resourced (Ratcliffe, 2013). When they fall outside the scheduled PD days of a school community, there is rarely adequate substitute teacher coverage in place to allow teachers to attend (Gelpieryn, 2023). Even when quality PD is offered for a day, most will observe that it remains conceptual and theoretical, and rarely offers attendees the opportunity to gain ownership over content and to experiment with translating it into practices

Universal Design for Learning Across Schools in the Global Context

in a hands-on way, or windows to interact actively with the speakers (Bergmark, 2023). PD on UDL falls squarely within these critical perspectives and can be said to be unconvincing at present in terms of frequency, scope, or quality. While there is growing focus on the need to integrate more UDL content in pre-service teacher training, it is clear that in-service PD also remains crucial in shifting mindsets in schools. It will be impossible to make headways with UDL implementation until this reality changes.

THEORETICAL AND METHODOLOGICAL STANCE

This chapter offers an introduction to the volume and serves as a basis for the development of the other chapters. Its theoretical stance is grounded in critical theory. Critical theory, as a research paradigm, is focused on identifying the way inequitable power dynamics articulate and weave the social canvas of daily interactions as well as professional relationships (Omodan, 2023). Critical theory seeks to bring these inequities to the surface, and to create awareness and a complex understanding of their impact on marginalized and oppressed minorities and communities (Wee et al., 2023). It eventually encourages the researcher to remain politically engaged with the world that surrounds them, to seek the erosion or elimination of these inequities, and to target transformative action in the field (McCarty & Lee, 2014; Brazant, 2023). Critical theory seems particularly well suited to this context as UDL highlights the inadequacies of traditional and historical school practices in relation to the inclusion of diverse learners. It highlights the urgency of transformation, as diverse learners remain otherwise stigmatized and marginalized by structures that adopt primarily a deficit model view of exceptional learners and are constantly perpetuated (Kasprisin, 2015; Patton Davis & Museus, 2019). Most UDL scholars and practitioners currently operate from a critical theory stance, as the work in this area focuses on shifting organizations and systems away from medical model practices towards a pedagogy that is authentically inclusive, empowering, and student-centered.

The methodological stance which is adopted for the writing of this chapter is a blend of phenomenology and narrative enquiry. The flavour of the methodological reflection is indeed phenomenological in part (Wertz, 2023). Phenomenology focuses on the individual meaning making of individuals, in order to understand their actions and motivations within social spaces (Badil et al., 2023; Dodgson, 2023). It targets and analyzes subjective constructs developed around social phenomena in order to understand and bring to the surface the complex ways individuals position themselves in relation to the social interactions they are confronted with daily (Neubauer et al., 2019; Patel et al., 2023). In the professional realm, and in educational spaces particularly, phenomenology has proven to be a powerful methodology to record and analyze lived experiences (Bonyadi, 2023; Stolz, 2023).

Phenomenology is particularly well suited as a methodological stance in the context of this chapter, as the author examines their lived experiences as UDL consultant and their overview of and insights into the various perceptions that exist in the field around UDL implementation. In their interactions with other stakeholders within this arena, the author constantly encounters personal and group constructs around UDL – and inclusion more generally - as a phenomenon. There is obviously objective evidence available in K-12 education, related to UDL initiatives, that is framed within the positivist paradigm and analyzed from a quantitative perspective (Almeqdad et al., 2023). In many respects, however, the subjective constructs and lived realities are perhaps more pertinent in this area of research as the basis for data collection, as resistance or progress in the management of change is often a perception rather than a question of hard facts. Understanding mindsets will be central and crucial to being able to monitor UDL implementation as a process of change.

The chapter also blends some elements of narrative enquiry (Weis & Johnson-Koenke, 2023). Narrative enquiry seeks to collect, analyze, and explore the story telling of individuals in order to extract emerging themes about the social phenomena these individuals encounter and how they position themselves in relation to these experiences (Clandinin, 2013; Rosen, 2021). The author uses story telling as they set to analyze and showcase some of their lived experience in the arena of UDL implementation across the Canadian K-12 sector. Story telling adds depth, authenticity, and nuance (Meegan, 2023), and is frequently used and borrowed - as a set of methodological tools and strategies – by phenomenological studies (Thompson, 2023).

ASSERTIONS

Uneven Development Across the Field

The way UDL adoption and implementation are fragmented across the field is of concern. Even across specific individual jurisdictions, there is great degree of discrepancy in relation to what is being achieved (LaRon, 2018). Many of the implementation initiatives are individual-led and occur in an ad hoc, uncoordinated way. There is no significant degree of sharing or collaboration occurring between these initiatives. In many ways, there is a process at play where everyone is 'reinventing the wheel' rather than building collaboratively on evidenced outcomes that might be pulled from past experiences. This is a process that inherently contradicts the very definition of the scientific process, which is traditionally seen as a process

Universal Design for Learning Across Schools in the Global Context

of collective building from others' outcomes. Fragmented, isolated initiatives are more likely to fail, and such dead ends are being observed across the sector. This is counter-productive in two distinct ways: the practitioner exhaustion is of concern in itself, in the sense that it means that these projects fail to yield the desired outcomes; secondly, the failure of so many ongoing initiatives inadvertently gives ammunition to skeptics in the field who may be resistant to UDL adoption. The negative impact on UDL growth is therefore two-fold.

Predominance of UDL in Certain Disciplines and Grades

While UDL has gained momentum in the K-12 sector, the majority of initiatives and projects have focused on specific subjects. Most documented and recorded implementation efforts have taken place in relation to literacy and numeracy. Some examples of UDL integration in teaching and learning in STEM have emerged. Other examples of UDL being used in Social Sciences class are also noted. There are, however, many disciplines and subjects which seem to be more resistant to UDL content. Many science and maths teachers will argue that they do not have time to 'get creative' with delivery when the curriculum content is vast and the number of hours of instruction insufficient. There are also some subjects where UDL adoption does not seem congenial, easy, or supported by a sufficient amount of teacher resources: second language classes and labs, art classes, physical education classes, etc. It is clear that there is a need for more tangible examples of what UDL integration might look like in such classroom spaces, which are less traditional in format and characteristics. It is also apparent that proactive efforts need to be deployed to change mindsets in certain subjects; there is indeed no evidence in the literature that UDL might be more challenging to integrate in certain subjects versus others. It all comes down to teacher mindset and perceptions.

There is also some evidence that certain grade levels may be more reluctant to adopt UDL than others. It is generally seen and perceived by the profession as adequate for higher grades when students becoming 'expert learners' appears feasible, as they are seen as more autonomous and reflective on their own learning by high school age. There is, however, no evidence in the literature that UDL might be more challenging to adopt in elementary education. It is likely that more examples of UDL experimentation in elementary and early years education are soon to appear. This volume goes to some lengths to debunk this myth and there are several chapters who offer examples of early years UDL implementation. Here again, the real issue is probably educator mindset and perception rather than real and documented tangible obstacles. These challenging perceptions will only be eroded through proactive efforts to alter educator attitudes and focus on growth mindset.

Concerns over Leadership for Inclusion

Leadership for inclusion has become a buzz word in the last decade but even a surface scratch of the literature in this area reveals just how limited this reflection is. There is a conceptual understanding that a certain type of scholarship is required to support and sustain inclusive provisions in schools. There is also an abstract discussion occurring as to what specific tradition within the literature on leadership might be most pertinent in supporting the implementation of inclusive policies, with transformational leadership, and distributive leadership as strong favourites (Collums, 2023). In the field, however, there is little evidence that a reflective process of alignment has begun to ensure that inclusion efforts are not led in silo and are embedded in a wider transformation of school leadership, This is very much also the case with UDL and there are few examples, either in school communities or in the scholarship, of clear, reflective, and actionable frameworks for a leadership for UDL to emerge.

Absence of Many Stakeholders From the Strategic Reflection

Even where a degree of reflection has begun in relation to management of change, and to strategic and organizational planning with regards to UDL implementation, this brainstorming generally fails to identify all key stakeholders or to involve them successfully. Four key groups of stakeholders have been absent at the table when UDL has been introduced or deployed in K-12 settings. First, parents are often forgotten in this landscape. While parents have been presented as key educational partners for now several decades by the literature, there have been very few efforts to involve them in UDL integration in schools. Often, they are contacted after the fact and may, by then, have misunderstood efforts around UDL, or may have developed problematic perceptions about it. It may be very challenging to undo the negative image that parents form of UDL – or any initiative they have not been kept abreast of, as has recently been argued in relation to sexual orientation and gender identity material within the curriculum (Poitras, 2023).

Students have also thus far been the absent stakeholder. Students, as a body, are rarely considered strategically by teachers or school leaders when developing UDL initiatives. It is often assumed that learners do not have the capacity to understand the rational behind UDL implementation; it is assumed that they will simply 'live' this pedagogical transformation and that they do not need to be aware of its complexity. Nothing could be more far from the truth and there is growing evidence that learners themselves can become suspicious of pedagogical change or transformation, if they do not clearly understand the objectives of this process. It is sometimes referred to as 'transitional friction' (Fovet, 2018). Much work is required in this area to make schools and leadership aware of just how crucial it is to involve learners as a stakeholder body. This is not limited to the K-12 sector. The situation is hardly different in the post-secondary sector, where students and student unions are rarely consulted.

Community, more widely, needs to have UDL introduced to it before implementation can begin. Community is a key partner in the educational relationship. It has an increasing degree of involvement in what is essentially a neo-liberal environment where community is seen as a 'market' (Kent et al., 2023). As a market, community decides to trust or not to trust a service provider such as a school or school board, and does so on the basis of information, communication, and public perceptions. If UDL is not embedded in communication with community, it is doomed to fail as an initiative, as it would then be misunderstood and implicitly rejected by a stakeholder which has considerable say in what succeeds and becomes sustainable and what does not. This is a fact that many industry leaders are highly aware of, but this awareness has not to date been fully developed by educational leaders who tend to underestimate the impact community push back can have on school initiatives.

Another key stakeholder which has been regretfully forgotten of dismissed in the current landscape around UDL implementation is teacher unions. Teacher unions have a key role to play in this process of change, as they often raise very pertinent questions in relation to teacher workload, recognition of new tasks such as redesign, and acknowledgement of the UDL tasks in performance reviews. A fear of push back has motivated school leaders to ignore teacher unions within the UDL discussions. It is unfortunate, as these teacher unions are likely to resist change if they do not feel that their concerns are being heard and addressed. The issue is so problematic that there is a tangible need, currently, for specific training and resources for leaders in this respect. They will need to see modelled and explained explicitly how they are to involve these unions without fear, within the UDL implementation process.

Fears and Needs in Relation to Training and Professional Development

A scan of the experimentations with UDL and of the recent literature evidence specific concerns in relation to the integration of UDL in pre-service training, in in-service PD, or even in relation to resources available for teachers (Rusconni & Squillaci, 2023). There is a significant gap between the discourse on UDL and the training that field practitioners have access to. This is observed globally. It is not just a contradiction in the process of UDL implementation but is actually a factor that threatens to permanently freeze UDL development unless it is tackled proactively and reflectively.

There are broad systemic and societal issues that slow down the process of transformation of pre-service teacher training globally. This process of reform normally includes a dialogue between government and tertiary sector, which is never organic, fast, or comfortable. It also involves a process of accreditation, or re-accreditation, which is usually burdensome, bureaucratic, and resource intensive. As a result, pre-service teacher training is finding it challenging to keep up with specific calls for reform emerging from the field.

In-service PD and the availability of pertinent resources for in-service teachers are also two areas of great concern. PD opportunities on UDL are few and far between. These narrow windows of exposure to UDL are usually perceived by teachers as frustratingly short and abstract. There are few opportunities for hands-on application, due to the very format of the PD delivery, which is usually concentrated into one day events. A further concern in this area is the commercialization of inclusion. The neoliberal flavour currently dominating the field of education has led to the imposition of a business model approach to school management. This leads to a dominant focus on productivity, competitiveness, resource efficiency, and branding. Inclusion does not escape this phenomenon, and UDL has not been left untouched. Although UDL advocacy has been led and energized by non-profit organizations, it has also been subject to very tangible market forces. UDL advocacy has become a business and a very profitable one, where organizations rival for a market share. This has led to inflated PD speaker costs, PD event formats that exclude many field practitioners, and a wide concern over the actual financial accessibility of this scholarship as an area of teacher development.

Strategic Hesitation in Relation to Future and Sustainable UDL Growth

At present, while the literature on UDL grows, there is in the field a very tangible hesitancy and feeling of ominous risk in relation to UDL implementation. Teachers have seen UDL projects come and go, fail and disappear. They foresee no imminent change within school leadership to support this process of transformation. They often feel exhausted and burnt out and may feel that the UDL efforts of advocates is not sufficiently sustainable to continue to impact practice. One of the chapters in this volume in fact discusses the gap that exists in Canada between scholarship and practice in relation to UDL. There is an urgent need for this issue to be resolved and for sustainable forward planning for UDL adoption across schools to take place. This will need to involve all stakeholders concerned and will require an innovative new

Universal Design for Learning Across Schools in the Global Context

funding model – quite distinct from the current targeted envelopes for individual interventions.

OUTCOMES

It is necessary to go beyond the assertions made in this chapter to consider their implications for the field. What are the changes and calls to action that emerge from this scan of the global UDL landscape?

Lack of Broad Strategic Reflection

Much of the work that discusses UDL has thus far focused mostly on convincing school leaders and classroom practitioners of the pedagogical advantages of UDL to create inclusive provisions for diverse learners; it has also focused on showcasing the benefits of inclusive design over retrofitting approaches; it has at times tackled the specific format UDL solutions can take in the K-12 classroom. What has been strikingly missing up to now is a broad and nuanced strategic reflection around UDL implementation as a process of change. There are many instances of sporadic, ad hoc UDL implementation initiatives around the world, driven by individual teachers or communities of practice. A historical scan of many of these initiatives sadly evidences the fact that many have been incapable of growing or of becoming sustainable.

The systemic, cross-institution scaling up of UDL initiatives is very complex. Any process of change across institutions is cumbersome, multilayered, and challenging to steer and monitor; all such processes will give rise to significant factors of resistance from stakeholders (Warrick, 2023). Educational institutions are not an exception (Konakli & Akdeniz, 2023), even if management of change in the field of education has traditionally, and perhaps naively, been seen as an instantaneous, overnight process. UDL implementation has suffered from this phenomenon and has been approached as a one-dimensional process that was simply about pedagogical evidence and desired outcomes. This unidimensional vision of UDL adoption has considerably limited the effectiveness of the scholarship, as it has ignored most of the operational hurdles that too often doom efforts to integrate UDL or amplify its pertinence. This chapter represents a call to action for scholars and practitioners to urgently focus on the organizational facet of UDL adoption, which represents the last frontier, and the shore where many projects unfortunately come to wreck themselves and fail.

Need for Overlap With Dialogue on Sustainability

The previous section of this chapter highlighted the danger of the short longevity of many UDL initiatives. While many UDL projects have failed to survive, a key characteristic of UDL as a framework is ironically its focus on sustainability. UDL represents a sustainable alternative to traditional inclusive frameworks because it shifts practitioners and institutions away from individual remedial interventions focused on retrofitting. Retrofitting amounts to a non-renewable expenditure of resources, from a systems perspective, as it addresses individual needs but does not alter or transform teaching and learning practices. In this sense retrofitting perpetuates a deficit model stance and continues to feed future learner needs because it shies away from addressing pedagogical practice. UDL, instead, directly targets educator practices and therefore ends up reducing future learner needs for individual interventions, since barriers to learning are progressively being eroded for all learners in the classroom. The more UDL is successfully integrated across a school, therefore, the more individual needs are being reduced in terms of accessibility. This also reduces, in the long term, the strain and burden on ancillary and parallel services (adaptions, teaching assistants, referrals, assistive technology requests, etc.).

The overlap between UDL and sustainability needs to be further emphasized and amplified by the literature. Academic scholarship can unfortunately become artificially siloed because of academics' formal training, their adherence to specifically delineated disciplines, and their theoretical stance. This has been the case in relation to the scholarship on sustainability and pedagogy. Pedagogy has rarely examined the issue of sustainability of teaching practices; vice versa the literature on sustainability has thus far mostly focused on operational and resource management. This is changing and the UN Sustainability Goals have squarely positioned education, social justice, and accessibility in the scope of sustainability. UDL advocates, implementers, and scholars will now need to ensure they are creating a bridge between both bodies of work. This will means stepping out of their zone of comfort to adopt more interdisciplinary approaches to UDL implementation. It will also require a sharing of vocabulary and terminology, so as to invite sustainability specialists into the UDL discourse (Fovet, 2021).

Ecological Fragility of the Model Within a Complex Geo-Political Context

This chapter has already discussed the relative absence of strategic and operational reflection around the UDL implementation process. It has highlighted, for example, the lack of leadership reflection around successful growth and development of such initiatives. Leaders are not the only stakeholders absent from this reflection. Teacher

Universal Design for Learning Across Schools in the Global Context

unions need to be considered as they play a key role in the process and can generate resistance of not successfully included. Students also represent a key stakeholder in a successful systemic process of UDL implementation across a school, and yet the learner voice has been entirely absent from this scholarship (Fovet, 2023). Parents and community are generally described in the literature as key partners, and yet they are entirely ignored by the UDL scholarship as well. Administrators and governance are also rarely considered in this process, but they have a considerable impact on the process as well, particularly in the sense that they perpetuate and shape funding processes, which themselves often embody bio-medical approaches to inclusion and run counter to the UDL objectives.

There is a need therefore for a theoretical overview that has the capacity to acknowledge these stakeholders, to analyze their relationships and interactions, to evidence the organizational complexity of the process of change, to offer nuanced systems-based solutions, and to map out an implementation process that avoids pitfalls and is not reductionist in flavour. Ecological theory will serve a useful role here in offering a framework that acknowledge systems thinking and the multi-layered complexity of this landscape. Ecological theory was developed by Bronfenbrenner in the context of social work as a tool to fully reflect the complexity of child behaviour (1993). It has been later used in educational contexts to map out the multiple systems that impact a child. In educational settings it has quickly become apparent that ecological theory can also help understand the complex reality that surrounds teachers as educators. In educational management, it is now frequently and effectively used to examine any stakeholder in educational institutions and their positioning, interactions, effectiveness, and efforts, within the context of any mandate they are seeking to advance. In the context if UDL, ecological theory will enable practitioners and scholars to reflect on the complexity, scope, and subtlety of the strategic dimension of such work (Fovet, 2021).

Need to Reflect a Wide Disparity of Socio-Historical Perspectives

There has been a tendency, historically to consider UDL and its implementation homogeneously, as if this reflection was identical irrespective of context. Even when examining the work of CAST in the US, the question comes to mind as to whether UDL can look the same in terms of pragmatic, contextualized implementation, in a federal context, one of such geographical, economic, and demographical diversity. Can any framework for inclusion genuinely purport to roll out universally and homogeneously across geo-political contexts that have few similarities? Beyond geo-political characteristics, UDL adopters and implementers will have to navigate a complex ecological reality, as has been highlighted in this chapter. This ecological reality will have to be acknowledged across UDL work, mapped out, and analyzed, as its characteristics will frame the shape of any UDL implementation momentum. This ecological reality is itself shaped by socio-historical factors that must be taken into account, in both the literature and field practices. Key dimensions of this socio-historical canvas will be legislative provisions, administrative policies, and funding models; these will vary from jurisdiction to jurisdiction The weight of historical contexts will also have a key impact on the range of stakeholders that are involved, and the flavour of the relationships between these stakeholders. One characteristic illustration of the subtlety of this type of socio-historical reflection on UDL implementation is the role played by teacher unions in the process; this varies greatly across contexts. Even a country such as Canada has 13 distinct realities, representing 13 socio-historical contexts; it has 13 divergent approaches to inclusion; this represents 13 subtly distinct contexts where UDL adoption and growth will end up looking radically different in terms of ecological nuance.

Need for an Acknowledgment of the Dichotomy Between Global North and Global South Voices

This chapter has begun a process of acknowledging the geo-political gaps that currently exist in the literature on UDL. Much of this scholarship has emerged from the Global North, however, more specifically from the United States. This is not representative of the reality of reflection and implementation occurring across regional contexts globally. The contexts currently reflected in the UDL scholarship are still predominantly middle class, urban, and racially homogenously Euro-Caucasian, and rapid change is required if this literature is to retain credibility. This chapter is a call to action for UDL researchers and advocates to focus on filling this gap and on facilitating and supporting the inclusion of diverse voices from around the globe into the UDL scholarship. The UN Sustainability Goals firmly assert that a key competency off the global citizen is the ability to considers issues, challenges, and themes from both a global and regional perspective, with equal ease and acumen. The regional perspective on UDL has thus far been missing from the scholarly reflection; this volume has triggered a movement of change by incorporating regional narratives, but this is a process that must be continued and amplified. A regional and local examination of UDL implementation will have a very different flavour, and significant specific nuances, when compared to a more global vision – often centered around Global North priorities.

Broader Need to Diversify and Reframe the UDL Discourse

The chapter has evidenced a siloing of UDL in respect to other scholarly literature (management of change, sustainability, leadership, etc.). The terminology of UDL can feel hermetical to outsiders as it is not necessarily immediately understandable by laypersons. UDL scholars and practitioners also tend to converge towards specific networks, PD events, and publications. There has therefore not been as much cross-pollination as necessary between UDL work and other areas of transformation in the educational landscape (open education, technological transformation, constructivist initiatives, experiential education among others). It is essential and urgent, therefore, to widen the discourse of UDL to invite in scholars and practitioners who may have divergent theoretical positioning (Fovet, 2019). Successful, transformative, student-centered, accessible inclusive education should be seen as an overlap of theoretical and philosophical traditions rather than the ownership of any specific model. This realization needs to be accompanied by a proactive and reflective effort of interdisciplinary collaboration. There is no evidence at present that this process has begun.

CONCLUSION

UDL implementation has been diverse in nature and fragmented in format over the last decade in the K-12 sector. It is a state of play that is both encouraging and concerning. The strength of the momentum is stimulating and brings hope; it reflects the general discontent that exists both in schools and in communities with medical model practices and with stigmatizing processes that are perpetuated without much reflection as to their impact. The uneven pattern of development of UDL across schools and school districts is, however, worrying. It reveals major ecological issues that weaken the effectiveness of training and PD, mentoring structures, leadership for inclusion, funding efforts, and sustainable future planning for growth. In many ways, it would be fair to assert that this point in time represents the end of the first wave of UDL development, a process mostly focused on spreading information, feeding curiosity, and encouraging field practitioners to get involved; it also marks the beginning of a second wave of UDL scholarship on UDL, one more focused on the hands-on implementation of the framework and on the strategic challenges of organizational change. This volume will go some way in contributing to this new, exciting wave of literature. It also represents a call to action for teachers to document their field reflection on UDL and their school based initiatives in order to develop the momentum related to this ecological mapping of strategic concerns.

REFERENCES

AHEAD. (2023). CPD - the Digital Badge for Universal Design in Teaching & Learning. *Training*.https://www.ahead.ie/udl-digitalbadge

Almeqdad, Q., Alodat, A. M., Alquraan, M. F., Mohaidat, M. A., & Al-Makhzoomy, A. K. (2023). The effectiveness of universal design for learning: A systematic review of the literature and meta-analysis. *Cogent Education*, 10(1), 2218191. Advance online publication. 10.1080/2331186X.2023.2218191

AlRawi, J. M., & AlKahtani, M. A. (2021). Universal design for learning for educating students with intellectual disabilities: A systematic review. *International Journal of Developmental Disabilities*, 68(6), 800–808. 10.1080/20473869.2021.190050536568615

Atlantic Technological University. (2023). Postgraduate Certificate in Universal Design for Learning (Online). Courses. *Faculty of Business and Social Sciences.* https://www.itsligo.ie/courses/postgraduate-certificate-in-universal-design-for -learning-online-2/#:~:text=Based%20in%20cognitive%20neurosciences%2C%20 UDL,designing%20capacity%20building%20learning%20experiences

Badil, D. D. M., Zeenaf Aslam, Z. A., Kashif Khan, K. K., Anny Ashiq, A. A., & Uzma Bibi, U. B. (2023). The Phenomenology Qualitative Research Inquiry: A Review Paper: Phenomenology Qualitative Research Inquiry. *Pakistan Journal of Health Sciences, 4*(3), 9–13. 10.54393/pjhs.v4i03.626

Basham, J. D., Blackorby, J., & Marino, M. T. (2020). Opportunity in Crisis: The Role of Universal Design for Learning in Educational Redesign. *Learning Disabilities (Weston, Mass.)*, 18, 71–91. https://files.eric.ed.gov/fulltext/EJ1264277.pdf

Bergmark, U. (2023). Teachers' professional learning when building a research-based education: Context-specific, collaborative and teacher-driven professional development. *Professional Development in Education*, 49(2), 210–224. 10.1080/19415257.2020.1827011

Bonyadi, A. (2023). Phenomenology as a research methodology in teaching English as a foreign language. *Asian Journal of Second and Foreign Language Education*, 8(1), 11. 10.1186/s40862-022-00184-z

Bray, A., Devitt, A., Banks, J., Sanchez Fuentes, S., Sandoval, M., Riviou, K., Byrne, D., Flood, M., Reale, J., & Terrenzio, S. (2023). What next for Universal Design for Learning? A systematic literature review of technology in UDL implementations at second level. *British Journal of Educational Technology*, 1–26. 10.1111/bjet.13328

Brazant, K. J. (2023). Disrupting the discourse: Applying critical race theory as a conceptual framework for reflecting on learning and teaching in higher education. *Equity in Education & Society*. Advance online publication. 10.1177/27526461231163325

Brillante, P., & Nemeth, K. (2022). *Universal Design for Learning in the Early Childhood Classroom: Teaching Children of all Languages, Cultures, and Abilities, Birth – 8 Years* (2nd ed.). Routledge. 10.4324/9781003148432

Bronfenbrenner, U. (1993). Ecological models of human development. In Gauvain, M., & Cole, M. (Eds.), *Readings on the development of children* (2nd ed., pp. 37–43). Freeman.

Capp, M. (2017). The effectiveness of universal design for learning: A meta-analysis of literature between 2013 and 2016. *International Journal of Inclusive Education*, 21(8), 791–807. 10.1080/13603116.2017.1325074

CAST. (2022). The Goal of UDL: Becoming Expert Learners. *Home*.https://www.learningdesigned.org/resource/goal-udl-becoming-expert-learners

CAST. (2023). About Universal Design for Learning. *Our Impact*. https://www.cast.org/impact/universal-design-for-learning-udl

Clandinin, D. J. (2013). *Engaging in Narrative Inquiry*. Routledge., 10.4324/9781315429618

Collums, D. (2023). *Exploring Transformational Leadership in a School Implementing Universal Design for Learning: A Case Study*. EdD Thesis, Southern Nazarene University. https://www.proquest.com/openview/756e9a6630490eae3802fd894dd60a33/1?pq-origsite=gscholar&cbl=18750&diss=y

Dodgson, J. E. (2023). Phenomenology: Researching the Lived Experience. *Journal of Human Lactation*, 39(3), 385–396. 10.1177/08903344231176453337278304

Dudley-Marling, C., & Paugh, P. (2010). Confronting the Discourse of Deficiencies. *Disability Studies Quarterly*, 30(2). Advance online publication. 10.18061/dsq.v30i2.1241

Dumont, H., & Ready, D. D. (2023). On the promise of personalized learning for educational equity. *NPJ Science of Learning*, 8(1), 26. 10.1038/s41539-023-00174-x37542046

Ewe, L., & Galvin, T. (2023). Universal Design for Learning across Formal School Structures in Europe—A Systematic Review. *Education Sciences*, 13(9), 867. 10.3390/educsci13090867

Fovet, F. (2014) Social model as catalyst for innovation in design and pedagogical change. *Widening Participation through Curriculum Open University 2014 Conference Proceedings*, 135-139.

Fovet, F. (2018) Exploring the Student Voice within Universal Design for Learning Work. *The AHEAD Journal, 8*. https://www.ahead.ie/journal/Exploring-the-Student-Voice-within-Universal-Design-for-Learning-Work

Fovet, F. (2019). Not just about disability: Getting traction for UDL implementation with International Students. In Novak, K., & Bracken, S. (Eds.), *Transforming Higher Education through Universal Design for Learning: An International Perspective.* Routledge. 10.4324/9781351132077-11

Fovet, F. (2020) Universal Design for Learning as a Tool for Inclusion in the Higher Education Classroom: Tips for the Next Decade of Implementation. Education Journal. *Special Issue: Effective Teaching Practices for Addressing Diverse Students' Needs for Academic Success in Universities, 9*(6), 163-172. http://www.sciencepublishinggroup.com/journal/paperinfo?journalid=196&doi=10.11648/j.edu.20200906.13

Fovet, F. (2020b). Beyond Novelty – "Innovative" Accessible Teaching as a Return to Fundamental Questions Around Social Justice and Reflective Pedagogy. In Palahicky, S. (Ed.), *Enhancing Learning Design for Innovative Teaching in Higher Education.* IGI Global. 10.4018/978-1-7998-2943-0.ch002

Gelpieryn, A. (2023, October 7) Substitute teachers are in short supply, but many schools still don't pay them a living wage. *CBS News*. https://www.cbsnews.com/news/substitute-teacher-shortage-living-wage/

Griful-Freixenet, J., Struyven, K., Vantieghem, W., & Gheyssens, E. (2020). Exploring the interrelationship between Universal Design for Learning (UDL) and Differentiated Instruction (DI): A systematic review. *Educational Research Review*, 29, 100306. Advance online publication. 10.1016/j.edurev.2019.100306

Griggs, N., & Moore, R. (2023). Removing Systemic Barriers for Learners with Diverse Identities: Antiracism, Universal Design for Learning, and Edpuzzle. *Journal of Special Education Technology*, 38(1), 15–22. 10.1177/01626434221143501

Haft, S. L., Greiner de Magalhães, C., & Hoeft, F. (2023). A Systematic Review of the Consequences of Stigma and Stereotype Threat for Individuals With Specific Learning Disabilities. *Journal of Learning Disabilities*, 56(3), 193–209. 10.1177/00222194221087383355499115

Jenson, K. (2018). Discourses of disability and inclusive education. *He Kupu, Special Edition, 5*(4). https://www.hekupu.ac.nz/article/discourses-disability-and-inclusive-education

Karisa, A. (2023). Universal design for learning: Not another slogan on the street of inclusive education. *Disability & Society*, 38(1), 194–200. 10.1080/09687599.2022.2125792

Kasprisin, L. (2015). Challenging the Deficit Model and the Pathologizing of Children: Envisioning Alternative Models. *Journal of Educational Controversy*, 9(1), 1. https://cedar.wwu.edu/jec/vol9/iss1/1

Kazmi, A. B., Kamran, M., & Siddiqui, S. (2023) The effect of teacher's attitudes in supporting inclusive education by catering to diverse learners. *Frontiers in Education, 8.*10.3389/feduc.2023.1083963

Kelly, O., Buckley, K., Lieberman, L. J., & Arndt, K. (2022). Universal Design for Learning - A framework for inclusion in Outdoor Learning. *Journal of Outdoor and Environmental Education*, 25(1), 75–89. 10.1007/s42322-022-00096-z

Kent, C., du Boulay, B., & Cukurova, M. (2022). Keeping the Parents outside the School Gate—A Critical Review. *Education Sciences*, 12(10), 683. 10.3390/educsci12100683

Kieran, L., & Anderson, C. (2019). Connecting Universal Design for Learning With Culturally Responsive Teaching. *Education and Urban Society*, 51(9), 1202–1216. 10.1177/0013124518785012

Konakli, T., & Akdeniz, R. K. (2023). The Emergence, Reasons and Results of Resistance to Change in Teachers. *International Journal on Lifelong Education and Leadership*, 8(1), 49–67. Advance online publication. 10.25233/ijlel.1107137

Lambert, R., McNiff, A., Schuck, A., Kara, I., & Zimmerman, S. (2023). 'UDL is a way of thinking'; Theorizing UDL teacher knowledge, beliefs, and practices. *Frontiers in Education*, 8, 1145293. 10.3389/feduc.2023.1145293

LaRon, A. S. (2018). Barriers With Implementing a Universal Design for Learning Framework. *Inclusion (Washington, D.C.)*, 6(4), 274–286. 10.1352/2326-6988-6.4.274

Lawson, A., & Beckett, A. E. (2021) The social and human rights models of disability: towards a complementarity thesis, *The International Journal of Human Rights,* 25(2), 348-379. 10.1080/13642987.2020.1783533

Lohmann, M.J., Hovey, K.A., & Gauvreau, A.N. (2023) Universal Design for Learning (UDL) in Inclusive Preschool Science Classrooms. *Journal of Science Education*. 10.14448/jsesd.15.0005

McCarty, T., & Lee, L. (2014). Critical Culturally Sustaining/Revitalizing Pedagogy and Indigenous Education Sovereignty. *Harvard Educational Review*, 84(1), 101–124. 10.17763/haer.84.1.q83746nl5pj34216

McKenzie, J., Karisa, A., Kahonde, C., & Tesni, S. (2021) *Review of Universal Design for Learning in Low- and Middle-Income Countries.* Including Disability in Education in Africa (IDEA). https://www.cbm.org/fileadmin/user_upload/UDL _review_report_2021.pdf

Meegan, J. (2023). Tensions and dilemmas: A narrative inquiry account of a teacher-researcher. *Irish Educational Studies*, 1–16. Advance online publication. 10.1080/03323315.2023.2236592

Neubauer, B. E., Witkop, C. T., & Varpio, L. (2019). How phenomenology can help us learn from the experiences of others. *Perspectives on Medical Education*, 8(2), 90–97. 10.1007/S40037-019-0509-230953335

Ok, M. W., Rao, K., Bryant, B., & McDougall, D. (2017). Universal Design for Learning in Pre-K to Grade 12 Classrooms: A Systematic Review of Research. *Exceptionality*, 25(2), 116–138. 10.1080/09362835.2016.1196450

Omodan, B. (2023). Unveiling Epistemic Injustice in Education: A critical analysis of alternative approaches. *Social Sciences & Humanities Open*, 8(1), 100699. Advance online publication. 10.1016/j.ssaho.2023.100699

Patel, V., Lindenmeyer, A., Gao, F., & Yeung, J. (2023). A qualitative study exploring the lived experiences of patients living with mild, moderate and severe frailty, following hip fracture surgery and hospitalisation. *PLoS One*, 18(5), e0285980. 10.1371/journal.pone.028598037200345

Patton Davis, L., & Museus, S. D. (2019). What Is Deficit Thinking? An Analysis of Conceptualizations of Deficit Thinking and Implications for Scholarly Research. *Currents (Ann Arbor)*, 1(1). Advance online publication. 10.3998/currents.17387731.0001.110

Piccolo, G. M. (2022). Pelo direito de aprender: Contibucioes do modelo social da deficiencia a la inclusao escolar. *Educação em Revista*, 38, e36926. 10.1590/0102-4698368536926

Poitras, J. (2023, May 8) N.B. reviews gender-identity policy in schools as supporters accuse minister of caving to anti-LGBTQ pressure. *CBC News*. https://www.cbc.ca/news/canada/new-brunswick/nb-education-gender-policy-1.6836059

Queen's University Faculty of Education. (2023). CONT691: Universal Design for Learning. *Professional Studies*. https://pros.educ.queensu.ca/courses/CONT691

Ratcliffe, R. (2013, October 7) Professional development in teaching: the challenges, solutions and status quo. *The Guardian*. https://www.theguardian.com/teacher-network/teacher-blog/2013/oct/07/professional-development-teaching-learning

Resch, K., Schrittesser, I., & Knapp, M. (2022). Overcoming the theory-practice divide in teacher education with the 'Partner School Programme'. A conceptual mapping. *European Journal of Teacher Education*. Advance online publication. 10.1080/02619768.2022.2058928

Rose, D., & Meyer, A. (2002). *Teaching every student in the Digital Age: Universal Design for Learning* (1st ed.). Association for Supervision and Curriculum Development. https://www.cast.org/products-services/resources/2002/universal-design-learning-udl-teaching-every-student-rose

Rose, D. H., & Meyer, A. (2006). *A practical reader in universal design for learning*. Harvard Education Press. Harvard Education Press.

Rosen, L. T. (2021). Mapping out epistemic justice in the clinical space: Using narrative techniques to affirm patients as knowers. *Philosophy, Ethics, and Humanities in Medicine; PEHM*, 16(1), 9. 10.1186/s13010-021-00110-034696799

Rusconi, L., & Squillaci, M. (2023). Effects of a Universal Design for Learning (UDL) Training Course on the Development Teachers' Competences: A Systematic Review. *Education Sciences*, 13(5), 466. 10.3390/educsci13050466

Sims, S., & Jerrim, J. (2022). *Traditional and progressive orientations to teaching: new empirical evidence on an old debate* (CEPEO Working Paper No. 22-08). Centre for Education Policy and Equalising Opportunities, UCL. https://EconPapers.repec.org/RePEc:ucl:cepeow:22-08

Stolz, S. A. (2023). The practice of phenomenology in educational research. *Educational Philosophy and Theory*, 55(7), 822–834. 10.1080/00131857.2022.2138745

Tefera, A. A., Artiles, A. J., Lester, A., & Cuba, M. (2019). Grappling with the paradoxes of inclusive education in the U.S.: Intersectional considerations in policy and practice. In Hartmann, M., Hummel, M., Lichtblau, M., Löser, J., & Thoms, S. (Eds.), *Facetten Inklusiver Bildung* (pp. 117–125). Klinkhardt.

Thompson, J. (2023). NASA resilience and leadership: Examining the phenomenon of awe. *Frontiers in Psychology*, 14, 1158437. Advance online publication. 10.3389/fpsyg.2023.115843737359869

Truth and Reconciliation Commission of Canada. (2023). *Exhibits*.https://exhibits.library.utoronto.ca/items/show/2420

Valencia, R. R. (2010). *Dismantling contemporary deficit thinking*. Routledge., 10.4324/9780203853214

Vargas-Hernandez, J. G., Rodríguez-Maillard, C., & Vargas-González, O. C. (2023). Organizational Ecology and Its Implications on Organizational Ecological Innovation. *Journal of Business Ecosystems*, 4(1), 1–16. 10.4018/JBE.320482

Vasilez, J. (2023). *Indigenizing Education: Universal Design for Learning and Indigenous Leadership Frameworks*. Ed.D. Thesis, Dissertations in Practice. University of Washington Tacoma. https://digitalcommons.tacoma.uw.edu/edd_capstones/76

Vostal, B. R., Oehrtman, J. P., & Gilfillan, B. (2023). School Counselors Engaging All Students: Universal Design for Learning in Classroom Lesson Planning. *Professional School Counseling*, 27(1). Advance online publication. 10.1177/2156759X231203199

Warrick, D. D. (2023). Revisiting resistance to change and how to manage it: What has been learned and what organizations need to do. *Business Horizons*, 66(4), 433–441. 10.1016/j.bushor.2022.09.001

Weiss, C. R., & Johnson-Koenke, R. (2023). Narrative Inquiry as a Caring and Relational Research Approach: Adopting an Evolving Paradigm. *Qualitative Health Research*, 33(5), 388–399. 10.1177/10497323231158619368 03213

Wertz, F. J. (2023). Phenomenological methodology, methods, and procedures for research in psychology. In Cooper, H., Coutanche, M. N., McMullen, L. M., Panter, A. T., Rindskopf, D., & Sher, K. J. (Eds.), *APA handbook of research methods in psychology: Research designs: Quantitative, qualitative, neuropsychological, and biological* (pp. 83–105). American Psychological Association. 10.1037/0000319-005

Winzer, M. A. (2007). Confronting difference: An excursion through the history of special education. In Florian, L. (Ed.), *The SAGE Handbook of Special Education* (pp. 20–30). Sage Publications. 10.4135/9781848607989.n3

Woodcock, S., Gibbs, K., Hitches, E., & Regan, C. (2023). Investigating Teachers' Beliefs in Inclusive Education and Their Levels of Teacher Self-Efficacy: Are Teachers Constrained in Their Capacity to Implement Inclusive Teaching Practices? *Education Sciences*, 13(3), 280. 10.3390/educsci13030280

KEY TERMS AND DEFINITIONS

Ecological Theory: A theoretical paradigm developed by Bronfenbrenner which highlights the vast number of systems which impact a child's life and behaviour, while also interacting with each other. Ecological theory enables educators to avoid knee jerk reactions by understanding and acknowledging the vast complexity of interactions within educational spaces.

Multiple Means of Action and Expression: This UDL design principle encourages educators to inject optimal flexibility in the ways we expect learners to provide information to teachers (within contribution, participation, completion of assessment, production of content, etc.)

Multiple Means of Engagement: This UDL design principles guides teachers as they reflect on flexibility and choice when defining and formulating expectations in relation to learner engagement.

Multiple Means of Representation: This is one of the three UDL design principles. It consists of integrating as much flexibility as possible in the way we offer learners information.

UDL Implementation: A process of management of change, quite distinct from the process of pedagogical adoption of UDL within a specific classroom. UDL implementation is going to be a process of organizational transformation, like any other, which encounters hurdles and triggers resistance. It must be planned for strategically and monitored with care.

Universal Design for Learning: A framework for inclusion that seeks to translate the social model of disability into practice and to shift educators away from deficit model practices. It translates the social model into classroom realities because it argues that UDL supports educators as they inject optimal flexibility in their instruction or assessment, with the use of inclusive design principles. UDL is a progressive, career-long process of eroding barriers from one's practice through a constant process or reflection and redesign.

Section 2
Case Studies

Chapter 2
How Universal Design for Learning Transformed My Teaching:
An Elementary Educator's Journey of Implementation

Jana Nicol

New Brunswick Department of Education and Early Childhood Development, Canada

EXECUTIVE SUMMARY

The purpose of this chapter is to provide a summary of research and recommendations for implementing Universal Design for Learning (UDL) in the elementary school setting through a review of the literature (2016 – 2021), one teacher's account of UDL implementation with elementary school-aged students (K-5) in a fully inclusive public education system in New Brunswick, Canada, and the findings of action research undertaken through a partnership between the New Brunswick Department of Education & Early Childhood Development (EECD) and University of New Brunswick (2013 – 2015). The goal of the action research was to determine what tools will help facilitate the implementation of UDL in elementary school classrooms to improve student engagement. Implementing UDL in the elementary school setting results in observable gains in inclusion, student engagement, and academic achievement. Teachers can take a personalized and incremental approach to UDL implementation guided by CAST's UDL Guidelines.

When I was an early career teacher, I was continually streamlining the process of offering accommodations to students who, for a variety of reasons, had difficulty meeting grade-level curriculum outcomes. I planned lessons for the "average" student and tried to provide prescribed accommodations to large numbers of students who

DOI: 10.4018/978-1-6684-4750-5.ch002

Copyright © 2024, IGI Global. Copying or distributing in print or electronic forms without written permission of IGI Global is prohibited.

had varying needs. Students' needs can be quite diverse given that I work within a fully inclusive public education system in New Brunswick, Canada, in which every student attends their community school and participates in the common learning environment. Given the vast variability in the educational, social, emotional, and physical needs of my elementary school students (grades K-5), offering accommodations that meet everyone's needs can be a monumental task. I was looking for ways to help my students meet me where I was teaching, and they had so many ways to get there. It was exhausting trying to reactively adjust lessons to meet everyone's needs. Why was this so hard? Because I was trying to teach to the average learner, which doesn't exist.

"Variability is the rule not the exception" – Todd Rose

As I learned about and began to gradually implement Universal Design for Learning (UDL) in my practice I discovered that I could reduce or even eliminate the accommodations I needed to offer to many students by reshaping the learning environment to consider their needs from the outset. UDL helped shift my focus from identifying deficits in learning so I could accommodate for them, to identifying barriers to access so I could proactively eliminate them through careful design of instruction and/or the learning environment. Identifying and eliminating barriers from the outset reduces and possibly eliminates the need for many accommodations. Instead of responding to variability, I began to anticipate it and plan accordingly. I offered choice. I focused on the goal of the lesson and considered multiple pathways that students can take to meet these goals, eliminating barriers wherever possible. For example, a student could use letter tiles or a device to spell words instead of completing pencil and paper tasks, as these can present barriers to students who struggle with fine motor tasks.

In a classroom that respects learner variability, students should not have to require a diagnosis or label to access options that help them experience success, and everyone is meaningfully included in the learning environment. The more barriers that can be identified and eliminated from the outset, the less there is a need to retrofit the learning experience in the moment in attempts to include everyone. Offering accommodations to everyone also destigmatizes them. For example, dark lined paper can be offered to all students to write on, not only those who have visual impairments or difficulties with fine motor planning. A variety of styles of paper (along with the option to use devices to complete work if this is feasible) to complete writing assignments could be available for everyone to choose from. This eliminates the need to ensure that certain students are the only ones who use different tools to complete work, and everyone can select the option that better meets their interests, plays to their strengths, and increases access to learning for all. This is the kind of classroom I aspired to have. I have been implementing the principles of UDL in my practice ever since, and have observed increased access to learning, higher levels of engagement, and positive gains in academic achievement among my students.

LITERATURE REVIEW

UDL and the Myth of the Average Learner

Traditionally, educators have focused on designing instruction to meet the needs of the "average" learner, retrofitting lessons after the fact in response to students who need accommodations to better access learning and demonstrate what they know. Universal Design for Learning (UDL) recognizes that there is no "average" learner. Learner variability is not limited to students who are identified as needing services. Everyone can benefit when lessons are designed to support a wide range of learners since each of us have different strengths, challenges, abilities, backgrounds, and interests (Berquist, 2017). Labeling students according to abilities or disabilities, learning styles, and preferences oversimplifies the neurological variability that exists among all of us and fails to consider our brain's plasticity and ability to change (Posey, 2018). Although UDL grew out of the need to accommodate students with disabilities, the continued review of neuroscience and classroom implementation makes it a helpful framework to use in any classroom, especially in inclusive settings where students of all ability levels are present (Nelson, 2021). Rather than adapting lessons as they are being administered, UDL focuses on proactively building supports throughout lesson goals, instructional practices, resources, and assessments (Ok et al., 2016).

The UDL framework is organized into three main principles of providing multiple means of engagement, multiple means of action and expression, and multiple means of representation. Included within are nine guidelines and 31 checkpoints, which are supported by research in neuroscience, learning science, and cognitive science, and represent practices that are effective in reducing barriers to learning to support the diverse needs of students (Ok et al., 2016). When implementing UDL, it is recommended to keep referencing the guidelines as they are essential to developing a better understanding of variability and barriers to learning. It is helpful to start small, making just one change in the learning environment at a time or focusing on goals (Posey & Novak, 2020). Integrating UDL in one's practice can take deliberate effort in the beginning, but the more familiar these shifts become, the less energy will be required to design learning experiences from the outset to support all learners by clarifying goals, providing options for learner variability, and prioritizing engagement (Posey & Novak, 2020). There is not a defined set of steps to follow when implementing UDL. It is a process of improving the cycle of learning through ongoing reflection and growth, and this will look different for every educator (Berquist, 2017).

Anticipating and Respecting Learner Variability

Following UDL to guide the design of the physical environment, instructional methods, curriculum materials, and assessments creates a more flexible and inclusive classroom that accommodates students of varied abilities and validates the learning capacity of every student (Craig et al., 2019). When teachers are guided by the belief that all students will succeed and keep this belief at the forefront of instructional planning, they are implementing UDL (Novak, 2016). In UDL, learner variability is not seen as a problem that needs to be solved; rather this variability is respected and considered from the outset of instructional design. Instead of trying to "fix" learners who aren't getting it, the focus is shifted to ways in which educators can reduce barriers in the learning environment to become more inclusive (Lowrey et al., 2017). When educators follow UDL, they value variability through the intentional design of engaging, flexible, goal-directed instruction to meet the needs of all learners, and in doing so the need to retrofit or reteach material is reduced or possibly eliminated (Posey, 2018).

UDL focuses on reducing barriers and lessons are designed from the outset using flexible methods, materials, and assessments to support the academic achievement of all students (Ok et al., 2016). Barriers are situations and structures that exclude students from full participation in the common learning environment. When designing the learning environment through the lens of UDL, teachers can consider which barriers may be present in the physical location, delivery of instruction, or within instructional materials themselves (Nelson, 2021). Teachers can use the UDL Guidelines as a reference to reflect on what and how they are teaching and as a guide to consider the possible barriers students may encounter in the learning environment. Instructional activities are designed to include flexible supports and scaffolds from the outset, reducing the need to make individual modifications (Berquist, 2017) to accommodate struggling learners.

Promoting Inclusion and Participation

UDL promotes inclusion and equity of access to learning for all students. Instructional practices, materials, and activities are designed with the flexibility to meet the strengths and needs of all learners so everyone can access what is being learned in the classroom (Smith Canter et al., 2017). When using the UDL framework to design the learning environment to be more flexible and accessible, educators are facilitating meaningful inclusion and increasing every student's access to the general education curriculum (Craig et al., 2019). When teachers consider how to include every student in a lesson, they are not only eliminating barriers; they are also helping create a stronger classroom community and more engaged learners (Lewis, 2018). All individuals vary in how they best learn and demonstrate their understanding in different contexts. Educators can reduce unintentional barriers to learning by being flexible and offering choice. UDL shifts the way teachers design instruction. Instead of asking how they can 'fix' students to fit into a learning environment, the focus shifts to how they can reshape the learning environment to better meet the needs of all our students (Posey, 2018).

Choice and Flexibility in the Learning Environment

Using the UDL framework as a guide, educators can create more opportunities for students to understand what is being taught by providing them with a variety of ways to perceive the information (e.g., see, hear, or physically manipulate). Teachers can also increase students' access to learning and opportunities to participate by offering a variety of ways for them to engage in tasks and demonstrate what they have learned (Nelson & Posey, 2019). All students should be given the opportunity to access learning in ways that meet their own kinesthetic strengths and needs (Vostal & Mrachko, 2021). The more information is presented through multiple sensory modalities (e.g., auditory, visual, tactile), the more students are likely to remember it (Posey, 2018). Teachers can also reduce barriers to learning by providing visual supports and graphic organizers in the classroom. These tools reduce barriers by helping learners better organize and understand information. Teachers can also prompt students to read written directions as they are being read aloud so they can receive visual and auditory information together and increase access to the task (Mrarchko, 2020). When given access to alternative modalities for expression as they engage in learning, most students can find the specific tools and processes to help them more easily demonstrate what they have learned. For example, pencil and paper tasks present barriers to learning for some individuals and educators can address these barriers by offering alternatives for physically responding to tasks and assessments (Vostal & Mrachko, 2021). Providing students with some basic additions to written and vocal directions not only increase their access to tasks, it also helps build their knowledge and problem solving capacity (Mrarchko, 2020).

With UDL, reaching every learner is not just about providing fun activities, materials, or using technology. It is about intentionally and purposefully designing the learning environment to include flexible options that allow students different ways to engage in learning (Posey & Novak, 2020). Decision making is an essential life skill. Offering choice in the classroom allows students to practice and refine this skill in a low-stakes environment (Mrarchko & Vostal, 2020). By giving students choice teachers are recognizing the strengths and contributions of every learner and helping them build intrinsic motivation to learn (Lewis, 2018). They are also giving students the opportunity to try new things, break ineffective habits, and take charge over their own learning. Students may not yet have all the skills needed to navigate choice and will benefit from a gradual release of skills and scaffolds as they develop proficiency (Posey & Novak, 2020). There are many ways to incorporate choice in the learning environment. Students can choose the type of media they use to demonstrate their learning. They can write a paper, make a poster, model, video, or give a presentation. When multiple tasks are planned, teachers can empower students to feel more in control of their learning by allowing them to choose the order in which they complete activities (Mrarchko & Vostal, 2020). When selecting possible choices for learners, it is important to remain focused on the goal of the lesson. Every choice offered should allow students to model proficiency on the chosen goal (Novak, 2016).

The Importance of Goal Setting

When implementing UDL, the goal is at the heart of any lesson. All resources, products, and activities used are intentionally selected to support the lesson goal (Nelson, 2021). Teachers can begin by sharing the goal with students. Goals can be posted on the board, on activities and assessments, and they are discussed regularly to help everyone understand the purpose of the goal, why it is relevant, and what steps are necessary to achieve it (Posey & Novak, 2020). Goals determine not only what students will learn but also the methods or materials they will use to learn and express what they know, therefore goals must be written with flexibility in mind. When the environment is designed to be responsive to learner variability, students are working alongside the same teacher and peers but may be engaged in different pathways to reach the same goal, depending on their learning strengths and needs (Nelson & Posey, 2019). Guided by the UDL framework, teachers can meet the varied needs of learners by offering different options to gain motivation, providing background information, identifying the purpose behind the content or skill, and helping students develop and work toward meeting goals (Nelson & Posey, 2019).

Modelling and discussing the process of goal setting helps support the executive functions of all learners. Executive functions include the processes students use to create and follow a plan and adjust flexibly to changes as they complete goal-oriented tasks (Vostal & Mrachko, 2021). Educators can support learners as they develop these skills by framing goals in age appropriate language. This helps keep everyone focused on desired outcomes and helps learners determine their own level of mastery as they work toward meeting a given goal in terms that they can understand (Nelson,

2021). Teachers can further support students by breaking up goals into manageable components, outlining the steps needed to achieve each part of the goal, and clarifying to the learners what success for each part looks like. Students attain higher levels of competency because they know where they are going and what they need to do to get there (Posey & Novak, 2020). Teachers can help develop working memory in students (which enhances executive functioning) through scaffolds such as planning templates, checklists, graphic organizers, and rubrics. These tools are useful because they organize information (visually and/or numerically) to help learners internalize the habit of breaking up goals into actionable steps while helping keep track of what they need to do to meet a goal (Vostal & Mrachko, 2021).

Limitations

UDL is an instructional design framework that is grounded in evidence-based practices. However, research on how to apply the framework to pedagogical practices is relatively nascent (Ok, Rao, Bryant, & McDougall, 2016), particularly in elementary education, where there is considerably less research than in other educational sectors. Emerging studies have found that UDL implementation results in increased engagement in learning, improved work completion, more collaboration between students with and without disabilities, and increased attitudes of kindness and caring among the classroom community (Lowrey et al., 2017). UDL has also been found to enhance the social-emotional development of all students, and academic performance on standardized test scores and other forms of assessment (Craig et al., 2019). UDL holds a lot of promise as an educational approach that promotes inclusion of all students in the learning environment, but the promise of this approach may not be realized until the research turns the corner from advocating to assessing and measuring the efficacy of the framework (Smith Canter et al., 2017). There is also a need for clear recommendations on ways in which the UDL Guidelines can be applied to instructional practice to support achievement for a wider range of learners (Ok et al., 2016), including elementary school-aged students.

Inclusion and UDL in New Brunswick, Canada

The public education system in New Brunswick has pioneered the concept of inclusive education through legislation and practice. Students with disabilities have been educated in community schools in the common learning environment with their non-disabled peers since 1986 (AuCoin et al., 2020). To build upon this initiative, the *Connecting Care and Challenge* (MacKay, 2006), and *Strengthening Inclusion, Strengthening Schools* (Aucoin & Porter, 2012) reports called for the need to provide a clear definition of inclusion, to outline better practices for schools and teachers, and to allocate resources more effectively. As a result, inclusive education by definition is not only about students with disabilities; it is about accommodating the variable and diverse needs of all leaners. All learners have strengths and challenges and are entitled to receive an education that allows them to learn alongside their peers in an inclusive learning environment (AuCoin et al., 2020).

In 2013, *Inclusive Education* Policy 322 was released, which applies to every public school in New Brunswick. It provides a clear definition of inclusive education and the common learning environment, and outlines supports for inclusion and the roles and responsibilities of superintendents, administrators, and teachers (New Brunswick Department of Education and Early Childhood Development, 2013). As a result of policy and practice in New Brunswick schools in which all students are included in the common learning environment, many teachers have embraced the UDL framework to better address the needs of all learners. New Brunswick teachers at all grade levels continue to engage in action research projects to further explore topics related to implementing UDL in the public education system (AuCoin et al., 2020).

METHODOLOGICAL STANCE

In 2013, school-based teams of teachers in New Brunswick public schools were invited to submit a proposal to engage in action research on a topic of their choosing involving UDL implementation. This was initiated by a partnership between the New Brunswick Department of Education & Early Childhood Development (EECD) and University of New Brunswick (UNB). Teams of teachers from throughout the province received professional learning, release time, and a $1200 grant to engage in action research. I led the action research team at Island View School in Saint John, New Brunswick, from 2013-2015, which was named *The UDL Project*. Island View School is an elementary school (kindergarten to grade five) attended by over 300 students from urban, suburban, and rural areas. Every classroom is equipped with a SMART board, and students have access to iPads and laptops. Students also engage in learning through hands-on activities, cross-curricular experiences, and outdoor learning is a part of the school culture. The school is adjacent to playgrounds, green space, a soccer field, an outdoor classroom, and wooded areas.

The action research team at Island View School included four teachers and represented a diverse range of grade levels (grades 2-5), disciplines (elementary education, education support services, and administration), and levels of experience with UDL (ranging from novice to proficient). Our team explored the following question through action research: what tools will help facilitate the implementation of UDL in elementary school classrooms to improve student engagement?

36

HOW UDL TRANSFORMED MY TEACHING: ONE BETTER PRACTICE AT A TIME: NARRATIVE OF A PROJECT IN THE ELEMENTARY SECTOR

Start Small

UDL is not a single practice. It is a framework representing a collection of better practices, so the idea of trying to take everything on at once can be overwhelming, therefore it is recommended to take an incremental approach to UDL implementation. I usually begin by referencing CAST's UDL Guidelines (CAST, 2018), which are useful because they break down UDL into a collection of research-based practices that can improve outcomes for students. The UDL Guidelines are like a menu at a restaurant: there are a lot of options and, as much as I would like to order one of everything right away, that would not be possible in a single sitting. My journey of UDL implementation has been gradual and personalized. I select one or two checkpoints from the guidelines that support my goals, reflect on progress along the way, and adjust goals or set new ones as needed to take my practice where I want it to go. I am continually implementing UDL, one better practice at a time.

As a teacher working with elementary school-aged students (ages 4-11), it is also important to think small when considering how to apply the framework to the needs of younger learners in mind, given that there is not yet a large body of research on UDL implementation for elementary educators to consult or adhere to. For example, checkpoint 9.3 – develop self-assessment and reflection (CAST, 2018), may seem like a big goal for young learners and some may argue, unconvincingly, that it is not developmentally appropriate for primary-aged students (ages 4-7). Part of developing as a proficient learner in the UDL framework, and working toward this checkpoint, would involve helping students learn how to monitor and regulate their emotions (CAST, 2018), goals which are already present in many elementary school settings, as evidenced by the use social-emotional learning programs such as *Zones of Regulation* or *Mind Up* in schools throughout Canada. Even the youngest students have been learning to use words to describe their own emotions and talk about strategies to regulate them. These activities are meaningful exercises in self-assessment and reflection while giving students important skills to help them function effectively in a positive learning environment.

Young learners can achieve UDL goals when teachers apply the guiding principles in developmentally appropriate ways, using age appropriate language. For example, elementary school teachers can support young learners with self-assessment and reflection through modelling and by using visuals, rubrics, and by providing timely feedback. Rubrics can be written in age appropriate language and supported by visuals, and educators can train students how to read them. We usually begin by showing the class a completed rubric filled in for a fictional student. We look at it together as a class and determine a strength and a goal for that fictional student based on the feedback. When I grade work with a rubric, upon returning it to students, I give them time to read and reflect and record a strength and a goal they have for the work. Then we confer, discuss their progress, talk about the goal, and try to figure out some steps that they can take to meet it. Students are learning how to reflect on their learning through this process and are on their way to becoming proficient learners.

Intentional Design of the Learning Environment

One of the first goals I set after starting the path toward implementing UDL in my practice, was to improve the spatial setup of my classroom to eliminate any physical barriers to learning and support a sense of inclusion. I began by considering the layout of the furniture and made changes to improve accessibility for students who use wheelchairs or other mobility aids. Every area of the classroom (i.e., meeting space, classroom library, options for working independently, and space to collaborate) is accessible to everyone. Students are given flexible seating options and can choose where they sit when engaged in independent and collaborative work. I have organized students' personal materials and shared classroom materials, so they are within reach of students. They are stored in consistent locations which are clearly labeled with print and visuals (braille labels could also be added to support students who have visual impairments). This, in combination with establishing consistent routines for accessing and returning materials, eliminates many barriers to locating and returning things they need to help them learn and complete tasks.

When designing the learning environment, teachers can eliminate the need to offer many accommodations to individuals by offering them to everyone. A large visual schedule can be posted in a prominent space in the room for everyone to follow, reducing or possibly eliminating the need for - sometimes multiple - personal visual schedules for individuals who benefit from their use. Text is supported by pictures, to reduce barriers to understanding experienced by emerging readers and to contribute to a print-rich learning environment. Although visual schedules are often a prescribed accommodation for students who have ASD, they can benefit all students. Everyone likes to know what the day will look like. Visual timers are another tool traditionally used to accommodate students who have ASD that can be used to benefit everyone in the learning environment. Following a visual timer can help students learn to prepare for transitions and manage their time effectively. Everyone in the class likes to know what to expect.

How Universal Design for Learning Transformed My Teaching

As an elementary school teacher in a fully inclusive public education system, I am often working with students and have already received a formal diagnosis. However, because students are so young, there may be some who have not received a formal diagnosis and may receive one when they are older. Given that early childhood is a phase of rapid development, formal psychoeducational assessments by a psychologist rarely occur before third grade. Assistive technology can also help eliminate barriers for these students. For example, a student who struggles with written output may experience more success with writing tasks if they use word prediction software. If using this software eliminates the barrier and allows the student to complete the task, then providing this tool is a reasonable accommodation to help students meet grade-level curriculum outcomes. The practice of having to wait for a diagnosis before giving permission or receiving funding to give students what they need to experience academic, emotional, and social success needs to stop.

Assistive technology could be offered to everyone in the classroom to eliminate barriers to benefit all students, not only those who have a documented need for it. Many students can benefit from extra help, or from taking advantage of things that can help make tasks simpler. People do this often, such as when choosing the escalator instead of the stairs to reach the same destination in the end. For instance, classroom FM systems may have been designed to benefit students who have hearing impairments, but they can also eliminate barriers for students who have auditory processing disorders or attentional difficulties, and they allow all students to hear the teacher more clearly. Therefore, to increase access for all students, I use the classroom FM system as a part of my general practice, instead of using it only as a prescribed accommodation for students who have hearing impairments. Everyone can hear me better; it is easier for some students to focus on my voice over extraneous noise, and I am intentionally reducing barriers to receiving information for students in the learning environment.

Teachers can make visual information more accessible by recording it on the computer and projecting it instead of using a chalkboard/whiteboard, so it can be screen shared by students who use devices. Students can then use the device's features as needed to review information, use speech-to-text, translate text, or complete work. Using the computer to display information also makes it easier to support that information with visuals. As amusing as it is to have the students tease my artistic abilities as I draw something, I can better convey the message with an actual photo, which makes the message more easily understood by emerging readers and English language learners and helps activate and supply background knowledge for everyone. Using the computer to display information simplifies the process of sending information to families who are helping support learning at home. For example, work can be emailed to families or saved on a drive that students can access from home if they need additional time to complete a task. Information about what

39

students are learning in class and instructional videos can be shared on a classroom website so students can watch them through repeat, asynchronous viewing, to see something they missed while absent, or for families to watch so they may support learning at home.

Embedding Choice Throughout Learning

Students love choice. By designing instruction and learning tasks to incorporate choice, educators are not only increasing access to learning, student engagement, and buy-in; they are also implementing UDL. The UDL Guidelines recommend optimizing individual choice and autonomy to promote student engagement (CAST, 2018). While it is not always possible or appropriate to change the goal of a lesson - what students are expected to learn -, we can be flexible on the means that students follow to meet a given objective. Standards or objectives-based curricula outline the destination – what students are expected to know or be able to do. While suggestions on how to help students meet the goals are generally always present, there can be many different pathways to achievement, and teachers can incorporate choice to allow students to choose the pathways to learning which better meet their strengths, needs, and interests.

There are many ways to embed choice throughout the learning environment. Students can be given the option to work alone or with others. They can choose where to sit while they are working. They may have access to a variety of flexible seating options (e.g., balance balls, wedge-shaped cushions, Hokki stools, yoga mats, standing desks, etc.). Educators can offer choice in how students access and demonstrate learning by offering a variety of activities that follow different pathways to meet the same goal. For example, if students are learning basic multiplication facts, they could choose among the following activities: using counters to form arrays that represent a multiplication sentence, matching multiplication sentences to their visual representations, using grid paper to draw arrays, writing a story problem to represent a multiplication sentence, using multiplication flashcards, playing multiplication war with a deck of cards, explaining strategies they use to solve multiplication problems, or finding the area of rectangles. While all activities are intended to help students learn multiplication, they offer a variety of pathways to get there. Some students may need or prefer to use concrete objects to work out products, while others may prefer activities that involve drawing or writing. Some may lean toward games or partner activities while others may prefer tasks they can work on alone. Everyone is working toward the goal of understanding multiplication, but each student is given options in how to achieve this objective, and the options offered are designed to meet the needs of learners who have diverse preferences, abilities, and needs.

40

How Universal Design for Learning Transformed My Teaching

As an elementary school teacher, it is important for me to be mindful that choice is offered in a manner that is developmentally appropriate for younger learners and promotes a positive learning environment. I have found it helpful to begin by limiting choice to two options, adding more over time as they become more comfortable with making choices. We can further support elementary school students in navigating choice by providing them with visual representations of the choices, not only to offer a reminder about what the choices are, but also to support students who integrate information better visually than auditorily, and those who may be dependent on devices to scan, read, or translate the text. Visuals could take the form of a list of choices, a bingo grid, or tangible items. For example, when presenting choices on a list to students learning to read and spell the *long a* sound, they could choose between reading decodable texts that feature the sound and includes a visual of books, or working on a picture sorting activity grouping words by their vowel sounds and includes a visual of the picture cards being sorted. Supporting text with visuals is also a great way to build literacy skills among emergent readers and English language learners.

I recommend communicating clear expectations when introducing choice to elementary school students. When young learners have a clear understanding of classroom routines and expectations, it is easier for them to focus their mental energy on learning. I find it helpful to involve learners in discussions about daily routines and record their ideas on an anchor chart for future reference. When co-constructing an anchor chart with students in the classroom, I may begin by asking, "what would _____ look like? What should I see you (students) doing? What would I (teacher) be doing?" I usually make a two-column chart and, in each column, we make a list of expected behaviours for both students and teacher during a given activity, stated in positive language. I use flexible seating in my classroom, which gives students the option to choose where they sit and what they sit on. They may choose between chairs, stools, benches, yoga mats, cushions, or scoop chairs. If a student feels more comfortable standing at their desk or sitting on the floor with a clipboard while working, they are afforded the privilege to do so. An anchor chart for flexible seating may remind the students to choose a seat and start work right away, sit in seats safely, remain in one spot, and work quietly. If a student is engaging in off-task behaviours that disturb others, they may temporarily lose the privilege of choosing where to sit or what type of seat they may use until they demonstrate readiness to engage in the desired behaviour (working quietly) while navigating choices.

Working in a fully inclusive public education system, in which every child participates in the common learning environment of their community school, I have encountered many students who need additional scaffolds to help them learn to navigate choice. Not all students are able to make choices with the same ease as their peers. It might be helpful to offer fewer options, inform learners in advance of a choice to come, set a visual timer to set a reasonable timeframe for making a choice, or give opportunities to practice and role play making choices in a safe environment. Most students find choice motivating and everyone is equally deserving of the opportunity to learn and refine the skill of making choices.

When accommodations and assistive technologies are offered to everyone, teachers are not only offering more choice to everyone, they are also helping destigmatize the use of these supports in the classroom. Earlier in my career I saw a significant amount of resistance among students when asked to take advantage of tools that would increase their opportunities for success, such as providing a visually impaired student with dark lined paper to write on or a version of a document that uses larger font so they could more easily read it. While some students accepted the accommodations, some declined them to avoid being singled out or treated differently. I decided to start increasing the font size of documents and giving dark lined writing paper to everyone in the class. Many students commented that they found it easier to do writing on dark lined paper, than on looseleaf, and preferred it. I also offer looseleaf as an option but both types of paper are readily available to everyone, and not only reserved for students who have a particular diagnosis or label. When educators destigmatize accommodations, they are not only creating a more equitable and inclusive learning environment; they are also offering more options that can maximize the learning potential of all learners.

The Importance of Goal Setting and Reflection

My students and I discuss goals frequently. We talk about what they need to learn and why they need to learn it. We break goals down into steps and talk about how to monitor progress along the way. We have discussions about goals as a whole class, in small groups, and I also meet with individuals, as students may be taking different pathways toward meeting the same goal. Goal setting is not only important for my students to help them become proficient learners; it is also an essential part of the process of improving my practice. In addition to managing the learning goals of every student in my classroom and facilitating a learning environment that equips every student to meet them, I continually set goals for myself as I embark on the journey of implementing UDL.

I have found it helpful to set manageable goals, reflect on progress, and adjust along the way as needed. I select one or two goals early in the school year and document them in my Professional Growth Plan (PGP). When selecting goals, I consider the UDL Guidelines and the areas in which I can adjust my practice to implement UDL more fully. Depending on the requirements of an organization's PGP, documenting goals can make one consider how UDL implementation aligns with school or district improvement plans, what resources are needed, and what the observable criteria are to determine whether goals have been met. When a goal has been met, it could be replaced by a different goal, or one could choose to develop the goal more fully and set new criteria to increase proficiency within a given area.

As teachers learn to set goals, create and follow a plan to meet goals, and reflect on progress along the way, they can also intentionally design lessons that model and teach these skills to their students, and in doing so they are implementing practices that are based on the UDL Guidelines. Following is an example of how a single checkpoint in the UDL Guidelines (8.1 – Heighten salience of goals and objectives) can be used to guide the implementation of UDL in an elementary school classroom.

Table 1. Sample goal and action plan

Goal: Increase student awareness of curriculum outcomes by heightening the salience of goals and objectives throughout instruction – CAST UDL Guidelines – checkpoint 8.1 (CAST, 2018)		
Action plan: • Display learning goals in age-appropriate language and refer to them often • Discuss goals with students in whole class, small group, and individual contexts and document student progress • Offer opportunities for students to reflect on progress toward meeting goals	**Resources needed:** • Time to collaborate with grade level team to develop bank of goals written in age-appropriate language in all subject areas • Area in classroom to display learning goals in age-appropriate language • Template for conferring notes to document student progress	**Evidence of achievement:** • Learning goals in age-appropriate language are visible in the classroom • Students can locate and explain posted goals • Students can discuss personal goals and reflect on their progress • Conferring notes reflect discussions with students about progress and next steps

Reflecting on progress toward meeting a goal is an ongoing process. Upon having met this goal, new goals could be added to continue to develop this checkpoint if desired. In addition to continuing the practice of displaying learning goals in the classroom in age-appropriate language, one could further engage students by having them state the goals aloud at the beginning of the lesson. This can be executed in different ways. In my elementary classroom, it is a class job and students take turns to be the "goal reader" each day. One could further heighten the salience of goals and objectives throughout a lesson by having goals visible on activities and assessments. Teachers can also intentionally create opportunities for students to reflect on their progress toward meeting goals, with questions designed to encourage student reflection for guided discussions, interviews, and exit slips. Following is an example of a possible next phase of implementing this same checkpoint.

Table 2. Sample goal and action plan

Goal: Continue to increase student awareness of curriculum outcomes by heightening the salience of goals and objectives throughout instruction – CAST UDL Guidelines – checkpoint 8.1 (CAST, 2018)		
Action plan: • Display learning goals in age-appropriate language and have students refer to it often • Display learning goals in age-appropriate language on activities and assessments • Offer opportunities for students to reflect on progress toward meeting goals through the use of guiding questions/prompts (i.e., pair and share, exit slips, interviews)	**Resources needed:** • Area in classroom to display learning goals in age-appropriate language • Time to edit documents (activities, assessments) to include learning goals • Time to collaborate with colleagues to create a bank of questions/prompts that guide student reflection toward meeting goals in a variety of contexts	**Evidence of achievement:** • Learning goals in age-appropriate language are visible in the classroom. Students can locate and read the goal at the beginning of a lesson • Learning goals are visible on activities and assessments • Students discuss progress toward meeting goals with teacher and peers, and record written reflections on exit slips • Guiding questions/ prompts are in use

One could continue to dive deeper into this checkpoint. Other practices that can heighten the salience of goals and objectives throughout instruction may include teaching students to formulate goals and how to break down larger goals into manageable steps. Involving students in co-constructing criteria for assignments and presenting rubrics to students before completing work can also help students develop in this checkpoint further. One could opt to continue to tackle this checkpoint or move onto another area of interest and return to this one when ready to develop it more fully. It depends on the interests of each educator and their desired approach to implementing UDL.

Teamwork and Collaboration

UDL recognizes the need for learners to be able to communicate effectively and work collaboratively. I was once hesitant to include a lot of partner or group work in instruction, in part because I was unsure that my young leaners were ready for it. Through efforts to implement checkpoint 8.3 from the UDL Guidelines, foster collaboration and community (CAST, 2018), I discovered ways to increase opportunities for students to work with others, and as a result observed positive gains in students' social and collaborative skills and an increased acceptance of differences. When teaching students how to work together, it helps to break down the larger goal of working collaboratively with smaller sub-skills, such as active listening, turn taking, sharing, being kind, participating in a discussion with a partner, participating in a discussion with a group, asking for help, offering help, settling disputes, and reaching an equitable division of labour within a group. Educators can design the

How Universal Design for Learning Transformed My Teaching

learning environment to include frequent opportunities for students to collaborate so they can practice these essential skills.

When building classroom community it helps to go beyond the typical "icebreaker" activities classrooms often engage in at the beginning of the year. *Pair and share* is a simple way to get students talking in a low-risk and low-pressure environment, especially if sharing with the class is optional. It is also brief, depending on the discussion prompt, and could range in time from less than a minute to a few minutes; it can be used throughout the day to discuss any topic. Teachers can help reduce barriers to discussion and facilitate more productive student discussions by offering scaffolds such as guiding questions or sentence starters. An example of a guiding question could be, "why is _____ your favorite character?", and a sample sentence starter to respond to this question could be, "_____ is my favorite character because _____ ". Offering scaffolds such as guiding questions and possible sentence starters can help build classroom community and can also teach about the structure of language, help students organize their ideas, offer a framework for students to discuss and review material, and support emerging readers.

Teachers can take on the role of 'student' and select one or more students to help them model a conversation for the class (which may also include modeling the use of sentence starters and guiding questions). Then the whole group can discuss their observations before beginning their own partner or small group conversations. Teachers can also build classroom community by facilitating opportunities for students to play games together. Games that are linked to what students are learning can be introduced in all subject areas. Educators can model how to play games, and essential social skills like taking turns, settling disputes, and being kind. Students could also be given opportunities to play board games and card games during unstructured times of the day, such as soft entry or indoor recess. Game play is an engaging way to learn and gives students authentic opportunities to develop oral language and practice social skills.

As I have continued to implement UDL in my practice, I have observed growth in my own collaborative skills and professional networks. Through independent research on UDL, I have discovered professional learning opportunities and online professional learning networks which include colleagues from across the globe who share my enthusiasm for UDL. In these groups, participants discuss topics related to UDL, share topics of interest, links to professional learning, and celebrate successes. These events and groups are informative and have at times resulted in opportunities to collaborate on specific projects, which helps provide a sense of personal and professional growth. UDL has also helped me form professional relationships locally. I have participated in and facilitated professional learning at the school, district, and departmental levels in the public education system in New Brunswick and, in doing so, have found colleagues, both within and outside of my school, who are implementing UDL. I have learned so much through our conversations and collaborations. One of the most memorable and productive of these relationships was the action research team at Island View School.

ACTION RESEARCH: SUMMARY AND FINDINGS

Summary

The UDL Project began in the fall of 2013, after a team of four teachers from Island View School were selected to participate in a UDL action research project in collaboration with the New Brunswick Department of Education and Early Childhood Development (EECD) and the University of New Brunswick (UNB). All team members were classroom teachers, with one member having a dual role between administration and grade four, and another member having a dual role of education support services and grade two. In our team's pursuit to determine what tools would help facilitate the implementation of UDL in elementary school classrooms to improve inclusion and student engagement, the team created universally designed lessons, executed the lessons in their own classrooms and evaluated their effectiveness through observations, reflections, and feedback from students. Our group searched for tools and materials, and created some of our own, designed to help teachers create lessons and materials that follow the principles of UDL. We wrote reflective journals about our experiences throughout this project.

In efforts to measure student engagement, we collected data from students in our own classrooms (88 students). In November 2013 and in April 2014, students were asked to describe how they felt about school and/or learning in one word, which they recorded on an index card. They were asked for only one word to make it easier to tabulate their responses as quantitative data. When students were asked to describe how they felt about learning in one word, the vast majority (85%) reported having positive feelings. When asked to describe how they felt about learning, more than half used words that were synonymous with 'awesome'; a quarter of the students used words synonymous with 'fun', and five percent used words synonymous with 'creative'. Five percent of students found school to be difficult, and the remaining students used words which were unclear (e.g., 'busy', 'math'). Results were almost identical in both sets of data (collected in November 2013 and April 2014), but more students used the word fun to describe learning in the second data set. It is noted that students who reported positive feelings about school, used better quality words in the second data set. While many students used words like 'good' in November, this word was rarely used in April, and was replaced by words like 'spectacular', 'fantastic', and 'interesting'. This data may indicate that students were more engaged in learning in April 2014 than they were in November 2013.

In November 2013, students engaged in a writing activity, responding to the prompt 'describe what the best day would look like in your favorite subject'. An overwhelming majority of students wrote about Physical Education or Art. Many upper elementary students wrote about cross-curricular activities (some used creative words like 'Mart' for Math/Art). Most students across all grade levels expressed a desire to have choices in what they were doing and/or who they could work with. In April 2013, students engaged in a writing activity responding to the prompt 'describe what the best day would look like in your Math/Language Arts/Science/ Social Studies classes'. The team decided to use this writing prompt to help students focus on specific subject areas to determine what they found most engaging about these subjects, and to guide our instruction so that we could increase engagement in all areas of the curriculum. Some recurring themes across all grade levels included preferences for: partner and group activities, having choices of activities, using manipulatives, doing hands-on activities, using technology, playing games, and reading.

The team wanted to determine the collective level of readiness for implementing UDL. We created an online survey using SurveyMonkey and emailed it to teachers in Island View School in November 2013. Most teachers (85%) responded to the survey, and all responses were anonymous. Teachers were asked about their level of knowledge about UDL, how often they implemented UDL in their practices, what the perceived obstacles to implementing UDL in their classrooms were, whether they would implement UDL more often if they had sample lessons to follow, and what their disposition toward UDL was. Another online survey was administered in January 2014 to get more information about the obstacles faced by teachers in the areas of planning and preparation, which was identified by respondents as a barrier to UDL implementation in the November 2013 survey.

According to the results of the online teacher surveys, most teachers (83%) believed that UDL was a step in the right direction, while the rest thought of it as just another passing fad. Levels of knowledge about UDL and how to implement it in teaching practices varied among respondents, ranging from knowing a little bit about UDL (12%) to being very knowledgeable about UDL and how to implement it in the classroom (29%). The majority fell in the middle, reporting that they had a good understanding of UDL, but were unsure as to how to effectively implement it in their teaching practices (59%). All respondents implement UDL in their teaching practices at least some of the time. All respondents indicated that they would implement UDL practices in their classrooms more often if they had sample lessons to follow. Planning and preparation, and time to plan and prepare, was the largest obstacle to implementing UDL, as indicated by 90% of respondents. This included: finding, creating, and adapting resources, collaborating with colleagues, teaching to diverse learning preferences, and finding or creating templates to facilitate the implementation of UDL.

Limitations

The main limitation of the team was time. The expectation that members would use part of their release time to collect and analyze data from students and colleagues and prepare a presentation of their work in May 2014 represented a significant workload and amount of planning time. Release time was also limited to a half-day per month, meaning it took months for the team to accomplish tasks, such as planning UDL lessons, finding and creating tools and templates to facilitate the implementation of UDL, collecting and analyzing data, and deciding how to use the budget to meet the schools' needs. This left the team feeling unprepared to share work with colleagues until the work was more developed, which was not until near the project's end. Therefore, it was not possible to use follow-up surveys with colleagues to determine whether this work helped them implement more UDL practices into their classrooms. It would have been worthwhile to have had the opportunity to continue the work for another school year to promote the implementation of UDL on a larger scale - school-wide - and solicit feedback from colleagues to improve the quality of the lesson plans, materials, and templates that were shared.

RECOMMENDATIONS

Respect Variability by Offering Choice and Flexibility

Students thrive when provided with choice in activities and assessments. They can work toward similar goals by completing activities that better suit their own interests and needs. The choices offered to students need to be grounded in the goal of the lesson and offer different ways to learn or demonstrate their learning. It is recommended that lessons and activities appeal to different sensory modalities - auditory, visual, tactile -, and consider the interests of students. Teachers can expose students to information in a variety of ways to appeal to multiple interests and sensory modalities by providing opportunities for students to engage in hands-on experiences and investigations, presenting information orally, and showing visuals and videos. Students should also be given opportunities to learn individually, with partners, and in small groups, and have choice embedded in these arrangements. For example, they could choose who to work with, what content to learn from a list of options, and how they will demonstrate their learning. Teachers can also promote inclusion and engagement through a UDL framework by integrating opportunities for arts-based education, technology, and physical activity in all subject areas, and by including games and hands-on learning experiences to increase choice and access for students.

Respect the Inclusion of All Learners by Anticipating Barriers and Planning Solutions

Learner variability is expected. Everyone learns differently and teachers can respect the inclusion of all learners from the outset by anticipating barriers students may encounter and considering possible solutions. In addition to offering choice, educators can better meet the needs of all learners by ensuring everyone can access and present information in ways that is better suited to their interests and abilities. Supports that are traditionally only offered to students who have diagnoses or Personalized Learning Plans could be offered to everyone. Teachers could offer anyone extra time, assistive technologies like word prediction software, and encouragement to use visuals or concrete materials to work through problems. In doing so we are not only destigmatizing the use of supports that some students rely on to access learning, but we are also increasing access to learning for everyone.

Teachers Need Improved Access to Professional Learning and Resources

Efforts to increase teacher readiness to implement UDL can be enhanced by improving access to resources and professional learning. School resources, such as manipulatives, books, and visual aids, should be well-organized and kept in known locations that are easily accessible by all teachers. It is also suggested that schools create databanks of digital and web-based resources, which are categorized by grade level, subject, and unit. Resources for student use should be selected to anticipate variability among learners. For example, students can access books about any science unit at a variety of reading levels so everyone can access the content whether they are an emerging or proficient reader. Teachers should be able to easily access UDL lessons, instructional materials, and templates to help facilitate implementation. Many such tools and sample lessons have been compiled and published on *The UDL Project* (Nicol, 2024), and it is also recommended that this website is shared with teachers. Teachers should also be given sufficient time to plan and collaborate to incorporate new learning into practice.

Continue Efforts to Conduct Action Research in UDL in the Public Education Sector

It is recommended that the New Brunswick Department of Education and Early Childhood (EECD) and the University of New Brunswick (UNB) continue to support efforts of school-based teams to conduct action research in topics related to UDL to develop teacher capacity for UDL implementation in public education schools. Participants in this project received instruction in action research and writing from UNB, and release time from EECD to develop a research question, conduct the research, develop recommendations, and present findings. Participants were then empowered to share their learning with colleagues; this can help increase UDL implementation at a grassroots level. When teachers see their colleagues having success with implementing UDL they may be more inclined to adopt this framework into their own practice. Additionally, creating opportunities for teachers to conduct and publish action research can serve to add to the body of research around UDL in the K-12 public education sector, and most importantly, allow the field to refine its practice to improve outcomes for all students.

CONCLUSION

UDL implementation has taken me down a path of continual professional learning guided by a framework that represents a collection of research-based practices. When this learning is applied in an intentional manner to remove barriers, promote inclusion, and deliver curriculum to all students through a goals-based approach, we can transform our teaching. Instead of designing instruction for the mythical "average" learner and trying to get all students to learn in one way, the focus has shifted in my practice to finding ways to design instruction for all learners, offering varied options that serve to meet a given objective in an environment that is intentionally designed to include everyone. Learner variability is not an inconvenience that requires accommodation or differentiation; it is an inevitability that teachers must plan for from the outset. It is recommended that teachers engage in professional learning and reference the UDL Guidelines as they follow a personalized approach to implementing UDL, one better practice at a time.

REFERENCES

AuCoin, A., Porter, G. L., & Baker-Korotkov, K. (2020). *New Brunswick's Journey to Inclusive Education.* https://inclusiveeducation.ca/wp-content/uploads/sites/3/2020/09/FINAL-UNESCO-Article-NB-Inclusion-Sept-2020-AuCoin-Porter-Korotkov.pdf

Berquist, E. (2017). *UDL: Moving from exploration to integration.* CAST Professional Publishing.

CAST. (2018). Universal Design for Learning Guidelines version 2.2. Retrieved from http://udlguidelines.cast.org

Craig, S. L., Smith, S. J., & Frey, B. B. (2019). Professional Development with Universal Design for Learning: Supporting Teachers as Learners to Increase the Implementation of UDL. *Professional Development in Education.* Advance online publication. 10.1080/19415257.2019.1685563

Lewis, S. (2018). Universal Design for Learning: A Support for Changing Teacher Practice. *BU Journal of Graduate Studies in Education*, 10(1), 40–43.

Lowrey, K. A., Hollingshead, A., Howery, K., & Bishop, J. B. (2017). More Than One Way: Stories of UDL and Inclusive Classrooms. *Research and Practice for Persons with Severe Disabilities : the Journal of TASH*, 42(4), 225–242. 10.1177/1540796917711668

MacKay, A. W. (2009). *Connecting Care and Challenge: Tapping our Human Potential – Inclusive Education: A Review of Programming and Services in New Brunswick.* https://www2.gnb.ca/content/dam/gnb/Departments/ed/pdf/K12/mackay/ReportOnInclusiveEducationSummaryDocument.pdf

Mrachko, A. (2020). Using the Universal Design for Learning Framework to Plan for All Students in the Classroom: Representation and Visual Support. *The Elementary STEM Journal*, 25(1), 22–24.

Mrachko, A., & Vostal, B. (2020). Using the "Universal Design for Learning" Framework to Plan for All Students in the Classroom: Engagement Through Choice. *The Elementary STEM Journal*, 25(2), 29–31.

Nelson, L. L. (2021). *Design and deliver: Planning and teaching using Universal Design for Learning.* Paul H. Brookes Publishing Co.

Nelson, L. L., & Posey, A. (2019). *A Tree for all; Your coloring book of UDL principles and Practice.* CAST Professional Publishing.

New Brunswick Department of Education and Early Childhood Development. (2013). *Inclusive Education* (Policy 322) https://www2.gnb.ca/content/dam/gnb/Departments/ed/pdf/K12/policies-politiques/e/322A.pdf

Nicol, J. (2024 February 28). *About the UDL Project.* The UDL Project. Retrieved from http://theudlproject.com

Novak, K. (2016). *UDL Now!: A Teacher's Guide to Applying Universal Design for Learning in Today's Classrooms.* Cast Professional Publishing.

Ok, M. W., Rao, K., Bryant, B. R., & McDougall, D. (2016). Universal Design for Learning in Pre-K to Grade 12 Classrooms: A Systematic Review of Research. *Exceptionality.* Advance online publication. 10.1080/09362835.2016.1196450

Porter, G., & AuCoin, A. (2012). *Strengthening Inclusion, Strengthening Schools.* https://www2.gnb.ca/content/dam/gnb/Departments/ed/pdf/K12/Inclusion/StrengtheningInclusionStrengtheningSchools.pdf

Posey, A. (2018). *Engage the Brain: How to Design for Learning That Taps into the Power of Emotion.* ASCD.

Posey, A., & Novak, K. (2020). *Unlearning: Changing your beliefs and your classroom with UDL.* CAST Professional Publishing.

Smith Canter, L. L., King, L. H., Williams, J. B., Metcalf, D., & Myrick Potts, K. R. (2017). Evaluating Pedagogy and Practice of Universal Design for Learning in Public Schools. *Exceptionality Education International*, 27(1), 1–16. 10.5206/eei.v27i1.7743

Vostal, B. R., & Mrachko, A. A. (2021). Using the "Universal Design for Learning" Framework to Plan for All Students in the Classroom: Encouraging Executive Functions. *The Elementary STEM Journal*, 25(3), 32–36.

Chapter 3
The Enactment of the Principles of UDL in Practice in an Irish Post–Primary English Classroom:
A Snapshot

Margaret Flood
Education Department, Maynooth University, Ireland

Louise O'Reilly
https://orcid.org/0000-0002-0785-1153
National Council for Curriculum and Assessment, Ireland

Elish Walsh
Kingswood Community College, Ireland

Sarah Dunne
Kingswood Community College, Ireland

EXECUTIVE SUMMARY

Due to the relative newness of Universal Design for Learning (UDL) in post-primary education in Ireland, there is a lack of examples that show teachers how the principles of UDL work in practice. This chapter addresses this gap through providing snapshots of learning, teaching, and assessment through the lens of representation, engagement, and action and expression. These snapshots take place in two junior cycle English classrooms. The teachers describe the goal and tasks of the lessons,

DOI: 10.4018/978-1-6684-4750-5.ch003

Copyright © 2024, IGI Global. Copying or distributing in print or electronic forms without written permission of IGI Global is prohibited.

take the reader through their UDL planning and actions, and finally reflect—and invite—student reflection on the lessons.

INTRODUCTION

Universal Design for Learning (UDL) is a relatively new concept in early childhood, primary, and post-primary education in Ireland (Flood & Banks, 2021). Efforts to embed UDL in learning and teaching in further and higher education are more established due to the work of the Association of Higher Education and Disability (AHEAD) and the training authority SOLAS in supporting educators develop inclusive practices in response to increasingly diverse student populations. The momentum has been slower in primary and at post-primary with arguments that there needs to be a focus on research evidence, analyzing examples of UDL in practice and their outcomes (Edyburn, 2005; Capp, 2017; Flood & Banks, 2021). This chapter begins to address this gap within the Irish context. It offers two snapshots in time of learning, teaching and assessment using a UDL approach in the junior cycle English classroom in a mainstream post-primary school in Ireland. The principles of engagement, representation, and action and expression permeated through both snapshots. However, for the purpose of this chapter, Snapshot One focuses on engagement and representation over two lessons in Second Year, and Snapshot Two focuses on action and expression over a unit of work in Third Year.

BACKGROUND

In Ireland, post primary education is divided into two stages: junior cycle and senior cycle. Junior cycle is the lower secondary stage of compulsory education and is guided by the *Framework for Junior Cycle* (DES, 2015). The introduction of this framework was a new departure for Irish education in that it sought to incorporate a shared understanding of how teaching, learning, and assessment practices should support "the delivery of a quality, inclusive and relevant education that will meet the needs of junior cycle students" (p. 6). The framework is guided by twenty-four statements of learning, eight principles, and eight key skills that are at the core of all subject specifications.

The Enactment of the Principles of UDL

LITERATURE REVIEW

In recent years, the conversation around inclusion in Irish schools has been shifting towards equitable education and the adoption of UDL (Bray et al., 2023; Flood & Banks, 2021; Reynor, 2021). However, inclusive education in Ireland has historically been viewed through the special education lens and until recently, the prevalent model of choice for including students with Special Educational Needs (SEN) in Ireland was differentiation (Flood & Banks, 2021). However, this deficit-based approach focused on what was perceived as wrong with the child rather than on addressing how the curriculum and lesson designs created barriers to their learning. To promote UDL effectively, it is essential to emphasize that it is not something adopted solely for some students, but rather a framework designed to benefit every student (Meyer et al., 2014).

The Irish government has made significant policy advancements towards inclusive education. Internationally, the Salamanca Statement (UNESCO, 1994) accelerated the inclusion trajectory globally, influencing Ireland to adopt more inclusive practices. Nationally, the Report of the Special Education Review Committee (SERC) (DES, 1994) led to the promotion of inclusion in mainstream schools for students with SEN, as the report's key outcomes highlighted the responsibility of schools to cater for all learners and the need for student-focused decision making and legislation (Banks & McCoy, 2011). Subsequent legislation, such as the Education Act (1998) and the EPSEN Act (2004), further supported the provision of supports for students with SEN in schools. The EPSEN Act redefined SEN to include any condition that impacts on a person's learning and emphasized the importance of inclusive education for children with SEN, encouraging their education alongside mainstream peers whenever possible. Despite not being fully enacted, the EPSEN Act has remained a blueprint for delivering resources to students with SEN (NCSE, 2014). The EPSEN Act is currently under review to ensure that legislation on education for students with SEN is adequate, fully operational, and reflective of the lived experiences of students with SEN and their families (DES, 2022).

Formally established under the EPSEN Act, NCSE has played a significant role in promoting inclusive education through various initiatives. Most recently, the NCSE published an interim report on special classes and schools in Ireland (NCSE, 2019). This report highlighted that Ireland was in contravention of Article 24 of the United Nations Convention on the Rights of persons with Disabilities (UNCRPD) (United Nations, 2008) which was ratified in Ireland in 2018. It argued that students with SEN should preferably - and possibly could - be educated in mainstream classes with their peers, while also pointing out that current school structures mean schools are not prepared to do this. The report went on to explore how Ireland could ensure students with SEN have a right to access equitable primary and post-primary education. The report outlined NCSE's exploration of New Brunswick's model of full inclusion based on UDL, as an approach to meet the rights of Irish students with SEN. However, it did acknowledge the variety of opinions concerning full inclusion in mainstream classes in Ireland, and the hesitation that might exist as to whether it is a desirable change. The report noted that for changes in inclusion to occur, teachers would require effective professional learning in inclusive teaching and learning practices.

As legislation continues to develop around special and inclusive education in Ireland, government bodies like the National Council for Curriculum and Assessment (NCCA) provide advice, guidelines, and directives to educators. The NCCA's work on curriculum access for students with SEN (NCCA, 1999, 2016, 2018) has emphasized that the principles underlying education for SEN students are the same as those for every student, reinforcing the inclusive nature of UDL. Embracing UDL as a guiding framework can help Ireland create more equitable and inclusive educational environments, ensuring that every student's unique needs are met and celebrated.

The concept of UDL was first introduced into Irish curriculum design in The Framework for Junior Cycle (FJC) (DES, 2015). Recognizing the diverse backgrounds, interests, and needs of students in junior cycle, the framework emphasized the importance of providing meaningful and valuable learning opportunities for all students. The subject specifications and short courses designed by the NCCA for junior cycle were crafted following the principles of universal design, aiming to provide "meaningful and valuable learning opportunities for students from all cultural and social backgrounds and from a wide variety of individual circumstances" to cater to the diverse student population (DES, 2015, p.26). By incorporating UDL in curriculum design, the framework supports inclusion by offering students multiple pathways to achieve the Junior Cycle Profile of Achievement (JCPA).

Exploring the junior cycle framework from a UDL perspective, evidence of UDL design can be observed beyond subject specifications and short courses, although there is no explicit relationship between UDL and the framework design itself. The junior cycle framework is designed to serve as one curriculum for every student, comprising eight principles, twenty-four statements of learning, and eight key skills. However, where UDL comes into action is through the provision of multiple pathways for students to achieve their JCPA. Students can choose from traditional level 3 subjects with Classroom Based Assessments (CBAs) and end-of-cycle state examinations, Short Courses with CBAs only, Level 2 Learning Programmes (L2LPs) for students with a General Learning Disability (GLD) in the low mild to high moderate range of ability, and Level 1 Learning Programmes (L1LPs) for students with a GLD in the low moderate to severe or profound range of ability. The flexibility of learning outcomes and framing within the specifications allows

The Enactment of the Principles of UDL

for various teaching approaches depending on the school context and student group, which aligns with UDL principles.

The integration of UDL within the junior cycle curriculum supports the goal of fostering inclusive education in Ireland. By offering diverse pathways, students with different abilities and needs can access the curriculum in ways that best support their learning and development. This approach acknowledges the uniqueness of each student and ensures that educational opportunities are tailored to meet their specific requirements. All specifications are learning outcomes focused and this is where UDL comes to the forefront. The broad flexibility and framing of these learning outcomes enable them to be taught in various ways depending on the context of the school and student cohort (Flood & Banks, 2021), creating a more inclusive and accommodating learning environment, promoting equitable education for all students.

APPLYING UDL TO THE FRAMEWORK FOR JUNIOR CYCLE

Universal Design for Learning as an approach to inclusive education offers a framework for teachers to embed inclusive practices into their planning, learning, and teaching, and reflective practices. As a proactive approach to learning, teaching, and assessment design (Meyer et al., 2014), UDL promotes an intentional design process that anticipates barriers to learning and student variability (varied identities, competencies, learning strengths, and needs). This predictable variability mindset supports teachers provide a variety of students with choices to understand content, create goals that are clear and specific to expected outcomes, and design flexible assessments that enable every student to demonstrate their knowledge, values, understanding, and skills in a variety of ways.

Three principles to reduce barriers, multiple means of engagement, multiple means of representation, and multiple means of action and expression, underpin UDL and reflect the intentions of the principles and key skills of the Framework for Junior Cycle (DES, 2015)

Principles

The underpinning principles of the Junior Cycle Framework (JCF) explicitly name inclusive education, engagement and participation, choice and flexibility, creativity and innovation, continuity and development, and learning to learn, as the core outcomes of students' learning at this level. Inclusive education in the framework is further defined as "inclusive of all students and contributes to equality of opportunity, participation and outcomes for all" (DES, 2015, p.11). The principle of engagement and participation states that "the experience of curriculum, assessment, teaching and learning encourages participation, generates engagement and enthusiasm, and connects with life outside the school" (ibid. p. 11). The choice and flexibility principle aims to "offer a wide range of learning experiences to all, and flexible enough to offer choice to meet the needs of students" (ibid, p.11). In seeking to realise these principles in the experience of the classroom, much can be gained from the application of UDL.

Key Skills

These UDL principles are also echoed in the key skills for learning identified in the curriculum documentation (Figure 1) *Communicating, being literate, Managing myself, Staying well, Managing information and thinking, Being numerate, Being creative and Working with others.*

The Enactment of the Principles of UDL

Figure 1. Key skills at junior cycle

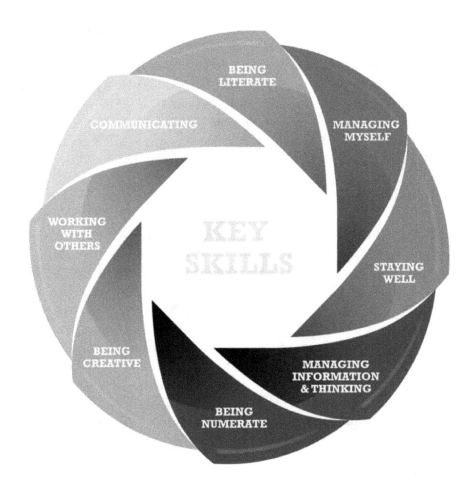

In striving to remove barriers, UDL emphasizes the need to develop agentic learners who are purposeful and motivated (engagement), resourceful and knowledgeable (representation), and strategic and goal-orientated (action and expression) (Meyer et al, 2014; CAST, 2018). Teachers intentionally incorporate the development of these key skills by providing a continuum of access, building understanding and agency. These key skills are integrated into the lesson or activity goals and are developed throughout each lesson. For teachers, this process starts with the learning outcomes set out within each strand of their subject specifications.

The JCF "outlines the curriculum and assessment arrangements that will provide students with learning opportunities that achieve a balance between learning subject knowledge and developing a wide range of skills and thinking abilities" des, 2015, p7). Traditional subject areas, such as English, mathematics, history and geography, were supplemented with a range of short courses in areas such as coding, digital media literacy, philosophy, and artistic performance. Wellbeing was introduced as an area of learning for all students, and a number of priority learning units were introduced for students with significant educational needs. All of the specifications for the subjects, short courses, and learning units were designed to align with the underpinning principles and key skills and enable the students to achieve the statements of learning.

English at Junior Cycle

The English specification (NCCA, 2015) is structured across three strands with three interactive and interdependent elements. The three strands (oral language, reading and writing) are described in terms of learning outcomes under the three element headings (Communicating as a listener, speaker, reader, writer; Exploring and using language; Understanding the content and structure of language). The learning outcomes detail the actions students should be able to undertake on the completion of the course and use verbs such as: deliver, choose, listen, engage, apply, collaborate, demonstrate, identify, select, and respond. A sub-set of the learning outcomes are identified as appropriate outcomes for students in the initial year of the programme, while others are identified as those on which the final assessment will be based. There is a dual approach to assessment in junior cycle consisting of two structured classroom-based assessments and a final externally assessed examination.

The alignment between the principles, key skills, statements of learning, and learning outcomes can be seen in the example given in Table 1.

Table 1. Principles, key skills, statements of learning, and learning outcomes

Principle	Key skill	Statement of learning	Learning outcome
Engagement and participation	Communicating	1. communicates effectively using a variety of means in a range of contexts	Strand: Writing Element: Communicating as a listener, speaker, reader, writer. LO5: Engage with and learn from models of oral and written language use to enrich their own written work.

continued on following page

The Enactment of the Principles of UDL

Table 1. Continued

Principle	Key skill	Statement of learning	Learning outcome
Creativity and innovation	Being creative	3. Creates, appreciates and critically interprets a wide range of texts	Stand: Oral Language Element: Exploring and using language LO10: Collaborate with others in order to explore and discuss understandings of spoken texts by recording, analysing, interpreting and comparing their opinions.

In the context of the English classroom, there are opportunities to incorporate UDL to achieve the inclusion, engagement, and creativity principles of the framework while also developing the key skills of literacy, managing information, and communicating. The English specification aims to encourage all students to "develop control over English using it and responding to it with purpose and effect through interconnected literacy skills of oral language, reading and writing" (NCCA & Department of Education and Skills, 2018, p. 5). The inclusion of oral language skills, in addition to reading and writing skills, allows for multiple means of engagement, representation, and expression to be incorporated into the classroom experience. Throughout the subject specifications, there are references to the inclusion of digital media, multi-modal texts, visual images, and soundtracks. Students are encouraged to explore these texts, develop their own responses, and create their own examples. In the contextual example explored here, UDL principles are applied to the specific aims of the English classroom while also incorporating the broader curricular principles of inclusion, engagement, and creativity.

METHODS

This paper focuses on two snapshots in time of learning, teaching, and assessment using a UDL approach in the junior cycle English classroom in a mainstream post-primary school in Ireland. It takes an action research approach to explore the application of UDL principles in the context of constructivism and the social justice model of inclusion. Action Research (Cohen, Manion & Morrison, 2011) is a participatory and iterative method of inquiry to address problems, improve prcatices, and create knowleddhe within a specific context, in this class promoting inclusion in the classroom. It is a procees of planning, acting, observing and reflecting to enable practioners to imlement change, access its impact and modift based on their learning throughout the process. This piece of action research considers an adaptive model of inclusion, which emphasizes adapting the learning environment to meet the diverse needs of all learners. The snapshots were gathered in a co-educational school setting, examing the experiences of two teachers.

Philosophical Framework

The philosophical foundation of this study aligns with constructivism and the social justice model of inclusion. Constructivism posits that knowledge is actively constructed by learners through their experiences and interactions with the learning environment (Crotty, 1998). This aligns with the UDL philosophy, which emphasizes offering multiple means of representation, engagement, and expression to cater to diverse learning needs (Meyer & Rose, 2002). The social justice model of inclusion emphasizes providing equitable opportunities and access to quality education for all students, regardless of their backgrounds or abilities (Slee, 2001). This model resonates with the goal of UDL to foster an inclusive learning environment that celebrates diversity and promotes equal opportunities for all learners (Meyer et al., 2014).

Data Collection Tools

Qualitative methodological tools were used to gain an understanding of the teachers' experiences, perceptions, and practices related to UDL implementation in order to present a snapshop of their practice in 2nd and 3rd year English classes. The lesson plans of these snapshot lessons were analyzed to examine how UDL principles are integrated into their instructional design and content delivery. Built-in student feedback as part of the teaching and learning process provided insights into the effectiveness of UDL practices from the learners' perspectives. Teachers' observations of their own instructional practices, interactions with students, and the level of engagement and participation among diverse learners informed teachers' reflections and adpatations. These teachers' reflections enabled continuous consideration of practice, challenges, and successes related to UDL implementation.

Limitations

Despite efforts to ensure rigour and trustworthiness, this study has certain limitations. As a small-scale action research study conducted in a single co-educational school with a limited population of two teachers, the findings may not be directly generalizable to other contexts or educational settings. The limited timeframe for data collection and analysis may restrict the depth and breadth of the study. A more extended research period could provide a more comprehensive understanding of UDL implementation and its long-term effects. Finally, despite efforts to minimize bias, the researchers' preconceptions and perspectives may still influence data collection and analysis. Openly acknowledging and addressing potential bias will be crucial to maintain research integrity

The Enactment of the Principles of UDL

CONTEXT

The examples of UDL implementation that follow were observed in a secondary school in south-west Dublin, Ireland. The school was established in 2015. It is a multi-denominational, co-educational school with 870 students, 60 teachers, and 10 Special Needs Assistants. It is a 1:1 Apple Distinguished school. The school prioritizes inclusion for every student in its community. UDL was introduced to school staff as part of a research project in 2018 to develop inclusive practices for students participating in their Level 2 Learning Programmes (L2LPs). However, it was quickly realised that this was an approach that could benefit every student and support teachers' planning, teaching, and assessment. Working with the researcher, teachers progressively developed their knowledge, beliefs, and skills in inclusion and UDL. The school now has a UDL team and a UDL strategic plan for continued growth of UDL implementation with the school community.

Two English teachers from this school employed UDL to design lessons for their junior cycle English classrooms. Their experiences are sahred through two snaps-shots in time: one from Second Year, consisting of two class periods, and one from Third Year. Both detail activities aimed at supporting students at different stages of their Classroom-Based Assessments (CBA) 2. The Collection of Texts (CBA 2) is the second of two CBAs to be completed by junior cycle English students. It requires students to produce at least four creative pieces of work, representative of different genres. With the support of their class teacher, students write, edit, and re-write their collection of texts during the second and third year of post primary. Students select two of their pieces for final assessment by their class teacher. CBA 2 was developed to support a number of the junior cycle English Learning Outcomes as detailed in table 2.

Although they will be highlighted separately, within the respective snapshots, the three principles of UDL can be seen to overlap and were considered as such in the design and delivery of these activities. It is important to note that UDL is not a checklist, but rather an approach to teaching and learning which considers all students capable of achieving the same learning outcomes through the effective, proactive removal of barriers and/or scaffolding carried out by students.

Table 2. Junior cycle learning outcomes focused on for CBA 2. Selected from junior cycle English specification (DES, 2015)

STRAND 1	Oral Language 1	Know and use the conventions of oral language interaction, in a variety of contexts, including class groups, for a range of purposes, such as asking for information, stating an opinion, listening to others, informing, explaining, arguing, persuading, criticizing, commentating, narrating, imagining, speculating

continued on following page

Table 2. Continued

STRAND 2	Reading 6	Read their texts for understanding and appreciation of character, setting, story and action: to explore how and why characters develop, and to recognise the importance of setting and plot structure
	Reading 8	Read their texts to understand and appreciate language enrichment by examining an author's choice of words, the use and effect of simple figurative language, vocabulary and language patterns, and images, as appropriate to the text
STRAND 3	Writing 1	Demonstrate their understanding that there is a clear purpose for all writing activities and be able to plan, draft, re-draft, and edit their own writing as appropriate
	Writing 4	Write competently in a range of text forms, for example letter, report, multi-modal text, review, blog, using appropriate vocabulary, tone and a variety of styles to achieve a chosen purpose for different audiences
	Writing 7	Respond imaginatively in writing to their texts showing a critical appreciation of language, style and content, choice of words, language patterns, tone, images
	Writing 13	Evaluate their own writing proficiency and seek remedies for those aspects of their writing that they need to improve

SNAPSHOT 1: REPRESENTATION AND ENGAGEMENT

This snapshop describes a series of lessons aimed at revising concepts learned in the previous school year and developing creative writing skills underpinned by the principles of representation and engagement. The aim of this snapshot is to explore how English teachers can create an authentic learning experience, while removing the barriers to imagination and creativity that are often experienced in the English classroom. The lessons took place in the October of second year. At that time, students were present in the classroom following a period of distance learning in the previous school year. The initial creative writing lessons took place during the COVID pandemic, and, as a result, the teacher found it necessary to develop this lesson of revision once the students were back in the physical classroom.

Lesson 1: Representation

When designing this lesson, the teacher identified the learning characteristics and the individual needs of the students within their classroom. In this mainstream class of 30 students, there were a variety of Addition Support Needs (ASN) identified. The ASNs within this class included dyslexia, developmental coordination disorder, autistic spectrum disorder, and dysgraphia. A clear understanding of the varied needs of the class allowed the teacher to determine what could be required to enable each student to succeed in the lesson; it encouraged the teacher to remove any possible barriers to understanding, engagement, and expression. Vital to their capacity to enact UDL successfully, is the fact that the teacher used their lesson

The Enactment of the Principles of UDL

objectives and learning goals to identify and remove barriers, by clarifying the goals and building UDL principles into the lesson planning.

The aim of this lesson was for students to revisit prior learning using creative writing techniques they had developed in their first year of post primary education in order to begin to scaffold the elements needed to write an extended piece for CBA 2: Collection of Texts. The objective of developing the key skill of literacy permeated throughout the lesson. As this was a revision lesson on this topic, the teacher used previously encountered images and symbols to promote connection to the learners' experience and their prior knowledge (Representation 2.1: Clarify vocabulary and symbols). By using a variety of texts incorporating multimodal means of representation, the educator was able to remove barriers to accessing content; this in turn supported each learner to be successful at achieving the learning objective.

This lesson began with a recall activity. Students were greeted with the five senses written on the board; each sense was accompanied by an image to represent their meaning. The symbols used were the same as those used during the initial learning experience: an eye, a nose, a mouth, a pointing finger, and an ear. The use of familiar images accompanying the words aimed to anchor any new learning within previous learning. Furthermore, it facilitated access for students whose primary language was not English (Representation 2.4: Promote understanding across languages). The goal of this recall exercise was for students to suggest words they could use to describe the five senses. Students had previously examined incorporating the five senses in descriptive writing from a theoretical lens (viewing other writers work in both short stories and poetry). This unit of learning was asking them to implement their learning on a practical level. Activating the students' previous knowledge (Representation 3.1: Activate or supply background knowledge) on the topic established a basis for their learning consolidation and progression, and also promoted the development of the key skill of literacy.

This activity was followed by time for students to connect and share their ideas with each other. A mind map was used to link words that had similar meanings, providing support and creating challenge for students. For example, when more complex words were suggested by a student, they were asked to use their iPads to search for an image to represent that word. Allowing students to provide their own images further developed the students' own descriptive writing skills, and extended everyone's vocabulary in the class. In terms of students achieving their goals, this section of the lesson was essential for laying the foundation for the piece of work they were to complete. It allowed the teacher to guide the exploration of a topic through an active discussion, and to introduce new learning in a safe and accessible manner.

For the main body of the lesson, students engaged in the collaborative exercise of 'Think-Pair-Share' followed by a period of independent work. Both of these activities prompted the devlopment of the key skills of communicating and managing

65

information. Used to develop the "Show! Don't Tell" method of creative writing, this exercise, introduced in year one of junior cycle English, asks the writer to use emotive writing and actions to allow the reader to experience the writing rather than being explicitly told how they should feel and think. The activity consisted of several elements, all of which asked the student to create "Show! Don't Tell" sentences as a response to a stimulus shown. Students had the opportunity to create their own sentence, share their work with their partner, and then discuss it as a class. The material was presented to students in the following formats:

- Develop basic sentences: they were asked to enhance sentences such as *'I am tired', said Mary.*
- Create pieces of writing based on an image and small video clip
- Decipher the technique: students read a short piece on the board (the piece was also available on our virtual learning environment (VLE) as an image and an audio clip) and were asked to highlight where they saw the method in action

To complete their lesson goal, students were asked to use vocabulary, understanding, and ideas developed throughout the lesson to work independently on a small piece of writing. Using a short video clip as a prompt students were asked to record what they saw or how they may have felt if they were experiencing it for themselves. Students were not required to write or develop a story or to have their sentences connecting. This was a 'record what you see/hear exercise' and removing the expectation for a structured written piece enabled both teacher and students to develop literacy, descriptive vocabulary, and creative ideas. This approach removed barriers by allowing students to focus on their thoughts and not the written word.

Lesson 2: Engagement

The goal of this lesson was for students to write an introductory paragraph to an extended creative piece of writing based on an image provided. The aim was to send students on a journey within which they created a piece of extended creative writing that they could add to their CBA 2: Collection of Texts. With creativity a key requirement to achieve this goal, the teacher sought to create an engaging and authentic learning experience based on the varied characteristics of the class and potential barriers that asking student to be imaginative might create. It was here the teacher decided to incorporate the principle of engagement to remove these potential

The Enactment of the Principles of UDL

barriers. Rather than have students write assumptively based on an image, the student learning would become experiential, and the stimulus image would 'come to life'.

This lesson began as students were entering the classroom. A stimulus image was on the board and on the VLE. This stimulus image was chosen to coincide with the time of year to allow for tangible links to be built with the natural environment the students entered, which would support students' engagement in later tasks in the lesson. At this point, students were asked to comment on how the five senses could be used to describe what they saw, and some examples were provided. By being given examples or prompts, students were able to see the desired outcome of this activity (Engagement 8.1: Heighten salience of goals and objectives). Having the image on the board and uploaded online allowed students, who may need more time to process what they were seeing, to have the added flecibility. Next, students were asked to explicitly state why they suggested certain words and exactly what part of the image inspired this. Student vocabulary was further enriched by creating a whole-class list of synomys for each of the students' words. While this activity was taking place, the words were being written on the board, allowing for an alternative to auditory information; this also nurtured the collaborative flavour of the classroom community (Engagement 8.3: Foster collaboration and community). Students were then invited to take a picture of the board, allowing for a visual representation of the discussion

Students were then given the objective of the lesson: Write a descriptive paragraph to serve as an introduction to an extended piece of writing based on a stimulus material (an image)[1] It should be noted that although language such as 'stimulus material' may be difficult for some learners, this language may appear in their Junior Cycle final exam and has been used continuously in the classroom.

Through a 'Think-Pair-Share' activity, students were asked to devise a set of 'success criteria' for their final piece of work, allowing students to participate in the design of their task (Engagement 7.1: Optimize individual choice and autonomy). Enabling students to set their own guidelines for success enables them to develop self-assessment and reflection skills, which are essential to Junior Cycle (Engagement 9.3: Develop self-assessment and reflection).

The main body of the lesson was designed for students to engage in an immersive experience. Using a worksheet, available as both a hardcopy and a softcopy on their iPads, students were required to explore their senses throughout the school grounds and describe what they saw, smelled, heard, felt, and tasted on the worksheet. Using the environment around them grounded the learning experience in reality, removing the abstract element that can otherwise be a barrier for some. Students did not just read from a book or watch a video. They created their own learning tools. They built on the knowledge learned in class and were able to implement it in a genuine way. The activity recruited the interest of the learners in a legitimate manner; they were learning from their experience. (Engagement 7.2: Optimize relevance, value, and authenticity).

The final activity saw students write their descriptive piece. They were given time to plan their piece. Students had access to examples of plans, highlighting good practice, but were also given the freedom to develop their plan in accordance with how they learn best. Additionally, the students had continuous access to both the stimulus image, their worksheet notes, and the earlier created 'success criteria' through the writing process.

SNAPSHOT 2: ACTION AND EXPRESSION

This second snapshot describes a series of activities with Third Year students, aimed at providing support to students tasked with producing two creative pieces of work that could be submitted for their CBA 2: The Collection of Texts. Activities detailed here were carried out with a 3rd Year junior cycle English class. These activities took place before Christmas of third year during the final stages of the study of a prescribed novel. The novel was positioned as a stimulus for the creative pieces; however, students were not restricted to it when it came to creative ideas.

The Lesson

The class group of 30 contained a varied profile of learners, including students with English as an additional language, students with a specific learning difficulty, mild general learning difficulty, uutism and attention feficit hyperactivity disorder, and exceptionally able. Considering the diversity of this group and the opportunity for choice within CBA 2, the action and expression principle of UDL was focused on. UDL requires the teacher to view the intended learning goal from the perspective of all students in their class and to consider the possible barriers to achievement. In this instance, the teacher considered the foremost barriers to be constrained means of creative expression and a lack of self-evaluation to aid improvement. The chosen response to this was to offer multiple modes of expression to students in their creative writing pieces and to include students in the assessment process.

To begin, the teacher outlined the learning goals of the unit of work and provided the students with the plan for the lessons. This was a student-friendly version of the teacher's lesson plans, with added scaffolding material for students to choose from. The teacher referred to this document as the road map. This term was chosen to emphasise its use in helping students reach their destination - creating two pieces of work. All elements of the roadmap are detailed belowand could be adapted to suit other topics.

The Enactment of the Principles of UDL

The roadmap had three stages: plan; create; assess. It was designed to ensure the students were aware of what they were to produce and how they could accomplish this throughout the process (Action and Expression 6.1: guide appropriate goal setting). This roadmap document was thoroughly explored with the group and provided to them on their Virtual Learning Environment (VLE)and in printed form. Students added their work to this document and referred to it during the process (Action and Expression 5.1: use multiple tools for communication*)*.

Stage 1: Plan

Students were given the option of chosing among four genres of language and four modes of expression (Action and Expression 5.2: using multiple tools for construction and composition*)*(table 3). They had the choice to match any one genre with any one mode of expression. Each mode and each genre could be selected only once to encourage students to challenge themselves in their exploration of different genres. From this initial selection, they would customise two pieces based on their preferred style and mode of expression. Also, as these pieces were being planned at the end of the study of a novel, students were able to use this text as inspiration and as source material.

Table 3. Teacher designed options for genres of language and modes of expression

Genre	Mode	Minimum work to be produced for chosen mode
Creative (short story, poem, diary entry, dialogue)	Handwritten document	2 A4 pages
Formal or Informal Letter	Presentation	15 slides
Exploration of Three Key Moments	Video	3 minutes
Production Design	Typed document	800 words

In groups of eight, students brainstormed ideas on an assigned genre. The groups were free to select their preferred mode of expression based on their ideas. Students were aware that they were not bound by the suggested ideas of their group; they could decide their individual pieces later. The following questions were provided to aid their discussion:

- What ideas/topics could feature under this genre?
- Which mode would you choose to represent this? Why?

The Enactment of the Principles of UDL

The groups collated their ideas and recorded them in their roadmaps. They shared their favourite ideas with the class. Students were encouraged to take notes on anything they found interesting. They could adopt any or all of a suggested ideas when planning their individual pieces (Action and Expression 6.1: supporting planning and strategy development). This feedback session not only supported students' creativity around the content that could feature in a genre, but also ensured thoughtful consideration of mode. One group suggested that a dialogue (genre) between the two main characters of the novel could work well as a video (mode) using a voice-over and accompanying images. Another group recognised that the pre-existing template for a formal letter (mode) on their Pages App would help them to structure their personal response letter to the author (genre). These considerations would also support students when it came to the reflection note which accompanies the Collection of Texts expectation, as this too requires students to explain their choices (Action and Expression 5.3: build fluencies with graduated levels of support for practice and performance).

Next, the success criteria and minimum requirements for each of the four genres was examined on the roadmap document. The students were familiar with these criteria from previous pieces of work, but the teacher assembled them here for ease of reference. Students were made aware that the success criteria directly translated to the grading rubric. Students were given time to ask questions on any of the criteria listed. In this way, all aspects of the assessment process were revealed to the students to help with planning and execution of their creative pieces.

As with any universally designed assessment, it was important here that the success criteria remained comparable, regardless of the mode of expression. This ensured high expectations, as well as equity of assessment across all options. For example, the success criteria in table 4 which was used for the "Exploration of Three Key Moments" genre could have been, and was, represented in a number of modes. There was no additional reward for choosing any one mode over another. The reward was in the students' ability to better represent their learning.

Table 4. Teacher designed success criteria - exploration of three key scenes

Success Criteria - Exploration of Three Key Scenes
Must have a clear introduction and conclusion
Must include direct quotes /evidence from the text (min of 4 quotes)
Must explain why these moments are important in the plot development
Must reference a studied theme within these key moments

The success criteria were easily translated into a grading rubric by weighing the categories based on their impact to the success of the piece, which in this instance was evenly. Each category was then divided into four scales of achievement in line

The Enactment of the Principles of UDL

with the Junior Cycle grade descriptors; Yet to meet expectations (1), In line with Expectations (2), Above expectations (3), Exceptional (4). Finally, the minimum requirement for each mode (table 3) was provided and discussed with students. This was not part of the success criteria, but was helpful to students to have an idea of length in each mode and to encourage students to see a parity between these modes In this way there was no "easy" option.

This planning stage took two 1hr classes. Students were not given homework, but were asked to think about what two pieces of work they would like to produce. Their choices were not only based on their individual preferences for genre and mode of expression, but were also aided by collaborative creative ideas, a clear grading rubric, and transparent expected requirements (Action and Expression 4.1: various methods of response and navigation). The students were now prepared to move onto the execution of two creative pieces.

Stage 2: Create

The creation process was a personalised experience for each student and involved minimal instruction from the teacher. The students had access to the scaffolding material within their roadmaps. In addition to this, the students were provided with one exemplar from each of the four genres. These sample pieces were accessible on the VLE but could also be printed. These were pieces of work completed by students during previous units of learning that had been collated by the teacher.[2] This supported students in understanding what excellence in these genres looked like. When comparing these exemplars to the rubrics, students could identify success in these pieces.

Having this variety of scaffolded material empowered students to customise not only their expression of learning but also the supports they wished to access while doing so (Action and Expression 6.2: support strategy and planning development). This freed-up the teacher to be able to move around the room and supervise progress. The teacher fielded questions and intervened at an individual levels, as needed. Students who needed additional support could signal to the teacher without having to stop the rest of the class from working. The creation of their two pieces took place over three 1hr classes and students could work on their pieces at home, if they wished, as no additional homework was given.

Stage 3: Assess

Using the grading rubric from their roadmap document, students self-assessed one of their pieces while the teacher assessed the other. As discussed in the planning section, the rubrics were simple and matched the success criteria with which students were familiar. The teacher requested that students also include one comment for improvement on their work. The students uploaded their work to the VLE. The teacher, over the space of a week, assessed their second piece using the relevant rubric This process can be effective without a VLE if students assess their work and complete a physical copy of the rubric. The teacher can evaluate the second piece and fill in the other physical rubric.

The teacher also reviewed but did not alter the students' self-assessment, as this would undermine the process.

From this process, students were better able to understand their level of achievement as well as routes to improve this (Action and Expression 6.4: enhance capacity for monitoring progress). In this instance, the teacher did not specifically request that the students implement this feedback due to time pressures. However, students were aware that they could redraft and submit either or both of these for their junior cycle English CBA 2: The Collection of Texts.

DISCUSSION OF SNAPSHOTS: TEACHER REFLECTIONS

Snapshot 1

Activities in Snapshot One were at the core of the students' learning, and were fundamental to allowing the students to access and engage with the material in a multimodal context.

The lessons were created to revise learning that had occurred during online learning over the period of the COVID pandemic. The teacher felt it a necessary exercise due to varied levels of interaction from students during the period of online learning. The teacher not only saw the need for, but also the value of, the scaffolding element to the lesson. The students engaged well with the initial recall activity. This created a sense of confidence that was vital for students throughout this lesson. The 'reuse' of the same symbols from the previous year was invaluable in allowing students to link to their previous learning. Many students were very quiet when it came to the class discussion element of the lesson. A way to counteract that would be to use the VLE to type their answers or to have them write their answers on post-it notes.

The main activity in the lessons, the collaboration and 'Think- Pair-Share' exercises, weas successful to a degree. The collaborative discussion worked well and, according to the teacher's observations, the students actively discussed the work and created effective creative sentences, but many pairs failed to complete the activity. There are two possible changes that could be made to improve this task in the future. One is to not have as many examples on the board, thus allowing the students to dedicate more time to each individual example. The second would

The Enactment of the Principles of UDL

be to have the examples available on their iPad, allowing students to work through them at their own pace and allowing them to choose the examples they would like to work on. In trying to create an authentic learning experience while ensuring the knowledge would be transferable to the requirements of the curriculum, it was clear from the teacher's observations that the students really enjoyed this lesson. It was successful in its goal, as many students chose to have this piece used as part of their CBA 2: Collection of Texts, at the end of 2nd Year. Having the students immerse themselves in the learning by bringing them outside was the most successful part of the lesson. The teacher was surprised that all students chose to use the hardcopy of the worksheet and wanted to leave their iPads in the classroom; many noted that it was simply easier to write on the hardcopy. When planning this lesson in the future, the teacher would allow for more time to be spent outside. Many of the students gravitated towards small groups and pair formations.

Through this learning and assessment process scaffolded material was released at a slow pace, building on previous knowledge and introducing new learning, offering each learner differentiated degrees of challenge. This allowed students to be comfortable in this deeply engaging learning setting. If this activity had occurred with no scaffolding in place, there may have been too many alternatives presented to students at once (visual, audio, or tactile). In turn, this would have created a barrier to learning and overwhelming students but, because the class was able to establish a strong foundation, students were equipped with the vocabulary and decoding skills needed to succeed. It was an activity that crossed language and learning barriers. It took a unit of learning that had been based in theory and made it practical. This is something that is usually more difficult to do in the English classroom.

The aim of the representation and engagement principles is to create expert learners who are purposeful and motivated. By recruiting students' interest and optimising the authenticity of the learning, it was clear that the activity succeeded in ensuring that pieces the students wrote became 'theirs'. Their efforts were sustained; they challenged themselves because they were writing about their experiences. They felt the crunch of the leaves under their school shoe; they felt the wind that blew their hair out of place. They were no longer writing about an image on the board. They were writing about what they had experienced.

A significant change the teacher might make would be to give students further options for the presentation of their work. The piece presented for the CBA does not have to be written. The teacher could offer varied avenues for success in this respect, by allowing students to present their work as a podcast, a video, or by diversifying the method of presenting written work.

Snapshot 2

The teacher was impressed with the quality and diversity of work submitted by this group. The creative genre was the most popular and was selected by 46% of students: 25% explored a key moment, 21% designed a production, and 8% composed a letter. The popularity of the creative genre might be explained by the fact that this option offered learners further opportunity for choice. Students created short-stories, poems, book reviews, and diary entries. Importantly, the variety of choices made by students both between and within the genres is an indication that they embraced the opportunity for individual expression. Lack of choice here would have greatly limited their creativity. The low up-take for the letter writing genre may indicate its lack of relevance in the lives of the students. This could be remedied with a more contemporary alternative, such as the composition of an email or blog post.

Of the four formats provided, 58% of students submitted a written piece, 33% chose the presentation, 8% chose the typed document, and 1% chose to display their learning through video. When surveryed on their choice of format, students' repsonses indicated an awareness of not only their personal preference, but also the merits of different formats. Their choices were based on the basis of what they perceived to be the best format for their purposes.

My creativity in embodying myself as the character works best in a handwritten format for a diary entry (Student 1).

I chose a presentation as I thought this was the best way to explain my answer best as well as using pictures and images. (Student 2)

I chose to present my work in a typed document/presentation. I chose that because, in my opinion, I feel like I can type more (therefore include more) content into each answer. I also don't have to worry about my handwriting being illegible as the text is uniform and I can chose the font, edit the size etc. I also think I can complete my work faster than if I were to write up my work. I picked a typed document for my creative writing poem because I could freely place the text wherever I wanted, edit the text and, if I didn't like the format, I could just 'undo'. (Student 3)

There was a notable lack of videos selected for the expression of learning. As students appear to be cognizant of the capabilities of their formats, it may be that the teacher has yet to offer a genre that would be best expressed through video. Perhaps more film focused options such as a trailer, documentary, or vlog would facilite expression through video. Also, videos - or more accurately highquality videos - take extensive amounts of time to create, more so than the other three formats. An option here could be to allow students to work in pairs or group and co-create their videos. This would reduce workload and encourage collaborative skills.

The Enactment of the Principles of UDL

RECOMMENDATIONS

The exploration of the above snapshots demonstrates that the aspects of UDL threaded across the junior cycle English curriculum can be, and in this instance are being, used to support teaching and learning to develop learners' confidence and capacity in the English classroom.. Thus, the potential of UDL to increase student engagement, participation, and achievement is actively demonstrated. However, this paper provides a snapshot of a much larger picture and more large-scale studies are required in order to explore these repercussions further. More national and international research providing evidence-based examples of UDL in practice and its outcomes will inform current research and also support teachers in their learning. (Edyburn, 2005; Capp, 2017; Flood & Banks, 2021).

Creating a solid foundation of evidence supporting UDL implementation is essential to drive policy change and foster development. It is crucial to establish a clear connection between the relevance and positive outcomes of UDL in promoting inclusive learning, teaching, and assessment in Ireland. This notion aligns with NCSE's (2019) findings on teacher learning and practice, which indicates that teachers require professional development before they can successfully develop inclusive practices, such as UDL. The teachers in this study had access to previous UDL professional development.. This is not the case nationally. Despite the fact that UDL is gaining momentum at secondary level in Ireland, professional learning opportunities for UDL remain limited at both Initial Teacher Education (ITE) and practicing teacher levels. To address the need for professional development (NCSE, 2019), a systematic approach to the provision of UDL professional learning programmes, alongside other inclusive teaching and learning development, is required. Indeed, embedding UDL in ITE and in all professional development programmes - for example subject, leadership, or assessment professional development -, will ensure an awareness of the potential role and usefulness of UDL for all teachers (Flood & Banks, 2021). UDL professional development requires clear policy directives and guidelines if systemic change is to occur. As the EPSEN Act (2004) is currently under review, this is an opportune time for its authors to consider what is required in terms of teacher professional development capacity building for inclusion and for them to address these needs as part of the review of EPSEN.

CONCLUSION

UDL as an approach to inclusive education has the potential to support and challenge students as they actively engage in their learning. Using snapshots of teaching, learning, and assessment, this chapter shows how the principles, and their accompanying checkpoints, translate into practice in the junior cycle English classroom. However, these are two small examples from one subject in one area of education in Ireland. For students, increasing experience of UDL in the classroom can lead to greater familiarity with accessing and representing learning in different ways and valuing the multiple means available to them. The traditional English classroom values written text above other forms of representation, which can create barriers for students. The reluctance of students in these snapshots to use the full range of multiple means available to them may be an indication of the greater value placed by educational settings on written text over other means of representation. The inclusion of classroom-based assessment in the Junior Cycle English course allows for greater means of representation to be utilised by teachers and students; this leads to a very different flavour and mindset than would have been created in a traditional pen and paper examination. The exploration of the full extent of the possibilities available requires a willingness to experiment with redesign and a sufficient degree of professional confidence to engage with the principles of UDL in the classroom.

The Enactment of the Principles of UDL

REFERENCES

Banks, J., & McCoy, S. (2011). A Study on the Prevalence of Special Educational Needs. In *National Council for Special Education*. https://www.esri.ie/publications/a-study-on-the-prevalence-of-special-educational-needs

Bray, A., Devitt, A., Banks, J., Fuentes, S. S., Sandoval, M., Riviou, K., Byrne, D., Flood, M., Reale, J., & Terrenzio, S. (2024). What Next for Universal Design for Learning? A Systematic Literature Review of Technology in UDL Implementations at Second Level. *British Journal of Educational Technology*, 55(1), 113–138. 10.1111/bjet.13328

Capp, M. J. (2017). The effectiveness of universal design for learning: a meta-analysis of literature between 2013 and 2016. In *International Journal of Inclusive Education* (Vol. 21, Issue 8, pp. 791–807). Routledge. 10.1080/13603116.2017.1325074

CAST. (2018). *The Universal Design for Learning Guidelines Graphic Organizer*. https://udlguidelines.cast.org/more/downloads

Cohen, L., Manion, L., & Morrison, K. (2011). *Research Methods in Education* (7th ed.). Routledge.

Crotty, M. J. (1998). *The Foundations of Social Research: Meaning and Perspective in the Research Process*. SAGE Publications, Limited. https://ebookcentral.proquest.com/lib/trinitycollege/detail.action?docID=6417765

Department of Education. (1993). *Report of the Special Education Review Committee*. SERC.

Department of Education. (2022). *Consultation Paper on the Review of the Education for Persons with Special Educational Needs Act 2004*. https://assets.gov.ie/287121/5a418b66-affe-4a47-bd31-2f8f3a858a25.pdf

Department of Education and Skills. (2015). A Framework for the Junior Cycle. In *National Council for Curriculum and Assessment*. https://ncca.ie/en/resources/framework-for-junior-cycle-2015-2

Edyburn, D. L. (2005). Universal Design for Learning. *Special Education Technology Practice, 7*(5), 16–22. https://elib.tcd.ie/login?url=https://search.ebscohost.com/login.aspx?direct=true&db=edo&AN=34232842

Flood, M., & Banks, J. (2021). Universal design for learning: Is it gaining momentum in Irish education? *Education Sciences*, 11(7), 341. Advance online publication. 10.3390/educsci11070341

Government of Ireland. (1998). *Education Act* (Issue 51). https://www.irishstatutebook.ie/eli/1998/act/51/enacted/en/html?q=education

Government of Ireland. (2004). *Education for Persons with Special Educational Needs Act (EPSEN)*. https://www.oireachtas.ie/en/bills/bill/2003/34/

Meyer, A., & Rose, D. H. (2002). *Teaching every student in the digital age: universal design for learning*. Association for Supervision & Curriculum Development.

Meyer, A., Rose, D. H., & Gordon, D. (2014). *Universal Design for Learning: Theory and Practice*. CAST Professional Publishing.

National Council for Curriculum and Assessment (NCCA). (1999). *Special Educational Needs: Curriculum Issues Discussion Paper*. https://ncca.ie/media/1834/special_educational_needs_curriculum_issues_-_discussion_paper.pdf

National Council for Curriculum and Assessment (NCCA), & Department of Education. (2018). *JuniorCycle_-English_-specification_amended_2018*. https://www.curriculumonline.ie/getmedia/d14fd46d-5a10-46fc-9002-83df0b4fc2ce/JuniorCycle_-English_-specification_amended_2018.pdf

National Council for Curriculum and Assessment (NCCA) & National Association of Boards of Management in Special Education (NAMBSE). (2019). *Level 2 Learning Programmes Guidelines for Teachers*. https://www.curriculumonline.ie/getmedia/38c33cf1-9e58-44f4-ad5b-ffbd9da20a6a/L2LPS-Guidelines-Jan-2019-version.pdf

National Council for Special Education (NCSE). (2014). *Delivery for Students with Special Educational Needs A better and more equitable way*. https://ncse.ie/wp-content/uploads/2014/09/NCSE_Booklet_webFINAL_10_06_14.pdf

National Council for Special Education (NCSE). (2019). *Policy Advice on Special Schools and Classes - An Inclusive Education for an Inclusive Society?* www.ncse.ie

Reynor, E. (2019). Developing Inclusive Education in Ireland: The case for UDL in Initial Teacher Education. In Gronseth, S. L., & Dalton, E. M. (Eds.), *Universal Access Through Inclusive Instructional Design* (pp. 258–267). Routledge. 10.4324/9780429435515-34

Slee, R. (2001). Social justice and the changing directions in educational research: The case of inclusive education. *International Journal of Inclusive Education*, 5(2–3), 167–177. 10.1080/13603110010035832

United Nations. (2008). *Convention on the Rights of Persons with Disabilities*. https://www.un.org/disabilities/documents/convention/convoptprot-e.pdf

The Enactment of the Principles of UDL

United Nations Educational Scientific and Cultural Organisation (UNESCO). (1994). The Salamanca Statement and Framework for Action on Special Needs Education. *Adopted by the World Conference on Special Needs Education: Access and Quality. Salamanca, Spain, 7-10 June, 1994.* https://unesdoc.unesco.org/ark:/48223/pf0000098427

Chapter 4
A Case Study Examining One School's Trek Towards More Inclusive Practice

K. Alisa Lowrey
University of Southern Mississippi, USA

Kathy Howery
University of Alberta, Canada

Leonard Troughton
University of Southern Mississippi, USA

EXECUTIVE SUMMARY

The purpose of this chapter is to discuss an in-depth case study involving one school's mission to increase inclusive practices through the utilization of Universal Design for Learning paired with evidence-based practices. Specifically, a K-9 private school in Canada approached a research team about utilizing a measurement tool to measure the inclusion of students with autism spectrum disorders in inclusive classrooms. After much discussion, the researchers and team agreed upon a year-long course of action to improve services for all students within the school, including those with ASD. A course of intervention was outlined that included pieces such as a needs assessment, training coaches, multiple observation assessments, intermittent coaching, and scheduled professional development. The purpose of this chapter will be to discuss the overall plan designed as well as lessons learned along the way.

DOI: 10.4018/978-1-6684-4750-5.ch004

Copyright © 2024, IGI Global. Copying or distributing in print or electronic forms without written permission of IGI Global is prohibited.

A Case Study Examining One School's Trek

PREFACE

In teacher education and research, researchers often discuss successful endeavors–those things that went right. Researchers and teachers discuss contributions that teach or inform us about evidence-based practices, proof of concept, or reliable and valid methods. Limitations, including errors, are often reduced or minimized to a paragraph of 'oops, we should've' or 'wish we would've'. There are lessons to be learned, however, in those missteps, in the things that were not foreseen. Evaluation of teacher practices is how the field improves (Mårtensson, et al., 2016). Self-reflection and self-evaluation are necessary components of any successful practitioner's growth process (Sullivan, et al., 2016), whatever the practice may be. Dissemination or sharing what one has learned is a key concept of academia (Head, 2020). It is with this in mind that this team decided to tell the story of its work with one school towards increasing their inclusive practices using the Universal Design for Learning (UDL) guidelines (CAST, 2018), evidence-based interventions, and communication strategies. In this chapter, the authors share their development and implementation plan, successes, failures, and reflections on their entire journey. It is hope that by doing so, the authors offer the readers the ability to take these lessons and develop a stronger model in their own work. It is also hoped that by recounting this trek, the authors encourage other practitioners to reflect on the broader challenges of bringing research to practice.

UDL PROFESSIONAL DEVELOPMENT

Implementing the UDL framework in K-12 schools has steadily grown with its inclusion in national policies like the United States' Every Student Succeeds Act of 2015 and the Higher Education Act of 2008. How implementation occurs is important to document; Professional development (PD) matters. Teachers can have a significant impact on students' learning (Waitoller & Artiles, 2013). Teacher impact is more significant than the effect of school on student learning (Nye et al., 2004). The Organization for Economic Cooperation and Development (2005) has identified teacher quality as the most important variable affecting student achievement. A critical element for any school system is the "capacity to nurture and develop teachers who have the understandings, skills, critical sensibilities, and contextual awareness to provide quality educational access, participation, and outcomes for all students" (Waitoller & Artiles, 2013, p. 320). PD packages should be directly tied to effective design of curriculum and instruction that itself leads to improved student outcomes for all students, including those with disabilities. The UDL framework is directly tied to effective curriculum design and instruction, appropriate for all content areas, and leads to improved student outcomes for all students (Cast, 2011). However, researchers found no studies on effective PD packages designed to help educators, within authentic settings, implement the UDL framework in ways that increase student outcomes.

CAST offers the widest range of professional learning opportunities as their website demonstrates (https://www.cast.org/our-work/professional-learning) making them potentially the leading PD provider on UDL in the United States. As the originator of UDL, this is not a surprising observation. CAST relies on an outsider, expert model of PD, meaning an expert comes into an environment to provide expert teaching and coaching to a group and then exits (Hargreaves, 2014). According to their website, "CAST invites school leaders, teams and teachers to work together toward sustainable, system-wide improvements through UDL. As a partner, CAST works with its partners to craft customized solutions which may include a blend of services and materials" (www.cast.org). While many pieces of PD are free and available online, districts and schools must pay for the specific blend of services and materials that promote a customized fit. CAST has partnered most recently with school districts in California, Indiana, Maryland, and New York City. PD packages most often are single day workshops, multiple day institutes, and blended (face-to-face workshops plus online learning). CAST does offer *A Tale of Four Districts*, a resource highlighting their work with four districts utilizing a UDL coach (Ganley & Ralabate, 2013). However, no published research studies have demonstrated effectiveness in terms of teacher outcomes, student outcomes, involvement of paraprofessionals, or efficacy of PD designs (Ok, et al., 2017). Additionally, because training is costly ($695 registration to the annual summit alone), few school professionals can attend. A replicable design of PD is needed to build capacity within districts or schools, in order to increase teacher and student outcomes when implementing the UDL framework. An outsider, expert model will not accomplish this in an authentic school setting (Hargreaves, 2014).

Prior to identifying or creating any authentic PD design, it is important to examine what PD designs have been effective in the past. In a review of research on PD for inclusive schools, six types of PD were identified by Waitoller & Artiles (2013). Those were action research, on-site training, university classes, PD schools, online courses, and a weekly newsletter. Of the studies included, 89% did not include measures of student outcomes resulting from the PD. Each of these types of PD can be found in the CAST model, and some of these have been used across the school-based models shared above. However, no data is available on the development, implementation, evaluation, efficacy, or in some cases, even the content of these components. Currently, for a school district to attempt to prepare educators to implement the UDL framework, it must either (a) piece together free components

A Case Study Examining One School's Trek

of online training and tools from organizations, states, and districts implementing UDL, or (b) hire an outside expert to facilitate implementation.

Waitoller and Artilles (2013) separated PD measurement into outcomes-based and process-based measures. According to Hill et al. (2013) most PD is 'home-grown.' In contrast to traditional outcomes-based measures, these authors recommend rigorous research of the design elements at the initial stages of development. Hill et al (2013) recommend that researchers focus on the identification of the best design practices in the development of PD, to connect effective PD to teacher knowledge, skills, change in instruction, and ultimately student outcomes. Developing several components of PD and comparatively evaluating them across participants during the initial implementation stages can lead to a more efficacious result. This maximizes cost, effort, and has the most desired effect on student achievement. As reported for current PD efforts in UDL implementation, many components of PD are utilized with no published measures as to which component(s) are the most effective in preparing educators to implement the UDL framework in their schools. Developing a PD model that can measure and identify each component, as necessary for the effective education and training of educators in the practice of implementing the UDL framework, is essential. The purpose of the following case-study is to share an attempt to develop a PD package that includes designing the PD to connect teacher knowledge to practice and supporting these teachers' changing practice through coaching, resources, and data-based measurement of implementation in authentic settings.

HOW IT BEGAN

Our trek begins in December of 2020 at the height of Covid-19. A school district in Canada utilizes what they term the 'Low Incidence Team' (LI Team). This team is comprised of a highly qualified special educator trained in significant disabilities, a speech therapist, and an occupational therapist. The purpose of this team is to support the teachers within district schools serving students with significant disabilities including Autism and other developmental challenges that result in students having complex communication and learning needs. Enhancing the ability of students with Complex Communication Needs (CCN) to communicate effectively had been identified by the local LI Team as a specific initiative for this school in 2020. By mid-December, the school team was looking for further direction in achieving their goals with students with ASD and CCN and they believed that communication opportunities would be vastly improved if teachers were supported in high quality inclusive practices. Researcher A was working to support school teams in Canada on their communication strategies, particularly for those students with CCN who needed Assistive and Augmentative Communication supports and strategies.

Based on the LI Team's perceived lack of success and a strong district focus on Applied Behavior Analysis (ABA) strategies that were difficult to implement with fidelity in inclusive classrooms, the team sought an approach that was more inclusively based, strategic and flexible to support students with autism spectrum disorders (ASD) and behavior challenges. In December of 2020, the book *Facilitating Evidence Based Practice for Students with ASD* by Carnahan and Lowrey (2018) was introduced to the LI team lead by Researcher A. The LI team felt that the evidence-based practices classroom observation tool (EBP-COT) within the Carnahan and Lowrey text could anchor the work, particularly because it is non-evaluative, therefore less threatening, and could be used as a lens from which to examine current practice, support teams to determine where they want to focus to improve their practice and measure the outcomes. With 27 students with diagnosed ASD, 8 students with significant physical medical needs, and 4 students with severe emotional behavioural needs registered for the 2021-22 school year from kindergarten to grade 9, the leadership team felt this learning would be good for the entire school community. Another boon for this approach is that the EBP-COT is grounded in UDL, a framework the district had embraced in the past and was attempting to reignite. With this in mind, a collaboration began between the LI Team lead and the researchers to design not only an implementation plan grounded in the text, *Facilitating Evidence Based Practice for Students with ASD,* but also a developmental evaluation process as the primary components of the research project. A primary aim of this collaborative project was to support the school in refining and developing inclusive practices so that students with significant support needs, in particular students with Autism, would be successful in their community school and not referred to the district segregated programs.

The initial collaboration was initiated between the researchers and the lead of the LI Team, beginning with a brainstorming phone call. The initial purpose of the call was to determine if Researcher B would train the LI Team on the EBP-COT (Carnahan & Lowrey, 2018). Both project researchers were interested in the implementation process and data reflecting teacher changes. Neither researcher was interested in a PD event ('sage on the stage') without coaching or measurement. The LI Team lead was intrigued by the idea of using formative data to shape PD and their coaching. After multiple meetings focused on determining goals, the focus of content, participation requirements, methods, tools, and support needs, Project STAR* was born. Project STAR* was a reciprocal relationship offering training and coaching support for which data was recorded and analyzed to determine the effects of the project.

A Case Study Examining One School's Trek

OBJECTIVES AND RATIONALE

The STAR project was designed to focus on meaningful inclusion for all students participating in inclusive classrooms at an identified school in Canada. Three primary objectives were identified for the project, as follows:
Objectives:

1. Educators (teachers, teaching assistants, and therapists) will design their classroom curriculum (goals, methods, materials, and assessments) utilizing the research-based framework of UDL.
2. Educators (teachers, teaching assistants, and therapists) will be able to utilize identified evidence-based practices within their UDL instructional design to facilitate better outcomes for all students, including those with significant support needs.

These EBP will specifically focus on the areas of:

inclusive instructional design that promotes the removal of barriers and student engagement
creating communicatively accessible environments
writing instruction

3. Educators will identify utilize a problem-solving model focused on formative assessment to create an iterative model of inclusive design.

As is the case in many schools, student success was prioritized in the school's mission statement. Supporting the diverse needs of students through best practice and responsive, flexible programming was identified as critical to this success as was whole-school approaches to capacity building around programming for the range of backgrounds and experiences students bring to school. Initial discussion stemmed around the school's need to tie UDL, inclusion of students with ASD and other disabilities, and communication together. Splintered initiatives do not have longevity and are often seen as fads or trends by educators (Ashkenas, 1994). Building a PD research package that met teacher-identified needs and addressed those through research-based methods and strategies was seen by the researchers as critical to the success of the STAR project.

To ensure that the project was grounded in meeting the needs of the school, the LI Team conducted a needs assessment in the spring of 2021. Teachers identified (i) the need for strategies that supported students with CCN in using their augmentative and alternative communication device (AAC) supports more effectively, (ii) the need for instruction that was engaging and less frustrating for students, and (iii) the need for writing instruction. All of these fit within utilizing the UDL framework for curriculum (goals, methods, materials, and assessment) design, and met the first two objectives of the project as listed above. Because the team also sought to use the EBP-COT (the initial focus of the first contact with the researchers), objective three was based on utilizing the EBP-COT as a formative assessment tool throughout the project. This project allowed further inquiry into UDL, as it applied to all students and their learning environments, but also positioned itself as a focused means to examine what happened for students with significant disabilities, including those who had a diagnosis of ASD when UDL was the foundation of learning for all, and specific evidence-based strategies were extended to meet individual needs.

PARTICIPATING SCHOOL RECRUITMENT AND CONSENT

The participating school was a public school operating in Canada. The school included grades Kindergarten through grade 9. The school served +/- 800 students, varying slightly throughout the year. Of those, 27 students were identified with ASD, 8 students were identified as having significant physical medical needs, and 4 students were identified with severe emotional behavioral needs. The school employed 41 teachers, 12 educational assistants, one behavior specialist, two behavioral therapy assistants, two occupational therapy assistants, and two speech/language therapy assistants for a total of sixty-one educators and related services personnel.

After receiving approval from the Institutional Review Board and the school district, recruitment was targeted at all sixty-one educators and related service personnel. Participants were recruited via an initial meeting of all faculty. Researcher A, the school principal, and the LI Team lead explained the purpose of the research, the time commitments involved, the data collection strategies, and confidentiality policies. Participants were informed that data collected would be anonymized by researchers for analytical purposes. Participants were informed that the research component was confined solely to the sharing of data with the researchers and was not required as a condition of employment. They were informed they could withdraw from the study (decline the agreement to share their data) at any time.

Because this project was linked to ongoing PD carried out by the school, consent for participation was solely around whether the participant's data could be used in the project. School faculty and staff were all expected to attend professional learning that was offered as a part of this initiative. The entire teaching faculty was required to attend all PD sessions and stay for the 2.5 hours. Assistants were required to attend until the end of the regular school day (1.5-2 hours) but left before the goal

A Case Study Examining One School's Trek

setting portions of the PD, due to pay differences. Coaching sessions were attended by both faculty and assistants when possible. These requirements were not related to participation in the project (consent to share data). However, everyone consented to participate in data sharing.

PROJECT DESIGN (METHODS)

It is important to note there was much discussion between the researchers as to whether or not to move forward with this project, as a program improvement project or as a research study. However, due to the lack of data on schoolwide UDL implementation and the expressed wish of the LI Team to specifically use the Classroom Observation Tool (Carnahan & Lowrey, 2018), the researchers decided to move forward, measuring what could be measured and understanding the lack of controls present in an active school environment. Tools were designed to measure observations, coaching logs, and pre/post learning. Outside of the topics selected for PD, everything else stayed in a 'business-as-usual' format.

Methods of inquiry and measurement were selected based on their efficacy for an authentic environment. Overall, we used a mixed methods design (Green et al., 2005) for the PD package that included (a) a needs assessment, (b) a numerically valued observation tool, (c) a coaching log, and (d) a pre-posttest. Together, these were administered as part of the PD package. The team has been selected to report this PD package here through a case study approach (Stake, 1995) utilizing a first person narrative.

The study was designed to extend through one academic school year (2021-2022) and included multiple components. In order to create a self-sustaining system utilizing an insider approach, researcher involvement within the school was limited. Within school time (whether via Zoom or on-site), researchers were only to lead PD, conduct observations for reliability purposes, and support LI Team members through problem solving.

Time out of classroom for participants coincided with regularly scheduled PD, faculty meetings, and team meetings. No additional time out of classroom was required. While coaching by the LI Team continued in a business-as-usual fashion, coaching logs and structured feedback were to be utilized in the study data analysis. No substitute faculty or staff were required to be hired for the purpose of this study. The project included monthly PD for the faculty/staff and twice monthly modeling and coaching sessions by the LI Team.

Instructional design utilizing the UDL framework can be difficult to measure (Smith, et al., 2019). In order to gain insight on how the school grew in their understanding and implementation of the selected topics, design elements, and strategies, a mixed methods design was utilized relying on both quantitative and qualitative measures. A total of four measures were designed or selected for use within the study. Those were a pre/post measure, the Evidence-Based Practice Classroom Observation Tool (Carnahan & Lowrey, 2018), Coaching Logs, and re-delivering the Needs Assessment from Spring 2021. Careful consideration was given to select tools that minimized personal involvement (pre-post measure; needs assessment) and/or could be completed with fidelity (Classroom Observation Tool; Coaching Log) Each measure is fully explained below.

Measure 1: Spring Needs Assessment

Occurring prior to the beginning of the study as a part of their program improvement initiative, the LI Team developed the needs assessment. Researchers did not participate in the needs assessment design or delivery as it occurred prior to the start of the study. This was developed and administered by the LI Team in Spring 2021 to all educators at the school employed in Spring 2021. For the purpose of program improvement, the plan was to deliver the needs assessment again at the end of the school year in 2022. Although not a part of the research study data itself, the initial results from the spring 2021 needs assessment drove the selection of topics for PD sessions in 21-22. When re-delivering the needs assessment in spring 2022, it was hoped that the LI Team could utilize results to show if gaps and/or identified PD needs had changed. Once this process was completed, the LI Team reviewed the data and established themes. These resulted in the LI Team identifying as themes: (i) faculty PD needs as instructional design goals to support inclusion, (ii) creating communicatively accessible learning environments, and (iii) writing instruction. Those became the focus of the PD calendar for the upcoming school year of 21-22.

Once these three main themes were identified, the LI Team reviewed those items that made up each theme to determine specific PD needs. In collaboration with the researchers, the following needs were identified in each area (See Figure 1). The researchers and LI Team lead agreed that UDL should be embedded throughout all PD, as it was the framework we were using for all instructional design. While the needs assessment developed by the LI Team is not shared here as it was developed prior to the beginning of the study, there are many resources available for developing needs assessments (Cuiccio & Husby-Slater, 2018).

A Case Study Examining One School's Trek

Figure 1. Professional development topics by theme

Inclusive Practices	Accessible Communication	Writing Strategies
• Utilizing Schedules • Visual Supports • Environmental Boundaries • Video Modeling • Technology Supports • Systematic Instruction	• Prompting communication in natural settings • Using Assistive Technology systems • Using peer supports • Systematic Instruction	• Utilizing the 6+1 Writing Traits (Voice, Ideas, Presentation, Conventions, Organization, Word Choice, Sentence Fluency) • Using technology to support • Utilizing progress monitoring • Systematic Instruction

Measure 2: UDL Pre/Post Test

The next step was to create a measure that could demonstrate basic, summative change across the year. The researchers in consultation with the LI Team lead decided a pre-post measure would be the best option to look at summative change in knowledge and understanding of the skills and strategies taught throughout the year. Researchers developed a UDL pre/post measure creating specific questions on inclusion, AAC, Evidence-based practices (EBPs), and UDL, using Sharma et al., (2011) for questions on inclusive education, and with questions on AAC and UDL in a style similar to that developed by the researchers.

In order to collect a baseline measure of knowledge, a UDL/Inclusive Practices Pre/Post measure was delivered during the initial meeting of the 21-22 school year on August 30. It was scheduled to be delivered again at the end of the 21-22 school year for comparative purposes. These measures were anonymous and were delivered via Qualtrics. Figure 2 provides a sample of a portion of the measure. Participants were provided time during the initial recruitment meeting to complete the measure. Participants were to click on the link and complete the measure, following directions within. All responses were anonymized within the school's permission-locked Microsoft Forms and aggregated within the system to determine the performance of the group. This tool was not used to determine or to disaggregate individual performance.

Figure 2. Portion of the pre/post measure

Evidence-Based Practice

I believe evidence-based practices are necessary to use in inclusive classrooms.

I can name at least five evidence-based practices for students with ASD and other developmental disabilities.

I believe many of the same evidence-based practices found effective for students with ASD are also effective for students with no disability.

I can teach someone else how to use at least one evidence-based practice for students with ASD.

I know how to measure the effectiveness of an instructional practice.

I know when to change an instructional practice that is not working.

When students with disabilities are included in my classroom, I must teach my regular lesson and a special lesson to meet their needs.

Identifying evidence-based practices is not important to my teaching.

I know which instructional practices are considered harmful for my students with disabilities.

I want to learn more about evidence-based practices for students with disabilities in inclusive settings.

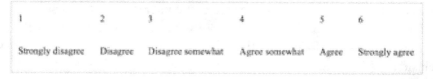

1	2	3	4	5	6
Strongly disagree	Disagree	Disagree somewhat	Agree somewhat	Agree	Strongly agree

Note: Modeled after Sharma, U., Loreman, T., & Forlin, C., (2011). Measuring teacher efficacy to implement inclusive practices. *Journal of Research in Special Education Needs* 12(1): 12–21. https://doi.org/10.1111/j.1471-3802.2011.01200.x

Measure 3: Classroom Observation Tool

The Evidence-Based Practices Classroom Observation Tool (EBP-COT) was a formative assessment designed utilizing the UDL Framework to be used by/with educators in inclusive classrooms serving students with ASD and other developmental disabilities (Carnahan & Lowrey, 2018). It relies heavily on standard EBPs identified for students with ASD and is appropriate for use in inclusive settings where special educator support may/may not be present. The EBPs were extracted from the Professional Development Center for Autism Spectrum Disorders (Steinbrenner, et al., 2020), where free web-based modules, exemplars, tutorials, and data sheets are

A Case Study Examining One School's Trek

available on their website (see https://autismpdc.fpg.unc.edu). The EBP-COT can be used by educators, mentors, and/or leaders as a goal setting tool for classroom teachers and others delivering services. It can also be used for self-rating. It does not pre-suppose an understanding of special education and/or autism spectrum disorder. The EBP-COT was not designed to be a summative evaluation of "good" or "bad" practices; rather, it was designed to help educators determine areas of focus for improvement and areas of strength. It is because it is characterized by this non-evaluative intent that the LI Team selected the COT. While the team used it to track change, it was also used for goal setting from the outset with teachers.

The EBP-COT is a discrete measure that allows basic scoring of 27 components on a 0 (n/a), 1 (no or limited implementation), 2 (partial implementation), or 3 (full implementation) scale. It includes a scoring guide to inform the scoring process as one observes. This also allows reliability of scoring to be determined as well as fidelity of implementation. It is arranged around three primary components: environmental arrangement, communication, and instructional considerations. Because it is copyrighted, it is not shared here. In Phase 1 of the EBP-COT use, members of the LI Team were trained on how to use the EBP-COT. The EBP-COT includes a protocol for delivery and scoring. During the week of August 26, 2021, the LI Team participated in case study training using the EBP-COT delivery and scoring protocol.

Utilizing case study videos of classrooms, interrater reliability was established. The team was not allowed to move forward with live observations until an interrater reliability score of 90% or above was reached on the case study videos. Once interrater reliability was at/above 90%, teammates conducted a week of shared, live observations making sure their interrater reliability stayed at or above 90%. The team wrote down any consistent differences in scoring of the EBP-COT and worked with researchers to determine a more complete definition of that component as observed in that school.

In Phase 2 of the EBP-COT delivery, observations were conducted with classroom participants in the month prior to any introduction of PD. The LI Team conducted one observation with each participating educator. Prior to them observing on their own, each member of the LI Team conducted observations with the LI Team leader until a reliability of 90% or greater was reached. Educators were also asked to complete a self-evaluation and submit that to the LI Team. One researcher conducted EBP-COT observations on 35% of the participants as well to establish a comparative measure between the LI Team and researchers.

Beginning in May 2022, this process was to be replicated, with all participants being observed by the LI Team using the EBP-COT, comparative observations by Researcher A taking place, and educators completing a self-rating on the instrument. By using this at the beginning and end of the year, the LI Team and participating educators planned to use the comparative data to determine the degree to which their annual goals had been met.

Measure 4: Coaching Logs

The LI Team lead shared the LI Team's standard coaching schedule of two visits per month; other visits were to occur as needed. The only addition to the LI Team's standard practice was to focus coaching on the practices supported through the EBP-COT, as well as their business-as-usual foci. Additionally, coaching procedures for Instructional Coaching (Knight, 2007) were reviewed with the LI Team. Their coaching log template was adjusted to be a collaborative template, adapted from the team's original coaching log, the coaching log included in the Carnahan and Lowrey text (2018), and The Best Foot Forward Project (Kane, 2015). See Figure 3 for final log used.

A Case Study Examining One School's Trek

Figure 3. STAR project coaching log

Date of meeting:
Instructional Coach: Educator:

Was an EBP-COT observation conducted? _____YES_____ No
Was a self-assessment conducted along with this observation? _____Yes _____No
Reason for the meeting: (describe primary goal for the meeting)

List 2-3 areas of strength noted in observation. If indicated, list 1 area of strength useable as a model for others within the school.

List one or two prioritized items for growth based on the school's identified priorities of inclusion, writing, and communication.

Identify Specific Next Steps:
(What needs to happen? Who is responsible? What resources are needed?)

Step	What needs to happen?	Who is responsible?	When will it happen (deadlines)?	Resources needed (list website, person, etc.)
1.				
2.				
3.				

Follow up:
(Who will follow up and when?)

Note: Modeled after Carnahan, C. R., & Lowrey, K. A. (2018). *Facilitating Evidence-Based*

Practice for Students with ASD: A Classroom Observation Tool for Building Quality

Education (1st ed.). Paul H. Brookes Publishing and The Best Foot Forward Project

(https://cepr.harvard.edu/files/cepr/files/13f_collaborative_coaching_log.pdf)

During the week of August 26, the LI Team reviewed the draft coaching log and procedures for implementation. During initial observations, coaching logs were completed by each team member. Upon consultation within the team, several tweaks were made to items logged to ensure it accurately captured each session and drove the LI Team coach and educator to review previously set annual goals. While this coaching log was used for all coaching sessions during school year 21-22, only those educators who had consented to participate had their logs scanned in as data. The LI Team leads established then reviewed all coaching logs to ensure completion.

Coaching Log Protocol was as follows, for September when the EBP-COT was also being conducted. Once initial observations were done, LI Team members skipped Steps 2 & 3 to complete the remaining steps of the protocol for ongoing bi-monthly coaching sessions.

1. Select a classroom for observation.
2. Observe the classroom using the EBP-COT for a minimum of 10 minutes, and a maximum of 20 minutes.
3. Score the EBP-COT for each indicator using the suggested 0-4 scale.
   * *if unsure about an indicator, review p.39-68 in text for indicator definitions, exemplars, and directions.
4. Identify strengths. Specifically, identify any indicator area in which this teacher or classroom is exemplary and could be used as a model for others in your school.
5. Prioritize areas of need based on identified needs assessment criteria (inclusive practices, communication, writing).
6. Complete initial coaching log notes in relation to conversations with teacher.
7. Meet with teacher to discuss observation, collaborate on strengths/needs, identify additional training or supports needed, and create an action plan.
8. Document results from #7 and any anecdotal notes in coaching log.
9. Submit log and completed, dated EBP-COT.

INTERVENTION: STAR INCLUSIVE PRACTICES PROFESSIONAL DEVELOPMENT AND ACTION PLANNING

The primary intervention utilized in this study was a PD package that included content sessions, goal setting, action planning, and supported coaching on educator-identified targets resulting from the spring 2020 needs assessment. The research team utilized standard PD opportunities occurring once every month on Thursdays for 2.5 hours to teach specific evidence-based practices highlighted in the EBP-COT and supported through the UDL framework as necessary for successful inclusion. These targeted practices were selected from the foci of the results of the spring 2020 Needs Assessment.

Topics were prioritized using two criteria. First, a least to most intrusive guideline was followed. Topics were selected based on their ease of implementation/least amount of effort for change by educators to the most intrusive implementation or most onerous need for change. The second criteria to use for prioritization was the

A Case Study Examining One School's Trek

needs assessment rankings. Overall, the needs assessment determined the following areas as priorities in general:

- Inclusive Instructional Design that Promotes the Removal of Barriers and the Increase of Student Engagement.
- Creating Communicatively Accessible Environments.
- Writing Instruction

UDL core principles, guidelines, and checkpoints were embedded throughout the intentional design and implementation of the PD.

PD was conducted using Zoom sessions supported via Padlet™ for housing all notes and resources provided during trainings. Because schools were under Covid-19 protocols and meetings were conducted with the researchers via Zoom, educators were grouped separately in computer equipped classrooms to allow for access to Zoom and to materials. The PD presentations were created with a very specific formula---content presentation should be 1/3 of the time; modeling/guided practice should be another 1/3; independent or group development for designing instructional practices, application to practice, reflection, and action planning/goal setting was the final 1/3 of the time.

Presenting real strategies that could be learned and implemented quickly was important to promote student and educator success. The LI Team was available to support coaching once educators selected the specific instructional strategy from the previous PD for implementation in their classroom. Using action planning with specific goals and strategies or implementation was critical to each session. Finally, tying all efforts back to each educator's annual goals helped them see that these were not trends or fads, but rather long-term practices that could improve their effectiveness as educators. Activities, reflections, and discussions were a routine part of training and any products or exemplars submitted by participants were stored in the ongoing anecdotal evidence files for the research project.

Action Planning

Creating and monitoring an action plan was embedded into the final third of every PD session. The process for action planning was as follows:

Identify 2-3 areas where you can make a change in your use of instruction or instructional supports.
Work with a colleague and/or the low incidence team to develop small group or individualized solutions for those changes.
Create an implementation plan

A Case Study Examining One School's Trek

When will you do this?
Where? In what space? Subject? Group?
How? What are the procedures?
With whom? Which students? Which adults?
How will you know it worked?

As this was a school improvement initiative, all faculty and educational staff at the school participated in the training sessions. Data was only kept from those faculty that consented to participate in the study. Table 1 provides a schedule of implementation for the calendar year.

Table 1. Planned schedule of implementation STAR Project Timeline & Checklist

Month	Professional Development			Team Activities	Research Activities
	Date	Topic	Lead		
Aug				Begin Inter-rater reliability	Consent Self-Rating Participant Goal Setting
Sept	Sept 7	All staff given copy of *Facilitating Evidence-Based Practice for Students with ASD: A Classroom Observation Tool for Building Quality Education* Share Information about Visual that the district currently has access too	LI T	Inter-rated reliability Observation Tool completed in Each classroom by Oct 13 Document any coaching done in classrooms	Check with Team re: scoring changes to Observation Tool Score 35% of classrooms ~ 14 rooms [Researcher A, (R-A)] by Oct 13 Data analysis
Oct	Oct 14	EBP	Researcher B (R-B)	Find and discuss each participant's goal(s) Observation Tool completed Classroom coaching logs	Analyze data gathered to date
Nov	Nov 18	EBP	R-B	Classroom coaching logs	
Dec	Dec 9	EBP	R-B	Classroom coaching logs	
Jan	Jan 13	Communication Strategies	R-A	Observation Tool completed Classroom coaching logs	Re-Score 35% of classrooms (R-A)
Feb	Feb 10	Communication Strategies	R-A	Classroom coaching logs	
March	March 10	Communication Strategies	R-A	Classroom coaching logs	

continued on following page

A Case Study Examining One School's Trek

Table 1. Continued

Month	Professional Development			Team Activities	Research Activities
	Date	Topic	Lead		
April	April 14	TBD	TBD	Classroom coaching logs	
May	May 12	TBD	TBD	Classroom coaching logs	
June				Observation Tool completed in Each classroom Wind Up – Celebrations, Next Steps	Re-Score 35% of classrooms (R-A) by… Data analysis Results sharing

HOW IT CONCLUDED

All projects come to an end, and it was no different for the STAR project, although regrettably the end came prematurely. In January 2022, Covid-19 infections flared up again, and teachers were once again working remotely. The LI Team requested that we postpone the January PD in order to allow educators to deal with the real crisis of delivering instruction remotely. Situations like these had become all too familiar to everyone these past years during the pandemic. During this hiatus, the LI Team lead became aware that two participants revealed they felt they were expected to participate in the research. Once the LI team leader shared this with researchers, the decision was immediately made to stop the project, even though this complaint was never directly shared with us by participants. We could not be sure that others did not feel that way as well. While it is true we could have most likely continued with a smaller subset (i.e., another round of consents and 'are you sure?' check-ins), it is against our code of conduct/ethics as researchers to continue when there is any hint that our participants may feel in any way obliged to continue with their participation. Even though all consent materials, initial recruiting session, and reminder messages made it clear that educators did not have to share their data if they chose not to, the reported feeling of these two teachers made us uneasy. As a result of this, we decided to destroy all data from the project. The needs assessment had been conducted by the LI Team for program improvement purposes prior to the start of the study, so we felt those results could be included given that all PD hinged on what they shared with us. However, all other data shared with the researchers that depended on consent from participants was destroyed.

So, what happens to over a year of work, designing interventions and measurement, getting approvals, creating presentations, conducting training, delivering measurements? As a researcher, does one destroy all of it? In reflection, we - the researchers - decided that if we analyzed the work we had carried out in the process of designing and implementing the project, others might learn from it as a case exemplar. We have obtained testimonials that changes were made in some classrooms prior to January. We have coaching logs that demonstrate that teachers were asking pertinent questions and utilizing resources shared in the training sessions. We have exemplars that were identified and used in our ongoing PD meetings. We were unable to conduct all of our spring (post) measurements to demonstrate the effects of the PD through formal analyzed data. We had learned some things we did not want to repeat and some things that went really well that we were excited to try again. Might others learn from the case of the Star Project? In light of the fact that others might be able to benefit from our design process and transparency, we submitted this chapter.

DISCUSSION

In the following section, we discuss what we, the researchers, thought went well, what we could have done differently or designed better, and what we had not foreseen; we examine what future PD models and frameworks may want to consider based on our experiences in this project. It is important to note that these last remarks represent the researchers' reflective take-aways based on notes, discussions, team feedback, and observations of PD sessions. We are, on the other hand, in the process of conducting a research study interviewing the LI Team to determine what their take-aways might be. In the meantime, what follows here are our own observations and conclusions.

What Went Well?

The time allotted to the study was a strength. Conducting the needs assessment during the spring that preceded the intervention, having the summer to plan, and embedding the research into standard PD and coaching times at the school, were all assets in this project. It is rare in the field of educational research that you have access to the time you need but, in this case, that was a well-designed component of the project.

The selection of tools seemed to be a good fit for the use the school identified. A needs assessment was the best place to start for both researchers and the LI Team. The process of doing the evaluating the school's needs based on collaborative discussion identified where they LI Team should focus. This led to their adopting the EBP-COT and to their taking a deeper dive into EBPs for students with ASD. By engaging in those activities together, the LI Team developed reliability in their

A Case Study Examining One School's Trek

understanding and measurement of the EBPs in the context of their work. They also began to use a systematic coaching procedure, which allowed more systematic discussion across classroom supports, needed resources and the identification of strengths. The action planning process as well as the EBP-COT provided a focus for coaching conversations. All of this led to a growing team consensus regarding what was important in supporting effective programming for students with ASD in inclusive classroom as well as how, by addressing the needs of those students, all students in the class would benefit.

The LI Team embraced and appeared to value the use of the EBP-COT as an observation tool. By using this tool, they were able to look at the whole class context while also focusing on the students who were identified as having LI disabilities. They established reliability as a team in how they measured specific items, even though the team was multidisciplinary. In PD sessions, the LI Team was charged to bring exemplars of quality evidence-based practices they'd seen implemented while conducting observations. They were able to share praise for teachers who'd increased their score in specific areas and offer exemplars of how teachers were changing their practices in their classrooms based on PD topics and what they observed using the EBP-COT.

Embedding UDL throughout inclusive practices training was also something that worked well. It made UDL less of an 'add-on' and more of a required design element for good inclusive practice. Researchers selected measurement tools that both looked specifically at UDL knowledge and embedded UDL within the components measured. This worked well for not mistakenly presenting UDL as an evidence-based practice strategy but rather a core component of high-quality inclusive design.

Finally, the design of the study overall was carefully planned and held great promise. The components of the study were very connected to what the school had identified as areas of needed improvement based on the needs assessment. The PD intervention was built into the regularly occurring school PD calendar. The design included participation of all educators employed at the school. The action planning process made the intervention flexible so that educators could select exactly what they wanted to work on based on their preferences and their score on the EBP-COT and tie that back to their annual evaluation if they chose. And, from researchers' perspectives, the design was replicable in terms of the intervention method and the measurement tools selected. Researchers hypothesized if this worked at this school, it could be implemented systematically elsewhere for systemic change.

What could Have Gone Better or Didn't Foresee?

In our efforts to keep this a sustainable, practical part of the school's daily practice, we diminished our presence on campus and our presence as the 'face' of the project. The LI Team leader was the manager of the project on-site. We thought having an 'insider' manage the project would increase buy-in and diminish the 'expert model' approach. We did not foresee the two teachers feeling as though they were expected to participate and not following consent procedures to drop participation when no longer desired. We may have had a knee-jerk reaction by stopping the study altogether and discarding all collected data based on our ethical guidelines for practice. We did not follow up directly with these participants to see if they were clear about what was optional research participation (data sharing) and what was required by their school (PD). They did not come to us with the concern. However, because we were not the on-site face of the study, we couldn't be sure that those two were the only participants that felt that way. That brings us to all the could've/should've/would've done differently.

We should've taken a stronger lead position in terms of the on-site management and implementation of the project. While it was valuable to have the active engagement of the LI Team lead, there were times when the researchers could/should have been more directly involved in the process. The researchers were at arm's length from the interactions with the school administration and the faculty/staff. While the LI Team lead worked appropriately in a dual role as the on-site research manager and practitioner on the LI Team, this duality and lack of a discrete role may have resulted in some confusion. Rather than the lead researchers speaking with school administration, the LI Team conducted those conversations. Researchers never discussed the research with the district or the school administration other than through written applications/responses to conveyed questions---that was all done through the LI Team lead. Directly clarifying research aims, permissions, challenges, and strengths with administration conversationally would have possibly benefited the study longitudinally. Administrator buy-in is critically important to success (Ruble, et al., 2018). We could easily 'say' we had administrator buy-in based on the permission granted to proceed and to subsume the entire PD calendar for the year. However, because we had no direct conversations, we are not sure how much administrator support was actually there for the day-to-day practices, measures, and general responses to teachers. Buy-in must be seen as greater than just permissions to proceed.

The duality of the LI Team leader also may have inadvertently led to perception and/or implementation issues. The LI Team's primary role was to support the teachers in the school, and as such needed to be seen as a valuable contributor to teachers in the school. Because the LI Team leader was included as an 'insider' in

A Case Study Examining One School's Trek

the development of the design, planning, and implementation, as well as considered the face of the project on-site, the duality of her role as the project manager within the school but also as the lead of a team that, to receive continued support, needed to be seen as a positive resource may have presented too many conflicting agendas (perceived or actual).

By reinforcing the non-obligatory participation in the study (sharing of their data) at the beginning of each interaction with school staff we may have eliminated any feelings of expectation to participate. Educators had to go to the PD sessions as part of the school improvement process; they did not have to elect to share their data. While this was stressed in the beginning and on consents, it could've been reiterated at every PD, and we could've made sure it was reiterated by any of the LI Team members. Doing so may have eliminated any feeling of expected participation.

If beginning a new project, we would be more engaged and have a stronger voice in the design of the needs assessment. Although the needs assessment was a positive contribution to the study and was conducted prior to the agreement of the school/district for this study to take place, the needs assessment drove much of the focus of the project. While it was important that it was done, it would have been valuable to have had it guided and particularly analyzed by the researchers who were not intimately involved with the support of the school prior to the project beginning. We believe that more initial exploration by the research team in teachers' current practices and/or current understanding of UDL, EBPs with regards students with ASD, and their perceived value or alignment with the teachers' own practices, was perhaps warranted and would have been of value to the overall development of the project.

There were challenges around the data. Regardless of the research aims, data was collected for school improvement purposes. Consents were used to determine those participants who agreed to share their data with researchers. All educators agreed to participate. The school district requirement was that the data all be gathered and stored by their staff using their data system. This was further complicated because we were under COVID-19 measures and digital collection of the data (rather than paper tools) was necessary. The LI Team leader managed the data to be shared with researchers. This made it challenging for the researchers to input measures and to analyze the information gathered. We were not the gatekeepers, and this complicated things.

One final thing we didn't foresee in our inclusive practices project was that measures might influence decisions of the administrators regarding removing students from inclusive classrooms. That had never even occurred to us in the formation of the project. Could we begin again, we would explicitly state in our initial proposal that our research measures should not be used for this purpose.

Making this goal more explicit, and more generally agreed to by all would have been of value.

Nowhere in the needs assessment was it identified that teachers needed to have tools and strategies to ensure students with disabilities would remain at their community school and be successful. This might be something to include more explicitly in any future research that embraces inclusive education as a foundational belief. The focus of the project was to increase/improve inclusive services.

What Future Implications Are There to Be Taken Away From the STAR Project?

Working in authentic settings of employment can be difficult. Working in an authentic setting during Covid-19 added layers of complication to an already difficult process. Trying to impose 'controls' for research practices in an environment that is constantly changing is one of the many contributors in the research-to-practice gap (Joyce, et al., 2020). In this project, we attempted to complete a year-long study demonstrating how we could increase inclusive practices by embedding the UDL framework into the planning and selection of specific EBP for students with ASD, while offering PD and coaching for those participating. In our efforts to diminish our role as outsiders/experts, we increased the roles of those on the inside as experts, specifically that of the LI Team and its leader. Doing this brought its own challenges. Although we provided some thoughts on this topic in the previous section, here are some addition suggestions we think should be considered for future research.

In order to obtain quality results that can be replicated in other settings, researchers need to be on-site for all or some of the process of the implementation. Conducting PD via Zoom once a month, and/or conducting reliability observations, was not enough on-site engagement to support distinct boundaries between what was 'research' and what was required by the school district/administration We identified the need for educators to see participation in the study as optional. Our concern is that, in this project, we over-embedded the 'insider' approach by making the LI Team leader the public face of the project. This blurred the lines between what was required for research purposes and what was required by the school.

The outsider/expert approach may not always be a bad thing and, in this case, might have improved the longevity and quality of this study. In future studies, we encourage you to consider that insider/outsider contribution and how having too much of one or the other may impact results. Participatory Action Research (PAR) may be the only place in which the blurring of those lines is not as critical. As educational researchers, it is important to continue to try to decrease the research-to-practice gap. It is also essential that the field continue to increase/improve research conducted in authentic settings. However, in order for systematic replication to occur, research methods must be reliable, valid, and implemented with fidelity. In some cases, expert

A Case Study Examining One School's Trek

implementation and measurement may be the best solution, particularly when no systematic implementation studies exist on the topic you are measuring.

In future research, creating a first-hand relationship with school administration will be necessary to the success of such a large and on-going project. While having relationships with teachers, teams, assistant principals, etc. may be beneficial, this project taught us the value of establishing a personal relationship with administration. We needed to ensure, through first-hand experiences, that the administrative team shared our goals and understood the implementation methods from the onset of the project; this is critical to the long-term success of the project. The readiness of the school administrative team and teaching staff - to change established practice must be fully established from the beginning.

Finally, the UDL framework supports high quality inclusive design. It should be embedded within existing opportunities to increase inclusive practices rather than as a separate agenda' that teachers have to adhere to. Additionally, school administration, teachers, and staff should have a shared understanding of, and a degree of general knowledge about the framework; there needs to be some consensus around the fundamental UDL practices. This understanding and knowledge should align with accepted research on UDL, as there is still some existing confusion in the field about what is and is not UDL.

Recommendations for Others Who May Undertake a Similar Project

The following recommendations are presented in bullet format to enhance clarity. All of these align with the Waitoller and Artiles (2013) concepts related to the development of PD in authentic settings.

Planning sufficient windows of time is critical. Setting aside one year to tackle the implementation was a good plan, together with allocating a month, the prior May, to setting the stage and conducting the interest inventory.

Utilizing on-site support is necessary for high quality, just-in-time supports and direction.

Coaching must be paired with PD training. Content is not sufficient in itself. Models - especially models which are drawn from the experiences of people who are implementing UDL successfully - - are necessary to help people connect that content to practice. Coaching extends the learning to actual practice.

Systematic measurement tools that collect different types of information are required; qualitative and quantitative data is needed for comprehensive growth. We were satisfied with the measurement tools we selected, in that they did not seem to create an undue burden for teachers but also gave us the information necessary to make decisions about training, schedules, growth, etc.

Similarly, adopting and using a systematic reporting database is recommended. We did not have one, as the school kept their own data. This made analysis clunky at best and somewhat challenging at worst.

Finally, direct and frequent contact with administrators is a necessity. We thought that, since we were working with a district team and the broader context was that of the pandemic, we did not have to be in such close contact with the administration at the school. This was incorrect. In the end, this was in all likelihood the undoing of the project.

CONCLUSION

Changing educational systems is a daunting task. Spearheading change through high quality PD can be complicated. Conducting high quality research is multi-faceted. Doing all three of those things in a manner that can be replicated successfully can be complex, requiring flexibility in some respects while other facets must remain fixed. In this chapter, we have shared our case study as an initial attempt at addressing the need for high quality PD that impacts practice and is replicable. We do this knowing hindsight is 20/20 and readers will be able to easily pick through our missteps as we now do. However, we have shared this case study because we think there are lessons to be learned here. We hope you think so too.

NOTE

STAR will not be spelled out in order to maintain confidentiality of the participating district/school as required by the university's Institutional Review Board application/approval.

REFERENCES

Ashkenas, R. N. (1994). Beyond fads: How leaders drive change with results. *People and Strategy*, 17(2), 25.

Carnahan, C. R., & Lowrey, K. A. (2018). *Facilitating Evidence-Based Practice for Students with ASD: A Classroom Observation Tool for Building Quality Education* (1st ed.). Paul H. Brookes Publishing.

CAST. (2018). Universal Design for Learning Guidelines version 2.2. Retrieved from http://udlguidelines.cast.org

Cuiccio, C., & Husby-Slater, M. (2018). *Needs Assessment Guidebook. American Institutes for Research* under U.S. Department of Education https://oese.ed.gov/files/2020/10/needsassessmentguidebook-508_003.pdf

Every, S. S. A. 20 U.S.C. § 6301 (2015). https://www.congress.gov/bill/114th-congress/senate-bill/1177

Ganley, P., & Ralabate, P. K. (2013). UDL implementation: A tale of four districts. CAST (https://www.cast.org/products-services/resources/2013/udl-implementation-tale-four-districts)

Greene, J. C., Kreider, H., & Mayer, E. (2005). Combining qualitative and quantitative methods in social inquiry. *Research Methods in the Social Sciences, 1*, 275-282.

Hargreaves, A. (2014). *Handbook of professional development in education: Successful models and practices, PreK-12*. Guilford Publications.

Head, G. (2020). Ethics in educational research: Review boards, ethical issues and researcher development. *European Educational Research Journal*, 19(1), 72–83. 10.1177/1474904118796315

Higher Education Opportunity Act of 2008, Pub. L. No. 110-135, 122 Stat.3078 (2008) https://www.govinfo.gov/content/pkg/PLAW-110publ315/pdf/PLAW-110publ315.pdf

Joyce, K. E., & Cartwright, N. (2020). Bridging the gap between research and practice: Predicting what will work locally. *American Educational Research Journal*, 57(3), 1045–1082. 10.3102/0002831219866687

Kane, T. J., Gehlbach, H., Greenberg, M., Quinn, D., & Thal, D. (2016). The Best Foot Forward Project: Substituting Teacher-Collected Video. https://cepr.harvard.edu/files/cepr/files/l4a_best_foot_forward_research_brief1.pdf

Mårtensson, P., Fors, U., Wallin, S. B., Zander, U., & Nilsson, G. H. (2016). Evaluating research: A multidisciplinary approach to assessing research practice and quality. *Research Policy, 45*(3), 593-603. https://doi.org/10.1016/j.respol.2015.11.009

Ok, M. W., Rao, K., Bryant, B. R., & McDougall, D. (2017). Universal design for learning in pre-k to grade 12 classrooms: A systematic review of research. *Exceptionality*, 25(2), 116–138. 10.1080/09362835.2016.1196450

Organization for Economic Cooperation and Development (OECD). (2005). *Teachers matter: Attracting, developing, and retaining effective teachers.* https://www.oecd.org/edu/school/34990905.pdf ISBN-92-64-01802-6

Ruble, L. A., McGrew, J. H., Wong, W. H., & Missall, K. N. (2018). Special education teachers' perceptions and intentions toward data collection. *Journal of Early Intervention*, 40(2), 177–191. 10.1177/1053815118771391 30774283

Sharma, U., Loreman, T., & Forlin, C. (2011). Measuring teacher efficacy to implement inclusive practices. *Journal of Research in Special Educational Needs*, 12(1), 12–21. 10.1111/j.1471-3802.2011.01200.x

Smith, S. J., Rao, K., Lowrey, K. A., Gardner, J. E., Moore, E., Coy, K., Marino, M., & Wojcik, B. (2019). Recommendations for a national research agenda in UDL: Outcomes from the UDL-IRN preconference on research. *Journal of Disability Policy Studies*, 30(3), 174–185. 10.1177/1044207319826219

Stake, R. E. (1995). The art of case study research. *Sage (Atlanta, Ga.).*

Steinbrenner, J. R., Hume, K., Odom, S. L., Morin, K. L., Nowell, S. W., Tomaszewski, B., Szendrey, S., McIntyre, N. S., Yücesoy-Özkan, S., & Savage, M. N. (2020). *Evidence-based practices for children, youth, and young adults with Autism.* The University of North Carolina at Chapel Hill, Frank Porter Graham Child Development Institute, National Clearinghouse on Autism Evidence and Practice Review Team.

Sullivan, B., Glenn, M., Roche, M., & McDonagh, C. (2016). *Introduction to critical reflection and action for teacher researchers.* Routledge. 10.4324/9781315693033

Waitoller, F. R., & Artiles, A. J. (2013). A decade of professional development research for inclusive education a critical review and notes for a research program. *Review of Educational Research*, 83(3), 319–356. 10.3102/0034654313483905

Chapter 5
Incorporation of Virtual Tour Guides Into Tourism Class as an Online Engagement and Retention Strategy

Haley Whitelaw
Fanshawe College, Canada

Frederic Fovet
https://orcid.org/0000-0003-1051-4163
Thompson Rivers University, Canada

EXECUTIVE SUMMARY

Universal Design for Learning (UDL) has been evidenced as a powerful framework for the inclusion of diverse learners in the K-12 sector. Little attention has been paid, however, to the sectors of further education, adult education, vocational training, and all other alternate forms secondary education can take beyond the mainstream or conventionally delivered grades 11 and 12. Yet, it is clear that UDL may have a greater impact in these alternate paths within which learner diversity is significant. This chapter examines the use of UDL within a vocational end of secondary alternate pathway program. It explores specific UDL strategies within a tourism course. The chapter discusses the implications of this case study within the wider global discourse on UDL integration in the classroom. It showcases a reflection around UDL in vocational secondary settings which is growing but still poorly documented in the literature.

DOI: 10.4018/978-1-6684-4750-5.ch005

Copyright © 2024, IGI Global. Copying or distributing in print or electronic forms without written permission of IGI Global is prohibited.

CONTEXT

Interest in Universal Design for Learning (UDL) as a framework for the inclusion of diverse learners is increasing rapidly in the K-12 sector (Rao, 2015; Unal et al., 2022). One area where this momentum has not been as noticeable is the vocational alternate secondary sector. In most jurisdictions around the world, despite growing insistence on mainstreaming, there exists alternate secondary pathways which involve a degree of vocational training and empower learners with real world skills for rapid entry to the employment market (Adamec, 2023; Guo & Wang, 2020). There is little literature documenting the use of UDL in these alternate vocational secondary pathways, and yet it is quite clear that UDL would be of particular relevance for these learner groups which are inherently diverse and usually experiencing barriers in traditional formats of teaching and learning (PwC, 2018; Roisin et al., 2022; Kelly et al., 2022). This chapter explores, through a case study, the use of UDL to engage learners in vocational secondary programs. It hopes to lay the ground for a specific and rich scholarship to emerge around this topic in order to fill a very noticeable gap in practice and research.

The adoption and integration of UDL in community college programs has begun over the last decade and there is therefore a fair amount of emerging scholarship relating to UDL in pre-university settings, as well as in trades and vocational programs at post-secondary level (McGuire & Scott, 2006; Hromalik et al., 2021). However, there is also an increasing amount of vocational and trades instruction that is happening at pre-postsecondary level (Kreisman & Stange, 2020; Matthewes & Ventura, 2022). In some countries these routes are sometimes formally described as the further education sector (Bowers, 2023; Eurydice, 2023). There is, to date, very little evidence or literature discussing the use of UDL in such alternate secondary programs, particularly those with a heavy trade or apprenticeship focus (Quirke & McCarthy, 2020).

The School-College-Work-Initiative discussed in this chapter is a program offering alternate pathways for struggling Grade 12 students to complete remaining credits towards their high school diplomas in Ontario, Canada. The Intro to Tourism course offering is considered a 'dual credit' - diploma and college credits - partnership between a large Ontario college and local school boards in a School Within A College (SWAC) setting. Any experiential learning initiative in alternate settings in the secondary sector is likely to experience certain tensions. It may sometimes be challenging to present in engaging, motivating, and meaningful ways employment related courses to students who may be feeling at risk of failure or exclusion, and may already have a tenuous relationship with or commitment to secondary education. These tensions were tangible in the Intro to Tourism course, but the challenges increased when instruction had to be further modified during the COVID pandemic.

Incorporation of Virtual Tour Guides Into Tourism Class

With an already challenging classroom environment, in terms of low student engagement and retention, the shift to online learning during the COVID-19 pandemic indeed added a complex layer of instructional hurdles. In this context, it was envisaged that incorporating Virtual Tour Guides into a Tourism class as an online engagement and retention strategy might be a solution in these times of low student engagement, considerable barriers to learning, and growing instructor burnout. Without being able to physically take the class out for place-based learning, this outcomes-based strategy aimed to recreate the benefits via guest speakers from a variety of locations around the world.

The goal of the initiative is to create opportunities for learning through a tourism lens and with an industry professional logging in live from the destination. SCWI liaison, Laura Elliott, was kind enough to join some of these sessions and she included it in the SCWI Spring 2021 newsletter as an item highlight in the Student Success through Innovation Section:

> *While the past year has brought many challenges to all aspects of work and family life, Fanshawe College staff has seized the opportunity to design new and creative approaches to engage students in the college experience. Haley Whitelaw, Professor, School of Tourism, Hospitality & Culinary Arts (STHCA) in the Introduction to Tourism Dual Credit course, connected through Zoom with her students and tour guide Pallavi, in Delhi, India for a live interactive workshop on Mandala Drawing! Students in Haley's class brought art supplies to this workshop as they learned how to design mandalas. Pallavi also provided a tour of her home and talked to dual credit students about her background and culture. See the photo of Haley and her creation, as well as Pallavi! (SCWI, 2021, 78)*

There are important lessons to draw from this initiative. Many of the outcomes will have immediate relevance to the further education and alternate secondary education sectors. More broadly the details of this project evidence the relevance of a UDL reflection in contexts where such a rethink in relation to teaching and learning has not yet otherwise begun.

OVERVIEW OF THE LITERATURE

There are various angles of the current literature on teaching and learning that will come into play to support the reflection undertaken in this chapter.

Experiential Learning in the K-12 Classroom

There has been growth in the use of experiential learning in the K-12 sector in the last decade (David & Weinstein, 2023). Experiential learning theory argues that rich and authentic learning occurs mainly within first-hand experiences with phenomena and observations (Rani & Tyagi, 2022). It can focus on first-hand exploration, observation, or making (AEL, 2023). Experiential learning can occur in two main ways: one involves the learner venturing outside the confines of the classroom to gain these first-hand experiences (Asfeldt et al., 2022); the other, more recent, perspective on experiential learning consists of bringing the world into the classroom, through the use of technology and virtual means (OET, 2023). This case study is innovative in its outlook as it examines how real-world interactive experiences can be brought into the classroom through virtual tools.

Experiential Learning Implemented Virtually

There is growing potential for experiential learning in the K-12 sector now that technology can serve as an affordance to bring real-world experiences into the classroom (Molenaar, 2022; Shemshack & Spector, 2020). In the past, costs, risk management, accessibility issues, and time restrictions have all made it challenging to offer K-12 students a broad range of experiential opportunities (Asfeldt et al., 2022; Roberts, 2018). The capacity of technology to bring into the classroom rich and authentic real-world experiences has radically increased with the development of web based and artificial intelligence solutions (Celik et al., 2022; Khosravi et al., 2022). In this case study, the technological supports discussed are fairly rudimentary, cost-effective, and widely available to educators. They mostly consist of using video and conferencing software. Contemporary technological solutions for classroom experiential learning no longer imply large costs.

Universal Design for Learning in Canada

UDL has gained in momentum in Canada rapidly over the last two decades. This interest began in the post-secondary sector, within a wider desire to address the growing diversity of higher education students and their expectations with regards to teaching and learning (Courts et al., 2023; Hills et al., 2022). This momentum and interest have later begun to manifest themselves in the K-12 sector as well (OK et al., 2016). It would be naïve, however, to claim that UDL integration in the K-12 sector has been rapid or seamless. While interest is high, detailed implementation is often complex and still challenging (Grillo, 2022; Scott, 2018; Smith Canter et al., 2017). Any emerging literature which evidences further and more effective ways to implement UDL within K-12 schools is therefore much needed and this chapter will contribute richly to this effort.

UDL and the Vocational and Further Education Sectors

There have been few examples of UDL implementation in trades education, in vocational training, or in further education programs. The appeal of UDL in these sectors that are focused on the immediate and fast acquisition of professional skills has been evident to researchers, and some literature has emerged, but it remains conceptual rather than applied (Quirke & McCarthy, 2020). These publications have generally proactively considered the potential use of UDL and its clear pertinence, but rare have been the articles that have documented real-world examples of implementation or offered lessons and suggestions to practitioners in these programs (CAST, 2023). It is a well-established fact that vocational programs attract a student population which is highly diverse and which will therefore have a wide range of expectations in relation to teaching and learning (Choy & Hodge, 2017). Some efforts have been deployed, both on terrain and in relation to research, in relation to UDL adoption in community college programs, but the majority of this scholarship focuses on pre-university courses, traditional classroom-based programs, and courses/ modules not specifically focused on vocational skills or trades (Smith, 2012).

Innovating with UDL

The UDL scholarship has been very dynamic over the last decade in Canada. There have been ample examples of UDL integration in both the K-12 sector (Levey, 2023) and the post-secondary environment (Espada-Chavarria et al., 2023). There have also been systematic reviews that have examined, categorized, and analyzed these initiatives (Almeqdad et al., 2023). While these developments have been encouraging, it is undeniable that the initiatives in questions have considerable commonalities and remain within a relatively narrow range of objectives and contexts: they are mostly examining the adoption of UDL in mainstream classrooms in K-12 education (Rao et al., 2014), and its integration in broad science and arts undergraduate courses (Casebolt & Humphrey, 2023). The key aim is readily apparent: evidencing the effectiveness of UDL for the broad range of mainstream students in conventional educational paths (Diaz-Vega et al., 2020). There is now a need for new, innovative, and bold literature that examines UDL implementation in non-traditional teaching and learning environments and spaces: language and science labs, outdoor courses, the graduate supervision relationship, visual arts programs, etc. (Fovet, 2020b). These spaces that are not structured as conventional classrooms present specific challenges and opportunities for the integration and use of UDL, and this chapter sets the ground for this scholarly exploration.

METHODOLOGICAL ORIENTATION

The chapter is constructed around a case study approach to data collection and analysis (Yazan, 2015; Yin, 2028). Case study approaches home in on specific examples drawn from the field to offer in-depth analysis of qualitative data which reveals itself in a window opportunity when access to practice allows this. Case studies set up small scale data collection processes that hope to serve as the basis for larger enquiries at a later stage (Shandana & Mujtaba, 2016; Takahashi & Araujo, 2020). They usually focus on exploring and showcasing emerging trends about social phenomena and do so in a time-efficient manner when large enquiry processes might not yet be possible (Ebneyamini & Moghadam, 2018; Schwandt & Gates, 2018).

This chapter also borrows and uses many tools from the narrative enquiry tradition (Finlay & Dela Cruz, 2023). Narrative enquiry uses story telling as the basis for data collection (Riley & Hawe, 2005; Rabelo, 2022), and much of the canvas on which this chapter is built is indeed the story of a classroom project which yielded surprising results. The thematic analysis and findings blend a two-perspective approach. On the one hand, the instructor who has designed and ran the initiative presents her practitioner stance on the content of the case study; this is contrasted with the co-author's commentary which offers a global perspective as to how this case study disrupts current work on UDL implementation in the scholarly literature.

THE CASE STUDY

The Reasoning Behind the Initiative

It can be challenging in any context to create authentic and meaningful opportunities of experiential learning in the K-12 sector. Such initiatives represent even greater challenges when they involve students in alternate education programs, who may already be feeling relatively disenfranchised and may have developed antagonistic relationships with school as an institution generally. Such challenges in relation to authentic and meaningful engagement in experiential contexts become monumental when physical collaboration and gathering, or social interaction, are impossible, as was the case during the online pivot that accompanied the COVID pandemic outbreak in most jurisdictions globally. It became essential, in order to remain meaningful, for the Intro to Tourism course within the SWAC setting to adopt a new format that might allow for equal or increased interaction, despite social distancing and the overnight adoption of online delivery. Considering many students within the SWAC setting may be diverse, and being mindful of the fact that it is this very diverse profile that has led many of these learners to feel it challenging to develop engagement in educational settings, it became immediately and pressingly urgent to ensure this course remained inclusive, fully accessible, but also highly engaging. Inclusive design and UDL therefore became key concerns during the online pivot of this course. Striving for inclusive representation was also a major factor in becoming creative with the course. It was previously made up of case studies on the 'pioneers of tourism & hospitality' which exclusively featured discussions related to Euro-Caucasian, mostly male, historical perspectives.

The Unfolding of the UDL Reflection

Here, there are two main UDL principles which come into play in the reflection on inclusive design. UDL is framed around three main principles of inclusive design: multiple means of representation (injecting optimal flexibility in the way information is presented to the learner), multiple means of action and expression (offering the learner optimal flexibility in the way they are presenting information or responding to directives), and multiple means of engagement (integrating an optimal degree of flexibility in the way educators construe engagement and frame expectations with regards to engagement). The main angles of reflection in this case study are multiples means of representation and multiple means of engagement.

The notion of an experiential learning opportunity is normally framed around first-hand interaction with content – rather than via educator led instruction. It may take the form of a visit, a physical discovery, or an autonomous process of hands-on action. It can also involve the act of making (Gravel & Puckett, 2023), or product creation. In this case, due to the COVID pandemic pivot to online teaching, it was impossible to offer field trips or the discovery of cultural or physical characteristics outside the classroom. Offering multiple means of representation implied a creative reflection as to how to substitute meaningful alternatives to this. Online virtual tour guides offered a flexible alternative to present this content, one that would be a much more interactive, playful, rich, and differentiated method than readings or unidimensional videos. The multiple means of engagement principle also came into the reflection, as attempting to re-engage disenfranchised students was very much at the heart of this SWAC initiative. It was apparent that traditional tasks such as asking the students to read and write about their readings would create low engagement, and possibly failure in this course. The virtual guide-led visual visits were able to offer the learners many personalized ways for them to interact and connect with the content. Multiple means of action and expression also come into play, to some extent, in this case study as there was a relative freedom in the ways learners could interact with the virtual tour or ask questions to the guides and facilitators.

The Observations

This section of the chapter will detail the classroom activity, which was designed to offer experiential capacity online, using a UDL reasoning.

Introduction to India

The activity selected for this region involved mandala drawing from Delhi. The aim of the session was for students to design their own mandala, while using their breath to clear their mind and create positive energy. While they were drawing, the students were able to explore the host's home/garden in Delhi, and talk about the tourism, culture, and religions of India.

The student responses were powerful and enthusiastic:

I really loved the lesson and enjoyed learning about their culture because everything was new to me. And I can't wait to hear from all the others that we see. – C.

It was nice learning about India and its culture. Would love to visit one day. I struggled with the Mandala designs, but I still had fun. – J.

Reflecting on my experience of my first virtual tour of India and Indian culture I enjoyed seeing the presenter's home and I learned how to draw Mandala's...or at least tried my best to learn how. Overall, this tour was a great experience for me and I am hopeful to see more activities like this as our semester continues! - A.

Exploration of Indigenous Contexts within Canada

This online activity involved Cree knowledge & storytelling of the Creation Story by Matricia Brown (2023). In this class, students experienced Canadian First Nation culture as it is shared with inbound & domestic tourists alike.

The responses from learners evidenced the effectiveness of the activity, which fell within this wider UDL reflection related to online delivery during the COVID pandemic:

I loved this class tour, it was very insightful and engaging. I especially enjoyed when the guest speaker was using her language being Cree, as I personally love to hear other cultures language. – A.

It was nice to learn more about the indigenous culture. It reminded me of the Indigenous culture back in the Philippines. Would love to learn more in the future! – J.

I love how their language gives everything meaning and purpose, I learned a lot today and I would be looking forward in learning more abut the language. – K.

I thought it was an amazing experience that I probably wouldn't have gotten if I wasn't in the class. She was very nice and helped with my questions. – H.

Discovering the Culture and Landscape of Jamaica

This activity was delivered by Adrian Harrison, of the Jamaica Tourist Board, who is also a member of Expedia Travel. Falmouth is a town that is historically significant because it grew out of the slave trade and sugar production. It was Jamaica's first planned town where every street was drawn on a blueprint before it was built. The town is known to have had piped water before New York City! Falmouth is also home to Jamaica's newest cruise port, and due to its history and resurgence, makes an interesting case study of the balance between tourism development and preserving heritage. We also examined who is benefiting from the presence of the cruise business: locals are concerned that Royal Caribbean has a 60% stake in the ownership of the port, and controls many of the shops, restaurants, and tours. This was a dialogical session of discovery, supported by a visual exploration of Falmouth.

The learner feedback evidences the success of the UDL strategy on engagement: "It was nice learning more about Jamaica and their culture. I really liked his Jamaican accent and the language of Patois". – D.

Interactive Activity Allowing a Discovery of Indonesia.

This virtual discovery of Indonesia was led and facilitated by Muhammad Khulaifi (Levi), a tour guide on the island of Lombok. Indonesia is made up of over 17,000 islands and is home to six official religions and over 300 different native languages. Participants learnt about the culture, traditions, religions, and foods of Levi's home island of Lombok, saw some sights, and explored how the pandemic has affected the island since it halted tourism. Levi guided students through the site of Lingsar Temple, one of the only sites in his area that was open at the time, within the context of the extended government closures surrounding the pandemic. The class discovered the importance of cultural sensitivity when traveling to religious sites – for example, guests are required to wear a sarong when entering the temple. Built in 1714, Pura Lingsar is considered to be a symbol of harmony between Hindu Bali Lombok and Islam Sasak Lombok. This dual heritage makes Pura Lingsar an important symbol of unity among the island's faiths. Levi showed the class that eggs are normally for sale on the temple grounds. These are not intended for peckish visitors but for the eels. The Wetu Telu section of the temple has a pool of holy eels that are said to represent the Hindu God Vishnu. Visitors are invited to gift them a hard-boiled lunch and they may be blessed, as a result, with sacred protection against evil.

An Online Virtual and Inclusive Exploration of Mexico City

This session was organized and facilitated by Ubish Yaren, of Mexico Underground. With experience as an international chef, Ubish conducts engaging tours centered on the food, art, and architecture of Mexico City. He features live-streaming tours from his city and the surrounding area, including street taco tours, the floating gardens of Xochimilco, hipster land, hidden neighborhoods, and city life after dark. While there was no direct feedback in writing collected in relation to these last two sessions, it was clear from mere observation during the virtual tours that the students especially enjoyed Ubish's live tour of his Mexico City neighborhood, including the market, tortilla factory, food stands, and monuments. The students especially enjoyed Ubish's live tour as he greeted them in his apartment and then affixed his camera as he took them out into the street, walking them through his local market to browse the fresh ingredients, then into a production shop nestled into the alley where a family makes and sells fresh tortillas. Next, the class visited food stands – specifically, taco stands. Ubish showed the participants the varieties of meat and toppings and the class could practically smell the tempting meal. The virtual tour wrapped up with some discussion on travel safety, as the learners' viewed monuments and the square where protests are frequent. The class was left feeling as though they really had just been walking through the streets of Mexico City.

ASSERTIONS

In this section of the chapter, both authors offer their respective perspective on the outcomes of the initiative, one from a theoretical perspective examining this innovative use of UDL, the other from a practitioner stance assessing impact on program outcomes.

The Practitioner Perspective

The level of engagement of the students during each virtual session with a guest was considerable and immediately palpable. As the class was taking place in the virtual environment, this growth in engagement became noticeable as students increasingly turned on their cameras, asked questions, showed interest, and generally being more involved with the content and more interactive with the guides and facilitators. In terms of retention of student interest throughout the course, key observations were possible. In a course of this type delivered face to face within the SWAC setting, it is not unusual for student attendance to diminish as the course progresses. A progressive decrease in student attendance was therefore something that was expected in this instance as well. Instead, Haley was able to "advertise" which country the next week's guest speakers were logging in from in advance and students seemed to specifically attend out of genuine interest in relation to the virtual destination. Overall, the success rate of students earning the credit for this class was 100%., when the usual success rate for this program; from the instructor's experience, is usually in the range of 60 to 70%. There is therefore tangible evidence that this particular innovative practice significantly increased the success of the students in this program.

The Researcher Point of View

This initiative represents a unique experimentation with UDL in online K-12 instruction and assessment. It is further unique in the sense that it relates to an alternative secondary education pathway. The project is also unique in the sense that it applies UDL reasoning and logic to the reformatting of experiential outcomes. There exists a degree of tension between UDL and experiential learning, as teaching approaches (Fovet, 2020). Indeed, much of the experiential learning observed in educational spaces remains inaccessible and may not prima facie be fully inclusive. Experiential learning is seen as highly engaging; it leads to rich and authentic acquisition of skills (Uyen et al., 2022), but it often involves travel, physical movement, long periods of time spent outside the educational institution, and sometimes a degree of risk (Pierce & Telford, 2023; Yildiz, 2022). This can create barriers for learners, that can be physical, social, or financial (Kelly et al., 2022; O'Connor et al., 2023). There has therefore not been much reflection to date as to how one might integrate UDL principles in experiential settings (Wilson & Mackie, 2018).

This initiative creates a blueprint and a precedent for the seamless application of UDL principles in experiential learning initiatives. It demonstrates that experiential learning opportunities can remain inclusive, and that in fact they do not necessarily require lengthy periods of time outside the classroom, or extended travel outside the institution. It also evidences the relevance of UDL within a reflection on engagement in a context that involves disenfranchised learners in K-12 settings and alternate pathways to secondary. This is a sector where little reflection related to UDL has, ironically, taken place to date. It can, indeed, be assumed that many students within alternate K-12 programs are diverse and require flexibility (Chen, 2017), but UDL implementation has thus far focused on the mainstream schooling environment.

Finally, this project is groundbreaking in the sense that it represents a UDL design process as applied to an online learning experience. Much was written during the COVID pandemic as to how useful UDL might be to support inclusion in the online pivot, but much of this reflection was after the fact (Seymour, 2023). The overnight pivot to online delivery, indeed, allowed for little proactive planning. This initiative is different in the sense that it represented a reaction to the COVID landscape and its challenges, but was a reflective process of adaptation to this reality. UDL was fully embedded in this process of change. A further pertinent facet of the initiative is that it opens a discussion as to the potential of UDL in the context of the acquisition of competencies for employment, of trades education, and of vocational training.

RECOMMENDATIONS

The case study represents a rich opportunity for reflection on practice within alternate secondary pathways and vocational training. It allows for broad recommendations for further exploration and ongoing analysis.

Overlap between UDL and Experiential Learning

UDL literature tends to be siloed and will often only focus on accessibility (Hartmann, 2015). There are, in fact, many overlaps between the intentions of UDL and the key objectives of experiential learning, despite their relative distance within the literature. Both in relation to multiple means of action and expression and to multiple means of engagement, experiential learning can serve as a tool or a vehicle for the objectives of UDL practitioners wanting to radically transform the expectations placed on learners. In both pedagogical frameworks, there is a desire to encourage learners to actively do, rather than passively integrate knowledge. There are therefore many commonalities between experiential learning and UDL, as reflective processes, and it will be essential in the future for scholars to blend these pedagogical approaches rather than consider them entirely separately. The K-12 sector appears as a particularly privileged environment for the blending of these scholarships.

Examining UDL and Learner Diversity
Beyond Disability and Impairment

This case study is particularly powerful in the sense that it applies a reflection around UDL and inclusive design in a broad landscape that is not limited to students with disabilities. It demonstrates the relevance and pertinence of UDL for all diverse learners. UDL has historically been focused mostly on the rights to inclusive provisions of learners with impairments, as most of the early scholarship has emerged from the work of accessibility specialists (Capp, 2017). There is now a need to widen the scholarship related to UDL to the full range of diverse learners, but few such examples exist so far (Gentile & Budzilowicz, 2022). This case study has opened the way for further work, both in terms of scholarship and field initiatives, to apply UDL for the inclusion of the full spectrum of diverse learners. It has been particularly powerful in establishing the relevance of UDL for learners who might be disenfranchised in school and needing reengagement through alternate pathways.

UDL in Online Teaching and Learning

There has not been much focus so far on the use of UDL in online instruction (Matteson, 2023). When such a focus has occurred, it has been in the post-secondary sector (Johnston, 2020). The COVID pandemic has obviously accelerated this implementation and this reflection on practice, as it has led almost all educators to suddenly consider inclusion in online delivery and assessment, as well as their stance as designers of an inclusive virtual experience (Li et al., 2023). Some of these experimentations have been more successful than others, but UDL has most definitely attracted increased interest from educators (Almeqdad et al., 2023). This chapter emphasizes the usefulness of UDL within a reflection on learner engagement in online delivery and assessment. It does so within a secondary alternate pathway and creates a useful and nuanced precedent for future research and on-terrain implementation in online instruction, in a post-pandemic landscape.

Considering all Three UDL Design Principles Simultaneously Versus in Isolation

Much of the scholarship on UDL considers the UDL principles in isolation. This can be criticized as slightly naïve and simplistic. Practitioners' reflections on inclusive design in fact rarely center on just one dimension of the learner's experience. There is therefore a need for scholarly analyses in relation to UDL that are complex, ecological in nature, and multidimensional. This case study analysis offers an encouraging precedent for design reflections that considers all three UDL principles simultaneously. Such field initiatives and scholarly commentaries will, in the future, offer the reader a more realistic overview of the wide reflection on practice that UDL implementation represents.

Need for a UDL Discourse Specifically Targeting the Vocational Secondary Sector

As was described in the scan of the literature on UDL, little attention and focus have thus far targeted vocational secondary sectors. UDL will increasingly be relevant and useful in alternate pathways that offer diverse learners, who are experiencing challenges in conventional teaching, more applied outcomes; these could be trade, sports based, apprenticeship, or professional alternatives. Vocational training in the K-12 sector has been seen critically in recent decades, while the focus on mainstreaming has been more pressing and tangible. Originally, vocational training in the secondary sector was seen as an effort to create a form of ability grouping that was detrimental to the development of learner potential and was challenging to later escape or exit for more traditional post-secondary avenues or options (Kim, 2023). In recent incarnations, therefore, vocational training and further education have had to reposition themselves in an innovative way – no longer as efforts at ability grouping, but more holistically as capacity building, student-centered alternatives that remain worthwhile, authentic, and genuinely lead learners to tangible life-long outcomes. UDL plays an important role in this reframing of vocational education in the secondary sector as it guarantees that it is accessible, inclusive, and meaningful (Hoekstra & Newton, 2017).

Need for a More Seamless Outlook on UDL Integration Beyond Formal Sector Delineations

Because this chapter and this case study are situated at the juncture of the K-12 sector and the vocational and further educational sectors, they set a useful precedent as to how UDL implementation, and the literature that accompanies it, must begin to bridge rigid sector delineations. It has been counterproductive that UDL implementation has thus far been seen as unique and different in each of the educational sectors that make up the contemporary institutional landscapes. The experiences of diverse learners are in fact not siloed or fragmented but span instead across sector delineations. It is therefore urgent that UDL scholars should begin to consider UDL integration as a process which bridges sector transitions and has commonalities across institutions. This process has begun, and this chapter sets the ground for further reflection around UDL adoption at the intersections of learner pathways.

Role of the Vocational Sector in Triggering a Deep Reflection Within the UDL Scholarship

Discussed above were observations as to how these case study findings provide innovative perspectives on how UDL might be pertinent and effective in reframing vocational pathways in the secondary sector, in inclusive ways that fully embrace learner diversity. This chapter also has a wider impact in relation to inclusive design and UDL implementation in vocational training more generally. There has thus far been very little exploration of UDL in vocational education, trades education, further education, field apprenticeships, and adult education. It is clear, however, that these streams focused on the acquisition of immediately applicable professional skills and competencies attract an extremely diverse learner population. UDL integration in these programs should therefore not be an afterthought but rather a central focus of the UDL scholarship, research, and on-terrain experimentation. This chapter sets the tone for a new and energized focus on UDL use in trades education, vocational programs, and further education programming.

CONCLUSION

This chapter highlights not just the impact of UDL strategies in a Tourism course. There are much wider outcomes showcased, pertaining to the use and relevance of UDL in any vocational alternate secondary program. The chapter illustrates the very specific pertinence of UDL in the context of all alternate K-12 pathways and other vocational training programs. The chapter will serve as basis for the development of an emerging scholarship on the use of UDL in further education, alternate K-12 pathways, and in vocational training. This piece will have immediate relevance for the international reader in the sense that it maps out possible UDL use in areas where challenges are considerable and where very little reflection around learner diversity or inclusive practices have occurred so far – in comparison to the literature discussing UDL in more conventional learning settings.

REFERENCES

Adamec, P. (2023). Teaching Vocational Subjects in Secondary School: A New Career or a Backup Plan? *International Journal of Engineering Pedagogy*, 13(5), 142–160. 10.3991/ijep.v13i5.37555

Almeqdad, Q. A., Alodat, A. M., Alquraan, M. F., Mohaidat, M. A., & Al-Makhzoomy, A. K. (2023). The effectiveness of universal design for learning: A systematic review of the literature and meta-analysis. *Cogent Education*, 10(1), 2218191. Advance online publication. 10.1080/2331186X.2023.2218191

Asfeldt, M., Purc-Stephenson, R., & Zimmerman, T. (2022). Outdoor education in Canadian public schools: Connecting children and youth to people, place, and environment. *Environmental Education Research*, 28(10), 1510–1526. 10.1080/13504622.2022.2061919

Association of Experiential Learning. (2023). *What is Experiential Education? AEL*https://www.aee.org/what-is-experiential-education

Bowers, S. (2023, August 29). 'Gamechanger' programme allows students to attain third-level degree outside CAO points race. *Irish Times.*https://www.irishtimes.com/ireland/education/2023/08/29/alternative-pathways-to-further-education/

Brown, M. (2023). *Warrior Woman.* https://warrriorwomen.ca/

Capp, M. J. (2017). The effectiveness of universal design for learning: A meta-analysis of literature between 2013 and 2016. *International Journal of Inclusive Education*, 21(8), 791–807. 10.1080/13603116.2017.1325074

Casebolt, T., & Humphrey, T. (2023). Use of Universal Design for Learning Principles in a Public Health Course. *Annals of Global Health*, 89(1), 48. 10.5334/aogh.404537484884

CAST. (2023) *Add Universal Design for Learning to Your CTE State Plan.* Home. https://www.cast.org/news/2023/universal-design-for-learning-udl-cte-state-plan

Celik, I., Dindar, M., Muukkonen, H., & Järvelä, S. (2022). The promises and challenges of artificial intelligence for teachers: A systematic review of research. *TechTrends*, 66(4), 616–630. 10.1007/s11528-022-00715-y

Chen, J. C. (2017). Nontraditional Adult Learners: The Neglected Diversity in Postsecondary Education. *SAGE Open*, 7(1). Advance online publication. 10.1177/2158244017697161

Incorporation of Virtual Tour Guides Into Tourism Class

Choy, S., & Hodge, S. (2017). Teaching practice in Australian vocational education and training: A practice theory analysis. In *Practice Theory Perspectives on Pedagogy and Education* (pp. 157–173). Springer. 10.1007/978-981-10-3130-4_8

Courts, R., Chatoor, K., Pichette, J., Okojie, O., & Tishcoff, R. (2023). *HEQCO's Dialogues on Universal Design for Learning: Finding Common Ground and Key Recommendations from the Sector*. Higher Education Quality Council of Ontario. https://heqco.ca/wp-content/uploads/2023/04/HEQCOs-Dialogues-on-Universal -Design-for-Learning-UDL-2.pdf

David, L., & Weinstein, N. (2023). A Gamified Experiential Learning Intervention for Engaging Students Through Satisfying Needs. *Journal of Educational Technology Systems*, 52(1), 52–72. 10.1177/00472395231174614

Diaz-Vega, M., Moreno-Rodriguez, R., & Lopez-Bastias, J. L. (2020). Educational Inclusion through the Universal Design for Learning: Alternatives to Teacher Training. *Education Sciences*, 10(11), 303. 10.3390/educsci10110303

Ebneyamini, S., & Moghadam, M. R. (2018). Toward developing a framework for conducting case study research. *International Journal of Qualitative Methods*, 17(1), 1–11. 10.1177/1609406918817954

Espada-Chavarria, R., González-Montesino, R. H., López-Bastías, J. L., & Díaz-Vega, M. (2023). Universal Design for Learning and Instruction: Effective Strategies for Inclusive Higher Education. *Education Sciences*, 13(6), 620. 10.3390/educsci13060620

Eurydice. (2023). *National reforms in further education and training and adult learning*. National Education Systems. European Commission. https://eurydice .eacea.ec.europa.eu/national-education-systems/ireland/national-reforms-further -education-and-training-and-adult

Finlay, J., & Dela Cruz, A. (2023). Reflexivity and Relational Spaces: Experiences of Conducting a Narrative Inquiry Study With Emerging Adult Women Living With Chronic Pain. *Global Qualitative Nursing Research*, 10. Advance online publication. 10.1177/23333936231190619061937576739

Fovet, F. (2020). Beyond Novelty – "Innovative" Accessible Teaching as a Return to Fundamental Questions Around Social Justice and Reflective Pedagogy. In Palahicky, S. (Ed.), *Enhancing Learning Design for Innovative Teaching in Higher Education*. IGI Global. 10.4018/978-1-7998-2943-0.ch002

Fovet, F. (2020b). Universal Design for Learning as a Tool for Inclusion in the Higher Education Classroom: Tips for the Next Decade of Implementation. *Education Journal, 9*(6), 163-172. http://www.sciencepublishinggroup.com/journal/paperinfo?journalid=196&doi=10.11648/j.edu.20200906.13

Gentile, A. L., & Budzilowicz, M. (2022). Empowering college students: UDL, culturally responsive pedagogy, and mindset as an instructional approach. *New Directions for Teaching and Learning*, 2022(172), 33–42. 10.1002/tl.20524

Gravel, B. E., & Puckett, C. (2023). What shapes implementation of a school-based makerspace? Teachers as multilevel actors in STEM reforms. *International Journal of STEM Education*, 10(7), 7. Advance online publication. 10.1186/s40594-023-00395-x

Grillo, M. (2022). The Administrator's Role in Universal Design for Learning's Successful Implementation. *Teaching Exceptional Children*, 54(5), 372–379. 10.1177/00400599211022030

Guo, D., & Wang, A. (2020). Is vocational education a good alternative to low-performing students in China. *International Journal of Educational Development*, 75, 102187. Advance online publication. 10.1016/j.ijedudev.2020.102187

Hartmann, E. (2015). Universal design for learning (UDL) and learners with severe support needs. *International Journal of Whole Schooling*, 11(1), 54–67. https://eric.ed.gov/?id=EJ1061020

Hills, M., Overend, A., & Hildebrandt, S. (2022). Faculty Perspectives on UDL: Exploring Bridges and Barriers for Broader Adoption in Higher Education. *The Canadian Journal for the Scholarship of Teaching and Learning*, 13(1). Advance online publication. 10.5206/cjsotlrcacea.2022.1.13588

Hoekstra, A., & Newton, P. (2017). Departmental leadership for learning in vocational and professional education. *Empirical Research in Vocational Education and Training*, 9(1), 12. 10.1186/s40461-017-0057-0

Hromalik, C. D., Myhill, W. M., Ohrazda, C. A., Carr, N. R., & Zumbuhl, S. A. (2021). Increasing Universal Design for Learning knowledge and application at a community college: The Universal Design for Learning Academy. *International Journal of Inclusive Education*. Advance online publication. 10.1080/13603116.2021.1931719

Johnston, S. (2020). *Universal design for learning to support remote learning*. EDUCAUSE. https://events.educause.edu/-/media/files/events/webinar/2020/eliweb2004/transcript.pdf

Kelly, O., Buckley, K., Lieberman, L. J., & Arndt, K. (2022). Universal Design for Learning - A framework for inclusion in Outdoor Learning. *Journal of Outdoor and Environmental Education*, 25(1), 75–89. 10.1007/s42322-022-00096-z

Khosravi, H., Shum, S. B., Chen, G., Conati, C., Tsai, Y.-S., Kay, J., Knight, S., Martinez-Maldonado, R., Sadiq, S., & Gašević, D. (2022). Explainable artificial intelligence in education. *Computers and Education: Artificial Intelligence*, 3, 100074. Advance online publication. 10.1016/j.caeai.2022.100074

Kim, R. (2023). Under the Law: CTE: A checkered legal history. *Phi Delta Kappan*, 104(6), 58–60. 10.1177/00317217231161544

Kreisman, D., & Stange, K. (2020). Vocational and Career Tech Education in American High Schools: The Value of Depth Over Breadth. *Education Finance and Policy*, 15(1), 11–44. 10.1162/edfp_a_00266

Levey, S. (2023). Universal Design for Learning. *Journal of Education*, 203(2), 479–487. 10.1177/00220574211031954

Li, Y.-F., Zhang, D., Dulas, H. M., & Whirley, M. L. (2023). The Impact of COVID-19 and Remote Learning on Education: Perspectives from University Students With Disabilities. *Journal of Disability Policy Studies*. Advance online publication. 10.1177/10442073231185264

Matteson, S. (2023). Universal Design for Learning in Asynchronous Online Instruction. In E. Langran, P. Christensen & J. Sanson (Eds.), *Proceedings of Society for Information Technology & Teacher Education International Conference* (pp. 2537-2540). New Orleans, LA, United States: Association for the Advancement of Computing in Education (AACE). Retrieved October 9, 2023 from https://www.learntechlib.org/primary/p/222153/

Matthewes, S. H., & Ventura, G. (2022) *On Track to Success? Returns to vocational education against different alternatives*. Discussion Paper 038. Centre for Vocational Educational Research. https://cver.lse.ac.uk/textonly/cver/pubs/cverdp038.pdf

McGuire, J. M., & Scott, S. S. (2006). Universal design for instruction: Extending the universal design paradigm to college instruction. *Journal of Postsecondary Education and Disability*, 19(2), 124–134. https://files.eric.ed.gov/fulltext/EJ844629.pdf

Molenaar, I. (2022). Towards hybrid human-AI learning technologies. *European Journal of Education*, 57(4), 1–14. 10.1111/ejed.12527

O'Connor, E., Marcogliese, E., Anis, H., Faye, G., Flynn, A., Hayman, E., & Stambouli, J. (2023). Adapting Experiential Learning in Times of Uncertainty: Challenges, Strategies, and Recommendations Moving Forward. *Engaged Scholar Journal: Community-Engaged Research, Teaching, and Learning*, 8(4), 49–56. 10.15402/esj.v8i4.70793

Office of Educational Technology. (2023). *Artificial Intelligence and Future of Teaching and Learning: Insights and Recommendations*. U.S. Department of Education. https://www2.ed.gov/documents/ai-report/ai-report.pdf

Ok, M. W., Rao, K., Bryant, B. R., & McDougall, D. (2016). Universal Design for Learning in Pre-K to Grade 12 Classrooms: A Systematic Review of Research. *Exceptionality*. Advance online publication. 10.1080/09362835.2016.1196450

Pierce, J., & Telford, J. (2023). From McDonaldization to place-based experience: Revitalizing outdoor education in Ireland. *Journal of Adventure Education and Outdoor Learning*, 1–14. Advance online publication. 10.1080/14729679.2023.2254861

PwC. (2018). *Inclusion of People with Disability in VET Cross Sector Project Environmental Scan*. https://www.skillsforaustralia.com/2018/02/02/inclusion-of-people-with-disability-in-vet-environmental-scan-released/

Quirke, M., & McCarthy, P. (2020) *A Conceptual Framework of Universal Design for Learning (UDL) for the Irish Further Education and Training Sector*. Solas. https://www.solas.ie/f/70398/x/b1aa8a51b6/a-conceptual-framework-of-universal-design-for-learning-udl-for-the-ir.pdf

Rabelo, A. O. (2022). The Importance of Narrative Inquiry in Education. *The Journal for Critical Education Policy Studies*, 19(3), 112–138. https://eric.ed.gov/?id=EJ1340278

Rani, K., & Tyagi, T. K. (2022). Experiential Learning in School Education: Prospects and Challenges. *International Journal of Advance and Applied Research*, 10(2), 178–183. 10.5281/zenodo.7652609

Rao, K. (2015). Universal design for learning and multimedia technology: Supporting culturally and linguistically diverse students. *Journal of Educational Multimedia and Hypermedia*, 24(2), 121–137. https://scholarspace.manoa.hawaii.edu/server/api/core/bitstreams/c273b37c-5b7b-450e-8667-fdd7d15e182a/content

Rao, K., Ok, M. W., & Bryant, B. R. (2014). A Review of Research on Universal Design Educational Models. *Remedial and Special Education*, 35(3), 153–166. 10.1177/0741932513518980

Riley, T., & Hawe, P. (2005). Researching practice: The methodological case for narrative inquiry. *Health Education Research*, 20(2), 226–236. 10.1093/her/cyg12215479707

Roberts, J. (2018). From the Editor: The Possibilities and Limitations of Experiential Learning Research in Higher Education. *Journal of Experiential Education, 41*(1), 3-7. 10.1177/1053825917751457

Roisin, D., Heelan, A., & Tobin, T. J. (2020). *AHEAD Ireland FET Project.* Paper presented at the Pathways15. https://www.atend.com.au/resource/119/pathways15 -keynote-ahead-ireland-fet-project/

Schwandt, T. A., & Gates, E. F. (2018). Case study methodology. In Denzin, N. K., & Lincoln, Y. S. (Eds.), *The Sage Handbook of Qualitative Research* (pp. 600–630). Sage Publishers.

Scott, L. A. (2018). Barriers with implementing a Universal Design for Learning framework. *Inclusion (Washington, D.C.)*, 6(4), 274–286. 10.1352/2326-6988-6.4.274

SCWI. (2021) School College Work Initiative 2021. *Newsletter, 1*(6). https://www .scwi.ca/resources/flipbook/SCWI_Newsletter_Spring_2021_V2/inc/html/4.html ?page=1

Seymour, M. (2023). Enhancing the online student experience through the application of Universal Design for Learning (UDL) to research methods learning and teaching. *Education and Information Technologies*. Advance online publication. 10.1007/s10639-023-11948-637361769

Shandana, S., & Mujtaba, B. G. (2016). Use it or lose it: Prudently using case study as a research and educational strategy. *American Journal of Education and Learning*, 1(2), 83–93. 10.20448/804.1.2.83.93

Shemshack, A., & Spector, J. M. (2020). A systematic literature review of personalized learning terms. *Smart Learning Environments*, 7(33), 33. Advance online publication. 10.1186/s40561-020-00140-9

Smith, F. G. (2012). Analyzing a College Course that Adheres to the Universal Design for Learning (UDL) Framework. *The Journal of Scholarship of Teaching and Learning*, 12(3), 31–61. https://scholarworks.iu.edu/journals/index.php/josotl/article/view/2151

Smith Canter, L. L., King, L. H., Williams, J. B., Metcalf, D., & Rhys Myrick Potts, K. (2017). Evaluating pedagogy and practice of Universal Design for Learning in public schools. *Exceptionality Education International*, 27(1), 1–16. 10.5206/eei.v27i1.7743

Takahashi, A. R., & Araujo, L. (2020). Case study research: Opening up research opportunities. *RAUSP Management Journal*, 56(1), 100–111. 10.1108/RAUSP-05-2019-0109

Unal, N. U., Karal, M. A., & Tan, S. (2022). Developing Accessible Lesson Plans with Universal Design for Learning (UDL).*International Journal of Disability Development and Education*, 69(4), 1442–1456. 10.1080/1034912X.2020.1812539

Uyen, B. P., Tong, D. H., & Lien, N. B. (2022). The Effectiveness of Experiential Learning in Teaching Arithmetic and Geometry in Sixth Grade. *Frontiers in Education*, 7, 858631. 10.3389/feduc.2022.858631

Wilson, M., & Mackie, K. (2018) Design. In *Learning by Doing: Postsecondary Experiential Education*. Open Library. https://ecampusontario.pressbooks.pub/adultedpseee/chapter/developing-ee-design-phase/

Yazan, B. (2015). Three approaches to case study methods in education: Yin, Merriam and Stake. *The Qualitative Report*, 20(2), 134–152. 10.46743/2160-3715/2015.2102

Yildiz, K. (2022). Experiential learning from the perspective of outdoor education leaders. *Journal of Hospitality, Leisure, Sport and Tourism Education*, 30, 100343. Advance online publication. 10.1016/j.jhlste.2021.100343

Yin, R. K. (2018). *Case study research - design and methods* (6th ed.). Sage Publications.

KEY TERMS AND DEFINITIONS

Alternate K-12 Pathways: There may be many reasons why learners may not feel able to remain in mainstream inclusive secondary pathways. Across jurisdictions, initiatives and projects may seek to offer alternate routes for students to remain in education when they might otherwise drop out. These formats may involve adaptations to the curriculum and to assessment; they may also involve modifications of criteria and program objectives.

Further and Continuing Education: This terminology relates to various formats of teaching and learning across a wide range of jurisdictions globally which seek to offer opportunities for learners, who would otherwise not feel able to finish secondary education, or to continue with education in some format or other.

Universal Design for Learning: This is a framework for inclusion which focuses on the inclusive design of instruction and assessment rather than on the exceptionality of students. UDL, as a teaching and learning model, presumes that there is a considerable degree of learner diversity in every class and encourages the proactive design of the learning experience along simple inclusive principles of design. The three UDL principles recommend optimal use of flexibility in relation to the way information is presented to learners, to the way students are asked to interact with the content, and in the ways educators create expectations in relation to engagement.

Vocational Secondary Programs: Vocational secondary programs seek to create alternate pathways to graduation that offer increased opportunities for experiential learning, the acquisition of competencies in trades, or the development of specific competencies for rapid employment.

130

Chapter 6
Perspectives From an In–Service Teacher UDL Action Research Project

Lauren Tucker
Southern Connecticut State University, USA

EXECUTIVE SUMMARY

Including universal design for learning in graduate programs for in-service teachers is crucial to increasing the application of the framework in practice. This chapter will introduce an action research assignment within an American UDL graduate course and its impact on teacher practice and student learning. Eight case studies across disciplines and levels will be shared. During this process, teachers identified a classroom challenge, developed a UDL intervention, analyzed student data, and shared implications. In-service teacher reflections will be shared on the continued use of a UDL approach beyond their course work and its impact on their teaching practice. The chapter will begin with an introduction to the context of the implementation, investigation questions, methodology, case study presentation, discussion, and conclusion.

INTRODUCTION

Within an American university's special education and curriculum and instruction and regular graduate programs, all students take a course titled *Universal Design for Learning (UDL) to Access Curriculum.* For the majority of students, it is the first course in their graduate program. The course was designed to model universal design for learning throughout its hybrid delivery while teaching about the framework. The goal is to provide substantial background on UDL while modeling its

DOI: 10.4018/978-1-6684-4750-5.ch006

Copyright © 2024, IGI Global. Copying or distributing in print or electronic forms without written permission of IGI Global is prohibited.

Perspectives From an In-Service Teacher UDL Action Research Project

implementation for teachers to apply in their subsequent courses and to learn content they can immediately implement in their classrooms. A key assignment focuses on a mini-action research paper focusing on UDL. These papers were utilized as the foundation of the eight UDL implementation case studies shared within this chapter. Before the teachers were asked to implement UDL practices, they learned about the framework in UDL designed learning experiences.

KEY ELEMENTS IN THE LITERATURE

UDL Based Course Delivery

Before expecting teachers to implement UDL in their practice, the instructor consistently modeled UDL within the content delivery. The hybrid course modeled universal design for learning throughout the 8-week semester with the goal of enhancing the learning experience of graduate students (Cumming & Rose, 2022; Polly et al., 2020) while simultaneously modeling UDL implementation (Engleman & Schmidt, 2007; Evmenova, 2018). The course embedded learner choice, deadline flexibility, multiple methods to engage with content, and options to express learning, which can all enhance learner access to content (Cumming & Rose, 2022). The instructor explicitly highlighted some of these UDL components during the course and others were simply embedded. At the culmination of the semester, each graduate student completed a "UDL Scavenger Hunt" to reflect on the various design and instructional choices aligned with UDL. They were asked to provide specific examples of each component integrated within the class. Table 1 provides examples of the course evidence graduate students supplied for each UDL component.

Table 1. Examples of UDL within graduate course

UDL Component	Course Example Provided by Graduate Students
Multiple Means of Engagement	"Would activate background knowledge by having us think about our own classroom environments and what we are ALREADY doing that might be UDL." "Notes available online and on board in class, could have online materials read-aloud, consistent activation of background knowledge, regular connections/relationships drawn between UDL and other topics discussed, certainly maximized transfer and generalization with numerous assignments and discussions (observation, UDLify lesson, action research)." "UDL course content was age appropriate for graduate students, it aligned with specific standards and goals, it was well organized and the content was valuable and authentic."

continued on following page

Table 1. Continued

UDL Component	Course Example Provided by Graduate Students
Multiple Means of Representation	"Providing choice in assignments, course content is already relevant/valuable/authentic but discussions and resources highlighted this consistently, varied resources used, certainly fostered collaboration and community amongst our cohort, provided great feedback." "The professor provided expectations that optimized motivation. She minimized threats, distractions and barriers. She optimized the relevance and value of UDL." "Many alternatives of how to receive the information, many scaffolds used to teach us, examples of assignments."
Multiple Means of Expression	"Provided choices in how to complete various assignments, let us know about AT available (having text read aloud was hugely beneficial), supported planning and progress monitoring with chunking of workload and reminders of when large assignments were due." "So much choice!!! I loved the amount of choice for our larger assignments, including being able to work with a partner for one." "The course provided multiple means of action and expression by allowing students different ways to demonstrate that they mastered a very clear objective."

This information has been included to provide context around this exploratory investigation. As the research of Craig et al. emphasized, training in-service teachers on the UDL framework needs to include research-based practices (2022). McGuire-Schwartz and Arndt (2007) researched the use of action research to implement the UDL framework. They emphasized the value of not only reflecting and continuing to evaluate student learning, but of also emphasizing action research as a method that promotes reflective practices (McGuire-Schwartz & Arndt, 2007). The action research method was introduced to practicing teachers to stimulate critical thinking and problem solving using the UDL framework.

Implementing UDL in Action Research

Action research can be defined as a "process of concurrently inquiring about problems and taking action to solve them" (Pine, 2009, p. 30). Introducing action research to practicing teachers can complement the implementation of universal design principles by demonstrating the impact of increasing access to learning. Facilitating this experience through a graduate course scaffolds the process for teachers. This support is crucial because action research can be time consuming and challenging for teachers to complete independently (Aguilar-de Borja, 2018; Burns & Westmacott, 2018; Mertler, 2021; Wulandari et al., 2019). When they have engaged in action research, teachers acknowledged the teaching and learning values for their students and themselves (Aguilar-de Borja, 2018; Burns & Westmacott, 2018; Polly et al., 2020). The course structure described in this chapter allowed the teachers to collaborate with classmates and their instructor through each step of the process.

METHODOLOGY

The goal of this exploratory study was to analyze teachers' experiences with UDL through a facilitated action research assignment within a UDL course. Data was primarily collected via their submitted action research papers and a whole group class discussion during presentation. However, the course design was also important to support the students' conceptualization and implementation of UDL, as emphasized within the Introduction section.

Investigation Questions

The goal of this investigation was to explore teachers' perceptions of UDL implementation through an action research project. The questions being investigated were:

- How does an action research approach to UDL implementation effect teachers' perceptions?
- What are teachers' perceptions on implementing UDL in their classes?
- What are teachers' perceptions on UDL after a UDL designed course and reflecting on implementing UDL in their classes?

Within a graduate course, current practicing teachers were introduced to the components of UDL and were asked to chronicle their action research process in a paper. With participant permission, papers were analyzed and summarized into the eight case studies presented within the chapter to illustrate UDL implementation within a variety of disciplines.

Paper Analysis

First, the teachers' final paper was utilized to develop the case studies presented. During the assignment, teachers were asked to align a current challenge with the UDL guidelines, therefore situating UDL as an intervention to solve a problem. Fornauf and Erickson (2020) warn against applying UDL only as a response to students with disabilities. The true goal of UDL is to focus on issues of design and removing barriers within curriculum and instruction, instead of "fixing" students (Fornauf & Dangora Erickson, 2020). To avoid this association within the course, the teachers were asked to focus on a whole class challenge. While some teachers did discuss challenges related to specific students struggling within their class, the intervention needed to focus on changing their own instructional behavior with the whole class. Teachers were asked to analyze a challenge and track progress of all students. The goal of the assignment was two-fold, encouraging the implementation of UDL practices and increasing the teachers' buy-in based on the classroom results (Moore et al., 2018), using an action research approach. The case studies developed from these papers are organized by: Background, Challenge, Intervention, Results, and Reflection.

Part of the action-research assignment required each teacher to also engage with existing research to validate the interventions and adjustments they were implementing. This requirement was meant to address the gap between educational research and practice which is complicated and multi-dimensional (Farley-Ripple et al., 2018). Specifically, timely access to research is a crucial factor (Oliver et al., 2014). Farley-Ripple et al. identified specific issues contributing to the gap: "usefulness of research products; the nature and quality of research; problems that research addresses; the structures, processes, and incentives surrounding research production and use; and the relationships between" (2018, p. 240). To promote engagement in the research, the graduate class analyzed one action-research study together focusing on the essential components of research studies. Searching research databases and using search terms was also modeled and facilitated during class. Engaging teachers in action-research can empower them to enhance their professional growth and development and become "agents of change" (Johnson, 2012, p. 20). Requiring teachers to engage with existing research to directly impact their practice highlighted the benefits of evidence-based practices and attempted to begin bridging the gap between research and practitioners.

Action Research Assignment Structure

When the assignment was first introduced, teachers were asked to brainstorm about challenges they were currently facing in their classroom. Collectively, they worked together to individually narrow their focus and discuss the UDL component which might best address their challenge. The teachers then took baseline data to quantify the difficulty within the classroom. Subsequently, they researched strategies around the specific UDL guideline to implement. The teachers planned the specific intervention period and data to collect after the completion of their project. After the implementation, the teachers reviewed the data and reflected on the impact of the UDL implementation. Promoting action-research is crucial to fill the gap between research and practice (Johnson, 2012) especially in relation to UDL (Craig et al., 2022; Smith et al., 2019). In addition to addressing their classroom challenge with UDL, teachers were able to tangibly see and collect specific data on the impacts of their UDL implementation. Each graduate student wrote their action-research paper and presented their findings to the class. The backgrounds of the teachers varied across discipline and grade-level; this information is included in the table below.

Perspectives From an In-Service Teacher UDL Action Research Project

Each case study summary includes the background, challenge encountered, UDL intervention, results, and each teacher's reflection.

Table 2. Case study descriptions

Case Number	Pseudonym	Teaching Level	UDL Implementation	Time Period
Case 1	Aliyah	Elementary PE	Visuals to support instruction	Fall 2020 – Virtual learning
Case 2	Brielle	High School Music	Interactive virtual content	Fall 2020 – Socially distant teaching
Case 3	Chanda	8th grade Math	Student choice board	Fall 2020 – Socially distant teaching
Case 4	Dahlia	Special Education Pre-school	Visuals for transition & visual timer	Fall 2021 – Socially distant teaching
Case 5	Estelle	4th Grade Classroom	Word bank	Fall 2021 – Socially distant teaching
Case 6	Fei	6th Grade math English Language Arts	Sentence stems	Fall 2020 – Hybrid teaching
Case 7	Gabriella	High School Spanish	Student feedback & choice	Fall 2020 – Socially distant teaching
Case 8	Haylie	Alternative High School Science Teacher	Student choice	Fall 2021 - – Socially distant teaching

CASE STUDIES

As mentioned in the methodology section, the case studies originated from submitted action-research papers. In this assignment, teachers chronicled their classroom challenge, baseline data, UDL implementation, results, and implications. The case studies shared within this chapter were completed in the fall of 2020 and 2021. During this time, many teachers were still experiencing restrictions as a result of the global COVID-19 pandemic. Some teachers focused their case studies on adapting to the virtual learning or social distancing requirements. Summaries of the cases are included below.

Perspectives From an In-Service Teacher UDL Action Research Project

Case 1: Aliyah

Background

In fall 2020, when her school was completely virtual, Aliyah, an elementary school PE teacher, was having difficulty during virtual learning with her English Language Learner (ELL) kindergarten class of eight students. Aliyah explained that the developmental stage of her students impacted the availability of resources to be utilized within a virtual setting. In addition to emerging literacy skills, this kindergarten class was experiencing all of their school online. Typical behavioral routines and expectations explicitly taught in the classroom were adapted to a virtual setting. Aliyah also reflected that the students were not able to establish strong personal connections with each other or with teachers because they began their school experience online. Not having these established, trusted, in-person relationships contributed to reluctant student engagement in the lessons.

Challenge

In typical physical education classes students have the opportunity to move about, practice skills using equipment, interact with each other, and communicate their learning either by demonstrating or explaining a skill. This setting is usually favorable for ELLs because the activities are generally kinesthetic and participatory in nature (Nguyen & Watanabe, 2013). However, promoting engagement in distance learning through the computer screen is challenging for all students, especially those learning English. ELLs often have difficulty following oral directions and can become confused about what they are being asked to do (Nguyen & Watanabe, 2013). This confusion was compounded by an online classroom environment and the lack on in-person behavioral routines and relationships.

Given these conditions, the challenge emerged that many prompts were needed to elicit participation from the students during PE class. All students needed at least one prompt within a lesson and two students needed consistent prompting during the one-hour class. During the baseline data collection, 44 verbal prompts were needed in a 60 minute lesson.

Intervention

Aliyah investigated the UDL guidelines and focused on multiple means of representation with the goal of increasing engagement. Her action research question focused on the following question: What impact do visual aids have on student engagement and comprehension for ELL kindergarten students, as measured by

136

Perspectives From an In-Service Teacher UDL Action Research Project

the number of teacher prompts used to promote participation and engagement in virtual physical education class activities? Her goal of the project was to increase student participation in the activities and reduce prompting throughout the virtual class sessions.

She began by analyzing her challenge through the UDL Guidelines. After this investigation, she aligned guideline #1 for Multiple Means of Representation, "offer ways of customizing the display of information" (CAST, 2020) and guideline #7.3 for Multiple Means of Engagement "optimize relevance, value, and authenticity" (CAST, 2020). The teacher decided to implement visual supports and Spanish videos during virtual instruction. For the next three weeks (1 hour class per week), visual aids were incorporated into the distance learning lessons. In the first week, picture cards with action words were introduced during the PE activity. The second week, picture cards with vocabulary words were introduced including Spanish translation. In the third week, in addition to the picture cards, Spanish language activity videos were embedded into the lesson.

Results

The first week, action picture cards were utilized and 25 prompts were needed for the 60 minute lesson, a 43% reduction in verbal prompts. In week 2, picture cards with the Spanish translation were implemented and 17 prompts were needed during the class, a 61% reduction from baseline. Finally in week 3, Spanish language videos were incorporated into the lesson in addition to the visual cards with Spanish translations. Given these instructional supports, the whole class needed 11 prompts, a 75% reduction from baseline. Overall, with the implementation of the culturally relevant videos and picture cards, Aliyah decreased the verbal prompts needed for her class and increased her instructional time and student engagement.

Reflection

When reflecting on her intervention in her paper, Aliyah shared that the integration of the visual supports and culturally relevant videos had a high impact on increasing student engagement in her virtual ELL kindergarten physical education lessons. In a typical in-person lesson, modeling specific movements so all students know what action to do and using large vocabulary cards have been useful in past practices. Teaching virtually, however, has limited her ability to model locomotor movements due to space limitations and the small screen of the computer. The picture cards proved to be very helpful in communicating what locomotor movements and actions were to be practiced by the students. These visuals were particularly useful in playing one of the students' favorite activities called the "Freeze Game". In this game the teacher holds up a cue card with the action word, calls out and models (if necessary) what locomotor movement to do when the music is on; when the music stops, students must stop or "freeze". The visuals with pictures were very effective in improving students' engagement and participation in this game during online learning. The picture cards were also useful for body part identification activities.

Aliyah also shared the implications of her implementation of the UDL principles as a result of her graduate coursework. She explained that her experience of using picture cards during this project resulted in her incorporating these low-tech visual aids into all of her elementary physical education lesson plans for both in-person and remote teaching. Aliyah also explained that she was now able to provide more formative feedback on students' locomotor movements instead of corrective prompts to keep students actively engaged.

Case 2: Brielle

Background

Brielle, a high school music teacher, needed alternative ways for her inclusive special education music class to interact with the content more meaningfully with less prompting. She chose to focus her project on an inclusive music class with 14 students with a range of disabilities including Down's Syndrome, Cerebral Palsy, and Mowat-Wilson Syndrome. Her class also included regular education students acting as "positive coaches" to demonstrate appropriate and productive musicianship.

Challenge

Before the pandemic, the class did copious amounts of activities that were very "hands-on" including physical movements in close proximity to each other, singing throughout each lesson, and using tactile tools and manipulatives for students to touch and share during class. For example, prior to Covid, class began with a "Hello" song, vocal warm-ups, reading lyrics, and it concluded with a "Goodbye" song. All of these methods were utilized to demonstrate students' understanding of the content. These strategies were typically effective in highlighting the students' strengths and opportunities for reinforcement. However, almost none of these methods were compliant with the safety protocols during the pandemic. This necessitated identifying alternate ways for the students to access their music experience and demonstrate their learning in class, while still maintaining engagement and participation.

Baseline data was collected on students' engagement during music class across two sessions within a week. Brielle tracked individual student engagement across the 60 minutes. She shared that 8 out of 14 students engaged for more than 75% of the class period. She measured engagement by tracking eye contact with the teacher/instruction, physical responses to verbal cues, and student responses focused on the class content. Brielle acknowledged that the social distancing requirements negatively impacted her instructional practices because so many of her activities did not comply with safety guidelines. She was eager to adjust her instructional practices to improve her students' learning experience, but was not clear what adjustments should be made.

Intervention

When analyzing her challenge through the UDL framework lens, she identified needing to focus on guideline #5 in Multiple Means of Action and Expression, checkpoint 5.1 - "use multiple media for communication" (CAST, 2020). After investigated the UDL guidelines and resources, Brielle stated: "My goal is to provide options for recruiting interest by implementing strategies such as hands on activities using technological tools, provide instruments that do not need to be shared and create more manipulatives for students to visualize concepts." Conducting more research, she investigated the book "Accessing Music; Enhancing student learning in the general music classroom using UDL" by McCord et al. (2014) which emphasized the need for manipulatives during teaching and assessment to improve access and flexibility. Given her unique situation with limited manipulatives, she was eager to answer the following questions:

- How can students with diverse needs be actively engaged in the music classroom without singing?
- How can a flexible learning environment be established in a diverse classroom while still upholding safety protocols?
- What kind of an impact will the incorporation of new UDL strategies in the inclusive music classroom have and how will it affect the curriculum when/if there is a return to pre-pandemic practices?

After some research, Brielle decided to implement the use of hand signs (Kodaly Solfege), body percussion, and sign language to actively engage in the songs where students would be singing. She also utilized a variety of music websites to practice note recognition and musical staff line identification. Previously, she had not implemented these technology aspects in her classroom. Finally, Brielle utilized Google Slides to create an interactive platform for her students to create percussion patterns. Students would use a bank of rhythms to create their own song. Then the class used body percussion to "play" each student's song. Brielle was also able to assess if the students were able to apply the specific concept introduced in class using the Google Slides interactive activity.

Results

After implementing these new strategies for two classes, she collected data on student engagement once again. Across two classes, student participation increased from 57% to 100% for at least 75% of the lesson. Over time, as these practices became more routine, she observed that all 14 students actively participated in a meaningful way during these exercises.

Reflection

Brielle reflected that allowing the students to have multiple opportunities to show their learning through alternate means, besides mostly singing, has already proved to be beneficial and opened up endless possibilities for the students. From the start of her data collection, through the use of technology and UDL practices, she observed tremendous growth in participation. Now she also has additional methods to gather tangible evidence of the students' learning and skills. When discussing the implications of her project, the teacher stated in her paper:

This has been "eye opening" for me on numerous levels. For one, I truly believed that I was lucky to teach the content that I do because it had the innate ability to engage students through its performance based qualities. Because of this, I think I became complacent in thinking that I was optimizing students learning opportunities through their performance. However, in reality, this didn't give students who have many other abilities and skills the opportunity to show what they are capable of and challenge them to go further with their music education. I will be sure to continue to explore these opportunities for learning and have honestly enjoyed learning how to be a better teacher for all of my students. Through their success it has energized me to become a more successful UDL teacher.

Case 3: Chanda

Background

During the COVID pandemic hybrid instruction, Chanda, an 8th grade Math teacher, was experiencing low student engagement and low performance on tests. She initially reflected that the social distancing and cohorting restrictions limited

Perspectives From an In-Service Teacher UDL Action Research Project

student movement throughout the day and negatively impacted student morale and participation. Chanda also suggested that traditional math instruction – presenting information on the board, and students copying it down and trying to memorize it – posed significant challenges for the majority of students. In fact, recent studies show that many students learn better through different methods (Sharp et al., 2019).

Challenge

An 8th grade class with 16 students including five students with special education services was utilized for Chanda's UDL implementation project. Her baseline data indicated that only 2-3 students consistently participated during class. In addition to low participation, the students' first quiz indicated that only 62% of the class scored a 70% or above - score equivalent to 'proficient' - on the content. Chanda emphasized the importance of students mastering this content because the remaining units built on these foundational concepts.

Intervention

Chanda was looking to increase student participation during class, to provide increased opportunities for physical movement, and to improve student mastery of the content. She aligned her challenge to the UDL guideline #7 in Multiple Means of Engagement, "optimize individual choice and autonomy" (CAST, 2020) and "optimize relevance, value, and authenticity" (CAST, 2020). She was interested in answering the following question: will providing students with a menu of options (to demonstrate their understanding of adding and subtracting rational numbers) while learning outdoors result in improved engagement and an enhanced quiz performance?

After researching strategies, Chanda became interested in incorporating an outdoor component to her classroom. Learning outdoors can engage students by "exposing them to new and interesting natural items" (Harte, 2013, p. 19). She decided to implement a choice board where students were able to choose how they interacted with the content around rational numbers. The choices included: making a poster, making a digital poster using Canva or Glogster, creating a quiz on Kahoot, making a video on Flipgrid, or writing a song or a poem. This project was conducted primarily outside of the school building and students were given about two weeks to complete it.

Results

Throughout the two-week long project, Chanda observed students who were excited about the change of pace and were happy to spend time outdoors without masks. The students would sit in a circle with their materials working on their projects. Tables were available to work on their devices or on posters. Chanda first brainstormed with the group and provided specific completed examples of the project. She stated it was noticeable that more students began participating in the daily discussion and seemed more involved in daily tasks. Ultimately, she was most impressed with the creativity they were able to express through their work.

As students worked on their project, they demonstrated original and unique ideas while simultaneously participating in math discussions. After an entire week, twice as many students (7-8 hands up) were engaging in class discussions. They also appeared to interact more efficiently with the material presented and even collaborated to achieve lesson objectives. Providing choices and opportunities for collaboration while creating a safe learning environment was key to boosting student engagement. Chanda also shared that she used more questioning techniques and a friendly approach to help establish a positive rapport with students. After the project, in addition to an increase in student engagement, proficiency on the math content quiz increased from 62% to 87.5%. In addition to increased quiz scores, the class had a noticeable improvement when given options catering to their learning preferences as well as being outdoors. By providing a plethora of choices, students did not feel restricted on how to learn and were better able to interact with the course material. Additionally, students started collaborating and had fun with their project while using their chosen method.

Reflection

When reflecting on the experience, Chanda stated in her paper:

Overall, this study has been eye-opening and insightful in regard to students learning behaviors and particular learning methodologies. In order to successfully cater to the needs of all students, an educator must be flexible and accommodating as necessary. If a student needs help, it is so important, now more than ever, to provide various ways to learn. In the time of a global pandemic, it is vital to keep a sense of normalcy and enjoy every day. By the same token, an educator must be focusing on students' well-being while maintaining rigor. This experience taught me to keep an open mind on ways to present material, assess, and give students choices to improve performance. Everyone learns in a slightly different manner and needs

Perspectives From an In-Service Teacher UDL Action Research Project

different strategies to reach their full potential. Our students' performance depends on how well and how fast the teacher can adjust and change gears when necessary.

Case 4: Dahlia

Background

A pre-school special education teacher, Dahlia, with a class of four students, three diagnosed with autism spectrum disorder and one with a developmental delay wanted to focus her intervention on providing behavior supports. Specifically, the class's transitions between activities was taking 5-7 minutes for them to clean up from one activity and transition to the next.

Challenge

Successfully transitioning for many of her students was an individual education program (IEP) goal. Dahlia's baseline data indicated that, in addition to transitions taking more than 5 minutes, one of her students would wander from their assigned activity. A teacher or paraeducator would need to continuously prompt the student to remain in the activity. Other students would mirror this behavior and it would result in ineffective activities and classroom chaos.

Intervention

Dahlia aligned guideline #1 for Multiple Means of Representation, "offer alternatives for auditory information" (CAST, 2020) and guideline #7 for Multiple Means of engagement focusing on recruiting interest. She was interested in answering the following questions:

- How can instructional time be maximized by managing routines and transitions throughout the day?
- How can students' transitions be supported to increase independence and efficiency?

Based on Dahlia's data and questions, she designed a multi-stage intervention. She decided to implement strategies to supplement her verbal directions based on recommendations in the UDL Guidelines; "…information conveyed solely through sound is not equally accessible to all learners and is especially inaccessible… for learners who need more time to process information or for learners who have memory difficulties" (CAST, 2020). Many of her students have demonstrated memory difficulties and were at a developmental stage where verbal reminders were consistently needed. She designed interventions for two different times: center time and during transitions. She implemented a visual timer during each center where students could "see" how much time they had left in the center. She also implemented a two-minute clean-up song and video to play during their transition period.

Results

Dahlia collected weekly average data on the length of time it took her students to clean-up and transition, in addition to their behaviors during this process. In Week 1, it took students an average of 73 seconds to clean up, 57 seconds during Week 2, and 46 seconds during Week 3. After implementing the visual count down timer, she noticed a 50% decrease in behaviors, when transitioning between centers using the visual timer. She noticed students watching the visual timer and anticipating moving to the next center. For example, half of her students recognized when the yellow circle was almost empty and anticipated the center change. The students started looking at the timer for longer periods of time or continued glancing at the visual timer while trying to clean up before it went off.

Reflection

When reflecting on her project in her paper, Dahlia stated that the transitions and routines in her classroom were more manageable because of the UDL strategies that had been implemented. The classroom expectations were also clear and consistent between all adults in the classroom to assist in reinforcing expected behaviors. When using more visuals in the classroom, she noticed her students had a reduction in negative behaviors during transitional times. Through learning and implementing new transitional strategies and systems, her students moved though the classroom more independently and she was able to maximize teaching time and focus.

Case 5: Estelle

Background

Estelle, a 4th grade classroom teacher, identified that her students were having difficulty with adding elaboration with character traits into narratives. Her class of twenty 4th graders included eight students identified as multi-lingual learners (ML) and English language learners (ELL). She explained that students are expected to be able to elaborate using character traits by 4th grade.

144

Challenge

When teaching literacy, Estelle was noticing foundational gaps in her students' writing skills. To further identify their challenges, she conducted a baseline assessment using the 4th grade writing rubric criteria. On this formative assessment, 80% of her class scored at 3rd grade expectations. Their stories were very brief with no details for characters or actions; for example: "My friend and I went to six flags. When we got to six flags, we went on rides and got food. Then we went home." When analyzing their work, the teacher realized that students knew what elaboration was but were unaware of what to add to their writing that might qualify as details/elaboration. They were also unable to distinguish the difference between a "feeling" and a "trait", or unable to demonstrate a character trait within a story. After gathering her baseline assessment, Estelle met with her special education teacher to discuss the class' challenges and possible universal supports she could integrate into her classroom.

Intervention

Using the UDL guidelines #1 and #2 in Multiple Means of Representation that focuses on "offering ways of customizing the display of information" (CAST, 2020) and "promoting understanding across language" (CAST, 2020), she decided to implement visual supports within her lessons. Estelle also incorporated guideline #4 of Multiple Means of Action and Expression, "optimize access to tools and assistive technology" (CAST, 2020), by providing a word bank and sentence starters to increase her students' access to elaboration within their writing. Her research questions focused on:

- What impact does providing visuals have on student learning?
- What type of visuals are best for helping students improve their elaboration in writing?
- How much will students improve when given a word bank/visuals on character traits to help with elaboration in their stories?

Estelle began modeling character traits and elaboration during rea-d-alouds within class. She collaborated with the special education teacher to design a slideshow that included a variety of character traits with visuals. The visuals depicted the specific character trait and were utilized during instruction with the goal of increasing all students' understanding of the traits (Jaime & Knowlton, 2007). Sentence starters were also included to model how to incorporate elaboration into writing. The sentence starters, available to all students, were specific to effectively incorporating elaboration within their personal narratives, a benefit of using this strategy (Grapin et al., 2021). For about 4 weeks, the slideshow was utilized during instruction to identify character traits and details with the class' shared reading of books. When the students began their independent writing, they were prompted to utilize the slideshow while drafting. During the students' individual writing conferences, the teacher also modeled the use of the slideshow to identify moments of elaboration and identify opportunities for growth.

Results

After the implementation of the supports, 100% of the class added elaboration of character traits at grade level expectations. Estelle also noted that students naturally reduced their dependence on the slideshow support, as they developed their confidence with the concept. She also noticed that students were utilizing the sentence starters and character traits in their writing across other subject areas as well, demonstrating their transfer of the skill.

Reflection

When reflecting on the project, Estelle shared:

After my data collection and research on my students with elaboration, I've come to the realization that providing visuals (word banks, graphic organizers, sentence starters, etc) benefits ALL my students. I used to think that visuals should only be provided to students who have "visual aids" written in their IEPs, but why not use it for all? I think many teachers in this field have that same assumption. We forget that the support we provide to our special education students can be used for our class as a whole. At least giving students the CHOICE and ACCESSIBILITY of a visual tool may surprise teachers in the improvements they see across the board when it comes to certain content skill areas.

Estelle's revelation reflected the true essence of universal design for learning and the impact of providing universal supports during instruction.

Perspectives From an In-Service Teacher UDL Action Research Project

Case 6: Fei

Background

Fei, a middle school English Language Arts teacher, focused on a challenge she was having in her 6th grade class. The whole class was demonstrating challenges with reading responses, but she identified two students who were consistently struggling to gather data on their progress during the project. During a typical reading work-shop lesson, Fei begins by introducing a strategy pertaining to becoming a stronger reader. After her mini-lesson, students are asked to read for 15 minutes and write a response based on their thinking while they are reading. Students are presented with the following question: "What were you thinking, as you were reading today?" They type their responses and submit them on the class learning management system. When responding to the text, the class utilized a rubric to guide their work. The rubric awards up to 3 points dependent on their ability to convey their thoughts about the text, to provide evidence for their thinking and to use appropriate grammar.

Challenge

In the baseline assessment, both students were asked to respond to the question "What were you thinking today?" after their independent reading. Both students scored a 0/3 after reflecting on their independent reading passages. One student's response was: 'when Gregg and Rodrick had to change the door they made one mistake the new door did not have a lock but when their dad saw it he just thought he was going crazy.'

Fei's feedback utilized the rubric and provided additional guidance to improve their reflection,

Great job telling what is happening in the story. I also like how you remembered to capitalize the names of the characters. Remember, when writing a response, please tell what you were thinking as you were reading and give evidence from the story to support your thinking. What were you thinking when you read that Greg and Rodrick made a mistake? Why were you thinking that?

Intervention

Fei identified an opportunity to incorporate guideline #5 under Multiple Means of Action and Expression to enhance the quality of the students' responses. Specifically, she was focusing on guideline 5.2, "use multiple tools for construction and composition" (CAST, 2020), and 5.3 - "build fluencies with graduated level of support for practice and performance" (CAST, 2020). These graduated supports can promote a students' effective learning and application of the concepts (Owiny et al., 2019). Sentence stems provide scaffolds for students to focus on the content rather than the organization (Rodriguez-Mojica & Briceño, 2018). Her research question focused on: What impact does providing sentence stems have on students' ability to write sentences that convey content and are grammatically accurate?

Fei modeled sentence stems in four lessons and provided the resource for all students as they completed their reading responses. The sentence stems promoted reflective thinking after reading, rather than simply summarizing. Examples of the sentence stems are included below:

- I wonder… because...
- I don't understand… because...
- I like/dislike… because...

  - This character reminds me… because...

Results

When comparing the baseline with the post intervention data, the target students improved their rubric scores from 0/3 to 2/3. The students utilized the sentence stems to share their thinking and provide evidence within the story. However, the students were still producing work with grammatical errors (run-on sentences, no capitals, etc.). The results of this action-research indicate that sentence stems have a positive impact on students' ability to write sentences that convey meaning. The project did reveal that additional grammatical supports and instruction are needed for students to produce accurate and high-quality correct sentences within their reading responses.

Reflection

When reflecting on the implications of her project, Fei emphasized the value of sentence stems across content areas in her paper. She also stated:

Teachers who implement the usage of sentence stems can aid their students' ability to write sentences that convey meaning. They can be used for students who are writing as well as aid in classroom conversation. As a classroom teacher, it is important to understand what the student knows and understands and sentence stems can assist the student in portraying their knowledge without the extra cognitive piece of having to figure out how to phrase their answer.

Fei's reflection addressed the core of UDL and focused on the essential learning of the activity and removing barriers (Meo, 2008) for her students.

Care 7: Gabriella

Background

Gabriella, a high school Spanish teacher, identified an introductory class of 12 students who consistently missed assignments and were disengaged during class. In this class, 10 of the 12 students were receiving special education services or had accommodation plans.

Challenge

After learning more about the UDL framework, Gabrielle identified that many of her assignments incorporated UDL already, especially multiple means of representation. For her baseline data collection, students were asked to create a 5-slide presentation on weather. During her instruction, vocabulary and expressions were accompanied by visuals to facilitate understanding of the Spanish terminology. By the due date, 7 out of 12 students completed the assignment (58%). She also shared that the majority of students were reluctant to complete missing work.

Intervention

Gabriella began with analyzing other areas of UDL she could focus on to improve her students' work submissions. She aligned her challenge with guideline #8 in Multiple Means of Engagement, "increase mastery-oriented feedback" (CAST, 2020), reflecting that increased teacher feedback might improve student work completion and motivation. She also aligned with guideline #7, "optimize individual choice and autonomy" (CAST, 2020). Before implementing the specific UDL strategies, Gabriella facilitated a reflective discussion with students around challenges within the class and corresponding assignments. She gathered their feedback about the previous assignment and what factors would improve their performance or task completion. After meeting with each student, Gabriella focused on increased feedback towards the learning goal and student choice. Therefore, her research question focused on: How does student choice, feedback, and extended timelines impact assignment completion?

For the next unit, Gabriella offered students a choice in how they completed the assignment. Students were able to submit a video response, a slide presentation, a song, or a written response to the introductory expressions that were reviewed. She also created extended deadlines to encourage increased assignment completion.

Results

Gabriella met with each student while working on the assignment and provided guiding feedback, while working on their project, based on her expectations. Ultimately, after incorporating student choice and increased feedback, 10 out of 12 (83%) students completed at least one choice for the activity. Her individual meetings and student choice increased her students' assignment completion by 25%.

Reflection

When reflecting on the project in her paper, Gabriella emphasized the benefits of choices for all students, but most importantly for students with disabilities. She also highlighted that the use of technology when completing assignments can improve motivation. Her final reflection focused on her feedback cycle: "In order to understand what the student is struggling with, frequent reflections in written or verbal form should become part of the routine. These check-ins may help the student to accurately self-assess." Teacher and student reflective meetings can be extremely powerful to positively impact instruction and learning (Hoban & Hastings, 2006). Gabriella's insight on the power of valuing student feedback and increasing instructional feedback was crucial. Her experience with her assignment enhanced her perspective on the relationship between feedback and motivation, more than reading an article or engaging in a lecture. It also provided the opportunity for her to implement these practices within her instructional routine.

Case 8: Haylie

Background

Haylie, a science teacher at an alternative high school, focused her project on a class of 13 students, 9 of which were receiving special education services. Completing written assignments was a consistent challenge for many students within her class.

Perspectives From an In-Service Teacher UDL Action Research Project

Challenge

To establish a writing baseline, students were asked to complete a one-paragraph written response. Their response was analyzed by completion, number of sentences, and a rubric score. The rubric included three factors: how well did the student answer the question/ was it on topic, flow/ coherence of the writing, and use of complete sentences and proper grammar. For the baseline, 9 of 13 students (69%) completed the assignment with an average of 4.3 sentences. For a typical high school student, Haylie was expecting a paragraph to be around 5-7 sentences long, coherent, use proper sentence structure, and be grammatically correct. The average of 4.3 sentences was slightly below what was typically expected. The substantial weaknesses in coherence and grammar were below the grade-level expectations for a written response of this nature.

Intervention

Haylie focused on the UDL guideline #4 of Multiple Means of Action and Expression, "vary the methods for response and navigation" (CAST, 2020). When analyzing her students' strengths and weaknesses, she noted that many of her students who were weakest in writing were very strong in oral discussion and verbally answering questions. She began researching to find a way to capitalize on the strengths of these students and to improve their written work. The use of technology, specifically speech recognition, presented a viable option. Speech recognition can remove writing barriers (Batorowicz et al., 2012) and reduce stress (Murawski & Scott, 2019) for many students. Haylie also realized that speech recognition was available for each of her students on their dedicated district provided devices. Haylie was looking to answer the following question:

When students are given the choice of typing, handwriting, or dictating a paragraph in response to a prompt relating to course material, how will the quantity and/or quality of responses be impacted compared to only being given the option to type?

Haylie integrated student choice during assignment completion across two class periods. Students were able to type, handwrite, or use speech recognition to complete their paragraph. Before providing the option to students, Haylie modeled speech recognition through her device platform multiple times.

Results

In the two different trials, all students chose to continue typing their responses. The completion rate increased to 10 of 13 (77%) in the first trial and decreased to 6 of 13 (46%) in the second. There was a slight increase in sentence length, but the quality remained consistent. Haylie was interested in why students did not utilize the speech recognition option when it should have removed barriers within the assignment. She decided to conduct individual consultations with her students. Some shared they chose typing simply because it was the "easiest" and others explained they did not want to seem "dumb" or be the only one choosing speech recognition.

Reflection

Upon reflecting on the project, Haylie shared that when she was teaching the students to use voice typing, almost every student reacted positively. Many students commented about it being "cool" and not having known it was built into their devices. She explained that she will continue modeling using speech to text during her instruction and hopefully students will remember these options. Hopefully her students will use it in the future when there is less peer pressure.

Haylie shared this experience has led her to consider trying an alternative methodology for a follow-up investigation. She would like to give three separate assignments, one using each method of response (typed, handwritten, and dictated using speech to text), to give the students an experience with each. Then she could give them one assignment with the choices again to see what option for the students would choose. This critical analysis reflected Haylie's instructional process evolving to include the elements of teach action-research to gather data on her instructional decisions. Haylie continued her reflection and shared:

In my practice, I plan to continue to implement interventions and strategies relating to UDL, despite this particular attempt being ineffective in improvement. Giving the options does not add any workload for myself and while none of these particular students used the options given, maybe another student would and could benefit from the choices being available.

The realization that integration of UDL might not immediately provide results, but might impact a future decision of a student, is a pivotal mindset for continued implementation.

DISCUSSION

The majority of teachers included within the case studies (7 out of 8) were regular education teachers across a variety of disciplines and levels. The action-research assignment was a catalyst for them to design and implement instructional changes with the goal of positively impacting student learning. The majority witnessed a positive impact on student learning, and all acknowledged the overall benefit of UDL practices for all teachers. Providing this hands-on experience for regular education teachers to learn, implement, and evaluate UDL in action can be crucial to promoting effective inclusive classroom. Highlighting the benefits and shared responsibility for regular and special education colleagues to work together to establish an inclusive learning experience for all students is vital to the successful implementation of UDL practices (Scott, 2018). Similar to what is discussed in the work of Baran et al. (2021) the scaffolded action-research process was vital to the teachers' experiences. Approaching the implementation of UDL as a teaching and learning process for in-service teachers – beginning with learning about UDL and transitioning to implementing it with support from their professor – positively shaped their perceptions towards the value of UDL within their classroom. Contributing to the existing work around in-service teacher professional development and UDL (Craig et al., 2022; Rao et al., 2014) the cases highlighted within this chapter demonstrate the impact of authentic learning, application, and reflection within a graduate course environment.

Whole Group Reflections

At the end of the course, each graduate student shared their action-research project and reflected on the experience. Their classmates asked follow-up questions around challenges, next steps, and results. When the teachers shared their projects with each other, meaningful discussions were held around changing instruction and lesson design. Seven out of eight teachers demonstrated improved student participation or learning through the implementation of UDL practices. These results are similar to those found in other studies that promote modeling, practice, and implementation of the UDL framework (Craig et al., 2022; Katz, 2015; McGuire-Schwartz & Arndt, 2007). Each teacher demonstrated a willingness to adjust their practices given these results. On the course evaluation surveys, many teachers reflected that they would continue using the UDL tools and strategies beyond their course. For example, one teacher shared that the course.

introduced me to many highly effective technology tools that enhanced my learning and I will use in my day to day instruction. The practice piece [action research project] helped me to really understand UDL and how to apply it in my work as an educator.

Most notability, the individual teacher reflections shared within the case studies revealed powerful transformations among teachers after their action-research concluded. Brielle, the high school music teacher, explained that the project pushed her out of complacency and inspired her to continue exploring new ways to integrate UDL. Establishing this honesty and true self-reflection revealed the community that was built within the course. Similar to the findings of Katz (2015), where a three-block model was used to implement UDL, the teachers reflected deeply on the impact of implementing UDL within their practice and student learning. Comparably, Chanda emphasized keeping an "open mind", as a regular education teacher, to adjust her instruction and content to accommodate students with different learning preferences. Establishing a UDL mindset within regular education can be crucial to creating a successful inclusive class (Scott, 2018). Estelle expressed similar sentiment when she shared that providing choice and accessibility to her whole class resulted in improvements for all students.

When some teachers were contacted approximately a year after their course concluded, they were eager to share that they were continuing to utilize UDL in their practices. For example, Aliyah shared, "I've been UDL-ifying my lessons since taking your course and it has vastly simplified my lesson planning. Teaching P.E. during a pandemic has been interesting and stress filled but rewarding nonetheless." Others shared a perspective change on their classroom routine and reported thinking reflectively about UDL in their daily practice and instructional routine.

CONCLUSION

Although the results shared in this chapter were gathered from one university, they mirror other studies on the impact of UDL instruction on in-service teachers (Craig et al., 2022; Evmenova, 2018; Katz, 2013; Navarro et al., 2016). As Mertler (2021) posits, practicing teachers are well versed in instructional trial-and-error. Providing the structure for teachers to engage in systematic classroom action-research can perpetuate "career-long learning and professional growth" (Mertler, 2021, p. 11). The case study results and subsequent reflections indicate that utilizing a supported action-research design for teachers to apply UDL principles within their classrooms and reflect on the impact can result in an increase in inclusive practices and perspectives for regular and special education in-service teachers.

ACKNOWLEDGMENT

Thank you to all the teachers who agreed to have their hard work represented in this chapter. I appreciate you.

REFERENCES

Aguilar-de Borja, J. M. (2018). Teacher action research: Its difficulties and implications. *Humanities and Social Sciences Reviews*, 6(1), 29–35. 10.18510/hssr.2018.616

Baran, J., Cierpiałowska, T., & Dyduch, E. (2021). Transformations of the Teaching–Learning Process Towards Inclusive Education as a Result of the UDL Approach Implementation. In *Improving Inclusive Education through Universal Design for Learning* (pp. 95–118). Springer. 10.1007/978-3-030-80658-3_5

Batorowicz, B., Missiuna, C. A., & Pollock, N. A. (2012). Technology supporting written productivity in children with learning disabilities: A critical review. *Canadian Journal of Occupational Therapy*, 79(4), 211–224. 10.2182/cjot.2012.79.4.323210371

Burns, A., & Westmacott, A. (2018). Teacher to researcher: Reflections on a new action research program for University EFL teachers. *Profile: Issues in Teachers'. Professional Development (Philadelphia, Pa.)*, 20(1), 15–23. 10.15446/profile.v20n1.66236

CAST. (2020). *Universal Design for Learning Guidelines.* https://udlguidelines.cast.org/

Craig, S. L., Smith, S. J., & Frey, B. B. (2022). Professional development with universal design for learning: Supporting teachers as learners to increase the implementation of UDL. *Professional Development in Education*, 48(1), 22–37. 10.1080/19415257.2019.1685563

Cumming, T. M., & Rose, M. C. (2022). Exploring universal design for learning as an accessibility tool in higher education: A review of the current literature. *Australian Educational Researcher*, 49(5), 1025–1043. 10.1007/s13384-021-00471-7

Engleman, M., & Schmidt, M. (2007). Testing an experimental universally designed learning unit in a graduate level online teacher education course. *Journal of Online Learning and Teaching*, 3(2), 112–132.

Evmenova, A. (2018). Preparing Teachers to Use Universal Design for Learning to Support Diverse Learners. *Journal of Online Learning Research*, 4(2), 147–171.

Farley-Ripple, E., May, H., Karpyn, A., Tilley, K., & McDonough, K. (2018). Re-thinking Connections Between Research and Practice in Education: A Conceptual Framework. *Educational Researcher*, 47(4), 235–245. 10.3102/0013189X18761042

Fornauf, B. S., & Dangora Erickson, J. (2020). Toward an Inclusive Pedagogy Through Universal Design for Learning in Higher Education: A Review of the Literature. *Journal of Postsecondary Education and Disability*, 33(2), 183.

Grapin, S. E., Llosa, L., Haas, A., & Lee, O. (2021). Rethinking instructional strategies with English learners in the content areas. *TESOL Journal*, 12(2), e557. Advance online publication. 10.1002/tesj.557

Harte, H. A. (2013). Universal design and outdoor learning. *Dimensions of Early Childhood*, 41(3), 18–22.

Hoban, G., & Hastings, G. (2006). Developing different forms of student feedback to promote teacher reflection: A 10-year collaboration. *Teaching and Teacher Education*, 22(8), 1006–1019. 10.1016/j.tate.2006.04.006

Jaime, K., & Knowlton, E. (2007). Visual supports for students with behavior and cognitive challenges. *Intervention in School and Clinic*, 42(5), 259–270. 10.1177/10534512070420050101

Johnson, A. P. (2012). *A short guide to action research* (4th ed.). Pearson.

Katz, J. (2013). The three block model of universal design for learning (UDL): Engaging students in inclusive education. *Canadian Journal of Education*, 36(1), 153–194.

Katz, J. (2015). Implementing the Three Block Model of Universal Design for Learning: Effects on teachers' self-efficacy, stress, and job satisfaction in inclusive classrooms K-12. *International Journal of Inclusive Education*, 19(1), 1–20. 10.1080/13603116.2014.881569

McCord, K., Gruben, A., & Rathgeber, J. (2014). *Accessing music: Enhancing student learning in the general music classroom Using UDL*. Alfred Music.

McGuire-Schwartz, M. E., & Arndt, J. S. (2007). Transforming universal design for learning in early childhood teacher education from college classroom to early childhood classroom. *Journal of Early Childhood Teacher Education*, 28(2), 127–139. 10.1080/10901020701366707

Meo, G. (2008). Curriculum Planning for All Learners: Applying Universal Design for Learning (UDL) to a High School Reading Comprehension Program. *Preventing School Failure*, 52(2), 21–30. 10.3200/PSFL.52.2.21-30

Mertler, C. A. (2021). Action Research as Teacher Inquiry: A Viable Strategy for Resolving Problems of Practice. *Practical Assessment, Research & Evaluation*, 26, 1–12.

Moore, E. J., Smith, F. G., Hollingshead, A., & Wojcik, B. (2018). Voices From the Field: Implementing and Scaling-Up Universal Design for Learning in Teacher Preparation Programs. *Journal of Special Education Technology*, 33(1), 40–53. 10.1177/0162643417732293

Murawski, W. W., & Scott, K. L. (2019). *What really works with Universal Design for Learning*. Corwin Press.

Navarro, S. B., Zervas, P., Fabregat Gesa, R., & Sampson, D. G. (2016). Developing Teachers' Competences for Designing Inclusive Learning Experiences. *Journal of Educational Technology & Society*, 19(1), 17–27.

Nguyen, H. T., & Watanabe, M. F. (2013). Using Visual Supports to Teach English Language Learners in Physical Education. *Journal of Physical Education, Recreation & Dance*, 84(8), 46–53. 10.1080/07303084.2013.818432

Oliver, K., Innvar, S., Lorenc, T., Woodman, J., & Thomas, J. (2014). A systematic review of barriers to and facilitators of the use of evidence by policymakers. *BMC Health Services Research*, 14(1), 2. Advance online publication. 10.1186/1472-6963-14-224383766

Owiny, R. L., Brawand, A., & Josephson, J. (2019). UDL and Literacy. *What Really Works With Universal Design for Learning*, 21.

Pine, G. J. (2009). Teacher action research: Building knowledge democracies. *Teacher Action Research: Building Knowledge Democracies*. 10.4135/9781452275079

Polly, D., Burchard, K. P., Castillo, C., Drake, P., Horne, S., Howerton, A., Peake, S., & Schmitt, K. (2020). Examining Action Research and Teacher Inquiry Projects: How Do they Help Future and Current Teachers? *School-University Partnerships*, 12(4), 36–47.

Rao, K., Ok, M. W., & Bryant, B. R. (2014). A Review of Research on Universal Design Educational Models. *Remedial and Special Education*, 35(3), 153–166. 10.1177/0741932513518980

Rodriguez-Mojica, C., & Briceño, A. (2018). Sentence Stems That Support Reading Comprehension. *The Reading Teacher*, 72(3), 398–402. 10.1002/trtr.1705

Scott, L. A. (2018). Barriers With Implementing a Universal Design for Learning Framework. *Inclusion (Washington, D.C.)*, 6(4), 274–286. 10.1352/2326-6988-6.4.274

Sharp, L. A., Bonjour, G. L., & Cox, E. (2019). Implementing the math workshop approach: An examination of perspectives among elementary, middle, and high school teachers. *International Journal of Instruction*, 12(1), 69–82. 10.29333/iji.2019.1215a

Smith, S. J., Rao, K., Lowrey, K. A., Gardner, J. E., Moore, E., Coy, K., Marino, M., & Wojcik, B. (2019). Recommendations for a National Research Agenda in UDL: Outcomes From the UDL-IRN Preconference on Research. *Journal of Disability Policy Studies*, 30(3), 174–185. 10.1177/1044207319826219

Wulandari, D., Shandy Narmaditya, B., Hadi Utomo, S., & Hilmi Prayi, P. (2019). Teachers' Perception on Classroom Action Research. *KnE Social Sciences*, 3(11), 313. 10.18502/kss.v3i11.4015

KEY TERMS AND DEFINITIONS

Action Research: A research method that can be utilized to solve a problem (Pine, 2009) on the impact of UDL practices.

Case Studies: Summaries of graduate student experiences on integrating UDL in their classes. Names have been changed for anonymity.

Course Delivery: The graduate course described within the chapter delivered the UDL content in a hybrid format and was designed to model specific UDL practices and increase accessibility for all learners.

English Language Learner (ELL): This term is utilized for a student in the American educational system whose primary language is not English. They are learning English while attending an English language-based school.

Multiple Means of Engagement: One component of UDL that focuses on motivating and engaging learners within the learning process. This component includes minimizing barriers, goal setting, authentic learning, and meaningful content (CAST, 2020).

Multiple Means of Expression: One component of UDL that focuses on allowing learners to demonstrate their learning or understanding in a variety of ways. For exam (CAST, 2020).

Multiple Means of Representation: One component of UDL that focuses on providing options for learners to engage with content. For example, providing a video, transcript, infographic, audio file, and text document (CAST, 2020).

Section 3
Wider Conceptual Considerations

Chapter 7
Achieving Genuinely Inclusive Bilingual K–12 Education:
Using UDL to Shift the Bilingual Classroom Irretrievably Away From Deficit Model Practices

Frederic Fovet
https://orcid.org/0000-0003-1051-4163
Thompson Rivers University, Canada

EXECUTIVE SUMMARY

This chapter examines the pervasive and perpetuated deficit model perspective which informs much of the second language instruction which occurs, in relation to diverse learners—particularly learners with disabilities—in the Canadian K-12 sector. The chapter argues that Universal Design for Learning (UDL) has a key role to play in shifting language teachers away from deficit model views in this context and has the potential to revolutionize the bilingual classroom. The chapter also demonstrates the extent to which UDL aligns seamlessly with communicative method approaches in second language instruction. The chapter explores and analyses phenomenological data drawn from the author's lived experience as a second language teacher over a decade. The chapter considers the repercussions of this reflection on pre-service teacher training, in-service professional development, and leadership practices for inclusion.

DOI: 10.4018/978-1-6684-4750-5.ch007

Copyright © 2024, IGI Global. Copying or distributing in print or electronic forms without written permission of IGI Global is prohibited.

Achieving Genuinely Inclusive Bilingual K-12 Education

INTRODUCTION AND CONTEXT

For far too long bilingual education – in all its forms (traditional second language classes, bilingual classes, or full immersion programs) – has been off limits to students with disabilities, particularly those affected by learning disabilities (Hoover et al., 2018; Morgan et al., 2015). Myths have abounded and been perpetuated, claiming that cognitive disabilities made it impossible for students to acquire a second language (Tangen & Spooner-Lane, 2008). More recently, the literature has finally debunked these myths and highlighted that the limitations experienced by students with cognitive disabilities in second language acquisition have more to do with issues related to pedagogy than with their actual impairment (Sowell & Sugisaki, 2021). All evidence suggests that students with disabilities are just as able to acquire a second language and to navigate the bilingual classroom as their peers (Mady, 2017; Skinner & Smith, 2011).

This does not mean that, in practice, students with disabilities now have a more seamless access to the bilingual classroom. Despite all recommendations emerging from the scholarship on inclusion, the field is still reluctant to move away from ability grouping practices, from segregated education, and from a deficit model view of students with disabilities (Mady & Arnett, 2016). While the bilingual classroom is now conceptually seen as entirely suitable to the diverse learner, in the field, bilingual education remains an area that is rife with hurdles for these students because of teacher misperceptions and beliefs (Arnett & Mady, 2017; Bourgoin, 2016; Cioe-Pena, 2017). In many ways, bilingual education has in fact become a tool for schools to inconspicuously create ability streaming where such segregated practices are prohibited by the legislation or policy (Mathewson, 2020).

Bilingual education remains perceived as the playground of highly-performing – and behaviourally compliant – students (Delcourt, 2018). The reason why the field is so slow to evolve is that language educators are reluctant to acknowledge that acquisition of second language is not impossible for students with disabilities. They are reticent to accept that such a task is challenging only when language pedagogy is teacher-centered, conventional, rigid, and textbook focused (Cioè-Peña, 2020; Wight, 2015). When communicative methods are adopted, students with disabilities are perfectly able to integrate bilingual education and to flourish within these learning environments. When language pedagogy is furthermore inclusive and accessible by design, these students succeed seamlessly in these classes (Wise, 2012).

The first section of the chapter contextualizes the tension which has been described above between traditional bilingual education and the needs of students with disabilities. It unpacks this tension and analyzes the ways traditional language education creates barriers for students with disabilities because of its teacher-centric nature and design. The second section describes and analyzes the ways Universal

161

Achieving Genuinely Inclusive Bilingual K-12 Education

Design for Learning (UDL) can be a tool which allows for the creation of inclusive and accessible bilingual classroom. This section also examines the seamless overlap between UDL and communicative methods approaches in second language education. This section of the chapter relies extensively on the analysis of phenomenological data the author extracts from his lived experience as a second language educator having used UDL in the bilingual secondary classroom, within a Canadian context.

EXISTING LITERATURE

In order to fully grasp the extent of the tension being described, it is first essential to build a good overview of the literature that informs the various positions, stances, and policies within this field. There is also a need to delineate with precision some of the terminology frequently used in this area of the scholarship.

Bilingual Education in Canada

There are many benefits of early access to bilingual education. It offers cognitive benefits (Barac et al., 2014; Nicolay & Poncelet, 2015; Padilla et al., 2013), boosts literacy skills (Montanari, 2013), allows for social capital opportunity (Borsch et al., 2021; Coe & Shani, 2015; Collins et al, 2011), has experiential impact on employment and travel opportunities (Grasmane & Grasmane, 2011; Woll & Wei, 2019), and lastly aligns with 21st century global citizenship objectives (Carlson et al., 2017).

Within immersion education itself, there are three main categories of programs identified in Canada (Hayday, 2015): (i) French immersion programs targeting mainly English speaking students, (ii) programs known as heritage programs which mainly focus on the survival of non-official languages such as Ukrainian, Greek, German, and Mandarin (Aravossitas & Oikonomakou, 2020), and (iii) Indigenous language revival programs exclusively targeting Indigenous students (Dicks & Genesee, 2017; Lindholm-Leary & Genesee, 2014).

French immersion programs themselves are usually of four types. There are, first, full French Immersion programs where French is the language of instruction (Davis et al., 2019). A second category consists of extended core French programs, available in a few provinces, within which French is the language of instruction for one or two core subjects in addition to French classes themselves (Arnott et al., 2019). The third type of program is known as Intensive French; it is a more recent program which was launched in 1998 in about half the provinces and territories in Canada. In this last type of programs, intensive periods of instruction in French make up at least 70 percent of the school day (Arnott et al., 2019). A fourth, more basic approach to immersion, consists of simply teaching the regular French classes

162

Achieving Genuinely Inclusive Bilingual K-12 Education

through immersion techniques. It is commonly referred to as core French (Canadian Parents for French, 2013).

It is probably fair to say that, Canada being a country with two official languages, there is probably more bilingual education currently in place there than in many other jurisdictions. Beyond the academic, social, and cognitive benefits identified, bilingualism in Canada plays both a cultural and constitutional role, both of which are historically grounded in the development of the Federation (Early et al., 2017). Bilingual education has therefore been a political stake which has been embraced and advanced by nearly all national and provincial parties. It would be fair to assert that fervour for bilingual education in Canada goes well beyond the usual enthusiasm demonstrated elsewhere for its cognitive and developmental benefits.

Ambivalent Position of Bilingual Education Towards Diverse Learners

Early literature tended to argue that including diverse students in bilingual classroom distracted from targeted individual interventions and led to a detrimental impact on the development of these students (Wise, 2011). There is in fact no evidence of any negative impact of bilingual education on the development or inclusion of students with disabilities (Bialystok, 2018). Despite an increasingly large body of literature evidencing the benefits of bilingual education and immersion setting for students with disabilities, negative attitudes persist, nonetheless. It is difficult to change mindsets in this area or to debunk these myths among teachers. Many authors point to the need for more solid development of awareness in this area within pre-service teacher training (Arnett & Mady, 2018). Professional development for in-service teachers is also seen as at fault in the perpetuation of these misconceptions and requires reform (Hefferman, 2011). Leaders' beliefs and perceptions are also often mentioned in this context and must be targeted in the search for solutions (Mady & Masson, 2018). While policy clearly supports the inclusion of all learners in French immersion programs, a more realistic assessment of the landscape highlights the remaining challenges and the significant gaps that still exist between discourse and practice (Bourgoin, 2014; Muhling & Mady, 2017; Wise, 2012).

Dangers of Exclusionary Practices in Bilingual Education

As a result, bilingual education in Canada has become an ambivalent area in relation to inclusion. While immersion programs are prima facie open to all students, irrespective of disability, in practice, schools are restricting access to these programs to students who are seen as performant, and as free of challenging behaviours. It can be said that in fact this inequitable approach to bilingual education goes beyond

163

disability and impairment. Students who are seen as undesirable or as not fitting the mainstream are often made to feel that these programs are not for them. French immersion programs are de facto currently used at times to create streaming, or ability grouping, even in provincial jurisdictions where such practices are prohibited by law (Delcourt, 2018). Sadly, bilingual education can currently be seen as a tool for exclusion, rather than a process leading to genuine inclusion (Barrett DeWiele & Edgerton, 2021). These inequitable power dynamics have been exacerbated during the COVID pandemic when the pretext of force majeure has given schools even more lea way to steer diverse learners away from immersion programs at a time when systems were seen as battling exceptional challenges (Gallagher-MacKay, 2021).

A factor which contributes to the perpetuation of these myths in relation to the performance and success of students with disabilities in French immersion programs is the fact that most of these programs are understaffed, underfunded, and battle significant issues with teacher attrition and hiring (Mason et al., 2020). The number of French immersion teachers being trained and graduating currently in Canada is not sufficient to fill immersion positions (Pan, 2014; Theriault, 2014). This often leads to the hiring of non-licensed or non-accredited teachers on short term bases (Kline-Martin, 2018; Pruss, 2017). This lack of training, in turn, is likely to make teachers dealing with precariousness – both in terms of resources and employment status – less prepared to deploy fully inclusive pedagogical methods in the bilingual class (Jack & Nyman, 2019).

An essential reason why students with disabilities – particularly learning disabilities – encounter challenges in second language instruction is that too often poor-quality pedagogy is being deployed in the bilingual classroom, simply because immersion teachers have not been fully trained or are not fully equipped to deliver these classes. Textbook learning, in particular, is not adequate for second language acquisition but often represents the bulk of what is provided in schools (Lyster, 2015). Language teaching strategies which are not communication based will often indeed overly rely on print-based approaches and create significant barriers for learners with disabilities. It is not, however, the language acquisition that is problematic in these instances, but the mode of instruction (Asadifard & Koosha, 2013; Ceylan, 2019).

Communicative Methods and Diverse Learners

The debate around the inclusion of diverse learners in the second language classroom has, of late, become significantly refined. If these students experience challenges, it is increasingly clear that it is not because of inherent characteristics of these students but rather because of conventional and outdated pedagogical approaches which are still pervasive in the K-12 sector (Zulu, 2019). While the teaching of languages in the private sector and industry has, for several decades now, evolved

Achieving Genuinely Inclusive Bilingual K-12 Education

towards communicative methods (Toro et al., 2018), there are still many school landscapes where these techniques are not being used (Arigita-García et al., 2021; Dos Santos, 2020; Khatib & Tootkaboni, 2019; Zhang, 2020). The communicative method approach argues that the learning of languages – unlike other school subjects – is inherently linked to a context of communication and cannot therefore be taught using conventional methods such as lecturing, note taking, textbook reading, and conventional summative assessments (Larsen-Freeman, 2018). Instead, communicative methods will seek to give the learner an experiential feel for what using the language in context looks like and involves. Communicative methods focus primarily on learner motivation: the motivation to dialogue with others, the motivation to explore the target culture, and the motivation to develop an identity in the target language (Lai & Gu, 2011; Peng et al., 2021; Reinders & Wattana, 2014; Tyler et al, 2018). When communicative methods – instead of conventional pedagogy – are used in the K-12 language classroom, diverse students thrive and face no further barriers than their peers (Fernández-Villardón et al., 2021; Ivančević-Otanjac, 2016).

Universal Design for Learning

When it comes to the inclusion of diverse students in the K-12 classroom, there are certain established and historical approaches to the creation of classroom conditions that address the need of all learners. In the past, personalized learning and individualized learning have been two approaches that have been privileged and have been supported by legislative provisions, administrative policies, and funding provisions (Shemshack & Spector, 2020; Waxman et al., 2013). Personalized and individualized learning both rely on individual interventions, often outside the classroom itself. They differ in the sense that individualized learning provides additional support but does not alter curriculum content or format of assessment; it merely provides adaptations (Christle & Yell, 2010). The most frequent form of individualized learning is the provision of a Individualized Educational Plan (IEP) and of specific adaptations. Personalized learning, as defined before it was reappropriated by online learning theory, recognizes the fact that some students may be unable to achieve age-appropriate goals, and focuses therefore on modifying class content and assessment (Zaic, 2021).

More recently, differentiation has brought yet new techniques, strategies, and practices to the classroom as tools for the inclusion of diverse learners (Tomlinson, 2014). Differentiation has been explored within inclusive second language acquisition (Mady, 2018). Differentiation diverges from individualized learning and personalized learning in the sense that it avoids reliance on support outside the classroom and recenters the intervention in the classroom itself (Kuppers et al., 2023). It has been useful in providing whole class approaches that do not rely on deficit model views of students with disabilities. It also represents, however, considerable challenges – particularly for novice teachers – in the sense that it requires all educators to become experts at (i) identifying learner needs, (ii) creating multiple pathways to the class objectives in a just-in-time fashion; and (iii) leading all learners regardless of abilities towards the same assessment tools (Suprayogi & Valcke, 2016).

UDL has recently triggered further innovation and a shift away from these traditional approaches to inclusion by offering teachers a design based – and therefore more manageable and less overwhelming – approach to whole-class inclusion. Within UDL, teachers no longer need to identify individual needs. Instead, they can assume that the full spectrum of diversity is present in their classroom, and they can plan for diversity, through inclusive design, at the blueprint stage. When planning a new class, starting a new school year, choosing resources, or designing assessment, they can grasp opportunities to offer learners as much flexibility as possible (Navarro et al., 2016). This flexibility can be systematically embedded, in relation to all decisions educators make in the classroom, by examining three distinct dimensions of inclusive design: multiple means of representation (offering optimal flexibility in the ways educators present information to students), multiple means of action and expression (offering optimal flexibility in the ways educators require students to present information and content), and multiple means of engagement (offering optimal flexibility in the ways educators conceive and define a learner's affective engagement) (Ok et al., 2017). While inclusion - through differentiation - in the second language classroom seems a little utopian, it becomes a much more feasible objective once UDL becomes systematically embedded as a culture (Ferguson, 2019).

UDL and Bilingual Education

In fact, fully accessible second language education is a reality and has been achieved in some jurisdictions (Krausneker et al 2017; Krausneker et al., 2002.). Applying UDL to second language teaching is a very feasible, user-friendly, and sustainable approach to inclusion in this sector. There have not been many studies, or much practitioner generated scholarship, in relation to UDL and inclusion in the second language classroom (Kasch, 2019), but this is an interesting and promising intersection of literature (Almumen, 2020; Strangman et al., 2014). It will be argued, in this chapter, that despite the fact the use of UDL in second language acquisition is relatively new, the three UDL principles intersect with all of the very beliefs and values that serve as a foundation for communicative methods approaches: language acquisition should be contextualized, offered with flexibility, in ways that are immediately pertinent and useful to the learner (Chita-Tegmark et al., 2012). Both approaches also employ a variety of modes and flexible pathways to address the needs of learners (Kasch, 2018; Stephens & Kaiser, 2018).

Achieving Genuinely Inclusive Bilingual K-12 Education

METHODOLOGICAL REFLECTION

Much of the chapter focuses on the phenomenological analysis of the author's experiences applying both UDL and communicative methods in the second language classroom. Phenomenology is a qualitative methodology which focuses on the analysis of individuals' lived experiences and their efforts at meaning making when confronted with specific phenomena (Emiliussen et al., 2021). Phenomenology is increasingly popular in educational research as it allows investigators to explore and analyze the professional experiences of educators as they are confronted with challenges and new realities (Webb & Welsh, 2019).

The author has been a second language teacher for two decades and has continued to teach second language French even as his career led him to become a school leader, and later faculty. He has always taught in environments where learner diversity was a conspicuous reality and a primary priority. He has, as a result, explored the use of UDL extensively within his practice. He has also worked consistently and steadily, through his career, in corporate language training programs which has led him to explicitly acknowledge and embrace communicative methods in language teaching. The analysis presented here spans approximately two decades of his teaching, exploring, and reflecting on the potential of both UDL and communicative methods approaches in the teaching of second language in the K-12 sector – particularly in contexts with a strong focus on learner diversity and disability.

Specific examples related to the implementation of UDL and communicative methods, used in the section below, relate in particular to a two-year period where the author worked as French second language teacher, in a public Quebec school, and had the opportunity to adopt and showcase strategies which were not the norm in this environment. He taught two secondary classes through their last two years of school, in 2009 through 2011. Since these classes had to sit ministerial end of secondary language exams, the author was able to gauge the success of these strategies – applied in a landscape where the school had previously been resigned to either failures or exemptions in second language for most students - within the formal context of external provincial summative assessment.

OBSERVATIONS AND ASSERTIONS

This section presents the author's phenomenological analysis of his lived experience as a second language teacher and his exploration of both UDL and communicative methods in the K-12 classroom, particularly over a two-year period during which he was able to deploy these strategies in a public sector environment where they had not previously been favoured.

Traditional Language Education Creating Barriers for Students With Disabilities

There are still many ways pedagogy in the bilingual or in the second language classroom remains teacher-centric, conventional, textbook-based, and directive in flavour (Fareed et al., 2016; Misbah et al., 2017). When such approaches are adopted or perpetuated in second language teaching, a very small portion of highly performant students may succeed and achieve objectives, but a large percentage of students – for various reasons – disengage from second language acquisition altogether. This disengagement happens progressively, but steadily over time, and results in an explicit hatred for the target language and its culture; this in turn frequently leads to behavioural issues in these classes (Debreli et al., 2019).

From 2009 to 2011, the author worked in the public sector in Quebec, teaching French as a second language in the English-speaking section of a bilingual school. He taught grades 10 and 11, in classes where a large portion of students were identified as having learning disabilities. Operating under the mistaken – and pervasive - belief that students with disabilities were unable to acquire a second language, the school and its leadership had allowed for the creation of a two tier system in the second language classroom where some students were being taught proactively with end of secondary ministerial exams in sight, while students with disabilities were encouraged to see this as a class to be 'sat out'. Alternate curriculum was provided, often in the form of textbook exercises. Most students with disabilities and their parents were actively encouraged to apply for a ministerial exemption – a process which would see the students graduate without completing second language requirements, but unable to proceed to further or higher education, unless they persevered later - through adult education - to complete the language component.

The process of how these learners disconnect with the target language happens over many years in the K-12 sector, and includes instances of overly directive teaching, excessive use of textbooks, instruction overly focused on grammar and vocabulary acquisition through purely abstract processes, absence of group work and authentic communicative activities, etc. It is important to note, however, that the weakness of language instruction is not usually limited to this. Learners feel no affective connection to the content – which is often basic and not age appropriate. There is frequently no injection of the target culture in instruction, which leads to a lack of cultural awareness or competency. As this worsens, and particularly in landscapes where there may be political dimensions to bilingualism in some jurisdictions, the learner may feel so disconnected from the target language that they feel oppressed by the target culture. In the setting the author has described above, for example, students by age 16 were seeing themselves as oppressed and marginalized socially by a dominant language and culture – French in this case – which they could not

Achieving Genuinely Inclusive Bilingual K-12 Education

master or navigate. At a broader level, conventional and archaic language instruction practices fail to give the learner the opportunity to develop an identity in the target language, to connect the target culture and language to their own lived experience, or to be socially recognized and validated (Anya, 2017).

Universal Design for Learning as a Tool for the Creation of Inclusive and Accessible Bilingual Classrooms

This section offers examples of ways UDL can help address some of the challenges described above that still plague many K-12 language classroom. The author will again draw from his lived experience as a French as second language teacher and explain the way he transformed his pedagogy using the three UDL principles. Though more than half of the students present in two grade 10 classes he taught in 2009/11 were below grade level in French, all students in both classes passed their ministerial end of secondary exams at the end of grade 11, after having been taught for two years in a way that combined communicative method approaches and UDL strategies. For the sake of clarity, this section will be presented using the three UDL design principles as sub-headings. Breaking down the inclusive design process in this way can seem a little artificial, as the pedagogical reflection, within the class itself, frequently involves the use of several UDL principles at once. This presentation format, however, will offer the reader a convenient and user-friendly structure in the reflection they are encouraged to carry out here.

Multiple Means of Representation

Multiple means of representation is the UDL principle which encourages teachers to offer learners optimal flexibility in the way information is presented to learners. In the second language classroom, this will mean that instead of focusing on print and textbook instruction, activities and objectives are presented in a way that offers learners multiple pathways to achievement. A reflection around multiple means of representation normally focuses on the need to offer learners multiple formats such as print, audio and video. In the second language classroom, however, this reflection around multimodal formats can quickly gain depth and pertinence, and stretch beyond this basic brainstorming. Many learners will find engaging with age appropriate, richly pertinent material in the target language, in print format only, to be extremely challenging; this gives rise to multiple barriers. It may therefore become onerous for the teacher to find material that connects with learners' lives and their genuine interests. Using the multiple means of representation format, however, offers the educator a wealth of possibilities when it comes to infusing the classroom with material that is highly pertinent to the learner but also accessible

169

in ways that will not be excessively challenging or daunting to a student who is not fully confident in the target language.

While teaching second language French to grade 10 and 11 classes in the context mentioned above, the author was tempted to offer students material that was age appropriate and engaging for adolescents. This would be key to eventually eroding their defensiveness towards the target language and to encouraging them to develop motivation in the exploration of the target culture. Such material would, however, obviously be challenging to non-fluent learners with disabilities. Offering complex, culturally relevant material that would connect richly to these students' lives would present strategic hurdles, and require creativity in formatting. The author, nevertheless, succeeded in reading and exploring, with these classes, two full plays, *Le Diner de Cons* and *Le Malade Imaginaire*. These are two plays which have been filmed as stage productions, but also transformed into film productions. The classes were therefore able to tackle the text, in turn, in three different formats: (i) at times the text was read collectively in class; (ii) at other times, the stage production was watched while the students followed the text – and the filmed staging helped them support their understanding of content; (iii) at other times, the class watched the film adaptation and this helped the students follow the plot and engage richly with the story line. Complex original cultural artifacts – in an unabridged format - therefore became accessible to second language learners with learning disabilities, because flexibility in format was systematically and strategically adopted.

Multiples Means of Action and Expression

Similarly, students with disabilities who are struggling with fluency quickly become disheartened and disengaged in the second language classroom when the responses and contributions required of them are basic, simplified, and not age appropriate. Assessment is often 'dumbed down', and becomes dry, superficial, and disengaging. Students may be facing challenges with specific skills such as writing or written comprehension, but they have little motivation in improving these skills when the tasks that they are offered have no pertinence to their lives, interests, or their individual contexts and experiences. The challenge therefore becomes to design exciting, complex, age appropriate, and engaging tasks and activities, while ensuring that their format does not hinder the overall accessibility of requirements or these learners' ability to achieve the objectives.

An example of some of the UDL strategies the author deployed in his classroom, in relation to learner contribution, showcase how motivation and engagement can drive skills acquisition. Once the classes – in the context which has been described previously - felt comfortable with *Le Malade Imaginaire* and had completed the reading and analysis of their first Molière play, a request came from the French

Achieving Genuinely Inclusive Bilingual K-12 Education

section of the school asking if the students would be willing to teach classes about the play, and Molière more generally, to their French speaking peers who ironically had no yet encountered the author or 17th century French theatre in the curriculum. Students in the author's classes accepted the challenge and designed introduction sessions for their French first language peers.

They became so motivated by this task that they also widened the scope of the task and decided to immerse themselves more widely in the history of Versailles, and to include this exploration in the sessions they designed for their French speaking peers. Their exploration of French 17th century society, and Versailles more particularly, became the driving force with regards to their skills acquisition in their own class for several months. Choice, flexibility, and autonomy in roles had become the key to these students' success in the language. There was also no small amount of pride generated by this achievement. It furthermore helped create social capital opportunities with their peers in the French section of the school, with whom they otherwise had very little contact. This contrasts very sharply with the narrow tasks, inadequate requirements, and summative assessment most second language learners with disabilities encounter in K-12 classes.

Multiple Means of Engagement

Engagement is usually the area that involves the most friction for students with disabilities in the second language classroom. Learner engagement, in the conventional K-12 classroom, is defined and assessed narrowly as compliance, resignation to tasks that are not age appropriate or pertinent to the learner's life, adequate performance on assessment that is often so disconnected with the learner's interests as to appear meaningless, and perseverance in a subject were success is presented as unachievable. As a result, most diverse learners become unavoidably described as disengaged in the second language classroom. Reshaping the curriculum with learner engagement as a starting point, and with it then systematically in sight, is essential. Skill acquisition and language development follow.

One key process the author adopted, during his two years in the school context previously described as an example, is a deep reflection in relation to learner engagement. The starting point of his reflection, with the two classes he followed through grade 10 and 11, was to explore first how one might re-engage adolescents that had begun to see the target language as oppressive and marginalizing. Film, rap and hip-hop, advertising, contemporary visual art, and street art were all used as pillars for the reshaping of the curriculum. Linguistic tasks and the acquisition of competencies were embedded into this framework that aimed first at creating interest, curiosity, passion, and autonomy. This was very successful, and a tangible example of the reengagement which eventually occurred was a time when a classroom

171

proposed a field trip to a cinema to see a newly released film in which appeared an actor known to them from a movie they had watched in class as part of a lesson. They had independently explored this actor's career, had followed his other screen features, had read about his new release, and had developed autonomous interest in seeing more of his work. This was an outcome that had been achieved, in a 180 degree transformation, by learners who only a few months previously had lived and described the second language class as a pointless slot in their schedule, and a subject entirely disconnected from their lives and interests.

Seamless Overlap between UDL and Communicative Methods Approaches in Second Language Education

What becomes evident to the language teacher who experiments with UDL implementation is that there is a considerable overlap between UDL and communicative method approaches in language instruction. Both approaches recognize that language is not developed through an abstract and conceptual study of structures, but instead requires experiential first-hand involvement in communication tasks. UDL allows for this experiential learning because it encourages teachers to always offer students multiple pathways to the learning objectives. Some of these pathways will necessarily involve formats, activities, and materials that are experiential in nature rather than textbook based. Communicative method approaches advocate for the contextualization of language acquisition in practical situations requiring the learner to dialogue with others.

Eventually, both UDL and communicative studies reach beyond the acquisition of second language as just content, and encourage the teacher to consider teaching as a process of cross cultural exploration. Through both the UDL and the communicative method lens, it becomes rapidly clear that language acquisition is not solely about learning a language, it is about positioning oneself vis-à-vis a culture, a culture that is understood and fully appreciated within a socio-political lens of social justice, diversity, and equity. The overlap between, on the one hand, communicative method approaches in second language teaching and UDL, and on the other hand culturally responsive pedagogy becomes increasingly apparent with time (Waitoller & King Thorius, 2016). One never simply learns a language; a learner is at times member of a linguistic minority that must access a majority linguistic culture and is highly aware of the power dynamics at play. Alternatively, a learner could also be a member of a cultural majority who is curious and receptive to a language and culture that have minority status in their context and jurisdiction; such a learner will need to be equally conscious, aware, and sensitive to the power dynamics at play in this exploration. Culturally responsive pedagogy full acknowledges the complexity of this

Achieving Genuinely Inclusive Bilingual K-12 Education

landscape, and positions pedagogy not as a practice carried out in a void, but instead as a process that is always situated in a critical reflection on power (Tanase, 2021).

RECOMMENDATIONS FOR THE FIELD

This section of the chapter examines the repercussions this reflection has for the K-12 sector as a whole. Many of the aspects of the analysis presented lead, indeed, to specific recommendations with regards to transformation of the sector and of pre-service teacher training.

Embedding UDL in Pre-service Teacher Training

It is still difficult for in-service teachers to feel at ease with UDL when the framework and the literature that accompanies it are rarely explicitly present in pre-service teacher training programs (Lowrey et al., 2017). Even when UDL is discussed, it is briefly mentioned generically in relation to the inclusion of students with disabilities (Lowrey et al., 2019), but it is almost never mentioned specifically in relation to the teaching of second languages. It is conspicuously absent from pre-service teacher training programs which cater specifically to candidates for French immersion (Lanterman & Applequist, 2018). As has been made clear in this chapter, the mindset of teachers and teacher candidates in the immersion sector is entrenched in deficit model thinking, and it will therefore be difficult to implement UDL before intentional, in-depth, whole school strategic work takes place to shift mindsets in relation to bio-medical assumptions and perceptions (Baglieri et al., 2015; Tindall et al., 2015). It may be essential, in particular, to introduce some elements of Disability Studies scholarship to pre-service training, especially basic elements of the Social Model of Disability (Baglieri, 2020; Elder et al., 2021). It will indeed be difficult to lead pre-service teachers away from deficit model views of diverse learners until the Social Model of Disability is effectively incorporated into this training, and they acknowledge and embrace their role as designers who have the capacity to include or exclude through design. The social model sees disability as a social construct, not as an inherent characteristic of the individual (Barnes, 2020; Anastasiou & Kauffman, 2013). It sees and positions disability as a lack of fit between individual embodiments and the design of spaces, products, or experiences. The social model will readily encourage educators to see the challenges of learners with disabilities in the Immersion classroom, as caused by faulty design in instruction, and not by these students' lack of competency or potential in this subject.

Explicitly Connecting UDL and Communicative Method Approaches in Professional Development

Professional development (PD) for in-service teachers also needs to integrate the introduction of specific elements of Disability Studies scholarship, particularly as they relate to Critical Disability Studies and the Social Model of Disability (Elder, 2020). There is a significant paucity of PD focusing on Social Model approaches to inclusion. There is also a considerable need for further in-service PD focusing on UDL (Craig et al., 2019). At present, most of the work being carried out around UDL is being undertaken by individual teachers or communities of practice (Ganias & Novak, 2019), but there is very little systematic training on UDL being offered across schools (Israel et al., 2014).

This chapter has shown that UDL and communicative methods approaches to second language teaching are intimately intertwined. Unfortunately, PD focusing on communicative methods is also quite rare in the K-12 sector (Kheirabadi & Alavi Moghaddam, 2014). There is a significant discrepancy currently between the latest second language teaching practices developed in the private sector – which are firmly grounded in communicative methods at this stage – and those used and perpetuated in schools, still very reliant on traditional prescriptive, teacher-centered, textbook-based teaching (Vanorsdale, 2019). Although the literature stresses the inherent social nature of second language acquisition (Li & Jeong, 2020), change in second language pedagogy is slow to occur in schools. There is certainly little training on communicative method approaches offered in pre-service teaching, and it therefore is essential that such content be covered through PD in the field (Dos Santos, 2020). Unfortunately change is currently sporadic and when communicative methods approaches are developed in K-12 schools, these usually represent sporadic ad hoc initiatives developed by individual teachers, or by communities of practice. There is, at times, some lateral transfer of competencies when K-12 public sector educators work simultaneously in the private sector and are offered relevant PD by language schools where they are employed on a part-time basis, but this is not sufficient for systemic change to occur.

Supporting UDL Adoption in School From a Leadership Perspective

The main assertion of this chapter has been that UDL has unique potential as a tool to shift second language teachers away from deficit views of learner diversity, towards Social Model approaches. The chapter has also evidenced the perfect alignment that exist between UDL and communicative methods approaches in the teaching of second languages. It would be naïve, however, to consider this reflec-

Achieving Genuinely Inclusive Bilingual K-12 Education

tion solely from the perspective of pedagogy. Even if UDL and communicative methods approaches are ideally suited to create inclusive provisions in the K-12 classroom for diverse learners, this does not mean that their adoption in the field is strategically easy or seamless. There are considerable challenges that exist, from a leadership perspective, in rolling out UDL effectively across schools and there are very few examples of this being carried out successfully currently in the public sector (Fovet, 2020). The challenging task of implementing UDL successfully from an organizational perspective requires the use of ecological theory to fully grasp the complex and multilayered hurdles that must be addressed: this affects not just teachers, but school leaders, unions, administrative personnel, and parents (Fovet, 2021). Far too much of the literature around UDL currently ignores this dimension and focuses solely on the pedagogical benefits of UDL implementation (Fovet, 2020). While the potential of UDL to create sustainable inclusive provisions for all diverse learners is well demonstrated from a pedagogical point of view (Basham et al., 2018; Rao et al., 2019), little movement will be achieved in the field until strategic implementation within organizational settings is simultaneously explored and analyzed (Flood and Banks, 2021).

CONCLUSION

The myth that second language acquisition is challenging for students with disabilities is now debunked quite effectively by the literature, but this does not mean that diverse learners are not encountering barriers in these classes and programs. Far too many second language classrooms still adhere to traditional, textbook-based pedagogical strategies which fail to include diverse learners. Instead, UDL offers exceptional potential to develop authentic inclusive provisions in the second language classroom, by allowing learners to work with flexibility from a strength-based approach. UDL, though it is usually presented as an innovative framework for inclusion, actually has significant overlaps with communicative methods approaches in second language teaching. This makes the second language classroom an ideal environment for UDL implementation, and it is well possible that, as a result, in many K-12 environments, language teaching may one day end up leading the way in terms of UDL adoption and modelling implementation for other subject areas. This is not to say that the adoption of UDL across schools, or across language departments, is an easy task and there are specific strategic issues related to leadership which must be examined and have been explored in this chapter.

REFERENCES

Almumen, H. A. (2020). Universal Design for Learning (UDL) Across Cultures: The Application of UDL in Kuwaiti Inclusive Classrooms. *SAGE Open*, 10(4). Advance online publication. 10.1177/2158244020969674

Anastasiou, D., & Kauffman, J. M. (2013). The social model of disability: Dichotomy between impairment and disability. *The Journal of Medicine and Philosophy*, 38(4), 441–459. 10.1093/jmp/jht02623856481

Anya, U. (2017). *Racialized identities in second language learning: Speaking blackness in Brazil*. Routledge.

Aravossitas, T., & Oikonomakou, M. (2020). New directions for Greek education in the diaspora: teaching heritage language learners in Canada. In *Language diversity in Greece – Local challenges with international implications* (pp. 235-253). Springer. 10.1007/978-3-030-28396-4_18

Arigita-García, A., Sánchez-Cabrero, R., Barrientos-Fernández, A., Mañoso-Pacheco, L., & Pericacho-Gómez, F. J. (2021). Pre-eminence of determining factors in second language learning: An educator's perspective from Spain. *Heliyon*, 7(2), e06282. 10.1016/j.heliyon.2021.e0628233665442

Arnett, K., & Mady, C. (2017). Core or immersion? Canadian French-second-language teacher candidates' perceptions and experiences of the best and worst program options for students with learning difficulties and for English language learners. *Exceptionality Education International*, 27(1), 17–37. 10.5206/eei.v27i1.7744

Arnett, K. & Mady, C. (2018). The influence of classroom experience on teacher belief systems: New French second language teachers' beliefs about program options for English language learners and students with learning difficulties. *McGill Journal of Education / Revue des sciences de l'éducation de McGill, 53*(3). 10.7202/1058418ar

Arnott, S., Masson, M., & Lapkin, S. (2019). Exploring Trends in 21st Century Canadian K-12 French as Second Language Research: A Research Synthesis. *Canadian Journal of Applied Linguistics. Canadian Journal of Applied Linguistics*, 22(1). Advance online publication. 10.7202/1060906ar

Asadifard, A., & Koosha, M. (2013). EFL Instructors and Student Writers' Perceptions on Academic Writing Reluctance. *Theory and Practice in Language Studies*, 3(9), 1572–1578. 10.4304/tpls.3.9.1572-1578

Baglieri, S. (2020). Toward Inclusive Education? Focusing a Critical Lens on Universal Design for Learning. *Canadian Journal of Disability Studies*, 9(5), 42–74. 10.15353/cjds.v9i5.690

Achieving Genuinely Inclusive Bilingual K-12 Education

Baglieri, S., Valle, J. W., Connor, D. J., & Gallagher, D. J. (2011). Disability studies in education: The need for a plurality of perspectives on disability. *Remedial and Special Education*, 32(4), 267–278. 10.1177/0741932510362200

Barac, R., Bialystok, E., Castro, D. C., & Sanchez, M. (2014). The Cognitive Development of Young Dual Language Learners: A Critical Review. *Early Childhood Research Quarterly*, 29(4), 699–714. 10.1016/j.ecresq.2014.02.00325284958

Barnes, C. (2020). Understanding the social model of disability: Past, present and future. In N. Watson & S. Vehmas (Eds.), *Routledge Handbook of Disability Studies* (pp. 14–31). Routledge.

Barrett DeWiele, C. E., & Edgerton, J. D. (2021). Opportunity or inequality? The paradox of French immersion education in Canada. *Journal of Multilingual and Multicultural Development*. Advance online publication. 10.1080/01434632.2020.1865988

Basham, J. D., Blackorby, J., Stahl, S., & Zhang, L. (2018). Universal design for learning: Because students are (the) variable. In Kennedy, K., & Ferdig, R. E. (Eds.), *Handbook of research on K-12 online and blended learning* (2nd ed., pp. 477–507). ETC Press.

Bialystok, E. (2018). Bilingual education for young children: Review of the effects and consequences. *International Journal of Bilingual Education and Bilingualism*, 21(6), 666–679. 10.1080/13670050.2016.120385930288137

Borsch, A. S., Skovdal, M., & Smith Jervelund, S. (2021). How a School Setting Can Generate Social Capital for Young Refugees: Qualitative Insights from a Folk High School in Denmark. *Journal of Refugee Studies*, 34(1), 718–740. 10.1093/jrs/fez003

Bourgoin, R. (2014). Inclusionary practices in French immersion: A need to link research to practice. *Canadian Journal for New Scholars in Education*, 5(1), 1–11.

Bourgoin, R. (2016). French immersion "So why would you do something like that to a child?" Issues of advocacy, accessibility, and inclusion. *International Journal of Bias, Identity and Diversities in Education*, 1(1), 42–58. 10.4018/IJBIDE.2016010104

Canadian Parents for French. (2013). *An Overview of French Second Language Education in Canada.* CPF. https://sencanada.ca/content/sen/committee/412/OLLO/Briefs/2013-11-22CPFBrief_Addendum_e.pdf

Carlson, S., Gerhards, J., & Hans, S. (2017). Educating Children in Times of Globalisation: Class-specific Child-rearing Practices and the Acquisition of Transnational Cultural Capital. *Sociology*, 51(4), 749–765. 10.1177/0038038515618601

Ceylan, O. N. (2019). Student Perceptions of Difficulties in Second Language Writing. *Journal of Language and Linguistic Studies*, 15(1), 151–157. 10.17263/jlls.547683

Chita-Tegmark, M., Gravel, J. W., Serpa, M. D. L. B., Domings, Y., & Rose, D. H. (2012). Using the universal design for learning framework to support culturally diverse learners. *Journal of Education*, 192(1), 17–22. 10.1177/002205741219200104

Christle, C. A., & Yell, M. L. (2010). Individualized Education Programs: Legal Requirements and Research Findings. *Exceptionality*, 18(3), 109–123. 10.1080/09362835.2010.491740

Cioe-Pena, M. (2017). Bilingualism, Disability and What it Means to Be Normal. *Journal of Bilingual Education Research & Instruction*, 19(1).

Cioè-Peña, M. (2020). Bilingualism for students with disabilities, deficit or advantage? Perspectives of Latinx mothers. *Bilingual Research Journal*, 43(3), 253–266. 10.1080/15235882.2020.1799884

Coe, C., & Shani, S. (2015). Cultural capital and transnational parenting. *Harvard Educational Review*, 85(4), 562–586. 10.17763/0017-8055.85.4.562

Collins, B. A., Toppelberg, C. O., Suárez-Orozco, C., O'Connor, E., & Nieto-Castañon, A. (2011). Cross-Sectional Associations of Spanish and English Competence and Well-Being in Latino Children of Immigrants in Kindergarden. *International Journal of the Sociology of Language*, 208, 5–23.

Craig, S. L., Smith, S. J., & Frey, B. B. (2019). Professional development with universal design for learning: Supporting teachers as learners to increase the implementation of UDL. *Professional Development in Education*. Advance online publication. 10.1080/19415257.2019.1685563

Davis, S., Ballinger, S., & Sarkar, M. (2019). The Suitability of French Immersion for Allophone Students in Saskatchewan: Exploring Diverse Perspectives on Language Learning and Inclusion. *Canadian Journal of Applied Linguistics. Canadian Journal of Applied Linguistics*, 22(2), 27–63. 10.7202/1063773ar

Debreli, E., Ishanova, I., & Sheppard, C. (2019). Foreign language classroom management: Types of student misbehaviour and strategies adapted by the teachers in handling disruptive behaviour. *Cogent Education, 6*(1). 10.1080/2331186X.2019.1648629

Delcourt, L. (2018) Elitist, Inequitable And Exclusionary Practices: A Problem Within Ontario French Immersion Programs? A Literature Review. *Actes du Jean-Paul Dionne Symposium Proceedings*. 10.18192/jpds-sjpd.v2i1.3152

Dicks, J., & Genesee, F. (2017). Bilingual Education in Canada. In García, O., Lin, A., & May, S. (Eds.), *Bilingual and Multilingual Education. Encyclopedia of Language and Education* (3rd ed.). Springer. 10.1007/978-3-319-02258-1_32

Dos Santos, L. M. (2020). The Discussion of Communicative Language Teaching Approach in Language Classrooms. *Journal of Education and e-learning Research*, 7(2), 104–109. 10.20448/journal.509.2020.72.104.109

Early, M., Dagenais, D., & Carr, W. (2017). Second and Foreign Language Education in Canada. In Van Deusen-Scholl, N., & May, S. (Eds.), *Encyclopedia of Language and Education, 4* (pp. 197–208). Springer.

Elder, B. C. (2020). Necessary first steps: Using professional development schools (pds) to support more students with disability labels in inclusive classrooms. *School-University Partnerships, 13*(1), 32–43. https://eric.ed.gov/?id=EJ1249469

Elder, B. C., Givens, L., LoCastro, A., & Rencher, L. (2021). Using Disability Studies in Education (dse) and Professional Development Schools (pds) to Implement Inclusive Practices. *Journal of Disability Studies in Education.* 10.1163/25888803-bja10010

Emiliussen, J., Engelsen, S., Christiansen, R., & Klausen, S. H. (2021). We are all in it!: Phenomenological Qualitative Research and Embeddedness. *International Journal of Qualitative Methods*, 20. Advance online publication. 10.1177/1609406921995304

Fareed, M., Ashraf, A., & Bilal, M. (2016). ESL Learners' Writing Skills: Problems, Factors and Suggestions. *Journal of Education and Social Sciences*, 4(2), 81–92. 10.20547/jess0421604201

Ferguson, B. T. (2019). Balancing requirements, options and choice in UDL:Smorgasbord or nutritious diet? In Gronseth, S. L., & Dalton, E. M. (Eds.), *Universal Access Through Inclusive Instructional Design: International Perspectives on UDL* (pp. 96–102). Routledge. 10.4324/9780429435515-12

Fernández-Villardón, A., Valls-Carol, R., Melgar Alcantud, P., & Tellado, I. (2021) Enhancing Literacy and Communicative Skills of Students With Disabilities in Special Schools Through Dialogic Literary Gatherings. *Frontiers in Psychology, 12*, 1275. 10.3389/fpsyg.2021.662639

Flood, M., & Banks, J. (2021). Universal Design for Learning: Is It Gaining Momentum in Irish Education? *Education Sciences*, 11(7), 341. 10.3390/educsci11070341

Fovet, F. (2020). Integrating Universal Design for Learning in Schools: Implications for Teacher Training, Leadership and Professional Development. In Al Mahdi, O. (Ed.), *Innovations in Educational Leadership and Continuous Teachers' Professional Development*. CSMFL Publications. 10.46679/isbn978819484832513

Fovet, F. (2021). Developing an Ecological Approach to Strategic UDL Implementation in Higher Education. *Journal of Education and Learning*, 10(4), 27. 10.5539/jel.v10n4p27

Gallagher-MacKay, K., Srivastava, P., Underwood, K., Dhuey, E., McCready, L., Born, K.B., Maltsev, A., Perkhun, A., Steiner, R., Barrett, K., & Sander, B. (2021) COVID-19 and education disruption in Ontario: emerging evidence on impacts. *Science Briefs of the Ontario COVID-19 Science Advisory Table, 2*(34). 10.47326/ocsat.2021.02.34.1.0

Ganias, M., & Novak, K. (2019). A perfect pairing: UDL and PLCs. *eSchool News.* https://www.eschoolnews.com/2019/11/06/a-perfect-pairing-udl-and-plcs/

Grasmane, D., & Grasmane, S. (2011). Foreign language skills for employability in the EU labour market. *European Journal of Higher Education.* 10.1080/21568235.2011.629487

Hayday, M. (2015). *So they want us to learn French: Promoting and opposing bilingualism in English-speaking Canada.* UBC Press. 10.59962/9780774830065

Hefferman, P. J. (2011). Second-language (L2) teacher preparation and ongoing professional development in a world in need of social justice. *Journal of Interdisciplinary Education*, 10(1), 142–155.

Hoover, J. J., Erickson, J. R., Patton, J. R., Sacco, D. M., & Tran, L. M. (2018). Examining IEPs of English Learners with learning disabilities for cultural and linguistic responsiveness. *Learning Disabilities Research & Practice*, 34(1), 14–22. 10.1111/ldrp.12183

Israel, M., Ribuffo, C., & Smith, S. J. (2014). *Universal design for learning innovation configuration: recommendations for pre-service teacher preparation and in-service professional development.*https://kuscholarworks.ku.edu/bitstream/handle/1808/18509/10%20Universal%20Design%20for%20Learning-1.pdf;sequence=1

Ivančević-Otanjac, M. (2016). Students with language learning disabilities and difficulties in a foreign language classroom. *Specijalna edukacija i rehabilitacija, 15*(4), 461-474.

Jack, D., & Nyman, J. (2019). Meeting Labour Market Needs for French as a Second Language Instruction in Ontario. *American Journal of Educational Research*, 7(7), 428–438. 10.12691/education-7-7-1

Kasch, H. (2018). New multimodal designs for foreign language learning. Learning Tech–Tidsskrift for læremidler, didaktik og teknologi, 5, 28–59. 10.7146/lt.v4i5.111561

Kasch, H. (2019). Experimental Studies of the affordances of assistive multimodal learning designs: Universal Design for Learning in modern language classrooms. *JISTE*, 23(2), 93.

Khatib, M., & Tootkaboni, A. A. (2019). Attitudes toward communicative language teaching: The case of efl learners and teachers. *Íkala. Revista de Lenguaje y Cultura*, 24(3), 471–485. Advance online publication. 10.17533/udea.ikala.v24n03a04

Kheirabadi, R., & Alavi Moghaddam, S. B. (2014). New horizons in teaching English in Iran: A transition from reading-based methods to communicative ones by 'English for schools' series. *International Journal of Language Learning and Applied Linguistics World*, 5(4), 225–232.

Kline-Martin, E. (2018) *Yes Oui Can: Addressing British Columbia's Shortage of French Immersion Teachers.* Master's thesis. School of Public Policy, Simon Fraser University.

Krausneker, V., Becker, C., Audeoud, M., & Tarcsiová, D. (2017). Bimodal Bilingual School Practice in Europe. In K. Reuter (Ed.), *UNCRPD Implementation in Europe - A Deaf Perspective.* EUD

Krausneker, V., Becker, C., Audeoud, M., & Tarcsiová, D. (2020). Bilingual school education with spoken and signed languages in Europe. *International Journal of Bilingual Education and Bilingualism.* Advance online publication. 10.1080/13670050.2020.1799325

Kupers, E., de Boer, A., Loopers, J., Bakker, A., & Minnaert, A. (2023). Differentiation and Students with Special Educational Needs: Teachers' Intentions and Classroom Interactions. In Maulana, R., Helms-Lorenz, M., & Klassen, R. M. (Eds.), *Effective Teaching Around the World.* Springer. 10.1007/978-3-031-31678-4_36

Lai, C., & Gu, M. (2011). Self-regulated out-of-class language learning with technology. *Computer Assisted Language Learning*, 24(4), 317–335. 10.1080/09588221.2011.568417

Lanterman, C. S., & Applequist, K. (2018). Pre-service Teachers' Beliefs: Impact of Training in Universal Design for Learning. *Exceptionality Education International*, 28(3). Advance online publication. 10.5206/eei.v28i3.7774

Larsen-Freeman, D. (2018). Looking ahead: Future directions in, and future research into, second language acquisition. *Foreign Language Annals*, 51(1), 55–72. 10.1111/flan.12314

Li, P., & Jeong, H. (2020) The social brain of language: grounding second language learning in social interaction. *NPJ Science of Learning, 5*, 8. 10.1038/s41539-020-0068-7

Lindholm-Leary, K., & Genesee, F. (2014). Student outcomes in one-way, two-way, and indigenous language immersion education. *Journal of Immersion and Content Based Language Education*, 2(2), 165–180. 10.1075/jicb.2.2.01lin

Lowrey, K., Classen, A., & Sylvest, A. (2019). Exploring Ways to Support Preservice Teachers' Use of UDL in Planning and Instruction. *Journal of Educational Research & Practice*, 9(1), 261–281. 10.5590/JERAP.2019.09.1.19

Lowrey, K. A., Hollingshead, A., & Howery, K. (2017). A closer look: Examining teachers' language around UDL, inclusive classrooms, and intellectual disability. *Intellectual and Developmental Disabilities*, 55(1), 15–24. 10.1352/1934-9556-55.1.1528181885

Lyster, R. (2015). Using form-focused tasks to integrate language across the immersion curriculum. *System*, 54, 4–13. 10.1016/j.system.2014.09.022

Mady, C. (2017). Multilingual immigrants' French and English acquisition in Grade 6 French immersion: Evidence as means to improve access. *Language and Intercultural Communication*, 18(2), 204–224. 10.1080/14708477.2017.1364259

Mady, C. (2018). Teacher Adaptations to Support Students with Special Education Needs in French Immersion: An Observational Study. *Journal of Immersion and Content-Based Language Education*, 6(2), 244–268. 10.1075/jicb.17011.mad

Mady, C., & Arnett, K. (2016). French as a second language teacher candidates' conceptions of allophone students and students with learning difficulties. *Canadian Journal of Applied Linguistics. Canadian Journal of Applied Linguistics*, 18(2), 78–95.

Mady, C., & Masson, M. (2018). Principals' Beliefs About Language Learning and Inclusion of English Language Learners in Canadian Elementary French Immersion Programs. *Canadian Journal of Applied Linguistics. Canadian Journal of Applied Linguistics*, 21(1), 71–93. 10.7202/1050811ar

Mason, M., Larson, E. J., Desgroseilliers, P., Carr, W., & Lapkin, S. (2020) *Accessing opportunity: A study on challenges in French-as-a-second-language education teacher supply and demand in Canada*. Office of the Commissioner of Official Languages. https://www.clo-ocol.gc.ca/en/publications/studies/2019/accessing-opportunity-fsl

Mathewson, T. G. (2020, July 13). Boston schools deny some students with disabilities enrollment into dual-language programs. *Boston Globe.* https://www.bostonglobe .com/2020/07/13/metro/boston-schools-deny-some-disabled-students-enrollment -into-dual-language-programs/

Misbah, N. H., Mohamad, M., Yunus, M., & Ya'acob, A. (2017). Identifying the Factors Contributing to Students' Difficulties in the English Language Learning. *Creative Education*, 8(13), 1999–2008. 10.4236/ce.2017.813136

Montanari, S. (2013). A Case Study of Bi-literacy Development among Children Enrolled in an Italian–English Dual Language Program in Southern California. *International Journal of Bilingual Education and Bilingualism*, 17(5), 509–525. 10.1080/13670050.2013.833892

Morgan, P. L., Farkas, G., Hillemeier, M. M., Mattison, R., Maczuga, S., Li, H., & Cook, M. (2015). Minorities are disproportionately underrepresented in special education: Longitudinal evidence across five disability conditions. *Educational Researcher*, 44(5), 278–292. 10.3102/0013189X1559115727445414

Muhling, S., & Mady, C. (2017). Inclusion of Students With Special Education Needs in French as a Second Language Programs: A Review of Canadian Policy and Resource Documents. *Canadian Journal of Educational Administration and Policy*, 183, 15–29.

Navarro, S. B., Zervas, P., Gesa, R. F., & Sampson, D. G. (2016). Developing teachers' competences for designing inclusive learning experiences. *Journal of Educational Technology & Society*, 19(1), 17–27.

Nicolay, A.-C., & Poncelet, M. (2015). Cognitive Benefits in Children Enrolled in an Early Bilingual Immersion School: A Follow Up Study. *Bilingualism: Language and Cognition*, 18(4), 789–795. 10.1017/S1366728914000868

Ok, M. W., Rao, K., Bryant, B. R., & McDougall, D. (2017). Universal Design for Learning in Pre-K to Grade 12 Classrooms: A Systematic Review of Research. *Exceptionality*, 25(2), 116–138. 10.1080/09362835.2016.1196450

Padilla, A. M., Fan, L., Xu, X., & Silva, D. (2013). A Mandarin/English Two-way Immersion Program: Language Proficiency and Academic Achievement. *Foreign Language Annals*, 46(4), 661–679. 10.1111/flan.12060

Pan, C. (2014) *Falling Behind: 2014 Report on the Shortage of Teachers in French Immersion and Core French in British-Columbia and Yukon.* Canadian Parents for French.

Peng, H., Jager, S., & Lowie, W. (2021). A person-centred approach to L2 learners' informal mobile language learning. *Computer Assisted Language Learning*. Advance online publication. 10.1080/09588221.2020.1868532

Pruss, V. (2017, August 23). Anglophone Schools 'Desperate' for Supply Teachers as Early French Immersion. *CBC News*. https://www.cbc.ca/news/canada/new-brunswick/french-immersion-teacher-shortage-new-brunswick-ingersoll-1.4258892

Rao, K., Ok, M. W., Smith, S. J., Evmenova, A. S., & Edyburn, D. (2019). Validation of the UDL reporting criteria with extant UDL research. *Remedial and Special Education*. Advance online publication. 10.1177/0741932519847755

Reinders, H., & Wattana, S. (2014). Can I say something? The effects of digital game play on willingness to communicate. *Language Learning & Technology*, 18, 101–123.

Shemshack, A., & Spector, J. M. (2020). A systematic literature review of personalized learning terms. *Smart Learning Environment*, 7(1), 33. 10.1186/s40561-020-00140-9

Skinner, M. E., & Smith, A. T. (2011). Creating Success for Students with Learning Disabilities in Postsecondary Foreign Language Courses. *International Journal of Special Education*, 26(2), 42–57.

Sowell, J., & Sugisaki, L. (2021). Accommodating Learning Disabilities in the English Language Classroom. *English Teaching Forum*.https://americanenglish.state.gov/files/ae/resource_files/etf_59_1_pg02-11.pdf

Stephens, M., & Kaiser, M. R. (2018). A comparison of visual and audio scaffolds in L2 English reading. *Indonesian Journal of Applied Linguistics*, 8(2), 380–387. 10.17509/ijal.v8i2.13303

Strangman, N., Meyer, A., Hall, T., & Proctor, C. P. (2014). New technologies and universal design for learning in the foreign language classroom. In *Worlds apart? Disability and foreign language learning* (pp. 164–176). Yale University Press. 10.12987/yale/9780300116304.003.0009

Suprayogi, M. N., & Valcke, M. (2016). Differentiated Instruction in Primary Schools: Implementation and Challenges in Indonesia. *PONTE International Scientific Research Journal*, 72(6), 2–18. 10.21506/j.ponte.2016.6.1

Tanase, M. F. (2021). Culturally Responsive Teaching in Urban Secondary Schools. *Education and Urban Society*. Advance online publication. 10.1177/00131245211026689

Tangen, D., & Spooner-Lane, R. (2008). Avoiding the deficit model of teaching: Students who have EAL/EAL and learning difficulties. *Australian Journal of Learning Difficulties*, 13(2), 63–71. 10.1080/19404150802380522

Theriault, M. (2014). French Immersion: A Growing Concern with Growing Pains. *The Manitoba Teacher*, 92, 8–9.

Tindall, D., MacDonald, W., Carroll, E., & Moody, B. (2015). Pre-service teachers' attitudes towards children with disabilities: An Irish perspective. *European Physical Education Review*, 21(2), 206–221. 10.1177/1356336X14556861

Tomlinson, C. A. (2014). *The Differentiated Classroom: Responding to the Needs of all Learners*. ASCD.

Toro, V., Camacho-Minuche, G., Pinza-Tapis, E., & Paredes, F. (2019). The Use of the Communicative Language Teaching Approach to Improve Students' Oral Skills. *English Language Teaching*, 12(1), 110. 10.5539/elt.v12n1p110

Tyler, A. E., Ortega, L., Uno, M., & Park, H. I. (2018). *Usage-inspired L2 instruction: Researched pedagogy*. John Benjamins. 10.1075/lllt.49

Vanorsdale, C. (2019) Communicative Language Teaching in E-Learning: How Confident are the Instructors? *E-Learn 2017 Proceedings*, 489-493

Waitoller, F. R., & King Thorius, K. A. (2016). Cross-pollinating culturally sustaining pedagogy and universal design for learning: Toward an inclusive pedagogy that accounts for dis/ability. *Harvard Educational Review*, 86(3), 366–389. 10.17763/1943-5045-86.3.366

Waxman, H.C., Alford, B.L., Brown, D.B., Hattie, J., & Anderman, E.M. (2013). Individualized Instruction. *International Guide to Student Achievement*, 405–407

Webb, A. S., & Welsh, A. J. (2019). Phenomenology As a Methodology for Scholarship of Teaching and Learning Research. *Teaching & Learning Inquiry*, 7(1), 168–181. 10.20343/teachlearninqu.7.1.11

Wight, M. C. S. (2015). Students with Learning Disabilities in the Foreign Language Learning Environment and the Practice of Exemption. *Foreign Language Annals*, 48(1), 39–55. 10.1111/flan.12122

Wise, N. (2012). Access to Special Education for Exceptional Pupils in French Immersion Program: An Equity Issue. In *Proceedings of the Canadian Parents for French Roundtable on Academically Challenged Students in French Second Language Programs* (pp. 34-38). Canadian Parents for French.

Woll, B., & Wei, L. (2019). *Cognitive Benefits of Language Learning: Broadening our perspectives*. Final Report to the British Academy, British Academy. https://www.thebritishacademy.ac.uk/sites/default/files/Cognitive-Benefits-LanguageLearning-Final-Report.pdf

Zaic, B. (2021) A Personalized Learning Approach to Educating Students Identified with Special Education Needs. Project in MSc in Special Education, *Culminating Projects in Special Education, 98.* https://repository.stcloudstate.edu/sped_etds/98

Zhang, X. (2020). A bibliometric analysis of second language acquisition between 1997 and 2018. *Studies in Second Language Acquisition*, 42(1), 199–222. 10.1017/S0272263119000573

Zulu, P. M. (2019). Teachers' Understanding and Attitudes towards Communicative Language Teaching Method in ESL Classrooms of Zambia. *International Journal of Humanities Social Sciences and Education*, 6(6), 1–13.

KEY TERMS AND DEFINITIONS

Communicative Methods Approach: An approach to second language instruction, now very popular in the private sector, which insists that the learning of languages must be contextualized in a hands-on context of dialogue. It argues that structures in the target language are not integrated conceptually but rather adopted through repetitive use in authentic situations of communication.

Culturally Responsive Pedagogy: An approach to pedagogy which systematically contextualizes teaching and learning within a socio-political context where cultural diversity and inherent power dynamics are acknowledged and addressed. Inclusive pedagogy is conceived within this complex landscape of critical awareness and responsibility.

Multiple Means of Action and Expression: Represents one of the three UDL principles for inclusive design. Encourages teachers to offer optimal flexibility and choice in the way information is presented to learners.

Multiple Means of Engagement: Represents one of the three UDL principles for inclusive design. Encourages teachers to offer optimal flexibility and choice in the way learners are required to create, submit, or present information, class contributions, answers to assessment, content, and participation material.

Multiple Means of Representation: Represents one of the three UDL principles for inclusive design. Encourages teachers to rethink broadly the way they construe and define learner engagement, in order to offer learners optimal flexibility in the way they may demonstrate this.

Achieving Genuinely Inclusive Bilingual K-12 Education

Universal Design for Learning: A framework for inclusion which places the focus not on learner diversity, but instead on the educator's responsibility for, and role in, designing learning experiences inclusively. UDL assumes that learner diversity is the norm, not the exception, and that inclusive design that offers learners optimal flexibility is key to address this diversity.

188

Chapter 8
Beyond COVID–19:
Innovative UDL Implementation in Early Childhood Education

Liton Furukawa
Royal Roads University, Canada

EXECUTIVE SUMMARY

The pandemic impacts children's physical and mental health, and children are now experiencing increased mental health and physical challenges as a result of COVID-19. This chapter presents Universal Design for Learning as a framework for curriculum reform that will improve children's learning experiences and enable more effective planning towards a more inclusive and interactive education method in early childhood education settings. This chapter focuses on a pilot study employing a mixed-methods design that explored how an innovative UDL model—interactive multi-sensory physical movements (IMPM)—was implemented in a kindergarten in Canada. This research is an evidence-based ongoing interdisciplinary study that highlights this new model with the aim of incurring long term benefits for children, parents, and ECE professionals. This research will also benefit the international ECE industry, scholars, researchers, and informed policy makers.

INTRODUCTION

The COVID-19 pandemic initiated an unprecedented crisis across the world. The pandemic impacted children's physical and mental health, and children have experienced increased mental health and physical challenges as a result of COVID-19 pandemic and lockdowns. Traditional classrooms were gradually replaced with blended learning methods. However, difficulties and challenges have been increasing for young children adapting to these virtual methods, especially for children who are

DOI: 10.4018/978-1-6684-4750-5.ch008

Copyright © 2024, IGI Global. Copying or distributing in print or electronic forms without written permission of IGI Global is prohibited.

Beyond COVID-19

limited by physical disabilities or other difficulties. This chapter presents Universal Design for Learning (UDL) as a framework for curriculum reform that will improve children's learning experiences and enable more effective planning towards a more inclusive and interactive education method in early childhood education (ECE) settings. This chapter focuses on a pilot study employing a mixed-methods design that explored how an innovative UDL model – interactive multi-sensory physical movements (IMPM) – was implemented in a kindergarten in Canada. A case study approach was used, incorporating virtual interviews and observations designed to capture dynamic conversations with, and the experiences of, research participants. This research identified an improvement in ECE professionals' UDL-aligned instructional practices and positive attitudes toward using a new model to inform instructional enhancement through a feasible and accessible new innovative kindergarten model. The opportunities and challenges of applying this model for children at pre-school ages in both mainstream and special education settings with respect to the UDL implementation were discussed. This research is an evidence-based ongoing inter-disciplinary study that highlights this new model with the aim of incurring long term benefits for children, parents, and ECE professionals. This research will also benefit the international ECE industry, scholars, researchers, and informed policy makers.

The specific content of each section is described in the following paragraphs. The researcher describes the nature of the problem to be addressed and why it is significant, which serves as a background for this study. This is followed by a discussion identifying current gaps in the research and how these gaps are addressed in this project. There is also be a discussion on how the project draws on knowledge gained from previous research.

Background

The Canadian Institute for Health Information (2022) released the newest document, *Child and Youth Mental Health in Canada* (reporting data time until 2020), showing approximately 20% of Canadians aged five to 24 could develop a mental disorder. One in 11 youth in Canada will require medication for mental disorders as Figure 1 illustrates. There has been a 75% increase in visits to emergency departments and a 65% increase in hospitalizations for children and youth with mental illnesses since 2006 (Mental Health Commission of Canada, 2022). Mental illness can be cumulative, oppressive, and involve systemic issues that reappear in children's lives, causing adverse childhood experiences.

Figure 1. Child and youth mental health in Canada — Infographic (Canadian Institute for Health Information, 2022)

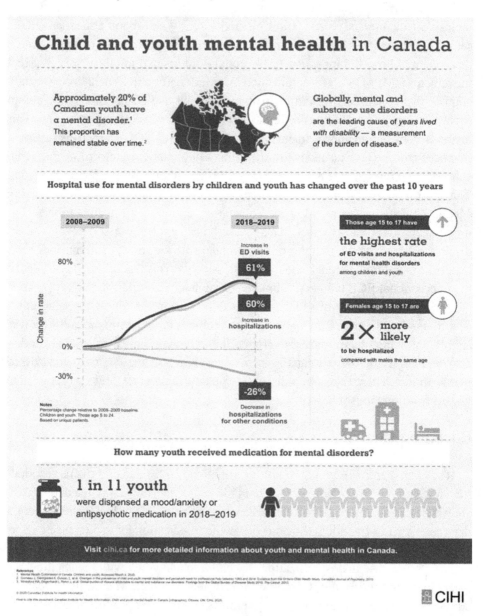

Especially as a result of the coronavirus disease (COVID-19) pandemic, opportunities for children to carry out their physical activities and have outdoor access have been impacted by school closures and physical distancing measures implemented by numerous governments. Numerous studies reported the severe risks of mental illness and substance use for vulnerable children, and that they have lost their focus on building academic and social skills as a result of COVID-19 (Golberstein et al., 2020; Hawke et al., 2020).

Evidence has shown that children are less active and more sedentary with an unstructured daily routine, according to Community Mobility Reports (Aktay et al., 2020), and this evidence is from global communities responding at the time to COVID-19, who have charted this trend over time and across the 15 countries involved. 15 preschool children's parents were interviewed in China, and scholars (Aktay et al., 2020) pointed out that children decreased their physical activity but increased sedentary screen time as a direct result of the COVID-19 pandemic lockdowns and online pivots. There are similar cases in South Korea, where 97 parents of young children were surveyed during the pandemic. In the report (Aktay et al., 2020), 81% of respondents indicated their children were spending more time on screens and 94% of 49 respondents indicated their children were having less play time and not using sports facilities. Reducing physical activities could lead to a higher risk of obesity (Rundle et al., 2020), mental health issues (Dalton et al., 2020), and myopia (Lanca & Saw, 2020). Children's physical and mental health has been a crucial consideration during the COVID-19 pandemic, and this will also be the case for post COVID-19 as governments, educators, and parents seek to establish a new normal and a long-term plan.

In response to the call for promoting children's physical and mental health and supporting them both during and after the pandemic, Universal Design for Learning (UDL) emerges as a systematically effective instructional framework that offers a strategy for positive learning environments. As the UDL framework incorporates a multidisciplinary approach, such as the science of learning, cognitive psychology, neuroscience, and education, its principles provide multiple means of (1) engagement, (2) action and expression, and (3) representation (CAST, 2022); it assists early childhood education (ECE) practitioners in designing positive learning experiences that are perceptual, comprehensive, and demonstrably accessible for supporting diverse learners in early childhood settings. This research aims to investigate the current challenges of ECE professionals and how they can support children in both mainstream and special needs' contexts and find an innovative ECE model to help educators facilitate diverse children's engagement within a positive learning environment.

This new innovative ECE model – interactive multi-sensory physical movements (IMPM) model is based on the UDL framework and encourages children using multiple senses when they engage in mental and physical activities and promotes different types of sensory learning through their auditory, visual, tactile, kinesthetic, gustatory, and olfactory senses. Teachers and parents are encouraged to involve themselves in the children's learning process and create an interactive multisensory learning environment. As one of BC's Early Years professionals, the researcher/author has been developing the IMPM model since she managed two early childhood education centers as a manager, led and participated in multiple associations, and developed intricate educational projects with national and international teams as a principal investigator. Her doctoral and postdoctoral training and research focused on children, families, and communities, with funding support from the Canadian government. The author's research skills are in the fields of early childhood education, curriculum studies, health promotion methods and applications, the interactive multisensory approach, and educational technologies. Her professional certifications include being a licensed early childhood education (ECE) educator in BC, Canada, and she has consistently built up her knowledge, skills, and abilities in caring for children and youth who deal with behavioral, emotional, and physical issues. Her past work experience included helping children with special needs, together with their families and communities, such as children with disabilities on the autism spectrum, those with Tourette Syndrome, and those with attention deficit hyperactivity disorder (ADHD). Her extensive research and work experiences have allowed her to become specialized in learning and teaching within different models and developing various mental and physical health strategies.

MAIN FOCUS OF THE CHAPTER

Research Gaps

In this section, the researcher discusses several research studies, learning approaches, and models, and looks at how they provide learning opportunities and educational resources for children. However, in the specific context of this study, there are very few studies addressing an innovative UDL approach and its implementation in the field of ECE.

While numerous efforts are underway to intervene and improve access to treatment and related services, it is crucial to first work toward prevention rather than intervention, as a parent, caretaker, or community member can collaborate with schools to help support children's mental and physical health (Coley, Lynch, & Kull, 2015). Mental health strategies that integrate physical exercises to support children's mental and physical health have made substantial contributions to child and adolescent health and health care. Some scholars have innovatively recommended resistance training as a way of developing long term and effective physical activity programs for children with special needs (Ten Hoor et al., 2016); other researchers have focused on emotional intelligence to promote sport practices to ensure that children learn to

Beyond COVID-19

better regulate and manage their emotions (Amado-Alonso et al., 2019). There are only a few reports that focus on mental-health strategies that are underpinned by physical activity in the development of true-self-awareness and personal growth in order to prevent adverse childhood experiences (Eime et al., 2013).

There is no simple solution to fix long-standing issues, and the pandemic lockdown has added to this difficulty of how to make incremental improvements for children's mental and physical health. "91% of the global student population" and "schools in 194 countries" were impacted due to the pandemic (Basham et al., 2020, p.84); how to overcome these issues both during and post pandemic and how to deal with these expected and unexpected challenges has been a struggle for children, parents, and ECE professionals. Although, certain researchers discussed and promoted the UDL framework for children in the COVID-19 pandemic context, especially regarding remote instruction and online learning environments (Basham & Blackorby, 2020; Carver & Rowe, 2021; Crosby, & Aguilar, 2022; Frumos, 2020), when children shifted their learning from an in-person to a virtual learning environment, remote learning presented unique challenges and barriers to young children, including those with different needs; and this is true even though school districts and community centers provided digital resources for children and families in an attempt to serve them in the context of school shutdowns. Many case studies indicated parents and ECE professionals became overwhelmed with remote learning (Carver & Rowe, 2021; Basham et al., 2020; Khan, 2022) and that children's mental and physical health became a critical issue. Some studies explored utilizing software and hardware as well as additional modalities to support children, families, and professionals (Morse, 2022; Mowrey & Cunningham, 2022).

Among these research projects, there is insufficient study of how mental-health strategies based on physical activities might work in a multi-sensory environment (MSE) for children, families, and communities. Parents and ECE professionals' need for a learning-centered framework, such as UDL, indicates the importance of examining whether and how to refine an ECE model in order to meet all children's needs.

Purpose of the Study

The purpose of this study is to apply the UDL framework and investigate how to implement a new UDL model – interactive multi-sensory physical movements (IMPM) – that will meet children's needs and result in an optimal learning experience beyond the COVID-19 pandemic. This study is evidence-based ongoing interdisciplinary research, and this chapter is focused on the first part of this research – a pilot study. In this section, research objectives and research questions will be discussed.

As the researcher discussed in the last section, there are very few studies addressing mental-health strategies based on physical activities with a multi-sensory environment approach, and one that would improve health outcomes using a model that depicts the relationship between psychological health and the frequency of the physical activities of children. This study aims to develop a new UDL model, an IMPM model, to meet children's mental and physical needs by integrating designed activities into scientific instruments (applications of holography) employing look/see, hear, touch, smell, taste, feel, think, speak, and full body motions. UDL provides a framework for guiding this research, and this model is feasible and accessible as a new innovative kindergarten curriculum/program. The IMPM model is, according to the UDL curriculum design framework, based on meeting the diverse needs of children, including curriculum objectives, methods, materials, and assessment. Based on the principle of UDL, the IMPM model incorporates digital media technology into the design of various elements of the course and enhances the flexibility and adaptability of the course from the two aspects of teaching and learning. IMPM does this by providing a variety of content presentation, expression, and participation methods, and provides children with suitable support to overcome the barriers and difficulties encountered within the traditional one-size-fits-all rigid curriculum, so that all children with different needs, especially children with mental and physical disabilities, can acquire knowledge, skills and learning like learners in mainstream settings.

A mixed method interdisciplinary approach was used with children from ages three to six for both mainstream and special education settings, the latter focusing on, for instance, children with developmental disorders (ADD, ADHD, autism, specific learning disabilities, dyslexia, and so on). From the UDL perspective, successful learning plans would have a flexibly designed curriculum with a proactive, positive, and equitable learning environment which, especially for those children with different needs, would decrease unnecessary challenges and barriers that impede children from interacting meaningfully with peers, teachers, and curricula (Kurniasari et al., 2021).

Research Objectives

This study explores a new UDL model in which children can access their own learning needs, parents and community members can be involved in a codesign process, ECE professionals can improve their learning, course designs, and lesson plans, ECE business owners can support the needs of a diverse group of children making ongoing adjustments for kindergarten programs and models, and policy

Beyond COVID-19

makers can better understand a critical issue by learning how UDL is being implemented within ECE in a holistic manner, thereby encouraging them to include UDL in their educational policies.

Research Questions

The primary research question of this study is: In what ways might a new ECE innovative UDL model – IMPM – contribute to the mental and physical development of both mainstream children and children with special needs?

The sub-questions are:

1. To what extent does context affect the delivery of the IMPM model given its team-based approach for establishing primary care homes/kindergartens/daycare centres?
2. What are the best practices and approaches for delivering an IMPM model using a team-based approach for establishing primary care homes/kindergartens/daycare centres?
3. How do the families of both mainstream children and children with diverse learners understand the concept of the new ECE UDL framework?
4. What do the families of both mainstream children and children with diverse learners see as the barriers and enablers to delivering the IMPM model?

METHODOLOGY AND EXPERIMENTAL DESIGN

In this section, the researcher articulates the methodology and methods, settings and participants, and procedures.

Methodology and Methods

In this study, the UDL framework was guided as a roadmap. There are three main principles integral to the UDL framework, which are (1) multiple means of engagement, (2) multiple means of representation, and (3) multiple means of action and expression. In the field of the ECE industry, ECE professionals have been increasingly adopting the UDL framework to design their curriculum/program, assess instructional strategies and practices, and adjust their learning content to support all children, including children with diverse abilities (Horn et al., 2016; Rao et al., 2017; Taunton et al., 2017). However, during and post COVID-19, the implementation of the UDL framework has needed to be adjusted and redesigned

Beyond COVID-19

in its processes, especially concerning the various ways of learning, and learning environments. In this pilot project, based on the core principles of UDL that foster learning and development for each individual, and given the goal of redesigning an ECE curriculum/program in the context of the ongoing COVID-19 pandemic situation and its aftermath, the researcher explores a new UDL model – mental-health strategies based on physical activities with a multi-sensory environment approach.

A case study approach was adopted, incorporating virtual interviews and observations designed to capture dynamic conversations with, and the experiences of, research participants. The key methodological considerations are employed using the case study approach to engage in an in-depth investigation of contemporary phenomena within its real-life context (Yin, 2014). The objective of this case study is to promote a better understanding of how the pandemic and post-pandemic impact children's physical and mental health, given that children are now experiencing increased mental health and physical challenges as a result of COVID-19 and its aftermath. Traditional classrooms are gradually being replaced using blended learning methods. However, difficulties and challenges have been increasing for young children adapting to these virtual methods, especially for children who are affected by physical disabilities or other conditions. Using a case study approach, the researcher can investigate a complexity of events that connect "directly to the common reader's everyday experience and promote an understanding of complex real-life situations" (Krusenvik, 2016, p. 9). Also, qualitative case study methods can engage in an in-depth inquiry that triangulates evidence from multiple sources to capture an authentic and holistic picture.

In this study, the researcher was able to obtain vivid and thick qualitative data from interviews with teachers, parents, management teams, a principal, and a business owner, as well as from teachers' journals, teaching reports, lesson plans, weekly meeting records, and teaching training reports. Also, data on instructional and learning activities gathered from classroom observations and implementation meetings have been collected. Through a series of meetings, interviews, teaching training, and document reviews, the challenges impacting the delivery of the IMPM model at the kindergarten in question were identified. This enabled the researcher to combine multiple sources of data to address the research questions and achieve a better understanding of this complicated case.

Settings and Participants

In order to maintain the anonymity of this pilot case study, the ECE center, and the research participants, the researcher only provides general contextual information that appropriately represents the settings in which the research took place. The pilot case study was conducted in a daycare center in British Columbia, Canada's

Beyond COVID-19

westernmost province, and the ECE business owner of this daycare center leads multiple educational business projects in Canada. The researcher chose one of their daycare centers to conduct a pilot study and further investigate other ones as this is an ongoing research project. In the next paragraphs and section, the author refers to this daycare center as Kindergarten C to distinguish it from other kindergartens or general use of the word kindergarten.

Ten adult participants have been involved in interviews, including two teachers, one teacher leader, one principal, one CEO, one owner of the ECE business, three parents from Kindergarten C, and one community member from the school district. Two classes of eight children from ages three to six have been observed virtually. These children include two individuals who speak English as an additional language and one child with Childhood Apraxia of Speech (CAS). A friendly rapport was purposefully established throughout the training sessions, interviews, and observations to enable the researcher to fully and authentically understand all research participants' perspective.

This pilot project was conducted following all the ethical requirements and policies of the university where the researcher is employed, those of the provincial health officer, and the requirements and guidance provided by WorkSafeBC. Research consent forms from children's parents, teachers, the CEO, business owner, and the community member were obtained. To ensure confidentiality, the names of the children and the ten adult participants were changed to pseudonyms in the report, such as: Kid#1, Kid#2, Kid#3..., and Kid#8 (they are also referred to as K1, K2, K3..., and K8 in the coding process) and Participant#1, Participant#2, Participant#3..., and Participant#10 (also referred to as P1, P2, P3..., and P10 in the coding process). No personal data or details that could be linked to a particular research participant were retained and all such data was redacted out of the transcripts. While writing the research report, the CEO, one owner of the ECE business, teachers, the teacher leader, and the community members were provided with information on the research results.

Procedures

There are five procedures employed within the research methods adopted, including meetings, interviews, model training sessions, documentations, and classroom observations. All virtual meetings, model training sessions, and interviews have used the organizationally licensed ZOOM platform to audio- and video-record the meetings with the participants' consent. The sessions of virtual classroom observations were recorded digitally and are summarized, in anonymous format, in the final research report. The researcher also took handwritten notes during meetings, interviews, model training sessions, and classroom observations. Participants'

Beyond COVID-19

comments have remained anonymous, and all documentation will be kept strictly confidential. All data files are securely stored on a password-protected computer, and all data analysis documentation, including any software use during the data analysis, were also password secured. All raw data collected for this pilot study was destroyed after the researcher finished the data analysis process.

1. **Meetings:** The researcher/author initially interviewed both the CEO and business owner of Kindergarten C to discuss the project and propose interview questions, to schedule teacher training and interviews, and to create a timeline for classroom observations. Each interview took around 30 minutes.
2. **Interviews**: In total, eight participants attended one-on-one interviews. Two teachers, one teacher leader, one principal from Kindergarten C, one community member from the school district, and three parents were separately interviewed for 30 to 40 minutes each. Three parents included one mother of a child who spoke English as an additional language and one father whose child has Childhood Apraxia of Speech (CAS). Besides participating in this study, the three parents also actively attended parents' meetings and community activities regularly before the COVID-19 pandemic.

Interviews were transcribed verbatim, and each participant was reviewed this document, which was standard practice in terms of the researcher communicating with these individuals in the past. The researcher has known the principal for six years and the other teachers for two to three years through the business owner, and was very familiar with their literacy level, vocabulary, and understanding of social norms in this particular kindergarten context. The researcher also sent the transcripts to the participants for triangulation.

3. **Training Sessions**: The researcher provided four virtual training sessions related to the IMPM model to the nine research participants including two teachers, one teacher leader, one principal, the CEO, the owner of the ECE business from Kindergarten C, and three parents. The training sessions did not exceed one hour each, and the researcher offered an open discussion forum at the end of each training session to see if participants had questions.
4. **Documentations**: (1) The teachers, teacher leader, and principal shared their teaching journals, teaching reports, and lesson plans. (2) Both the CEO and the owner of Kindergarten C provided their weekly meeting records and teaching training reports.
5. **Observations**: Ten sessions of virtual classroom observations, each 10 to 15 minutes, were conducted for this project. Kindergarten C currently runs two programs, that appeared suitable for observation, which are an IT Program (in-

Beyond COVID-19

fants and toddlers from six months to three years old) and a Creative Program (children with three to five years old). After discussion with the business owner and program head, the researcher decided to have two classes of eight children from ages three to six participate virtually in this pilot study. These children included two individuals who spoke English as an additional language and one child with Childhood Apraxia of Speech (CAS).

Limitations of the process

This chapter presented an initial study focusing on applying this new UDL model, but it has several limitations. For instance, the challenging timeframe due to the COVID-19 situation created hurdles. Beyond the provincial safety guidelines and university regulations for doing research that have had to be followed, in order to reduce the burden on research participants as much as possible during these challenging times, the researcher has tried their best to accommodate participants' schedules. As a result, the research plans often needed to change, and were many times interrupted by increased COVID-19 cases in the region where Kindergarten C is located. In addition, the classroom observations could not be conducted in-person, and some engagements with children's family had to be cancelled due to the provincial protocols.

DATA ANALYSIS

In this section, the author will examine how qualitative data was analyzed thematically using deductive approaches; the study also employed an inductive analysis to capture additional themes as they arose out of the data. To ensure rigor in the analysis, NVivo software (the version of NVivo 12 Plus) was utilized as a tool for qualitative data analysis. The researcher used the functions of Text Search to quickly find the required keyword paragraphs, a powerful drawing function which can draw concept maps, and a cluster analysis feature, which makes qualitative research analysis more accurate and faster. The thematic analysis used for this project included six phases: familiarizing oneself with the data; generating initial codes; searching for themes; reviewing themes; defining and naming themes; and producing the report.

To ensure the rigor of the collected data, the researcher asked participants to certify the written transcripts reproduced what they had expressed to confirm the accuracy of each participant's comments and to guard against the researcher's bias. In addition, a triangulation method was used in this qualitative data analysis that entailed drawing from multiple data sources to more comprehensively understand this pilot study's results.

Meetings

The business owner introduced their kindergarten's educational philosophy, the principles of their curriculum, their ECE programs, the core element of their daily teaching and learning routine, and the background of each employee; there was also a discussion with the researcher regarding the pilot project. The CEO provided detailed information on each ECE operational program and discussed with the researcher the issue of how they could improve their service both during and after the pandemic.

Interviews

From the thematic analysis, four major themes and their sub-themes emerged from the findings (Table 1): challenges and barriers to adoption, accommodating the model, issues with technologies, and collaborations and partnerships.

Table 1. Results of themes, sub-themes, sample quotations from participants, and the code totals

Themes	Subthemes	Sample quotations	Nos of occurrences of the code
Challenges and barriers to adoption	There was limited time to transition from the old models to the new UDL model	P2: "Our teachers are super busy since the pandemic started because we needed to double clean our facilities and make sure about safety issues. To ask them to adopt a new UDL model seems a challenge to us since it requires a transitional timeframe and my colleagues need to understand the model and its implementation." P7: "There are so many barriers now…for example, we need to have more time to modify the learning content for both teachers and children."	41
	Teachers have limited knowledge about how to Integrate the new UDL model	P1: "We used the Reggio Emilia approach, but it seems we need to have specific knowledge to understand the new UDL model." P3: "The BC Early Learning Framework and Gordon Neufeld's concept inspired my daily routines…it may change our daily routines if we started a new UDL model…that means we need to have new knowledge in order to overcome these challenges."	

continued on following page

Beyond COVID-19

Table 1. Continued

Themes	Subthemes	Sample quotations	Nos of occurrences of the code
	There are limited resources to facilitate the adoption of the new UDL model	P4: "There are so many barriers now…for example, we do not have enough resources in place right now." P5: "I am deeply concerned that there are not enough resources to fully accommodate this new UDL model…teachers may not be able to fully adopt this new model."	
Accommodating the model	To have the same learning goals and learning expectations	P1: "It is important to have the same goals for accommodating the new model." P6: "…what's critical to accommodating a new UDL model is to have the same goals." P8: "Our expectation is to have the same goals as teachers and parents do and hope this new model can help all children's learning needs."	37
	To have instructional strategies	P2: "I think to accommodate and best practice the new UDL model is to have instructional strategies; this means our teaching methods need to be flexible." P5: "…adjusting our current model to accommodate the new model needs to focus on teacher's instructional strategies through consistently monitoring the children's learning progress."	
	A variety of material to support the integration of UDL	P3: "We cannot only use simple and boring learning materials…we need to offer more options for our children" P7: "…the new media and APPs use in learning content would be a great idea."	
	To have multiple forms of assessment for all children	P4: "…accurately measuring children's knowledge, skills, and engagement seems an important part of accommodating the new model." P6: "I particularly care about having multiple assessments for all children, especially children with special needs…"	
Issues with technologies	Lack of experience using technologies	P2: "Since I have a background in CALL [computer-assisted language learning] and my husband works in the IT [Information Technology] industry, I know how to use these APPs… but other teachers do not have that experience, and may find it difficult to understand the process." P6: "I think teachers would have barriers to integrating new technologies into the new model."	30

continued on following page

Table 1. Continued

Themes	Subthemes	Sample quotations	Nos of occurrences of the code
	Lack of accessibility to technologies	P5: "I am just worried about the accessibility of using technologies…" P8: "…we work together as a team, but maybe there is an issue with accessibility in using technologies…"	
Collaborations and partnerships	Using a team-based approach	P1: "We support healthy developmental progress in every child with a team-based approach, so the new UDL model lines up with our core elements of a daily routine." P6: "…to build and manage healthy and meaningful relationships requires having a team-based approach."	15
	Partnerships with parents and communities	P7: "We are all social beings, it is vital for our kids to not only socialize with their peers and teachers, but also engage with communities." P8: "Interacting with a variety of groups, children need to adapt to different environments …and to connect with communities…"	

Training sessions

During the training sessions, the researcher shared with the participants the key characteristics of UDL framework used in this study and new UDL model – an interactive multisensory physical movements (IMPM) model. Open discussions offered opportunities for participants to ask questions in relation to various teaching and learning examples that applied UDL principles and the characteristics of the new model. It allowed participants to compare it to their older models and supported educators wanting to know how to adapt the new model to their current daily teaching context. The data from these four training sessions captured the participants' various levels of understanding of the concept of the new ECE UDL framework, how they planned to use this model for building and managing healthy and meaningful relationships as a team to promote children's mental and physical health, and how they could accommodate children with different needs. The actual training content included:

- Session 1 – Introduction to the UDL framework and the IMPM model. The researcher provided digital material as foundation for an introduction to the UDL framework and the IMPM model and sought to support the participants as they transitioned from their current learning and teaching practices to the new model; the session also sought to compensate for shortcomings in their initial preparation. The researcher also led participants through the profes-

Beyond COVID-19

sional handbook and the parents' guidebook. A sample lesson plan, together with a learning materials list, provided guidance regarding the variety of interventions available and offered information about agencies available to support professionals and parents.

- Section 2 – This incorporated the IMPM model utilizing the UDL framework. The section focused on teaching and learning strategies associated with the UDL framework and supported teachers' learning within their classroom contexts and family situations. The growing diversity of learners and how to actively use the IMPM model to support students were illustrated with video case studies in this session, and open discussions followed. Participants had the opportunity to get hands-on experience designing and practicing new teaching strategies using the IMPM model. They needed to prepare, using real examples of lesson plans, teaching, and learning instructions for the next session.

- Section 3 – This session focused on expert and peer support. The researcher invited two experts in the field of early childhood education and children's mental health to share their experiences. Participants presented their teaching and learning design/goals, lesson plans, sample learning materials, and they had a chance to review peer teaching and learning journals. Group discussions provided participants with an opportunity to see what good practices look like and implement the new IMPM model in their classroom and homes. An example of this was assisting children of different abilities achieve learning goals through a variety of technical aids. When printed text materials become an obstacle to some children's learning, these students can use digital media, such as digital text, digital images, and digital multimedia. These digital audio and video formats are extremely helpful, and children can use digital media to demonstrate what they have learned in a way that suits their personalities. In these group discussions, the researcher used an arts-based learning approach to support the participants' learning process and visual thinking strategies.

- Section 4 – This session offered opportunities for feedback and reflection. Participants received feedback from experts and their peers and made changes to their teaching and learning methods. The researcher created a safe learning circle that allowed participants to freely express their feedback and reflections. Multiple forms of feedback and reflection were used in this section, such as: written notes, oral comments, using the whiteboard, music, dancing, rhythmic gymnastics, and animation. The compatibility of UDL with other teaching practices deserves further discussion and was examined here as a topic. The session also explored how to remain up to date with teaching meth-

Documentations

The teachers, teacher leader, and principal shared their teaching journals, teaching reports, and lesson plans. Each day, the ECE licensed teachers and assistant teacher observed the children's play and recorded it in their teaching journals. All teachers created an electronic report each week and uploaded it in their Kindergarten C School Information System with their own separate passwords. Every Monday, the teacher leader held a weekly meeting to share lesson plans and discuss them with each team.

The CEO and the owner of the Kindergarten C provided their weekly meeting records and teaching training reports. The CEO and/or the business owner hold weekly meetings with teachers, and they have teaching training sessions on Fridays when children have nap time. One of programs is not open on Fridays, and thus teachers take turns attending professional development courses.

Observations

Observation enabled the direct investigation of what was happening in the classroom and allowed the researcher to record the participants' physical activity and behaviors (Graham et al., 2021). The researcher observed how the new UDL model was being applied in the children's classroom in line with the three UDL principles: (1) multiple means of engagement, (2) multiple means of representation, and (3) multiple means of action and expression. For example, the researcher recorded how often each child engaged in their role play activities by observing their verbal and non-verbal behaviors. In addition, the research explored the contextual and environmental characteristics present in play areas, such as how teachers equipped the play areas with multimedia and how teachers organized individual and group activities. These findings helped the researcher understand the effect of the delivery of the new UDL model; these observations also allowed the researcher to facilitate the exploration of the mental and physical development of both mainstream children and children with diverse abilities; they also examined what factors might influence the future development of interventions related to children's mental and physical well-bring.

Video clips from ten sessions of classroom observations captured the children's verbal and non-verbal behaviors and each class lasted approximately 10 to 15 minutes. Children of various groups and from three to six years of age, participated in this pilot study. The researcher referred to each child as K1, K2, K3..., and K8 in the coding process and each classroom activity was coded in relation to the total

Beyond COVID-19

number of observations. Raw data was processed in Microsoft Excel spreadsheets to produce a number for each classroom activity and the analysis focused on targeted content. The targeted content shifted from a wide to a narrow perspective and focused on particular details of each participant, as Merriam (1988) suggests; therefore, the researcher concentrated on each child's activities – how they interacted with teachers and peers, how children used vocabulary and key words in the conversation content, how their body moved with activities, how they used nonverbal expressions and gestures, and more.

RESULTS AND DISCUSSION

Based on the primary research question of this study: "In what ways might a new ECE innovative UDL model – IMPM – contribute to the mental and physical development of both mainstream children and children with special needs?", in this section, the researcher will present the data gathered from all methods and tools, and the discussion will be based on the four sub-questions.

Accessibility

The issue of accessibility has a major impact on the delivery of the new UDL model, given its team-based approach for establishing primary care in homes, kindergartens, and daycare centers. The integration of the IMPM model can be achieved through UDL approaches, that is by providing a variety of ways to present information, to allow children to express themselves, and to participate in the learning.

Based on the data extracted from interviews with both the CEO and business owner of Kindergarten C, it appears that the UDL principles line up with their kindergarten's goals of learning and teaching and that the new UDL model would help their children reach their individual potentials and would nurture them physically and psychologically. However, there were many challenges and hurdles encountered during the COVID-19 pandemic. First, COVID-19 resulted in schools being shut down from time to time, as the CEO indicated; he acted as a media point of contact to deal with these logistic issues. On the one hand, the kindergarten's operational system needed to follow provincial health and safety rules, and all children, parents, and staff faced further challenges when school closed. On the other hand, teachers had been trying to find useful resources for parents and children on the government website (Coronavirus disease COVID-19, 2022), as the CEO, Participant#1, Participant#5, and Participant#8 emphasized during their interview. "Anytime any children, parents, or staff in our kindergarten appeared to have COVID-19 symptoms and/or had a positive test result for COVID-19, we need to close our center and children will be learning from home", Participant#4 pointed out.

Second, when Kindergarten C closed at the beginning of the COVID-19 pandemic, all children needed to stay at home and had had to adapt to new types of learning. Parents and children became mentally fatigued, and teaching and learning changed dramatically. While remote learning can be structured to provide children with flexible learning content and parents may provide assistance, issues of accessibility have impacted the e-learning experience, as the majority of participants expressed during interviews and training sessions.

Third, given the data extracted from the teaching journals and teaching reports, it is apparent that some families have been struggling with learning environments. Participant#8 pointed out that "interacting with a variety of groups, children need to adapt to different environments…and to connect with communities…". The learning space and learning environment always affect children's learning experience, as a number of studies and reports have illustrated (Arnou et al., 2020; Khlaif, & Salha, 2020; Zhao et al., 2021). This issue can be identified in teachers' lesson plans and in their weekly meeting reports. Participant#5 stated that families could not access the internet or had trouble accessing the internet, and thus it was hard for them to receive digital learning material. As aftermath of the COVID-19 pandemic continues to impact children's mental health, parents play a huge role in supporting their children's mental well-being. To overcome this problem, the researcher provided a parent's guidebook to families during the training sessions, including hands-on teaching and learning materials for all children and containing a significant emphasis on designing children's physical learning space for their body movements. It has to be noted that the role of parent and family engagement is key to the development of this new UDL model; therefore, the parent's guidebook covers the challenges that a variety of parents faced while assisting children learning remotely and provides strategies to help children cope with the changes resulting from the COVID-19 pandemic and its aftermath. The IMPM model not only focuses on helping children develop their social and emotional skills, but also helps parents find resources for themselves in relation to taking care of their own mental health.

Design of Curriculum/Lesson Plans

UDL is essentially a new curriculum design framework guided by the organizational paradigm in special education research at the Center for Applied Special Technologies (CAST, 2022). Within this paradigm, students' learning challenges or disabilities are due to problems in the interaction between the learner and the curriculum model(s); they cannot simply be blamed on the inherent inabilities of the learner, as participants discussed in the training sessions. Participants compared the

Beyond COVID-19

traditional curriculum/lesson plan designs and their educational practice with the new UDL model. These redesigned classroom practices focused on a flexible approach to children's needs and interests and promoted the integration of diverse learners into the curriculum, not merely changes in teaching methods. Parents demonstrated how the sample lesson plans from the new UDL model could be applied at home and discussed the strengths and challenges they faced during the training sessions.

This point is also confirmed by the researcher's observational data. The new UDL model changed past practice, adjusted the current curriculum model, and filled learning gaps; it emphasizes that the curriculum should be changed according to children's needs and characteristics, rather than requiring that children adapt to a rigid curriculum. Teachers must be forward-looking, given the current situation, and analyze how they can adjust the curriculum/ lesson plans. Participant#3 described multiple situations that happened in their past teaching and suggested that difficulties that students might encounter should be reduced or eliminated from course design, rather than adjustments to students and courses be made after students encounter obstacles. The idea is to be proactive, not reactive. For example, in one of the observation sessions, teachers (one ECE licensed teacher and one licensed teacher assistant) adjusted the children's dancing class, which is part of the physical movement class, according to children's interests. Due to the rainy season, children brought umbrellas to Kindergarten C, but they wanted to make their own fun umbrellas during the morning circle 'walk and talk'. Therefore, teachers encouraged children to make umbrellas using different materials. The children's body movement class was adjusted to have the children listen to the sound of rain on the dancing floor, feel the vibration of raindrops, see the rainfall on the wall (applications of holography with analog rainfall), think about what they experienced and talk about how they felt in the rain that morning with their peers; then groups danced in the "rain" with their DIY umbrellas. During the activity, teachers repeatedly and clearly pronounced the new vocabulary for all children and paid special attention- but in natural ways, to the two individuals who spoke English as an additional language and to the one child with Childhood Apraxia of Speech (CAS).

Most parents and teachers mentioned in their interviews having an interest in understanding how to manage the long-term effects of the pandemic on children's mental health. In addition, participants in the training sessions had a chance to discuss how to cope with mental health during the pandemic, as well as study this topic in the parent guidebook and professional handbook. The IMPM model, especially, added the term and conditions of mental health and how to support families' well-being. Most teachers liked the professional handbook units on "the COVID-19 pandemic and mental health", "what is stress, anxiety, depression, and other common mental health terms", "how to support your child's mental and physical health", and "how to help your child process loss and grief during the COVID-19 pandemic".

Beyond COVID-19

The UDL framework provides guidance to create a flexible curriculum and teaching environments; the new UDL model uses technology to enable all children, including children with different needs, to maximize their potential. This kind of curriculum allows teachers to choose what information should be presented in the classroom and how to present information according to the children's needs and preferences, their physical, mental, and development characteristics, and their knowledge background.

Combining the New UDL Model With Technology

Technological learning and advanced teaching methods allow alternate approaches to one-size-fits-all conventional educational practices. The UDL framework features developments in education technology and promotes innovational learning and teaching methods using digital materials; many studies have explored this (Harris et al., 2018; Liu et al., 2017; Parette & Blum, 2015; Shambaugh & Floyd, 2018). After the COVID-19 pandemic started, the issue of technology became a critical topic in teaching and learning (Dickinson & Gronseth, 2020; Havens, 2020; Leonardo & Cha, 2021; Shores, 2021; Smith, 2020; Rogers, & Gronseth, 2021).

The availability of technology within remote learning at home and parents' use of technology to enhance their children's learning process became common concerns during the interviews, meetings, and training sessions. One of the teaching journals listed ways of communicating with parents, such as posting information in the Kindergarten C School Information System, which both teachers and parents can access; the teacher in question shared her thoughts and inspired parents to understand new ways of teaching during the pandemic. Since most parents felt insecure about using their group Facebook account, they started using the Kindergarten C School Information System to post their child/children's pictures, daily activities, and encouraged feedback, questions, and other comments. Participant#2 had voluntarily been managing the Kindergarten C School Information System, together with the CEO, after the pandemic started. Before the pandemic, only the CEO managed this platform, whereas nowadays, they are required to create digital task calendars for both teachers and parents, send reminders or alerts for events, and manage voice messages from the phone networks to improve Kindergarten C's everyday operational system. During the transitional period, when starting to use the new UDL model, teachers began using video-based instructions, visual teaching aids, audio messages to parents, google drive functions, and various other meeting applications to enhance communication.

Beyond COVID-19

Since I have background in CALL [computer-assisted language learning] and my husband works in the IT [Information Technology] industry, I know how to use these APPs... but other teachers do not have this experience and may find it difficult to understand the process (Participant#2).

Participant#4 also echoed this point during the interview: "we do lack experience using technologies, but using technology would benefit our teaching and enhance children's learning experience". Especially when it comes to children with diverse abilities, learning is combined with technology to present content that they are interested in and suits their physical and mental characteristics. One example of this, extracted from the observation data, was an instance where teachers hung a color-changing curtain that used sensory fiber optics, which was also a tactile experience for children as there is no electricity in fiber optics, only light; therefore, these curtains were safe to touch and hold. This practice is used to develop children's cause and effect skills, and their color recognition skills. An interactive dialogue between children and teacher occurred when they were engaged in a role play session and children easily and organically expressed their feelings. In 98% of teaching reports, the teachers validated the fact that employing technology in their classroom had benefits for the children's learning experience.

Goals and Methods of Assessment

The goal of the new UDL model is to provide all children with an appropriate level of challenge and difficulty reflecting the knowledge and skills that all children strive to learn. According to the results of a brain science study, "educators and learners need to be aware of the intended learning goals so that they can begin to build connections, connect to background knowledge, and practice for expertise" (CAST, 2018, p2).

Scholars believe that teachers advocating for UDL need to recognize the purpose of different learning goals, choose their course content, and determine teaching and assessment methods accordingly (Cook & Rao, 2018; Courey et al., 2013; Evans, Williams et al., 2010; Hall et al., 2015; Rose et al., 2018; Smith et al., 2019). Participant#1 agreed with this statement and said, "it is important to have the different learning goals for accommodating the new model." She elaborated the following point: "...different children may have different learning goals, as their teacher, our goal is to personalize the learning content as much as possible." Participant#5 added, "...adjusting our current model to accommodate the new model needs to focus on teachers' instructional strategies through consistently monitoring children's learning progress."

Beyond COVID-19

The goal of the new UDL model is to provide students with a variety of learning methods, so that students can choose the method that suits them according to their personal learning abilities and preferences, rather than restrict students to a certain method. One of the teaching reports suggested that the curriculum should reflect the principle of differentiation from the beginning of its design, and the obstacles and that difficulties that children may encounter in learning must be considered before teaching occurs. Therefore, to apply a new UDL model in home-based learning and/or daycare centers setting, Participant#3 emphasized that course/learning goals, methods, and assessments should be diverse and adaptable. To have multiple assessments for all children, Participant#4 noted: "…being concerned with accurately measuring children's knowledge, skills, and engagement seems an important part of accommodating the new model".

Participant#6 conveyed the following statement: "I particularly care about having multiple assessments for all children, especially children with special needs…". There are two children with an impairment in Kindergarten C, and they both need to have opportunities to engage in social activities; as Participant#7 said: "We are all social beings, it is vital for our kids to not only socialize with their peers and teachers, but also engage with communities." Indeed, in a team-based approach for establishing primary care homes/kindergartens/daycare centers, parents and communities are all involved in the children's learning process. The IMPM model covers general principles in the assessment of children's different learning goals and particularly focuses on the context of evaluation regarding an understanding and grasp of children's physical development and mental health.

RECOMMENDATIONS

The results of this pilot study suggest important implications for future research on implementing UDL in the field of early childhood education as a framework for guiding the design of inclusive learning environments using a team-based approach. Specifically, implementing this new UDL model to enhance children's engagement involves a team-based approach based on observing children's problem-solving ability, psychological characteristics, and progress made in different tasks/activities. This teamwork approach promotes common growth with children. Especially during these challenging times, given the pandemic and its aftermath, in addition to parental participation in the learning circle, an indispensable part of this circle, now that the community is fully opened up again, will be the activities of parents and children participating in the community. Such a comprehensive method will serve as an iterative process, which will provide a basis for teachers to choose and use

Beyond COVID-19

different teaching methods to transmit and display the knowledge and information included in the teaching materials.

CONCLUSION

In this pilot study, the researcher detailed the implementation of an innovative UDL model – interactive multi-sensory physical movements (IMPM) – which was implemented in a kindergarten in Canada. The focus of this study was to adopt the UDL framework and investigate how to implement this new UDL model in a way that will meet children's needs and result in an optimal learning experience both during and beyond the COVID-19 pandemic. Using multiple data sources from a series of meetings, one-on-one interviews, model training sessions, various documentations, and classroom observations, this project aimed to comprehensively (i) explore the context affecting the delivery of the IMPM model given its team-based approach for establishing primary care homes/kindergartens/daycare centers; ii) explore, as this pilot project emerges from a team-based process, the implementation of best practices to enhance children's engagement, as a shared new UDL model implementation goal that aligned with the children needs and the interests of Kindergarten C; (iii) share with parents a parent's guidebook and sample lesson plans/activities for home-based learning, as part of the new UDL model, to help them understand how the key concepts behind the new ECE UDL framework better support children's physical and mental needs; and(4) explore if parents exhibited positive attitudes toward using this new UDL model to address children's needs, particularly those of children with diverse abilities. Overall, based on the initial implementation process in this given context, several opportunities and challenges emerged with respect to applying the new UDL model to guide the design of engaging learning environments for mainstream children and children of diverse abilities.

As the author mentioned in the section on "Research Gaps", that there is no simple solution to fix long-standing issues regarding children and their families facing more challenges during and after the pandemic. This study highlighted how to make incremental improvements in children's mental and physical health through a new UDL model making accessibility the goal, that is by providing a variety of methods of information presentation, expression, and participation in curriculum design, children with different backgrounds, learning styles, and abilities, as well as children with various types of disabilities- can truly obtain and understand the curriculum. The IMPM model advocates the use of embedded and dynamic assessment; assessment is built into the usual learning, rather than be used as stand-alone summative assessment. This can reduce students' anxiety and fear of assessment and promote students' active participation in assessment. Especially for children

211

Beyond COVID-19

with mental health issues, teachers should provide a variety of selective and flexible learning and teaching methods based on their mental health status.

After this initial study, the researcher will continue investigating more case studies because this research is an evidence-based ongoing interdisciplinary study that highlights this new model with the aim of achieving long term benefits for children, parents, and ECE professionals. This research will also benefit the international ECE industry, scholars, researchers, and informed policy makers.

ACKNOWLEDGMENT

The author gratefully acknowledges the financial support of Mitacs, the Government of Canada, the Province of British Columbia, and partner organizations.

REFERENCES

Aktay, A., Bavadekar, S., Cossoul, G., Davis, J., Desfontaines, D., Fabrikant, A., Gabrilovich, E., Gadepalli, K., Gipson, B., Guevara, B., Kamath, C., Kansal, M., Lange, A., Mandayam, C., Oplinger, A., Pluntke, C., Roessler, T., Schlosberg, A., Shekel, T., . . . Wilson, R. J. (2020). *Google COVID-19 community mobility reports: Anonymization process description* (version 1.1). https://arxiv.org/abs/2004.04145

Amado-Alonso, D., León-del-Barco, B., Mendo-Lázaro, S., Sánchez-Miguel, P. A., & Iglesias Gallego, D. (2019). Emotional intelligence and the practice of organized physical-sport activity in children. *Sustainability (Basel)*, 11(6), 1615. 10.3390/su11061615

Arnou, C., Cornelis, G., Jan Heymans, P., Howard, S. K., Leemans, G., Nuyens, I., Tondeur, J., Vaesen, J., Van Den Driessche, M., Elen, J., & Valcke, M. (2020). *COVID-19 and educational spaces: Creating a powerful and social inclusive learning environment at home.* https://www.academia.edu/download/63264421/20200507_EN _create_a_learning_environment_at_home20200510-115155-1l3v4pe.pdf

Basham, J. D., & Blackorby, J. (2020). UDL next: The future of the framework. In Lowrey, K. A. (Ed.), *Critical issues in universal design for learning*. Knowledge by Design.

Basham, J. D., Blackorby, J., & Marino, M. T. (2020). Opportunity in crisis: The role of Universal Design for Learning in educational redesign. *Learning Disabilities (Weston, Mass.)*, 18(1), 71–91.

Canadian Institute for Health Information. (2022). *Child and youth mental health in Canada — Infographic*. https://www.cihi.ca/en/child-and-youth-mental-health -in-canada-infographic

Carver, L., & Rowe, A. (2021). Students with disabilities and online learning in a pandemic. *Interdisciplinary Insights: The Journal of Saint Leo University's College of Education and Social Services*, 3(1), 59–73.

CAST. (2018). *UDL and the learning brain*. CAST Publishing. https://www.cast .org/our-work/publications/2018/udl-learning-brain-neuroscience.html

CAST. (2022). *The Universal Design for Learning guidelines.*https://udlguidelines.cast.org/

Coley, R. L., Lynch, A. D., & Kull, M. (2015). Early exposure to environmental chaos and children's physical and mental health. *Early Childhood Research Quarterly*, 32, 94–104. 10.1016/j.ecresq.2015.03.00125844016

Cook, S. C., & Rao, K. (2018). Systematically applying UDL to effective practices for students with learning disabilities. *Learning Disability Quarterly*, 41(3), 179–191. 10.1177/0731948717749936

Coronavirus disease (COVID-19). (2022). *COVID-19 resources for parents and children.* https://www.canada.ca/en/public-health/services/diseases/coronavirus-disease-covid-19/resources-parents-children.html

Courey, S. J., Tappe, P., Siker, J., & LePage, P. (2013). Improved lesson planning with universal design for learning (UDL). *Teacher Education and Special Education*, 36(1), 7–27. 10.1177/0888406412446178

Crosby, C., & Aguilar, F. (2022). Navigating the Abyss: Early childhood educator perspectives on the impact of remote learning during a 21st century pandemic. In *Handbook of Research on Adapting Remote Learning Practices for Early Childhood and Elementary School Classrooms* (pp. 352-357). IGI Global.

Dalton, L., Rapa, E., & Stein, A. (2020). Protecting the psychological health of children through effective communication about COVID-19. *The Lancet. Child & Adolescent Health*, 4(5), 346–347. 10.1016/S2352-4642(20)30097-332243784

Dickinson, K. J., & Gronseth, S. L. (2020). Application of universal design for learning (UDL) principles to surgical education during the COVID-19 pandemic. *Journal of Surgical Education*, 77(5), 1008–1012. 10.1016/j.jsurg.2020.06.00532576451

Evans, C., Williams, J. B., King, L., & Metcalf, D. (2010). Modeling, guided instruction, and application of UDL in a rural special education teacher preparation program. *Rural Special Education Quarterly*, 29(4), 41–48. 10.1177/875687051002900409

Frumos, L. (2020). Inclusive education in remote instruction with universal design for learning. *Revista Românească pentru Educație Multidimensională, 12*(2supl1), 138-142.

Golberstein, E., Wen, H., & Miller, B. F. (2020). Coronavirus disease 2019 (COVID-19) and mental health for children and adolescents. *JAMA Pediatrics*, 174(9), 819–820. 10.1001/jamapediatrics.2020.145632286618

Graham, M., Wright, M., Azevedo, L. B., Macpherson, T., Jones, D., & Innerd, A. (2021). The school playground environment as a driver of primary school children's physical activity behaviour: A direct observation case study. *Journal of Sports Sciences*, 39(20), 2266–2278. 10.1080/02640414.2021.192842334080956

Hall, T. E., Cohen, N., Vue, G., & Ganley, P. (2015). Addressing learning disabilities with UDL and technology: Strategic reader. *Learning Disability Quarterly*, 38(2), 72–83. 10.1177/0731948714544375

Harris, L., Yearta, L., & Chapman, H. (2018). The intersection of the UDL and TPACK frameworks: An investigation into teacher candidates' use of technology during internship. In *Society for Information Technology & Teacher Education International Conference* (pp. 2175-2180). Association for the Advancement of Computing in Education (AACE).

Havens, G. (2020). Universal design in the age of COVID-19. *Planning for Higher Education*, 48(4), 14–24.

Hawke, L. D., Barbic, S. P., Voineskos, A., Szatmari, P., Cleverley, K., Hayes, E., Relihan, J., Daley, M., Courtney, D., Cheung, A., Darnay, K., & Henderson, J. L. (2020). Impacts of COVID-19 on youth mental health, Substance Use, and well-being: A rapid survey of clinical and community samples: Répercussions de la COVID-19 sur la santé mentale, l'utilisation de substances et le bien-être des adolescents: Un sondage rapide d'échantillons cliniques et communautaires. *Canadian Journal of Psychiatry*, 65(10), 701–709. 10.1177/0706743720940562232662303

Horn, E. M., Palmer, S. B., Butera, G. D., & Lieber, J. (2016). *Six steps to inclusive preschool curriculum: A UDL-based framework for children's school success.* Brookes Publishing Company.

Khan, I. (2022). Remote learning in early childhood and elementary schools: An unprecedented shift. In *Handbook of Research on Adapting Remote Learning Practices for Early Childhood and Elementary School Classrooms* (pp. 482–505). IGI Global. 10.4018/978-1-7998-8405-7.ch028

Khlaif, Z. N., & Salha, S. (2020). The unanticipated educational challenges of developing countries in Covid-19 crisis: A brief report. *Interdisciplinary Journal of Virtual Learning in Medical Sciences*, 11(2), 130–134. 10.30476/IJVLMS.2020.86119.1034

Krusenvik, L. (2016). *Using case studies as a scientific method: Advantages and disadvantages.* http://www.diva-portal.org/smash/record.jsf?dswid=5853&pid=diva2%3A1054643

Kurniasari, K., Masitoh, S., & Bachri, B. S. (2021). Learning planning development of Universal Design for Learning for autism in elementary school. *Budapest International Research and Critics in Linguistics and Education (BirLE). Journal,* 4(4), 1339–1350.

Lanca, C., & Saw, S. M. (2020). The association between digital screen time and myopia: A systematic review. *Ophthalmic & Physiological Optics,* 40(2), 216–229. 10.1111/opo.1265731943280

Leonardo, M. D. F., & Cha, J. (2021). Filipino Science Teachers' Evaluation on Webinars' Alignments to Universal Design for Learning and Their Relation to Self-Efficacy amidst the Challenges of the COVID-19 Pandemic. *Asia-Pacific Science Education,* 7(2), 421–451. 10.1163/23641177-bja10035

Liu, L., Li, W., & Dini, D. (2017). Accessibility of teacher education online courses: Design and assessment with a UDL infused technology integration model. In *Society for Information Technology & Teacher Education International Conference* (pp. 2521-2528). Association for the Advancement of Computing in Education (AACE).

Mental Health Commission of Canada. (2022). *Children and Youth.* https://me ntalhealthcommission.ca/what-we-do/children-and-youth/

Merriam, S. B. (1988). *Case study research in education: a qualitative approach.* Jossey-Bass Publishers.

Morse, K. (2022). Case studies in remote learning through COVID-19: Examples from one school district. In *Handbook of Research on Adapting Remote Learning Practices for Early Childhood and Elementary School Classrooms* (pp. 1–17). IGI Global. 10.4018/978-1-7998-8405-7.ch001

Mowrey, S. C., & Cunningham, D. D. (2022). Assessing technological tools for remote learning in early childhood. In *Handbook of Research on Adapting Remote Learning Practices for Early Childhood and Elementary School Classrooms* (pp. 18–38). IGI Global. 10.4018/978-1-7998-8405-7.ch002

Parette, H. P., & Blum, C. (2015). Including all young children in the technology-supported curriculum: A UDL technology integration framework for 21st-century classrooms. *Technology and digital media in the early years: Tools for teaching and learning,* 129-149.

Rao, K., Smith, S. J., & Lowrey, K. A. (2017). UDL and intellectual disability: What do we know and where do we go? *Intellectual and Developmental Disabilities,* 55(1), 37–47. 10.1352/1934-9556-55.1.3728181886

Beyond COVID-19

Rogers, S. A., & Gronseth, S. L. (2021). Applying UDL to Online Active Learning. *The Journal of Applied Instructional Design*, 10(1). Advance online publication. 10.59668/223.3748

Rose, D. H., Robinson, K. H., Hall, T. E., Coyne, P., Jackson, R. M., Stahl, W. M., & Wilcauskas, S. L. (2018). Accurate and informative for all: Universal Design for Learning (UDL) and the future of assessment. In *Handbook of accessible instruction and testing practices* (pp. 167–180). Springer. 10.1007/978-3-319-71126-3_11

Rundle, A. G., Park, Y., Herbstman, J. B., Kinsey, E. W., & Wang, Y. C. (2020). COVID-19–Related school closings and risk of weight gain among children. *Obesity (Silver Spring, Md.)*, 28(6), 1008–1009. 10.1002/oby.2281332227671

Shambaugh, N., & Floyd, K. K. (2018). Universal design for learning (UDL) guidelines for mobile devices and technology integration in teacher education. In *Handbook of research on digital content, mobile learning, and technology integration models in teacher education* (pp. 1-21). IGI Global.

Shores, M. (2021). Using UDL to explore best practices in teaching online statistics: The impact of COVID-19 on academic learning. In *SITE Interactive Conference* (pp. 257-261). Association for the Advancement of Computing in Education (AACE).

Smith, C. (2020). Challenges and opportunities for teaching students with disabilities during the COVID-19 pandemic. *International Journal of Multidisciplinary Perspectives in Higher Education*, 5(1), 167–173. 10.32674/jimphe.v5i1.2619

Smith, S. J., Rao, K., Lowrey, K. A., Gardner, J. E., Moore, E., Coy, K., Marino, M., & Wojcik, B. (2019). Recommendations for a national research agenda in UDL: Outcomes from the UDL-IRN preconference on research. *Journal of Disability Policy Studies*, 30(3), 174–185. 10.1177/1044207319826219

Taunton, S. A., Brian, A., & True, L. (2017). Universally designed motor skill intervention for children with and without disabilities. *Journal of Developmental and Physical Disabilities*, 29(6), 941–954. 10.1007/s10882-017-9565-x

Ten Hoor, G. A., Plasqui, G., Ruiter, R. A., Kremers, S. P., Rutten, G. M., Schols, A. M., & Kok, G. (2016). A new direction in psychology and health: Resistance exercise training for obese children and adolescents. *Psychology & Health*, 31(1), 1–8. 10.1080/08870446.2015.107015826155905

Yin, R. (2014). *Case study research: design and methods* (5th ed.). Sage Publication.

Zhao, L., Hwang, W. Y., & Shih, T. K. (2021). Investigation of the physical learning environment of distance learning under COVID-19 and its influence on students' health and learning satisfaction. *International Journal of Distance Education Technologies*, 19(2), 77–98. 10.4018/IJDET.20210401.oa4

KEY TERMS AND DEFINITIONS

ECE: In the context of using this term in this research, ECE refers to early childhood education, and it is described as a crucial period of education in children's mental and physical development, from birth to five years old.

ECE Professionals: In this pilot study, the early childhood education professionals worked in the daycare centre, and they were all licensed by the Government of BC and can legally work for any childcare facilities in BC.

ECE Programs: In the context of this research, two programs offered in the daycare facility in which the pilot study was conducted. One of the programs is for children under three years of age, and the other is for children from three to five years old.

IMPM: An interactive multisensory physical movements model that can be applied in the field of early childhood education. Specifically, this model is designed to meet children's mental and physical needs by integrating designed activities into scientific instruments (applications of holography) employing look/see, hear, touch, smell, taste, feel, think, speak, and full body motions.

Kindergartens/Daycare Centres: In the province of British Columbia (BC) in Canada, there are many different types of childcare facilities providing early learning for various groups of children. In this research, the author investigated a licensed childcare facility in BC providing muti-age childcare from birth to five years old.

Learning Environments: Within the context of UDL implementation in this research, learning environments not only refers to children's physical learning space, but it also means an interactive, dynamic, and situated learning space for children with diverse learning needs.

MSE: In the context of this research, it refers to a multi-sensory environment, but it is a supported active learning environment that provides personalized learning strategies employing muti-sensory equipment.

Chapter 9
The Shifting Landscape of Digital Accessibility for Students With Visual Impairments in K–12 Schools:
Inclusion, Diversity, Equity, and Accessibility

Natalina Martiniello
https://orcid.org/0000-0002-2739-8608
School of Optometry, Université de Montréal, Canada

EXECUTIVE SUMMARY

Technologies based on universal design foster greater inclusion and proactively embed accessibility for all learners. Today, the digital workflow of students with visual impairments incorporates universally accessible tools used alone or alongside specialized assistive technologies. At the same time, opportunities remain to address persisting gaps in inclusion, diversity, equity, and accessibility within the K-12 landscape. Among these priorities, there is a need to empower educators and administrators with the tools to ensure accessibility in classroom content, embed disability allyship in change management efforts, consider access equity within change measurement outcomes, and contemplate the empowering ways that accessible digital tools can be used to deepen student engagement and diversify the curriculum. This chapter traces the shift from traditional to mainstream digital accessibility for students with visual impairments, outlining how broader issues of inclusion, diversity, equity, and accessibility can inform and advance inclusive

DOI: 10.4018/978-1-6684-4750-5.ch009

Copyright © 2024, IGI Global. Copying or distributing in print or electronic forms without written permission of IGI Global is prohibited.

learning and UDL implementation efforts.

INTRODUCTION

The digital revolution of the 21st century continues to redefine teaching and learning by pushing the boundaries of inclusive pedagogy, shifting where and how learning takes place, and changing who has a voice in the classroom. Advancements in accessible educational technologies provide students with multiple means of representation, engagement, action and expression, enabling access for students with disabilities who have traditionally remained marginalized (Rose & Meyer, 2002). With a focus on students with visual impairments, this chapter explores how accessible educational technologies can also be harnessed to enhance broader equity, diversity, and inclusion within the curriculum.

Embedded accessibility - such as text-to-speech software on mainstream classroom computers - carries important implications from a cost equity perspective, but also recognizes the natural variability that exists among all learners by not limiting accessibility features to specific end-users (Fichten et al., 2014). In the process of encouraging students to become self-empowered expert learners, access to embedded accessibility solutions provides an opportunity for all students to explore their needs and preferences, and to potentially adopt new and more effective learning approaches that they may have not previously considered (Siu & Presley, 2020).

There is a growing emphasis placed on the accessibility benefits of digital classroom tools that proactively integrate universal design principles, and this is especially evident when considering the experiences of students with visual impairments in the K-12 landscape. For students who are blind or who have low vision, the last decade has seen the proliferation of innovative accessible and inclusive educational technologies that enable greater access to information (Candela, 2006; Kamei-Hannan et al., 2017). In fact, in the not-so-distant past, many published works were entirely exclusionary to end-users unable to read print, with a vast majority of blind students relying heavily on human readers, when such services were available (Page, 1980). The development of traditional assistive technologies, now shifting towards a more proactive mainstream accessibility model, continues to significantly change the landscape for these students. Unlike traditional assistive technologies designed and marketed to meet specialized needs, mainstream access technologies integrate these features for all users from inception (Martiniello et al., 2019).

Driven by the disability civil rights movement, this acceleration towards greater digital universal accessibility has been shaped by the social model of disability, which recognizes that disabling barriers encountered by learners can often be reduced or altogether eliminated through proactive inclusive design (Shakespeare,

The Shifting Landscape of Digital Accessibility

2021). Although impairments exist, the social model underscores that disability is often socially constructed and caused by barriers found within the environment (for example, inaccessible computers and classroom documents). Therefore, a blind student who is provided with an electronic document that is inherently accessible (without needing retrofitting or adaptations) is not disabled in that instance, though they are blind. The solution lies in changing the environment to better account for the natural diversity that exists among all learners (Novak & Rose, 2016). This is an empowerment-based notion that highlights the role collectively played by all people to either eliminate or maintain disabling barriers. This stands in contrast with the traditional medical model, which defines disability as a problem that inherently exists within the student (for example, a student cannot see) (Shakespeare, 2021). From this medicalized perspective, the solution lies in focusing on the student, through the use of specialized procedures or accommodations to enable them to function more like a perceived 'norm' (Davis, 1997). Students with disabilities are therefore expected to remain flexible enough to fit within a fixed curriculum that does not change.

While greater accessibility is unquestionably one of the more evident advantages of educational technologies based on universal design, the case of students with visual impairments provides a unique lens through which we can more critically examine the impact that such tools have on achieving broader equity, diversity, and inclusion. When harnessed to their full potential, accessible digital classroom tools, alongside traditional methods, can provide blind and low vision students with empowering opportunities for digital authoring, collaboration, and connectivity that challenge traditional narratives of disability (Auxier et al., 2019; Gleason et al., 2020). Using video authoring tools, digital communities of practice, and social media platforms, users with visual impairments are dispelling myths and misconceptions, elevating advocacy efforts, and creating communities where digital citizens with disabilities support one another (Asuncion et al., 2012; Della Líbera & Jurberg, 2020). Such avenues to amplify student voice through accessible digital classroom tools bring to light historically silenced narratives in the curriculum, provide more diverse representations within classroom contexts, and enable students with lived experience to reclaim stories that may have traditionally ben told by others. In this way, accessible digital tools can empower students to become both teachers and learners, a core tenant of UDL-thinking itself (Chardin & Novak, 2020).

To instigate more sustainable and effective implementation of UDL within the K-12 landscape, there is a growing recognition that we must move beyond considerations of accessibility alone, and creatively reflect on how inclusive technologies can also fill persisting gaps in equity, diversity, and inclusion. This chapter will trace the evolution from traditional assistive technologies to mainstream accessible solutions for students with visual impairments, highlighting the implications these tools have on inclusive education and broader UDL implementation. Through an increased awareness of the power of existing technologies and a recognition of persisting gaps, educators and administrators can become powerful agents for positive change who embed disability allyship at the core of what is needed to move inclusive education forward (Abes & Zahneis, 2020).

BACKGROUND

The Population: Students With Visual Impairments

The increasing heterogeneity of students with visual impairments provides clear support for the advancement of educational paradigms and technologies that proactively integrate flexibility and multi-functionality through universal design. According to the World Health Organization (WHO), there are approximately 253 million individuals with a visual impairment worldwide, roughly 36 million of whom are considered to be blind and 217 million of whom are identified as having a moderate or significant visual impairment (Ackland et al., 2017). A majority of Global North countries have adopted a legal definition of blindness based on visual acuity (the ability to see fine detail at a distance) and visual fields (the area a person is able to see when both eyes are fully open) to determine eligibility for mandated services, including educational accommodations and access to assistive technologies (Siu & Presley, 2020). Legal blindness is defined as a central visual acuity of 20/200 or less in the better eye with best standard correction, or a visual field that subtends an angular distance no greater than 20 degrees in the better eye (Koestler, 2004).

Although visual acuity and field measures provide an important starting point for understanding visual impairment and for tracking how vision might change in a student over time, such objective measures alone provide an incomplete portrait for understanding the extent to which visually-dependent activities might create disabling barriers in the K-12 classroom. In Canada, for example, of the 756,300 individuals who self-identify as having a 'seeing disability' that limits their daily activities, only 5.8% identify as legally blind (Bizier et al., 2016). Moreover, like other disability experiences, visual impairment is often highly contextual and shaped by external factors, bringing to centre stage the influence of learning environment and format. A student may be able to read standard print in most contexts or when testing conditions are ideal, but struggle depending on glare and poor lighting, fluctuating vision due to visual fatigue or the influence of health conditions, and the nature of the reading or writing task (such as colour, contrast and the duration of the activity) (Lee, 2020b). As a common example, many students with low vision may be able to read shorter print texts (such as labels, short instructions, and hand-

The Shifting Landscape of Digital Accessibility

outs), but quickly fall behind during more sustained reading tasks that are typical of higher grade levels, such as novels, textbooks, and articles. For these reasons, the term functional vision has been advanced to describe that a student may experience functional limitations even if they do not meet the criteria for legal blindness (Corn & Erin, 2010), which poses a particular barrier for students without a documented visual impairment who are unable to request traditional classroom accommodations.

Level of vision (ranging from low vision to no vision at all) is only one example of the broad diversity that exists among students with visual impairments today. Students may have congenital visual impairments identified early in life or might acquire a visual impairment later in adolescence or beyond. Although congenital visual impairment was most common in the mid-20th century, the prevalence of acquired visual impairment is projected to at least double in Global North countries over the next three decades (Varma et al., 2016). Age of onset carries important implications for educational practice. Students who are identified as having a visual impairment early in their education often have access to earlier learning opportunities that correlate with better educational and employment outcomes. For example, while braille (a tactile reading and writing system) can be learned at any age, children who are introduced to braille early in life will often exhibit better braille reading rates and comprehension (Martiniello et al., 2021; Ryles, 1996). Evidence drawn from neuroscience shows that earlier and more frequent opportunities to meaningfully engage with non-visual modes of access also contribute to cortical plasticity, where the visual part of the brain is recruited even during non-visual tasks, such as when blind students read braille or listen to text-to-speech software (Hannan, 2006). These ample opportunities to access educational content through diverse and multiple means of representation as early as possible not only increase access to the classroom but strengthen multisensory connections and literally rewire the brain (Sadato et al., 2002).

Recognizing the diversity that is attached to age of onset also carries important social implications for learning. Students who acquire a visual impairment in upper grade levels and who were previously sighted may carry unconscious but deeply rooted stigma and misconceptions about blindness that may shape their own identities and their willingness to disclose their visual impairments to others, including fellow peers and teachers (Tuttle & Tuttle, 2004). This is especially true when blind students lack meaningful opportunities to witness positive and realistic portrayals of blind individuals in the literature, media, and other classroom content they consume.

Reflecting on portrayals of blindness in popular culture, Jernigan, an early leader from the blindness advocacy movement who was also blind himself, noted that blind characters are often depicted as symbols of pity and charity, such as the trope of the blind beggar (Jernigan, 1974). Alternatively, there is what has been coined the 'super-crip' phenomenon, where blind characters are bestowed with super-human capabilities that compensate for what is perceived to be a deficit, as in the case of Dare Devil (Barnes, 1992; Jan, 2015). As illustrated through such tropes, blind characters are seldom portrayed as individuals who study, work, parent, and live full lives alongside their sighted peers, instead demarking blindness as the underlying characteristic of who they are. More recent studies also reveal that, when surveyed, members of the general public fear life with blindness above other disabilities, including potentially life-threatening conditions such as heart disease (Bowling, 2015). In this way, students with and without visual impairments may find it difficult to imagine how it would be possible to live as fully without sight, influenced both by cultural misrepresentations and the absent voices in the curriculum. These inaccurate depictions not only shape how sighted peers, parents and teachers may come to perceive and respond to blindness, but may also lead students with invisible disabilities (such as those with low vision) to feel reluctant about using specialized assistive devices and accommodations that reveal their visual impairment to others (Martiniello et al., 2019; Shinohara & Wobbrock, 2011).

To add to these layers of diversity, students with visual impairments may experience additional disabilities that limit the effectiveness of a monolithic one-size-fits-all educational approach. Many children born prematurely, for example, may also experience motor, intellectual or other developmental delays that may remain masked or overlooked if educational difficulties are wrongly linked to visual impairment alone (Wormsley & D'Andrea, 1997). The failure to consider the holistic experiences of students with visual impairments during the traditional accommodation process may lead to the provision of ineffective learning approaches. For example, it is estimated that up to 2% of individuals worldwide have some form of Deafblindness (Jaiswal et al., 2018; Minhas et al., 2022). Students with combined vision and hearing impairments may experience disabling learning barriers if it is wrongly assumed that all students with visual impairments are first and foremost auditory learners who will benefit from text-to-speech software.

Vignette 1: Katie

Katie is a 12-year-old student who experienced a traumatic brain injury. Katie's parents and teachers have noticed that she struggles with certain visual tasks. She is not always able to identify teachers and peers in the classroom. While playing a board game in her social studies class, Katie struggled to locate her token on the board and to track the movement of others in her group. Although she used to love physical education, Katie's teacher noticed that she struggles during class volleyball. After getting hit with the ball because she did not see it coming in time, Katie is no longer interested in participating. Katie also struggles with reading when

The Shifting Landscape of Digital Accessibility

given hard copy print handouts in class. Despite these difficulties, Katie's ophthalmologist did not identify an ocular visual impairment. With the added support of a teacher of students with visual impairments (TVI) who specializes in cortical visual impairment (CVI), Katie was eventually identified as having CVI. Katie is now able to read much more easily with her iPad. Her teachers share classroom documents electronically with all students who prefer to access it this way, and Katie can adjust the colour, size, and lighting to meet her needs. She has also discovered that highlighting specific words using colours she prefers allows her to better visually focus and process what she is reading. With the support of her TVI and classroom teacher, she has also discovered that using specific colours (especially solid, saturated colours like yellow and red), helps her track and identify items around her. Since Katie sometimes takes longer to process what she is seeing, Katie's physical education teacher has set up different stations in the gymnasium so that students can choose different physical activities to play. Although Katie can't easily play ball, she has discovered new talents and interests this way.

Although CVI is now the most common form of childhood visual impairment among Global North countries, it often remains invisible, undetected or misdiagnosed (Roman-Lantzy, 2007). This is because CVI is not a problem with the eyes, but a brain-based visual impairment caused by damage along the visual pathways or visual cortex, often a result of premature birth or later traumatic brain injury. In CVI, children may have eyes that appear typical using traditional ophthalmologic assessments when there is no damage to the ocular system, but still experience a visual impairment caused by problems at the cortical level, often resulting in reduced acuity and fields, delayed visual responses, a preference for specific colours, and the inability to interpret complex visual scenes (Roman-Lantzy, 2019b). Early identification, intervention and support is critical to improve visual functioning in CVI, highlighting the importance of interdisciplinary educational teams, including educators specializing in CVI (Roman-Lantzy, 2019a). However, the example in Vignette 1 also illustrates the importance of learning environments that can remain flexible and creative from the start, providing students with diverse learning and engagement opportunities, regardless of documented impairment.

Level of vision, age of onset, the presence of additional disabilities and the role of external factors are all important indicators that highlight the diversity among students with visual impairments; however, even these examples fail to properly account for the true impact of intersectionality, including the role of sex, gender, race and ethnicity (Milian & Erin, 2001). In recent years, educational leaders with lived experiences have increasingly emphasized the need to better include disability within broader equity, diversity and inclusion efforts (Swenor & Meeks, 2019; Wu et al., 2021). Similarly, recent discussions on UDL have highlighted the need to move beyond consideration of disability alone and to recognize the role of intersectionality as a means to address systemic barriers in inclusive learning (Rose et al., 2021). The evolution of assistive technologies for learners with visual impairments provides a unique lens to understand the broader impact of digital classroom tools for elevating inclusion, diversity, equity, and accessibility in the K-12 landscape.

Supporting a Multiplicity of Access Methods

Students with visual impairments access information through regular or large print on paper, screen magnification software (that magnifies electronic information), text-to-speech software (that reads aloud electronic information on the screen), braille (a tactile reading and writing system, which can be accessed on paper or through electronic devices), or through a combination of these methods (Siu & Presley, 2020). The decision to use a specific mode of access is influenced by many factors, including level of vision and visual prognosis, but also the classroom subject and, as is the case with any other student, personal needs and preferences (Holbrook & Koenig, 1992). For example, students with low vision who read print but who have a visual condition that is expected to deteriorate over time should have early meaningful and motivating opportunities to also learn and engage with non-visual reading and writing methods, such as braille (tactile) and text-to-speech (auditory) access (Wormsley & D'Andrea, 1997). These early opportunities to meaningfully engage with multiple means of representation during classroom activities introduce students to the diverse options available to them and can strengthen motivation when a specific mode of access is limiting their potential. It also equips students with the tools they need to better prepare for their future educational careers. For example, students can discover what they prefer and what works best for them for a given classroom subject, a process which deepens their growth as expert learners who are aware of their learning needs and preferences in different contexts and who are able to communicate this to others. At a practical level, such early learning also ensures that students become more proficient users of specific non-visual methods (such as braille and screen-reading software), facilitating the transition to these non-visual methods if they are needed even more in future as level of vision changes (Siu & Presley, 2020).

Vignette 2: Emma

Emma is 19 years old and had low vision throughout elementary and high school, relying primarily on large print and screen magnification software. However, her parents also advocated for her to learn how to read and write braille from a young age, to prepare Emma for the further vision loss that was expected in the future

The Shifting Landscape of Digital Accessibility

due to the nature of her visual impairment. From the start of her schooling, Emma met with a TVI daily to develop her braille literacy skills, and also had access to braille in the classroom throughout the day. Emma's TVI also signed her up to receive books in braille through the national accessible library service, based on her interests and favourite subjects.

Emma was reluctant to use braille at first since it made her feel different from her classroom peers. This changed when Emma was encouraged to bring along a friend to one of her braille lessons. In collaboration with the school librarian, Emma's TVI and classroom teachers also ensured that a collection of braille books were made available in the school library, for Emma to independently select and for other students to explore. Emma and her TVI also prepared Valentine's Day cards in braille for her classmates to decode. Suddenly, Emma was the coolest kid in class. Although Emma primarily used print in class, she loved that she could read braille books in the dark at home, even after everyone had fallen asleep. Emma also discovered that braille worked much better for her during certain activities, such as in math and science class where visual information was more difficult to read because of the spatial layout. She also found that she could more easily access her notes during classroom presentations by using braille, without having to put the pages so close to her face while trying to read visually.

Thanks to these early experiences and the support of her TVI and classroom teachers, the transition was straightforward when Emma eventually did lose more of her vision in college. She already had access to the tools she needed to know and understood when and how to use them to best achieve her goals. Although she still could read print in some situations, Emma was grateful that she also knew braille and how to use screen-reading software as her reading load increased. Since she felt comfortable with these different methods, Emma also discovered that she studies and remembers information best when she reads it in braille but prefers to use her screen-reading software for tasks that require less concentration, like reading email.

Although they didn't learn braille, Emma's peers also grew up knowing that there are all kinds of ways people can access information since examples of braille were always naturally integrated, and that blindness is only a disability when access to these options do not exist. This would have long-lasting implications for her peers who would grow up to potentially become parents, teachers, employers, or colleagues of individuals with visual impairments like Emma, or who would one day develop a visual impairment of their own.

The above vignette is an example of how access to diverse modes of representation carries important implications for student success, but also allows all students to learn important lessons about inclusion, diversity, equity, and accessibility. Braille is an example of a mode of access that is specifically used by students with visual impairments. Over the decades, a number of accessible technologies have been introduced which also provide multimodal access to other means of representation (such as text-to-speech software) used and applied by a diverse student profile (Lee, 2020a; Siu & Presley, 2020).

Traditional Assistive Technologies Designed to Meet Specialized Needs

The earliest assistive technologies were simple hand-held and mechanical devices that provided the first non-visual methods for reading and writing and are still part of a blind student's repertoire. The slate and stylus, akin to the pen and pencil for sighted users, has undergone different iterations but was initially used by Louis Braille in the 1800s, the inventor of the braille code who himself was blind (Dixon, 2000). While developing his raised tactile system consisting of dots arranged in a 3 x 2 matrix (see Figure 1), Braille used a guide with holes corresponding to the 6-dot braille configuration (the slate) and a sharp tool (the stylus) to punch braille symbols onto paper (Cheadle, 2007). Small and inexpensive, the slate and stylus is still used today as a handy portable note-taking tool, though is increasingly being supplemented by digital options for longer writing tasks, much like the pen and pencil for sighted users.

The Shifting Landscape of Digital Accessibility

Figure 1. Diagram depicting the structure of the braille cell and the braille alphabet. Different combinations of the six dots are used to form all the letters, numbers, and other characters needed to write in over 133 languages worldwide

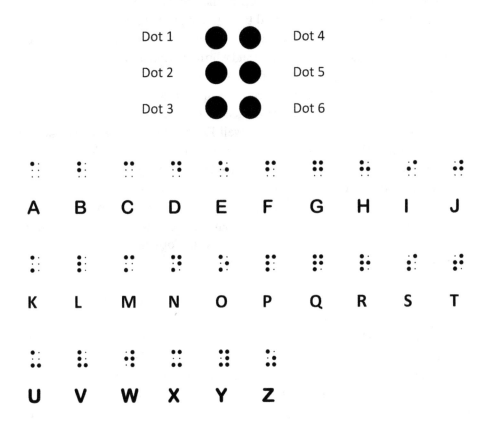

In 1892, one of the first braille writing machines was developed by Frank Hall, with later versions modified by leaders in blindness education, including Perkins School for the Blind (Dixon, 2000; Koestler, 2004). The braillewriter resembles a standard mechanical typewriter, with input keys corresponding to the six braille dots, a carriage to control the cursor position, and knobs to insert and remove the paper manually (Abbott & Connors, 2020). Although not portable, it remains a very popular and standard method for writing braille manually because it provides instant access to braille on paper and is simple to use. Many blind students begin to write with a brailler, before also being introduced to other methods (Abbott & Connors, 2020). Blind adults often comment on the convenience that the brailler provides, as a tool to keep close by the phone or computer for taking braille notes on paper (such as phone numbers or route instructions) that can then easily be transported (Cryer & Home, 2011; Martiniello et al., 2020).

Some of the earliest electronic specialized assistive technologies for students with visual impairments were introduced in the 1960's and 1970's. These technological developments were prompted by both the growing disability civil rights movement and the significant increase of blind and low vision students who were being integrated into mainstream schools and who had to function within a classroom inherently designed for sighted, print readers (Koestler, 2004). In 1976, Raymond Kurzweil, a graduate of M.I.T., invented the Kurzweil Reading Machine, the first optical character recognition (OCR) device to translate print (visual) text into computer-spoken (auditory) words (Kurzweil Education, n.d.). Inducted into the National Inventors Hall of Fame, Kurzweil is recognized worldwide as a pioneer for proving that information could be presented in multiple formats using the power of technology and artificial intelligence (AI). The earliest Kurzweil machines were large and expensive stand-alone computers, available only to consumers who could afford them (musician Stevie Wander was famously one of the first to acquire a Kurzweil Reading Machine) (National Inventors Hall of Fame, 2002).

Similar specialized solutions were developed during this time to meet the needs of students who accessed information visually. For example, Tieman developed one of the first video magnifiers for users with low vision in the 1970s, a stand-alone hardware device that uses a camera to capture and magnify printed text based on reader preferences (Optelec, n.d.). Since this initial invention, many specialized video magnifiers have been introduced, ranging from desktop versions to small portable devices that can be carried from class to class (Faubert & Overbury, 1987). Video magnifiers also typically enable other capabilities, including improved colour contrast and polarity (for example, displaying white print on a black background or vice versa), while others also integrate text-to-speech software to provide students with a multisensory learning experience (Lee, 2020b).

The level of sophistication and portability of current day traditional assistive technologies has significantly changed the playing field for students who have access to these specialized tools. Today, screen magnification software (such as ZoomText) and screen-reading software (such as Job Access for Speech, or JAWS) enable students to access mainstream computers once this third-party software is installed and students are taught how to use it (Lee, 2020a). Many screen-readers such as JAWS integrate advanced capabilities above and beyond basic text-to-speech, including a wide range of keyboard-based commands to navigate with ease in documents, on websites and in other common programs, without the use of a mouse that requires the ability to see the pointer on the screen.

The Shifting Landscape of Digital Accessibility

These same specialized advancements have also drastically changed access for students who prefer or who learn best through braille and tactile information for a range of educational tasks. Most notably, refreshable braille displays and braille note-takers now provide students with instant access to braille in an electronic format (Cryer & Home, 2011). Connected to accessible computers, tablets and smartphones, these specialized assistive devices translate what is on the screen into braille, through a series of pins that rise and fall to form braille symbols on a built-in display. Today, these devices are available in multiple sizes, ranging from small portable models that can easily be transported from class to class, to those that are desktop models with longer displays used for more extensive reading. Students can typically use these devices with or without additional screen-reader support, providing multimodal access (Abbott & Connors, 2020; Siu & Presley, 2020, ch. 3). Significantly, the proliferation of braille displays has drastically expanded the amount of classroom content available to students in braille, since any documents and websites that are designed to be accessible can be read with these tools. However, current day braille displays cannot display tactile images and will only present a single line of braille at one time, limiting the extent to which students can use these devices for classroom content that relies heavily on spatial information, such as science, technology, engineering and math (STEM), where blind students remain significantly under-represented (Maurer, 2009; Mealin & Murphy-Hill, 2012; Swenor, 2021). A number of innovators are prototyping lower-cost multiline displays that can also convert images into a tactile format to address these gaps (Marshall & Moys, 2020; Runyan & Carpi, 2011), but the current context highlights the continued need for paper-based braille as well. Other traditional assistive technologies are used to address a variety of additional reading needs. Specialized book readers, for example, are designed for listening to audiobooks or for recording notes in class, while providing maximum colour contrast of buttons and integrated voice support to facilitate use (Kelley, 2020).

While the evolution of these assistive technologies provide blind and low vision students with more equitable access to information, the shift towards greater mainstream digital accessibility further enhances inclusion and accessibility in the K-12 classroom.

The Shift Towards Mainstream Digital Accessibility

Despite their benefits, the abandonment of traditional assistive technologies is estimated to range between 30% to 50% on average, with some reports suggesting an under-use or abandonment rate of 70% or higher for some tools (Fuhrer, 2001). Among the factors influencing under-use and abandonment, traditional assistive technology users have highlighted the role of cost, technical support, stigma, limited multifunctionality and portability (Martiniello et al., 2019).

Although some jurisdictions maintain governmental or alternative funding programs to purchase traditional assistive technology and software for blind and low vision students, this remains inconsistently available worldwide, and is typically lacking in low income countries (World Health Organization, 2022). Even when such programs are maintained, rigid eligibility criteria may restrict the provision of traditional assistive devices to specific end-user categories (AccessATCanada, 2019). In Quebec, Canada, for example, assistive technologies used by students with visual impairments are loaned at no cost through the provincial healthcare system, but not all service users are eligible (Régie de l'assurance maladie du Québec, 2018). In some jurisdictions, students have access to a list of specific pre-approved devices, but often must choose between different mutually exclusive modes of access. For example, a student who has already been provided with screen magnification software (visual mode) may not be able to request dedicated text-to-speech software or a braille display (non-visual mode). In many jurisdictions, students may be eligible for a specific device for school (such as a braillewriter) but cannot request another one for home.

Such restrictions limit the extent to which students can draw on multiple formats, or access these assistive technologies at home to further support learning and motivation. Similarly, students who do not meet specific eligibility criteria based on visual acuity and fields, due to fluctuating or non-traditional vision impairments, often fall between the cracks.

This is especially problematic given the cost of many traditional assistive devices, that are often expensive due to the niche market that is being targeted. For example, third-party screen-reading software typically costs $1,000 or more, with braille displays typically costing a minimum of $2,000 for the smallest models and an upward of $10,000 for the largest models used for more extensive reading (Martiniello et al., 2021). From a cost equity perspective, students from low-income families and those without permanent citizenship status are often at the greatest disadvantage. The bureaucratic burden to obtain traditional assistive devices has also been identified as an especially disabling barrier in previous reports (Fichten et al., 2012).

The highly specialized nature of traditional assistive devices also limits the extent to which those in a students' network, such as parents and classroom teachers, are able to provide or locate technical support and assistance (Gitlin, 1995). Similarly, traditional assistive technologies designed for specific populations must typically be sent to specialized vendors when technical problems arise, sometimes leaving the end-user without a device to use in the interim.

The Shifting Landscape of Digital Accessibility

As touched on earlier in this chapter, stigma associated with the use of technologies that disclose an otherwise invisible impairment to others may lead to a reluctance to use these tools for students with invisible impairments or who are still adjusting to a newly acquired disability. In a study exploring factors influencing device abandonment, authors found that users with invisible disabilities (such as low vision) are more likely to abandon a traditional assistive technology if they had not yet accepted their disability, if the technology had led them to feel excluded by others, or if they appeared different from the norm (Pape et al., 2002). While all students should learn about the strength that exists in diversity and should gain the confidence to use whatever tools are best for them, this perceived stigma may delay the use of otherwise helpful tools for such learners. The tendency to design for a specific disability group has also been highlighted as a limitation of many traditional assistive devices (Martiniello et al., 2019). While these tools may integrate improved colour, contrast, and size to increase the visibility of buttons and other visual features, they often do not incorporate other functionalities, such as the ability to improve sound, supports for users with learning or motor difficulties, or who have needs that go beyond vision alone.

In the past decade, there has been a marked increase in mainstream technologies (computers, smartphones, and tablets) that are used by everyone but that also incorporate a range of accessibility features to address different user needs (Martiniello et al., 2019). Educational technologies based upon universal design principles incorporate the same concepts borrowed from universal design in architecture, learning and other environments, and reflect a shift from the medical to a social conception of disability. The concept of universal design in technology therefore highlights the importance of flexible devices that enable all users to access a wide range of accessibility functionalities (such as screen magnification and text-to-speech software), without the need to purchase expensive third-party solutions (Rose et al., 2005).

When technologies are proactively designed to be accessible, it is often observed that all users will benefit. For example, although talking books were initially developed for blind users, the global success and popularity of the booming audiobook industry through services such as Audible, Kindle and iBooks highlights the value this has had for multiple consumers (Rubery, 2016). Sighted users can listen to books while driving, performing other household tasks, or when they simply want to unwind. Sighted students who were otherwise uninterested in reading can become enchanted and motivated when they also have the option to listen to a story being read, or can both read the text while listening to it, as an added learning support. Similarly, although voice assistants such as SIRI on Apple products were initially developed for all users, this has also become a powerful accessibility tool for blind users or for others who prefer to voice their commands. Users who may not have otherwise considered text-to-speech, including students with low vision who may feel initially reluctant, have opportunities to discover these multimodal functions within the basic settings available to everyone, and users can activate multiple functions (such as increased contrast and size, text-to-speech and hearing aid support) on a single portable device. Likewise, when devices integrate built-in text-to-speech software and applications are designed to follow existing accessibility standards, users can connect their braille displays to access this information through a tactile format when they choose.

In 2005, Apple introduced Mac OS X 10.4 Tiger, which also included built-in text-to-speech software called VoiceOver as part of their computer operating system. This was followed by the integration of VoiceOver on the iPhone in 2009 and on the iPad in 2010 (Maccessibility, 2011). Alongside this screen-reader support, Apple products have also introduced a suite of additional accessibility features that continue to be updated and maintained, including Zoom (magnification software), supports for users with hearing, motor, and learning disabilities (such as modified wait times for performing gestures), and a wide range of features that can be customized to meet specific visual needs (such as colour, contrast, size, polarity, icon size, and highlighting capability) (Apple Inc., n.d.). Users can also select among a variety of built-in typing and input features that they can activate and change depending on the context. In addition to the standard on-screen QWERTY keyboard, users can connect a Bluetooth physical QWERTY or braille keyboard to their device or activate an on-screen braille keyboard for typing in braille (where the user places their fingers onto the screen corresponding to the position of dots within braille characters), or alternatively use the dictation feature available across the platform (Morales, 2015). Students can trial these different options to discover what they enjoy and find most efficient in different contexts, such as dictation in quieter environments and one of the standard keyboard typing methods in others. Similar "born accessible" features have continued to be incorporated into other mainstream devices, including Google Android and Microsoft Windows, with the level of capability differing among products as these innovations continue to progress (Google, 2022).

Vignette 3: Tommy

Tommy is 15 years old and in the 10th grade. He uses a wide range of digital tools inside and outside the classroom. While he continues to use specialized screen-reading software on his PC computer for reading and writing homework assignments, browsing the Internet and emailing assignments to teachers, he also loves his iPad which his sighted friends use in class as well. With the collaboration of classroom teachers and a TVI, Tommy learned how to perform the gestures needed to navigate non-visually on the screen with VoiceOver, so that he could

The Shifting Landscape of Digital Accessibility

use his tablet alongside his peers during classroom activities. While exploring the different apps on the home screen, he discovered YouTube, which he was happy to learn was fully accessible to him as a VoiceOver user. He was thrilled when his teachers made him aware of a YouTube channel hosted by a blind influencer who shares tips and resources for using different accessible technologies. The host also uses a guide dog. Curious to learn more, Tommy has also been browsing videos on what it is like to have a guide dog and recently chose to speak about this as part of a class presentation, where he also shared a portion of the video with his class-mates. In class last week, the teacher used a spelling application to introduce new vocabulary words to her students, but first confirmed that the application would be accessible with VoiceOver as well. Tommy loves that he can connect his braille display for these activities, since he has discovered that this is an easier way for him to tactually observe how new words are spelled, in addition to hearing how they sound. Tommy is learning more about what works best for him in different contexts, but has also had opportunities to discover new interests thanks to the multiple apps that have been installed on his tablet.

The above vignette illustrates the learning advantages of mainstream accessible technologies that can be used on their own or alongside specialized tools, such as refreshable braille displays. These advantages move beyond enabling accessibility, and open the door to content that may not otherwise be available to students, as-suming the applications used are designed to be proactively accessible.

Mainstream Digital Accessibility: From Products to Applications

In addition to the proliferation of mainstream accessible technologies, the shift towards universal design has also inspired a proliferation of accessible applications (apps) that can be accessed on smartphones and tablets, such as Google Android and Apple products (Senjam et al., 2021). When accessibility features such as text-to-speech software, screen magnification or braille display connectivity are activated, students with visual impairments can use built-in applications alongside their peers to strengthen their own metacognitive learning skills and to develop an awareness of strategies that will support their success. For example, older stu-dents can use built-in reminder and calendar applications to manage tasks and to maintain a list of upcoming class dates. Table 1 provides some examples of how integrated accessible applications available to all learners can also provide new empowerment-based learning opportunities for students with visual impairments.

Table 1. Examples of how integrated accessible applications provide new empowerment-based learning opportunities

Application	Task
Reminder apps	To keep track of upcoming dates and class deadlines (maintain a to-do list)
Calendar	To keep track of important dates (develop organization strategies)
Email	To communicate with teachers/peers, submit assignments, and receive accessible feedback
Web browser (e.g. Safari)	To explore topics of interest (develop research skills and curiosity)
Messages (or accessible age-appropriate social media apps)	To communicate with teachers and peers, discussion groups)
Podcast Apps	To explore topics of interest and learn about podcasting as a communication tool
Accessible book apps (e.g. iBooks, Kindle, Audible, Gutenbirg, Librivox, EasyReader, VoiceDream)	To read books of interest in preferred format (print, audio or braille) alongside peers (opportunity to develop awareness of reading interests, often not possible in a traditional library for blind students, where catalogs are not accessible)

Such an emphasis on universal design has also led to examples of greater accessibility within mainstream computer programs. For instance, virtual conference calling programs such as Zoom embed accessibility for text-to-speech users in addition to other accessibility features, such as automatic captioning and transcripts that can be configured in meeting settings.

Alongside these mainstream applications, born accessible products have also inspired developers to launch a growing number of specialized applications to address real accessibility barriers encountered by users with visual impairments of all ages. For example, Microsoft has developed Seeing AI, a freely available optical character recognition application that enables users to read printed information and access other visual features from the environment using their mainstream smartphones and tablets (Microsoft Corporation, 2022). Through Seeing AI, students with visual impairments can take pictures of paper-based print and have it read aloud, identify inaccessible currency, gain basic information about the visual environment, and read bar codes on common household items all while using a single accessible mainstream device. While users will still require accessible desktop solutions for more extensive stationary tasks, the growing number of applications available through proactively accessible mobile tools minimizes the number of traditional devices that students will need to carry throughout the day.

While not meant to be exhaustive, the following sections highlight a number of important considerations for educators and administrators to address persisting gaps in inclusion, diversity, equity and accessibility through the use of universally accessible digital learning tools.

The Shifting Landscape of Digital Accessibility

SOLUTIONS AND RECOMMENDATIONS

Support Equity in Access to Information

Equality is the notion that all students should have the opportunity to participate in the same activities and accomplish the same tasks as their peers. Equity is the nuance that students may require different tools, supports and strategies to accomplish those activities, and that there may be a great amount of diversity in the path followed to achieve that goal and in the ultimate destination itself (Souto-Manning et al., 2019). For example, a teacher may design an assignment for students to demonstrate their learning about representations of disability in children's literature. Students might do this through the writing of a research paper, but if the ultimate goal is to demonstrate knowledge rather than to specifically write a research paper, students may feel more inspired to create a video, publish a blog, give a presentation, initiate a social media thread, or create an artistic representation of what they learned (Novak & Rose, 2016). Ultimately, all students learn about disability representations, but may use different methods to get there. The flexibility to select among diverse means of action and engagement enables students to explore new forms of expression but, at a deeper level, also acknowledges the importance of preference and enjoyment that should accompany all learning. In this same way, having access to accessible formats will not necessarily provide students with equitable access to information if these options do not take into account what students need in a given learning context.

Vignette 4: Baylee

Baylee is in the 12th grade and about to start an advanced statistics course. He is excited because this course is a prerequisite for the computer programming degree he hopes to pursue next year in college. Baylee requested the course textbook in hard copy braille because, although he uses text-to-speech for some other subjects, he feels that he needs full page access to physical braille for content that relies heavily on spatial orientation and for performing calculations, like math and science. The original electronic version of the textbook provided by the publisher was born accessible (designed to be accessible from inception). This meant that although transcription and proofreading would still be needed to ensure that content would translate properly into an embossed tactile format, much of the initial heavy lifting and work was significantly reduced. Unfortunately, Baylee experienced push back from a member of the educational team who questioned his need for braille, stating that a previous blind student was able to function well with text-to-speech software alone. Given that the textbook was already available in an electronic format that *could be accessed with a screen-reader, Baylee felt as though he had to justify his request for braille. This seemed unfair to Baylee since the sighted students in his class were not being asked to justify their right to print. Due to these circumstances, Baylee began his course without access to braille, using only the electronic format he had been provided. He quickly fell behind and found it very difficult to conceptualize the equations being discussed in class, without physical access to full page braille. Although Baylee eventually did receive his textbook in braille, he was left feeling discouraged and wondering whether he should pursue computer programming as a career path. Thankfully, Baylee had the opportunity to meet a blind computer programmer who served as an invaluable mentor and who provided insights about how she addressed similar barriers throughout her studies. With access to braille, Baylee ended up excelling in his course.*

Unfortunately, there are other students whose stories remain untold or who fall between the cracks, with multiple studies pointing to a higher attrition rate among postsecondary students with disabilities (Fichten et al., 2016; Martiniello & Wittich, 2019). There is growing attention devoted to the burden of disability labour – the often additional and unpaid work that students with disabilities must negotiate to have equitable opportunities to participate alongside their peers (Brown & Leigh, 2018). This In part, this may include the burden of having to continually explain, justify, and advocate to those with decision-making power. This can feel especially jarring to students with visual impairments who were accustomed to an inclusive learning environment where they had access to accessible tools and materials in earlier grades. When added to the additional time needed to negotiate assignments that may not be proactively constructed to be inclusive or the need to juggle other health conditions, this additional labour to self-advocate contributes to lower student engagement and higher educational abandonment (Fichten et al., 2016).

On the surface, Baylee (Vignette 4) was provided with an accessible format, yet this was not an accessible and inclusive learning experience for him, because it was not the format he needed. In this way, increased access to information is only truly inclusive if students have equitable opportunities to select the method that is best for them. This is especially relevant in STEM subjects (science, technology, engineering and math), where access to specific formats such as braille is often limited (Ajaj, 2020). The lack of tactile graphics may impede students with visual impairments who learn best tactually from truly grasping content introduced in class, especially if access to other methods (visual or auditory) are viewed as more conveniently available (Rosenblum & Herzberg, 2015). Pre-service and in-service K-12 teachers require meaningful opportunities to learn about the diversity that exists among all students, including students with visual impairments, and to recognize that no two students are the same. Likewise, students with visual impairments require equitable

The Shifting Landscape of Digital Accessibility

opportunities to gain competency in multiple modes of access so that they can select the ones that are best for a given activity, particularly as they approach postsecondary studies and may need to advocate for this on their own. At a broader level, the nuance of equitable access to information in a student's preferred format also highlights the importance of centering student auto-ethnographies and personal testimonies within UDL literature, as important sources of evidence to capture themes that may play a significant role but that may nonetheless remain overlooked (Fovet, 2018).

Filling the Accessibility Gap: Developing Accessible Classroom Documents

While significant attention has rightfully been paid to the importance of technological advancements, students with visual impairments nonetheless continue to confront a variety of accessibility barriers. These obstacles highlight the vital need to ensure that the content (classroom documents, platforms, and websites) being accessed through different technological solutions are proactively designed to conform with existing accessibility standards. Studies and personal testimonies underscore that document and textbook accessibility remain a pervasive problem, often requiring students to wait for alternative versions of inaccessible files to be provided, leading students to fall further behind their peers (Schuck et al., 2019).

To address these persisting accessibility barriers, there is an ongoing need to ensure that pre-service and in-service teachers are educated on how to design accessible classroom documents. Likewise, there is a need for administrators to recognize the importance of selecting accessible products and platforms at the procurement stage, to facilitate more proactive systemic change.

Accessibility refers to environments (physical or virtual spaces) that are designed to be inclusive to a variety of user needs, minimizing the need for retroactive approaches. The Web Content Accessibility Guidelines, for instance, provide clear recommendations for web developers to ensure that websites are proactively designed to be accessible and usable to diverse end-users, including those with little or no sight (W3C., 2018). Despite the long-standing existence of these guidelines, inaccessible websites remain a pervasive problem, particularly in jurisdictions where web accessibility is not entrenched into policy. This pervasive inaccessibility has led to barriers for students attempting to access online information and course management platforms (Arias-Flores et al., 2021). Consequently, students with visual impairments may have access to text-to-speech software but will still experience inaccessibility if the content they attempt to read with that software is not designed to be accessible. This is akin to a person who may have access to a wheelchair, but nonetheless is excluded if the environment they wish to access is not equipped with ramps and elevators.

The Shifting Landscape of Digital Accessibility

Many resources exist to guide educators in the development of accessible classroom documents (Canadian Institutes of Health Research, 2022; CAST, n.d.).

One common example of an accessibility barrier relates to images that frequently appear on websites, in textbooks, and in electronic classroom handouts. Visual images (photos, memes, graphs, and figures) are inherently inaccessible to students who are visually unable to see them, but also pose barriers to other students who may access information through text-to-speech software, including students with learning disabilities. Visual images are pervasive throughout the K-12 curriculum as an engaging and simple method to communicate information to young learners (for example, pictures in class workbooks). Text-to-speech software will indicate that an image is present in a document, without providing any information or interpretation of what that image contains. This significantly limits comprehension and the ability for students to access vast amounts of information being communicated, particularly in subjects where visual content is commonplace, such as math, geography, language learning, or science (Rosenblum & Herzberg, 2015). Alternative text (also called *alt text*) is a method whereby individuals can append a written description to any electronic image. This description will then be read aloud by text-to-speech software whenever a student encounters that image (W3C., 2018). Educators can easily add descriptions to images in recent versions of Microsoft Word or Microsoft PowerPoint by right clicking on the image and selecting the *Edit alt text* option. A text field will appear where a written description can be appended (see Figure 2). Similarly, schools that regularly use social media as a form of engagement can easily incorporate image descriptions for memes and photos included in their posts as a proactive form of inclusion, regardless of whether they are aware of end-user needs.

The Shifting Landscape of Digital Accessibility

Figure 2. Screenshot of editing alternative text on an image in Microsoft Word

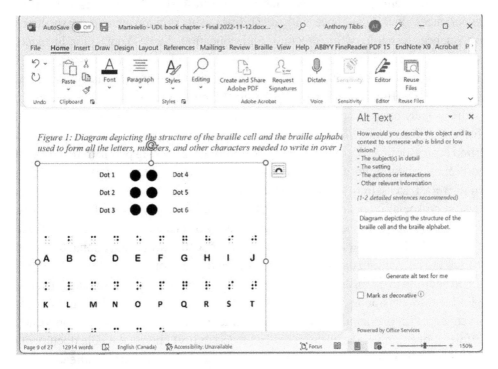

Deepening Diversity and Inclusion Through Mainstream Digital Accessibility

Beyond accessibility itself, there is a growing body of evidence suggesting that accessible digital classroom tools can also open the door to new forms of engagement that deepen diversity and inclusion and provide a platform for previously silenced narratives within the curriculum.

Educators can harness accessible educational technologies and online tools to address disability misconceptions, highlight historical leaders with disabilities in math, science, art, and other disciplines, and provide students with new forms of empowerment and engagement. Accessible websites, such as the online museum of the American Printing House for the Blind, provide new insights on social studies and history by documenting the history of blind people in America (American Printing House for the Blind, n.d.). The Netflix series *Crip Camp: A Disability Revolution* (available with audio description for blind viewers) brings to light first-hand voices and aspects of history that often remain untold, and is accompanied by a curriculum with additional lesson plans and activities to extend this learning (Laureano

& Turman, 2020). TED Talks, which are also available through a currently accessible mainstream application, provide a platform to diverse speakers with lived experiences, including those with disabilities who provide unique perspectives on science, technology, architecture, and education. Stella Young, for instance, voices the problems that exist when disability is solely viewed through a lens of inspiration and difference (Young, 2014). Similarly, users with disabilities have harnessed YouTube and online blogs to share their experiences and, by extension, address many misconceptions about what people with visual impairments can do. In the YouTube series *Planes, Trains and Canes*, for example, Dr. Mona Minkara (a blind professor from the United States) travels the world using public transportation to highlight how blind individuals travel, the barriers she encounters, innovations in universal accessibility, and the impact of public perceptions and environmental design on social inclusion (Minkara, 2019). While it is important for students to avoid generalizations and to understand that no two perspectives are the same, these examples highlight how access to accessible applications and educational tools can enrich the curriculum and broaden diversity and inclusion.

In addition to opportunities to incorporate first-hand voices across subject areas, blind and low vision technology users are also harnessing accessible digital tools to engage with one another, change the online narrative, and strengthen advocacy efforts. For example, the hashtag #a11y (accessibility) on social media documents the many online discussions around accessibility and allyship that have already taken place, including examples of where accessibility barriers persist and how people with lived experiences and their allies are responding. Inspired by the online disability movement, Global Accessibility Awareness Day (#GAAD) provides opportunities for social media users to highlight current accessibility issues, advancements and experiences at a global level (GAAD Foundation, n.d.). The accessibility of social media platforms broadens the voices who have access to these channels, but also offers empowering opportunities to learn about themes and lived experiences that are not always as easily learned from a textbook.

Accessible online tools are also providing blind and low vision users with opportunities to teach and learn from each other, providing forms of mentorship traditionally not available. For example, a growing number of social media communities of practice (such as online groups) have been initiated by users with visual impairments to ask questions about technology, education, employment, and other aspects of social participation and to provide resources, training, and allyship to one another. For example, the Getting Together with Technology program is a grass-routes online peer-support program for technology users with visual impairments in Canada (Canadian Council of the Blind, n.d.). AppleVis is an online accessible global community run by and for blind and low vision Apple users, providing access to numerous user-made tutorials, resources and discussion forums to trouble-shoot accessibility issues and maximize technology usage (Goodwin et al., n.d.). Likewise, a recent study explored the use of WhatsApp, a currently accessible messaging platform, as a powerful discussion tool for students with visual impairments to communicate with each other and to develop social skills (Della Líbera & Jurberg, 2020). While issues around privacy and safety should remain central considerations, with educators and parents helping to guide students towards age-appropriate opportunities, these universally accessible digital resources provide learners with new avenues for engagement and expression.

Accessible platforms and applications that widen access to reading materials (such as audiobooks and ebooks) also introduce new voices to the language arts curriculum, fostering important discussions about equity, diversity, and inclusion. *Born accessible* published works are available to blind and low vision students with access to accessible technologies on the day of release (Benetech, 2022). This accessible publishing movement ensures that students with visual impairments have increased access to the same books as their peers, though it has also inspired a growing generation of diverse authors. For example, Haben Girma, the first deafblind woman to graduate from Harvard law school, narrates her own audiobook where she describes her educational and employment experiences while drawing connections to broader issues of social equity and inclusion (Girma, 2019). The National Center on Disability and Journalism has published an accessible online disability language style guide to educate others on how to write about disability in journalism while raising awareness of problematic and ableist approaches, which can be harnessed to instigate discussions on diversity and inclusion in mass media and writing courses (National Center on Disability and Journalism, 2021). Collectively, these examples broaden the content and opportunities available to extend learning and to deepen diversity and inclusion both within and outside of the classroom.

FUTURE DIRECTIONS AND CONCLUSION

As technologies based on universal design continue to evolve, it is imperative to strive towards a day when all educational technologies are inherently more accessible. As educational leaders look to the next frontier, opportunities also remain to address persisting gaps in inclusion, diversity, equity, and accessibility.

Among these priorities, there is a need to ensure that the functionalities of mainstream accessible technologies continue to expand, while ensuring that lower cost options for specialized solutions (such as refreshable braille displays) are also introduced. Collectively, these efforts will increase access to equitable choice, an important aspect to consider in inclusive learning outcomes.

The Shifting Landscape of Digital Accessibility

Similarly, the content (documents, websites, and applications) consumed through accessible educational technologies must conform to existing accessibility standards, to address the inaccessibility barriers that persist. Educators require meaningful and empowering opportunities to learn how to create accessible documents from inception, calling upon pre-service university programs to incorporate these competencies within teacher education mandates. Similarly, accessibility must be considered by administrators at the procurement stage, when purchasing decisions about curricular resources and digital learning platforms are made. Effective change flourishes through allyship and when accessibility and inclusion are positioned as priorities not only by those who are directly affected, but by all individuals in positions of power.

This also underscores the importance of initiatives that elevate inclusion within professional training and career advancement, to better ensure that educators, administrators, researchers, and other educational leaders reflect the diversity of the students they serve. Several studies explore the experiences of pre-service teachers with disabilities but additional research and ethnographies are needed to explore these themes in greater depth (Flanagan et al., 2014).

The past decade has represented a significant and positive step towards greater inclusive learning and effective UDL implementation. As we look to the future, proactive consideration of broader aspects of equity, diversity, inclusion, and accessibility will foster more inclusive learning environments for all students.

REFERENCES

W3C. (2018). *Web Content Accessibility Guidelines (WCAG) 2.1*. Retrieved June 9 from https://www.w3.org/TR/WCAG21/

Abbott, P., & Connors, E. (2020). Braille and other tactile forms of communication. In Lee, H., & Ottowitz, J. (Eds.), *Foundations of Vision Rehabilitation Therapy* (4th ed., pp. 199–243). APH Press.

Abes, E. S., & Zahneis, M. E. (2020). A Duoethnographic Exploration of Disability Ally Development. *Disability Studies Quarterly*, 40(3). Advance online publication. 10.18061/dsq.v40i3.7038

AccessATCanada. (2019). *AccessATCanada: Find out which government and charity programs offer assistive technology funding and services in Canada and its provinces and territories*. Retrieved November 12 from https://www.accessassistivetech.ca/programs

Ackland, P., Resnikoff, S., & Bourne, R. (2017). World blindness and visual impairment: Despite many successes, the problem is growing. *Community Eye Health*, 30(100), 71–73. https://www.ncbi.nlm.nih.gov/pmc/articles/PMC5820628/29483748

Ajaj, R. (2020). Navigating the World of Higher Education as a Blind or Visually Impaired Student: Unequal Opportunities for Academic Success.

American Printing House for the Blind. (n.d.). *APH Museum: A museum dedicated to ordinary people doing extraordinary things*. Retrieved November 12 from https://aphmuseum.org/

Apple Inc. (n.d.). *Apple VoiceOver Guide - Chapter 10 - Using braille displays*. Apple Inc. Retrieved November 3 from https://www.apple.com/voiceover/info/guide/_1129.html

Arias-Flores, H., Sanchez-Gordon, S., & Calle-Jimenez, T. (2021). Analysis of the Level of Accessibility of Scientific Online Conferences for Blind Participants. International Conference on Applied Human Factors and Ergonomics.

Auxier, B. E., Buntain, C. L., Jaeger, P., Golbeck, J., & Kacorri, H. (2019). #HandsOffMyADA: A Twitter Response to the ADA Education and Reform Act. Proceedings of the 2019 CHI Conference on Human Factors in Computing Systems.

Benetech. (2022). *Born Accessible: A Benetch Initiative*. Retrieved November 12 from https://bornaccessible.benetech.org/

Bowling, E. (2015). What's the value of eye care? *Optometry Times, 7*(1), 3. https://www.proquest.com/openview/32cd8c656e0e087bea741d2e4c4d4a84/1?pq-origsite=gscholar&cbl=2029739

Brown, N., & Leigh, J. (2018). Ableism in academia: Where are the disabled and ill academics? *Disability & Society*, 33(6), 985–989. 10.1080/09687599.2018.1455627

Canadian Council of the Blind. (n.d.). *Get Together With Technology (GTT)*. Retrieved November 12 from https://ccbnational.net/shaggy/get-together-with-technology/

Canadian Institutes of Health Research. (2022). *Resources: Accessibility and eliminating systemic ableism*. CIHR. Retrieved November 13 from https://cihr-irsc.gc.ca/e/52842.html

Candela, A. (2006). Legends and pioneers of blindness assistive technology, Part 2. *AccessWorld, 7*(5). https://www.afb.org/aw/7/5/14437

CAST. (n.d.). *National Center on Accessible Educational Materials*. CAST. Retrieved November 13 from https://aem.cast.org/

Chardin, M., & Novak, K. (2020). *Equity by design: Delivering on the power and promise of UDL*. Corwin Press.

Cheadle, B. (2007). A parent's guide to the slate and stylus. *Future Reflections, 26*(1). https://nfb.org/images/nfb/publications/fr/fr25/fr07spr18.htm

Corn, A. L., & Erin, J. N. (2010). *Foundations of low vision: Clinical and functional perspectives*. American Foundation for the Blind.

Cryer, H., & Home, S. (2011). *Use of braille displays* (RNIB Centre for Accessible Information, Issue. Davis, L. J. (1997). Constructing normalcy. *The disability studies reader, 3*, 3-19.

Della Líbera, B., & Jurberg, C. (2020). Communities of practice on WhatsApp: A tool for promoting citizenship among students with visual impairments. *British Journal of Visual Impairment*, 38(1), 58–78. 10.1177/0264619619874836

Dixon, J. (Ed.). (2000). *Braille into the next milennium*. National Library Service for the Blind and Physically Handicapped.

Faubert, J., & Overbury, O. (1987). Active-passigm paradigm in assessing CCTV-aided reading. *Optometry and Vision Science*, 64(1), 23–28. 10.1097/00006324-198701000-000043826273

Fichten, C. S., Asuncion, J. V., & Scapin, R. (2014). Digital technology, learning, and postsecondary students with disabilities: Where we've been and where we're going. *Journal of Postsecondary Education and Disability*, 27(4), 369–379.

Fichten, C. S., Asuncion, J. V., Wolforth, J., Barile, M., Budd, J., Martiniello, N., & Amsel, R. (2012). Information and communication technology related needs of college and university students with disabilities. *Research in Learning Technology*, 20, 20. 10.3402/rlt.v20i0.18646

Fichten, C. S., Nguyen, M. N., Asuncion, J. V., Martiniello, N., Jorgensen, M., Budd, J., Amsel, R., & Libman, E. (2016). An exploratory study of college and university students with visual impairment in Canada: Grades and graduation. *British Journal of Visual Impairment*, 34(1), 91–100. 10.1177/0264619615616259

Flanagan, T., Benson, F. J., & Fovet, F. (2014). A multi-perspective examination of the barriers to field-placement experiences for students with disabilities. *Collected Essays on Learning and Teaching*, 7(2), n2. 10.22329/celt.v7i2.3993

Fovet, F. (2018). Exploring the student voice within Universal Design for Learning work. *The Ahfad Journal*, (8), 1–6.

Fuhrer, M. J. (2001, July). Assistive technology outcomes research: Challenges met and yet unmet. *American Journal of Physical Medicine & Rehabilitation*, 80(7), 528–535. 10.1097/00002060-200107000-0001311421522

GAAD Foundation. (n.d.). *Global Accessibility Awareness Day*. GAAD Foundation. Retrieved November 12 from https://accessibility.day

Girma, H. (2019). *Haben* [Audio Recording]. Hachette Audio. https://www.audible .ca/pd/Haben-Audiobook/B07VWKKNMT?language=en_CA

Gitlin, L. N. (1995). Why older people accept or reject assistive technology. *Generations (San Francisco, Calif.)*, 19, 41–46.

Gleason, C., Valencia, S., Kirabo, L., Wu, J., Guo, A., Jeanne Carter, E., Bigham, J., Bennett, C., & Pavel, A. (2020). Disability and the COVID-19 pandemic: Using Twitter to understand accessibility during rapid societal transition. The 22nd International ACM SIGACCESS Conference on Computers and Accessibility.

Google. (2022). *Android developer documentation: Build accessible apps*. Google. Retrieved November 12 from https://developer.android.com/guide/topics/ui/accessibility

Hannan, C. K. (2006). Review of research: Neuroscience and the impact of brain plasticity on braille reading. *Journal of Visual Impairment & Blindness*, 100(7), 397–413. 10.1177/0145482X0610000704

Holbrook, M. C., & Koenig, A. J. (1992). Teaching Braille Reading to Students with Low Vision. *Journal of Visual Impairment & Blindness*, 86(1), 44–48. 10.1177/0145482X9208600119

Jaiswal, A., Aldersey, H., Wittich, W., Mirza, M., & Finlayson, M. (2018). Participation experiences of people with deafblindness or dual sensory loss: A scoping review of global deafblind literature. *PLoS One*, 13(9), e0203772. 10.1371/journal.pone.020377230212504

Jan, G. (2015). The problem of the supercrip: Representation and misrepresentation of disability. In *Disability Research Today* (pp. 204–218). Routledge.

Kamei-Hannan, C., Lee, D. B., & Presley, I. (2017). Assistive Technology. In C. K. Hannan, C. Holbrook, & T. McCarthy (Eds.), *Foundations of Education: Volume II: Instructional Strategies for Teaching Children and Youths with Visual Impairments* (3rd ed.). APH Press.

Kelley, S. (2020). Access to information: Electronic listening, recording, and reading devices. In Lee, H., & Ottowitz, J. (Eds.), *Foundations of Vision Rehabilitation Therapy*. APH Press.

Koestler, F. A. (2004). *The Unseen Minority: A Social History of Blindness in the United States.* https://www.afb.org/unseen/book.asp?ch=Koe-00toc

Kurzweil Education. (n.d.). *The history of text-to-speech technology.* Retrieved October 30 from https://www.kurzweiledu.com/about-kurzweil/history-of-text-to -speech.html

Laureano, B. I., & Turman, A. (2020). *Crimp Camp Curriculum.* Netflix. Retrieved November 12 from https://cripcamp.com/curriculum/

Lee, H. (2020a). Keyboarding and Access Technology. In Lee, H., & Ottowitz, J. (Eds.), *Foundations of Vision Rehabilitation Therapy* (4th ed., pp. 313–355). APH Press.

Lee, H. (2020b). Low Vision Skills. In Lee, H., & Ottowitz, J. (Eds.), *Foundations of Vision Rehabilitation Therapy.* APH Press.

Maccessibility. (2011, November 12). Blind faith: A decade of Apple accessibility. *M12Y.* https://maccessibility.net/2011/02/10/blind-faith-a-decade-of-apple -accessibility

Marshall, L., & Moys, J.-L. (2020). Readers' experiences of Braille in an evolving technological world. *Visible Language*, 54(1-2).

Martiniello, N., Barlow, M., & Wittich, W. (2021). Exploring correlates of braille reading performance in adults and older adults with visual impairment: A retrospective study. *Scientific Studies of Reading*. Advance online publication. 10.1080/10888438.2021.1969402

Martiniello, N., Eisenbarth, W., Lehane, C., Johnson, A., & Wittich, W. (2019). Exploring the use of smartphones and tablets among people with visual impairments: Are mainstream devices replacing the use of traditional visual aids? *Assistive Technology*, 1–12. 10.1080/10400435.2019.168208431697612

Martiniello, N., Haririsanati, L., & Wittich, W. (2020). Enablers and barriers encountered by working-age and older adults who pursue braille training. *Disability and Rehabilitation*. Advance online publication. 10.1080/09638288.2020.183325 333053313

Martiniello, N., & Wittich, W. (2019). Employment and visual impairment: Issues in adulthood. In Ravenscraft, J. (Ed.), *Routledge Handbook of Visual Impairment* (pp. 415–437). Routledge. 10.4324/9781315111353-26

Maurer, M. (2009). The difference the dots make: A personal history with Braille. *Journal of Visual Impairment & Blindness*, 103(4), 196–198. 10.1177/0145482X0910300402

Mealin, S., & Murphy-Hill, E. (2012). An exploratory study of blind software developers. 2012 IEEE Symposium on Visual Languages and Human-Centric Computing (VL/HCC).

Milian, M., & Erin, J. N. (2001). *Diversity and visual impairment: the influence of race, gender, religion, and ethnicity on the individual*. American Foundation for the Blind.

Minhas, R., Jaiswal, A., Chan, S., Trevisan, J., Paramasivam, A., & Spruyt-Rocks, R. (2022). Prevalence of Individuals with Deafblindness and Age-Related Dual-Sensory Loss. *Journal of Visual Impairment & Blindness*, 116(1), 36–47. 10.1177/0145482X211072541

Minkara, M. (2019). *Planes, Trains & Canes*. Retrieved November 12 from https://monaminkara.com/ptc

Morales, T. (2015). *VoiceOver turns 10*. Retrieved October 31 from https://www.applevis.com/blog/voiceover-turns-10

National Center on Disability and Journalism. (2021). *Disability Language Style Guide*. Walter Cronkite School of Journalism and Mass Communication. Retrieved November 12 from https://ncdj.org/style-guide/

National Inventors Hall of Fame. (2002). *Raymond Kurzweil: Optical character recognition (U.S. Patent No. 6,199,042)*. National Inventors Hall of Fame. Retrieved September 30 from https://www.invent.org/inductees/raymond-kurzweil

Novak, K., & Rose, D. (2016). *UDL Now!: A teacher's guide to applying universal design for learning in today's classrooms*. CAST Professional Publishing.

Optelec. (n.d.). *About Optelec: History*. Optelec. Retrieved November 12 from https://in.optelec.com/about/History

Page, D. D. (1980). Securing and Maintaining Qualified Readers for Visually Impaired College Students. *Journal of Visual Impairment & Blindness*, 74(2), 71–75. 10.1177/0145482X8007400206

Pape, T. L.-B., Kim, J., & Weiner, B. (2002). The shaping of individual meanings assigned to assistive technology: A review of personal factors. *Disability and Rehabilitation*, 24(1-3), 5–20. 10.1080/0963828011006623511827155

Régie de l'assurance maladie du Québec. (2018). *Tariff for insured visual aids and related services, CQLR c A-29, r 8.1 (Health Insurance Act)*. http://canlii.ca/t/53hjp

Roman-Lantzy, C. (2007). *Cortical visual impairment: An approach to assessment and intervention*. American Foundation for the Blind.

Roman-Lantzy, C. (2019a). *CVI & Autism: Shared Behaviors, Not Diagnoses*. Retrieved July 18 from https://youtu.be/EFPB9r-dIlA

Roman-Lantzy, C. (2019b). *Teaching and Learning in Phase I CVI*. Retrieved Aug. 15 from https://pcvis.vision/educators-and-therapists/phase-i-cvi/

Rose, D., Gravel, J. W., & Tucker-Smith, N. (2021). *Cracks in the foundation: Personal reflections on the past and future of the UDL Guidelines*. CAST. Retrieved November 12 from https://www.cast.org/products-services/events/2022/01/cracks -foundation-past-future-udl-guidelines-rose-gravel-tucker-smith

Rose, D. H., Hasselbring, T. S., Stahl, S., & Zabala, J. (2005). Assistive technology and universal design for learning: Two sides of the same coin. *Handbook of special education technology research and practice*, 507-518.

Rose, D. H., & Meyer, A. (2002). *Teaching every student in the digital age: Universal design for learning*. ERIC.

Rosenblum, L. P., & Herzberg, T. S. (2015). Braille and tactile graphics: Youths with visual impairments share their experiences. *Journal of Visual Impairment & Blindness*, 109(3), 173–184. 10.1177/0145482X1510900302

Rubery, M. (2016). *The untold story of the talking book*. Harvard University Press. 10.4159/9780674974555

Runyan, N. H., & Carpi, F. (2011). Seeking the 'holy Braille' display: Might electromechanically active polymers be the solution? *Expert Review of Medical Devices*, 8(5), 529–532. 10.1586/erd.11.4722026617

Ryles, R. (1996). The impact of braille reading skills on employment, income, education, and reading habits. *Journal of Visual Impairment & Blindness*, 90(3), 219–226. 10.1177/0145482X9609000311

Sadato, N., Okada, T., Honda, M., & Yorekura, Y. (2002). Critical period for cross-modal plasticity in blind humans: A functional MRI study. *NeuroImage*, 16(2), 389–400. 10.1006/nimg.2002.111112030824

Schuck, L., Wall-Emerson, R., Kim, D. S., & Nelson, N. (2019). Predictors Associated with College Attendance and Persistence among Students with Visual Impairments. *Journal of Postsecondary Education and Disability*, 32(4), 339–358.

Senjam, S. S., Manna, S., & Bascaran, C. (2021). Smartphones-Based Assistive Technology: Accessibility Features and Apps for People with Visual Impairment, and its Usage, Challenges, and Usability Testing. *Clinical Optometry*, 13, 311–322. 10.2147/OPTO.S33636134866955

Shakespeare, T. (2021). The Social Model of Disability. In L. J. Davis (Ed.), *The disability studies reader*. Routledge (Taylor & Francis Group). 10.4324/9781003082583-3

Shinohara, K., & Wobbrock, J. O. (2011). In the shadow of misperception: Assistive technology use and social interactions. CHI 2011, Vancouver.

Siu, Y.-T., & Presley, I. (2020). *Access technology for blind and low vision accessibility*. APH Press, American Printing House for the Blind.

Souto-Manning, M., Rabadi-Raol, A., Robinson, D., & Perez, A. (2019). What stories do my classroom and its materials tell? Preparing early childhood teachers to engage in equitable and inclusive teaching. *Young Exceptional Children*, 22(2), 62–73. 10.1177/1096250618811619

Swenor, B. K. (2021). Including disability in all health equity efforts: An urgent call to action. *The Lancet. Public Health*, 6(6), e359–e360. 10.1016/S2468-2667(21)00115-834051160

Swenor, B. K., & Meeks, L. M. (2019). Disability inclusion—Moving beyond mission statements. *The New England Journal of Medicine*, 380(22), 2089–2091. 10.1056/NEJMp190034831141629

Tuttle, D. W., & Tuttle, N. R. (2004). *Self-esteem and adjusting with blindness: The process of responding to life's demands.* Charles C. Thomas Publisher Ltd.

Varma, R., Vajaranant, T., & Burkemper, B. (2016). Visual impairment and blindness in adults in the United States: Demographic and geographic variations from 2015 to 2050. *Journal of the American Medical Association: Opthalmology*, 134(7), 802–809.27197072

World Health Organization. (2022). *Global report on assistive technology.* https://apps.who.int/iris/bitstream/handle/10665/354357/9789240049451-eng.pdf

Wormsley, D. P., & D'Andrea, F. M. (1997). *Instructional Strategies for Braille Literacy.* American Foundation for the Blind.

Wu, Y.-H., Martiniello, N., & Swenor, B. K. (2021). Building a More Accessible Conference for Researchers With Vision Impairment. *JAMA Ophthalmology*. Advance online publication. 10.1001/jamaophthalmol.2021.561334967843

Young, S. (2014). *I'm not your inspiration, thank you very much.* TEDx. https://www.ted.com/talks/stella_young_i_m_not_your_inspiration_thank_you_very_much?language=en

Chapter 10
Navigating the Gap Between Theory and Practice in UDL Implementation Within the K–12 Sector:
Understanding an Ongoing Tension

Pamela Gurney
Thompson Rivers University, Canada

Frederic Fovet
https://orcid.org/0000-0003-1051-4163
Thompson Rivers University, Canada

EXECUTIVE SUMMARY

This chapter examines the gap which exists between theory and practice in the K-12 Canadian school system in relation to Universal Design for Learning (UDL) implementation. It blends the voices of two academics, one examining UDL adoption from a theoretical and conceptual point of view, and one presenting observations from the field. The chapter argues that the current academic discourse related to UDL integration in schools is misleadingly optimistic, when the reality of on terrain integration is radically grimmer. The chapter argues that this glossy perception of progress must be unpacked and re-examined as it otherwise is at risk of creating and perpetuating a false narrative regarding the efforts that remain to be applied in the area of inclusive design and UDL adoption. The chapter's recommendations

DOI: 10.4018/978-1-6684-4750-5.ch010

Copyright © 2024, IGI Global. Copying or distributing in print or electronic forms without written permission of IGI Global is prohibited.

include a more pragmatic and realistic assessment of the work that remains to be achieved in the field before UDL can be considered in the process of becoming a reality for teachers and students.

INTRODUCTION AND CONTEXT

Universal Desing for Learning (UDL) is a framework for inclusion which radically alters the perspective of teachers on learner diversity (Lambert et al., 2023). Instead of presenting learner diversity as exceptionality, it posits that learner diversity is a given in any context. UDL scholars therefore argue that teachers can prepare to address this diversity proactively in the design of their instruction and assessment before they even observe any learner struggling with format. UDL in this sense translates the social model of disability into action and classroom practices (Fovet, 2014). It argues indeed that disability is not an inherent characteristic of the leaner but is rather a tension which emerges when the learning environment is not designed with learners' variability and diverse embodiment in mind (Saia, 2023). UDL has been discussed within the K-12 sector for now over two decades. The amount of scholarship focusing on UDL integration in schools has risen sharply within Canada, and this may suggest that there is a degree of success when it comes to spreading this framework to all provinces and territories.

Instead, the on-terrain reality seems much more complex and there seems to be evidence that UDL implementation is not an easy, linear, or sustainable process yet at this stage. There is little evidence of sustained growth, and instead the many initiatives observed around the country appear sporadic and short lived. There is evidence of pilot projects on UDL integration losing steam and momentum (BCUDL, 2010).

This chapter seeks to explore the degree to which this tension is a reality. It seeks to explore the reasons that cause the resistance, slow progress, and frequent failure associated with UDL integration efforts taking place in the Canadian K-12 sector. It highlights the varied and complex factors which contribute to this tension that manifests itself as a clear gap between theory and practice in this area. The way this chapter structures its approach is to combine two narratives: one voice is that of a scholar reflecting on her recent experiences with UDL in the field; the other is the perspective of a scholar more focuses on promoting UDL theoretically. The combination and weaving of these narratives offer a wide scope and ecological insight into this complex and rapidly evolving phenomenon.

Navigating the Gap Between Theory and Practice

OVERVIEW OF THE LITERATURE

Inclusive Provisions in the K-12 Sector

There is considerable legislative support in most Global North jurisdictions for the inclusion of diverse learners (USDofE, 2023). It can fairly be asserted, therefore, that students with disabilities benefit from a significant degree of statutory and constitutional protection (Cera, 2015; OHRC, 2018). The nature of this protection, however, can be problematic. Indeed, the overall flavour and intent of legislative protection for students with disabilities are grounded in a medical model approach to inclusion which perpetuates a deficit model view of students with exceptionalities (Fovet, 2023). In many ways, therefore, while legislative protections and human rights considerations continue to grow significantly in relation to students with disabilities, there is little growth when it comes to inclusive teaching and learning that might create whole class provisions for all diverse learners (Dignath et al., 2022). Instead, the provisions continue to amount to retrofitting, meaning the provision - after the facts - of individual interventions to erode existing discrimination in access to learning (Finnerty et al., 2019). In many ways therefore there is frustration in the field at the slow evolution of field practices towards more authentic inclusion (White, 2015).

Emergence of UDL

Universal Design for Learning is a framework for the inclusion of diverse learners. It comes at a later stage historically in a legislative and policy tradition that has focused predominantly on adaptations and modifications, as well as individual interventions (McKenna et al., 2023). UDL instead seeks whole class inclusion through inclusive design (King-Sears et al., 2023). UDL in many ways translates the social model of disability which positions disability – not as an individual characteristic – but more as a social construct and importantly as the friction that occurs between individual embodiments and the design of experiences and spaces that is not always optimally inclusive (Disability Nottinghamshire, 2023; Saia, 2023). UDL translates this vision into classroom practices by steering teachers away from deficit model views and supporting them as they acknowledge and grasp that it is their reflection, or absence of reflection, on design that can alternatively include or exclude leaners (Levey, 2021). UDL advocates will argue that a teacher has the capacity to prepare for learner diversity and can proactively use inclusive design to inject as much flexibility as possible into teaching and learning, so that diverse learners can work from a strength-based position using strategies that are their own.

(Tobin & Behling, 2018). The emphasis is very much on forward proactive planning and design, rather than on retrofitting.

There are three UDL principles: multiple means of action and expression, multiple means of representation, and multiple means of engagement (Kelly et al., 2022). These three facets of the design process respectively mirror the three main transactional dimensions of teaching and learning, i.e., the ways learner produce material, the ways teachers offer students information, and the ways the content of instruction connects with learners' interests and lived experiences (Rao & Meo, 2016). Redesigning a teaching experience or a lesson inclusively can be daunting for a teacher who has never previously adopted a design mindset, and the three UDL principles can support teachers in their design work, allowing them to break down the experience into bite size opportunities for reflection on their practice (Lowrey et al., 2017; Almumen, 2020). UDL redesign, as opposed to differentiated instruction, is not done in the moment and does not require the development of pathways in response to the identification of specific needs among students in the classroom (Griful-Freixenet et al., 2020). Instead, UDL represents a desire to redesign inclusively for learner diversity, whenever forward planning allows or opportunities for an overhaul of existing practices occurs (Rose et al., 2012).

Integration of UDL in the K-12 Sector

There has been a significant degree of UDL growth over the last two decades, both in the K-12 and the post-secondary sector (Almeqdad et al., 2023). Whether UDL has spread faster in the K-12, or the post-secondary landscape seems to differ from jurisdiction to jurisdiction, but it seems fair to assert that eventually both sectors become equally interested in the model – out of frustration with existing deficit model approaches and medical model practices. It is also fair to assert that eventually sector feeds from the momentum that exists in the other. In the end, there seems to be a desire across the educational landscape to better address the needs of diverse learners and to do so using whole class approaches that rely on proactive inclusive design that can lead to sustainable change in teaching and learning practices.

In the K-12 landscape, the growth of UDL has been steady but not even, across geo-political landscapes (OK et al., 2017). Even in a country such as Canada, it is necessary to stress that the development of UDL has not been universal, seamless, or linear (Fovet, 2018). Instead, there has been an abundance of pilot projects, teacher-led initiatives, and communities of practice that have experimented, created interest, and to some extent grown resources and professional development opportunities (Ok et al., 2016). There has definitely been some growth in the scholarship of UDL in schools, with particular emphasis being placed on assessment (Salvia et al., 2009), as well as the move away from print-based practices (Spina, 2020). There

Navigating the Gap Between Theory and Practice

has also been some exploration of the use of UDL in STEM contexts (Thoma et al., 2023). The majority of work around UDL implementation has thus far focused on high school, but there is now emerging literature examining the use of UDL in early years (Lohmann et al., 2022).

UDL and Learner Diversity beyond Impairment

Early UDL work has been given momentum by the accessibility community and had focused mostly on learners with disabilities (Cumming & Gilanyi, 2023). This reality has recently evolved, however, and in the last five years there has been an increasing amount of interest for UDL in relation to learner diversity construed more widely to include the full spectrum of 'non-traditional' learners. Cultural and linguistic diversity in particular is increasingly the focus of UDL initiatives and projects in the K-12 arena (Mahoney & Harsma, 2021). Using UDL to create inclusive provisions for Indigenous learners is also a topic of growing interest (Vasilez, 2023). This widening in the scope of UDL work mirrors an overall growth in the scope and width of diversity as a concept (Bobongie-Harris & Youse, 2023). Many recent societal events and movements have undoubtedly nurtured and supported this reflection around diversity and inclusion, as umbrella concepts that reach right across the canvas of our communities and go well beyond disability and impairment (Wolbring & Nguyen, 2023).

Recent Trends in UDL Adoption

There is emerging literature examining UDL in the wider spectrum of K-12 classes and subjects. While original initiatives have focused on STEM, English, and social sciences (Mackey, 2019), there is now a desire to see UDL being applied in less traditional teaching settings (Ewe & Gavin, 2023). There is interest in examining how UDL translates and can be adapted to physical education lessons (Haegele et al., 2023), to art classes (Coleman et al., 2015), to language labs (Novak, 2018), and to science labs (Miller & Lang, 2016; Thoma et al., 2023). There is also increasing development of UDL in early years education (Gauvreau et al., 2019). There is some discussion in the scholarship, regarding the degree to which UDL requires technology (Bray et al., 2023); it usually appears that UDL can in fact be implemented without technology (Moore & Nichols Hess, 2020), but there is no doubt that technology, as an affordance, speeds up UDL integration and widens the possible choice of design solutions (Ender et al., 2007; Edyburn et al., 2017). There has also been growing research, since the onset of the COVID pandemic, into the use of UDL in online instruction (Kilaptrick et al., 2021; Hu & Huang, 2022; Smith & Harvey, 2014).

UDL and Strategic Leadership

UDL implementation does not involve solely teachers. It is clear that school leaders have an important role to play in this process (Bouakir, 2019; Fovet, 2023b), and yet the literature on UDL and school leadership is still slim. It is assumed that leaders will automatically and inherently grasp how to support UDL, but leaders often have but limited understanding of UDL themselves. Even though leadership for inclusion is itself a term often used, there is some confusion as to exactly what this involves in terms of tangible skills and competencies. There is actually very little scholarship related to what leadership styles might even be best aligned with the development of inclusive practices or the development of UDL.

METHODOLOGICAL STRUCTURE

The chapter is firmly grounded in the narrative enquiry tradition (Finlay & dela Cruz, 2023). Narrative methodology is usually focused on story telling and seeks to extract themes through the analysis of personal narratives (Weiss & Johnson-Koenke, 2023). Narrative methodology is frequently used in the contemporary landscape to examine professional experiences and to dive deep into stakeholder perspectives and motivations (Chaaban et al., 2021; Ni & Wu, 2023). It has been particularly powerful as a methodology within educational research (Tafazoli & Meihami, 2023; Keskin, 2023). This chapter builds on traditional narrative methodological processes and enriches them by blending two voices, and by analyzing codes and themes in parallel between both these voices. It therefore integrates an element of comparison between the narratives. The comparison in turn is particularly effective to highlight the tension that exists between policy and practice. This is a technique sometimes described as the collection of composite narratives (Johnston et al., 2023).

CONFLICTING REALITIES

The findings in this project bring together two distinct professional perspectives. One author is focusing on the implications of this analysis in relation to on-terrain UDL implementation. The other considers the repercussions of this analysis from the perspective of the research and scholarship which is developing in relation to UDL implementation.

Navigating the Gap Between Theory and Practice

Practitioner Perspective

Sporadic Evidence of Successful Implementation

There is some evidence of pockets of successful implementation of UDL practices.

I think it is important to recognize the progress made and the potential for further growth in the future. For example, in some schools, educators and administrators have recognized the transformative power of UDL and have actively worked towards integrating that UDL principles into their teaching practices. They are seeing the positive impact of UDL on student engagement, motivation, and achievement. It's interesting because as they share their success stories with colleagues in their local school districts and beyond, more educators are seeing the potential benefits for neurodiverse learners in mainstream classrooms.

What strikes practitioners, however, is the fact that these pockets are isolated and fragmented, and that there is no unified or large-scale successful integration of UDL into school districts, or even across individual schools.

I have done numerous UDL presentations for educators. but the overall scale of implementation is still lagging. Yes, there are pockets of excellence where teachers engage in intentional and proactive planning. And yet, there are educators who remain reluctant and/or remain disinterested in this approach. Thus, implementation remains sparse and inconsistent.

What this highlights, is that there are issues around access to training and to professional development. There are also variations in the nature of leadership support available for such initiatives. Geo-political discrepancies exist cross Canada, and even within provinces. Much, in relation to the introduction and the development of UDL, is connected to communities of practice. The inherent nature of communities of practice is that they vary in effectiveness from region to region; they may also adopt very different approaches in how they address needs and target objectives (Ghamrawi, 2022). The fragmentation of the UDL landscape in schools, and the unevenness of the UDL knowledge available in the field, have now become fixtures of this landscape.

Difficulty of Teachers to Break Out of Deficit Model Practices

UDL implementation requires teachers to move decisively and permanently away from deficit model thinking and from medical model practices (Sandoval Gomez & McKee, 2020).

There is a feeling of uncertainty despite multiple workshops and dissemination of information. Shifting to inclusive design means that educators need to look at the strengths of the whole class. But there also appears to be a general anxiety that teachers will neglect the specific needs of struggling learners. It's a balancing act. And yet, moving away from the deficit model remains a challenge. For example, a myth remains that adaptations apply only to students with ministry designations. However, designing inclusively for the whole class requires a reimagining of instruction, being flexible, and knowing each student's strengths and stretches. It involves being open to resources that don't always involve textbooks and looking through the lens of teaching and learning in holistic ways. It's a leap of faith. And that leap can be too big for people.

It is difficult for teachers to navigate this change in mindset and there are many environments where a fixed mindset is on display (Xin et al., 2023; Lyra, 2023).

Letting go of the deficit model is like breaking up with an old habit. The deficit model is comfortable, familiar, and teachers have been conditioned to think that way for so long. The deficit model has been around for many years, that's how many of my colleagues and I were trained while in the Bachelor of Education program. It's so deeply ingrained with many teachers' belief systems. Shifting to inclusive design with the whole class in mind feels like your swimming upstream.

The medical model and deficit approach are associated with the funding model currently in use. It is challenging to shift teachers away from an emphasis on the bio-medical, when funding is intrinsically connected and tied to administrative practices that require the production and archiving of diagnostic nominal information (Sharma et al., 2019). There is therefore often a degree of wishful thinking when teachers are encouraged to adopt the social model of disability and to implement UDL, but they remain tied in administrative processes that contradict the PD they are receiving. The notion of 'hidden curriculum' comes to mind in this area, a dissonance that often occurs in schools when the values explicitly formulated are not aligned with the values, norms and habits otherwise perpetuated (Kärner & Schneider, 2023). It would be fair to say that the hidden curriculum in schools often contradicts any explicit policy on UDL adoption. This hidden curriculum

Navigating the Gap Between Theory and Practice

that contradicts the UDL vision or objective of the school usually manifests itself in the way few resources are dedicated to supporting teachers. They may not have adequate time for redesigning, not obtain coverage for training, and generally not feel that it is treated as a priority by the establishment.

Another obstacle that I've seen teachers experience and express involves having limited time to plan for instructional UDL. There are many demands in classrooms such as behavioral outbursts, evaluations, meetings, extracurricular, etc. that UDL planning falls to the wayside. If only more people could create a fire plan so that less fires need to be put out.

Uneven Standards of Leadership for Inclusion

Just as the development of UDL has been haphazard and uneven in the field, so have experiences of leadership support been in this respect too. There are anecdotal documentations of effective leadership reflection regarding what UDL growth implies and requires. There is also clear evidence that some school leaders are not addressing the needs of their communities when it comes to UDL integration.

In some schools UDL is embraced. It's welcomed and their leaders champion its implementation. But in other schools, leaders have no clue. Maybe they don't fully understand the potential of UDL or perhaps it's not part of the school's vision or mission. It's unfortunate because it's simply a blip on their radar, and they focus on other priorities. On a positive note, there are leaders who really understand the power of UDL and strive to intentionally create those inclusive learning environments. They are the administrators who carve out the first 15 minutes during staff meetings and teach a small component of UDL. They are leaders who provide the necessary resources, the professional development, and the ongoing support. But these champions, they don't just theorize it and talk about it, they model it and have other leaders model it to colleagues within the school. It's amazing how one champion, just one person, can be that transformative leader when it comes to supporting and implementing UDL.

Hypothesizing about the dichotomy that is observed in the field leads one to question the adequate training of school principals in relation to UDL and the conceptual redesign it requires. There is clear evidence as well that funding envelopes do not currently allow school leaders to effectively support the shift of mindset to social model practices and UDL. With this funding structure comes a very rigid and bureaucratic set of administrative processes that involve the collection of diagnostic information, the vetting of this documentation, the categorization of this clinic information within school district designations, and the subsequent allocation of funds on the strength of this documentation. School leaders will often find this process to be so rigid as to leave little room for work on mindsets and pedagogy.

It may also be useful to examine the hesitancy of leadership in relation to UDL implementation through a wider lens which stresses the lack of time and resources more broadly available to school leaders in the current landscape. In a climate of expansion of neoliberalism within the K-12 sector, the dominant stance is distinctly one of business model efficiency (Bailey & Gibson, 2023). When public sector educational institutions are treated as competing enterprises responding to free market pressures, school principals are increasingly seen as managers rather than leaders; the level of accountability is such that resources allocated to vision and pedagogical transformation become limited (Stein, 2016). This is, in all likelihood, a phenomenon that significantly hinders school leaders' commitments to authentic and deep change, and to UDL adoption cross institutions.

Poor Access to Training and Resources

There are issues in the K-12 sector with regards to PD generally (Karsenty & Brodie, 2023; Sims et al., 2021; Schwartz, 2023). This has been evident in the past in relation to such diverse agendas as technological integration (Montero-Mesa et al., 2023), the management of challenging behaviours (Gildlund, 2018), update of literacy strategies (Basma & Savage, 2023), and inclusive provisions generally (Arnaiz-Sánchez et al., 2023). Much care will therefore need to be given to the design of PD that is effective and actually equips teachers with authentic knowledge in relation to UDL, and actionable competencies, as there is growing evidence of low attainment of outcomes in much of teacher training currently deployed in the sector (Patfield, et al., 2021).

Sometimes there is a resistance to change. I know some educators who take one look at the 3 pillars of UDL from CAST and say: 'forget it.' They're accustomed to traditional teaching methods that they remain hesitant to change their instructional practices. Perhaps they find the 3 pillars overwhelming or challenging to implement effectively and realistically. Another one is that maybe teachers are not familiar with the concept of UDL, or even its potential benefits. For example, during non-instructional days, there are so many workshops that teachers often choose something that has nothing to do with UDL or inclusion. Consequently, they don't receive the adequate training or professional development. Unfortunately, the shift to implementing or adopting UDL remains unchanged until they intentionally choose professional development that is UDL focused. Another obstacle, I think, is

Navigating the Gap Between Theory and Practice

not having additional resources to implement UDL effectively, such as technology tools, specialized instructional materials, or assistive technology. I know so many schools that have budget constraints or limited access to these resources, and it really makes it difficult to fully embrace UDL, Dl, and above all, provide those diverse learning options for all students.

If PD on UDL is ineffective in equipping teachers with skills and knowledge that have impact, there will be concerned too as to the access to training that school leaders themselves have in relation to UDL (Sims et al., 2021).

I also believe that school leaders need to play an active role in championing UDL. I've seen far too many leaders who go into this profession and have not participated in relevant UDL training. Their mindsets haven't changed and yet, they need to provide guidance, financial support, and, of course, that much needed ongoing feedback to teachers, as well as ensuring that UDL is aligned with school district strategic plans or the school's vision and mission. When school leaders can do that, then they can also advocate for more resources, grants, and have that funding allocated towards UDL initiatives.

Lack of Fit between Training Format and Teacher Expectations

Teachers have very specific expectations when it comes to PD on UDL. They have questions, require clarifications, and will want to personalize their understanding of the model by accessing a variety of resources. This broad opportunities for in-depth UDL adoption and integration have not been available within the PD that has been offered. Often, teachers are left with a simple taste of what UDL might look like but rarely have opportunities to go beyond this initial discovery, or to feel that their thirst for understanding in relation to UDL is satisfied. PD on UDL will have, in particular, to model UDL practices and the inclusive design mindset been promoted. Instead, there is usually a considerable contradiction between the values of inclusive design which are being preached, and the format of the PD which is being offered (Fovet, 2017).

I believe UDL professional development can be designed to be flexible and accessible. It can involve a mix of in-person workshops, online modules, and self-paced resources that teachers can engage with at their own convenience. Again, if we consider the heavy workloads that teachers face, I believe it's important to design a universally designed PD, in a flexible and accessible matter, maybe have a mix of in-person workshops, some self-pace modules, and perhaps asynchronous and synchronous webinars. When school districts offer a variety of PD formats, they model what UDL can look like for teachers, not just for students. Teachers would also benefit from real case studies where they can practice applying the UDL strategies. Theory is great but application is important too. Again, PD needs to be manageable. It must be realistic bite-size pieces that support professional growth amid a demanding and stressful profession. Another option is to maybe have mentoring or coaching in place, having that one-on-one support in the classroom can help teachers with the implementation. Maybe the mentor or coach can provide specific suggestions for improvement, and perhaps some resources like templates, graphic organizers, and UDL focused lesson plans. These would be wonderful approaches to help teachers gain the confidence and skills to implement UDL.

Lack of Awareness of Parents and Community around UDL

There is no significant awareness in relation to UDL among parents and community. There is, on the other hand, considerable understanding of what differentiated instruction represents. It can therefore be difficult for parents to feel fully informed about what UDL objectives might be or to fully grasp how UDL differs from differentiated instruction.

Not a lot of parents know what UDL is, at least the ones I've met. If they do, they're often teachers themselves. Community agencies that work with schools are starting to understand UDL, and they became aware of this when I explained it to them in my interactions with them. The issue is that some stakeholders may believe that UDL is just for students with special needs, but when it's explained to them, they certainly have a better understanding of the term and absolutely love it. The solution, I think, to helping parents in communities know more about UDL is through competency-based IEPs, which are now being used by more than 50% of school districts in the province of BC. Stakeholders need to understand UDL because there is a specific section allocated to it in a competency-based IEP.

There will need to be considerable work done in relation to parents and community across country if resistance from these important stakeholder groups is to be eroded. The literature has argued for some time that parents must be allies in any transformational process in education, and there can be no successful large scale UDL integration envisaged without parental support. Ironically, parents who are not informed adequately about UDL may see the provision of inclusive design to all students in a whole class approach as a loss of specific support and services for

Navigating the Gap Between Theory and Practice

their child. It will be essential that this transition in approach, from retrofitting to UDL, be accompanied by structured and planned information campaigns for parents.

Researcher Perspective

Lack of Sustainable Reflection

The literature offers ample evidence of implementation attempts across the Canadian K-12 landscape, but there is little documented record of successful, cross-organization, sustainable implementation. It has been significantly frustrating for UDL advocates, scholars, and teachers to see initiatives come and go, and to observe UDL pilot projects appear, thrive, and fail within a rapid time frame. It has been extremely counter-productive, as it feeds suspicion among the stakeholders that have yet to be convinced of the usefulness of UDL as a model.

What the literature tells us is that there is a large gap between the assessment that we make about future development of UDL, its potential use, and the receptiveness of the field, and what is actually happening on the ground. I think that the most challenging parts of my research actually focuses on examining the number of initiatives and pilot projects that have failed over the last ten years and disappeared into the cobwebs of the net, with no trace. There's been a lot of wasted energy and we're certainly not seeing all literature on UDL translated into practice; it feels like planning in a way that is informed by evidence is still something challenging.

It has created exhaustion among stakeholders and advocates who have invested personal efforts and time into projects that never grew or developed. There is a need to reassure the sector as a whole that UDL implementation is feasible, achievable, measurable, and sustainable. Short of this, it will begin to be perceived as a wasteful trend that cannot deliver the desired outcome over time.

So, the main obstacles that teachers face in implementing UDL from a theoretical point of view, or a conceptual perspective, or looking at the scholarship, would definitely have to do with workload management. If we situate ourselves within a neoliberal perspective on the current educational landscape, we see teachers struggling to keep up with workload, accountability measures, growing responsibilities, and they are left literally to focus on professional development in their own time, in their time off as well. So, there's a lack of structured sustainable vision with regards to growth and growth mindset within the teaching profession. The second obstacle is more structural. At present, we don't even have teachers' unions involved in the UDL dialogue. We are not thinking about the remuneration for UDL work, for redesign work. We are not really examining exactly when teachers might be expected to carry on that redesign work; there is no tangible, realistic, and pragmatic examination of the cost element for teachers, and I think that's one of the major obstacles and that's completely absent from the literature.

Impact of Failings in Leadership

It is apparent in the current literature on UDL that there is little space given to a strategic reflection around the role that must be played by school leaders in this process.

The school leadership issue is really problematic. In the literature we have a significant body of literature that talks about leadership for inclusion, but I would argue that that term is often very shallow. In fact, in the field, we don't really see a leadership style, or conceptualisation of leadership, or construct of leadership that actually adequately addresses the needs of inclusive education, or more particularly UDL implementation. So, this is probably one of the areas where we have the most striking gap between theory and practice, with literature that often appears as wishful thinking on what we would like leadership to look like for UDL implementation, but very few instances where we see this illustrated or evidence in practice.

Far too much of the scholarship on UDL thus far has focused on the teacher role in UDL implementation. Many of the experimentations discussed in research also focuses on teacher-led pilot projects where the only variables examined are (i) the student-teacher relationship, (ii) the impact of UDL integration on learning outcomes, or (iii) the mindset of the teachers carrying out these projects (UNB&DEECD, 2014). Instead, the process of UDL implementation should be considered more widely as an organizational process. The involvement of school leadership will need to be examined with care and framed conceptually in the future. There is also a need for specific UDL PD for school leaders, and a sparsity of available resources for this stakeholder group.

Absence of Reflection on Administrative and Environmental Variables

There is a lack of awareness in the literature on UDL implementation in the K-12 sector in relation to the complexity of the landscape. This section of the chapter has discussed teachers, and school leaders, but all administrative and support services are affected by this process of change. If UDL is to be adopted systemically across

Navigating the Gap Between Theory and Practice

organizations, it is essential that training, resources, and professional reflection dribble down to all layers of these institutions. All staff must gain a mastery of UDL as a framework to be able, in order to understand how it will transform their role, their job description, and the messaging they give others. As UDL represents a move away from deficit model practices, it affects all aspects of the current service delivery model, and shifts the entire organization away from deficit thinking, not just educators.

There is also an ecological need to infuse all relationships of the school, and all facets of its work with external stakeholder, with UDL principles and values. At present, this is not happening. Community and parents, for example, are rarely involved in the dialogue on UDL; nor are they strategically invited into this reflection.

So, when it comes to community, there is simply not much of a focus in the scholarship and literature on partnership with community and it's striking. In every other respect, the literature describes parents and communities as the essential partner in school life particularly in management of change, but we have not to date really considered parents and community within the literature or the research that focuses on UDL. They may in fact have questions, need information, and they may have misperceptions about Universal Design for Learning, and also they may simply feel reluctant to embrace UDL because they have not been part of the process from the start.

Failures of Pre-service Teacher Training and In-service Professional Development

The scholarship on UDL highlights that pre-service teacher training is not adapting quickly enough to provide teachers with sufficient resources; nor does pre-service teacher training offer opportunities for the implementation of inclusive design competencies.

The issue of pre-service teacher training and in-service teacher professional development is problematic. In the literature or the scholarship on UDL, we tend to assume that pre-service candidates and in-service teachers will simply pick up resources and training on the cuff, and that's not going to happen. So, we need to see a drastic redesign of pre-service teacher training and in-service professional development on UDL, if we want teachers to be able to access authentic, substantial, and effective resources and to have access to training that is more than lip service.

Navigating the Gap Between Theory and Practice

Even when UDL is brought up and discussed in PD, this material fails to offer tangible and pragmatic opportunities for authentic integration and application in context. When UDL concepts are introduced in relation to the classroom environment, these principles are not used and developed during the field placements or the practicums (Flanagan et al., 2014; Lowrey et al., 2019). There has been a reflective and historical move away from any professional development in pre-service teacher training that might be construed as perpetuating medical model and deficit model approaches, such as 'special needs' or 'special education' categories (Sharma, 2018). This shift in focus is logical and does have a beneficial impact on pre-service teacher candidates' perceptions and beliefs, and on their mindset. The specialized content and instruction candidates used to receive in special education should, however, be replaced by substantial exposure to UDL and by authentic opportunities to apply the UDL design principles in context (Massouti, 2021; Rusconi & Squillaci, 2023); this is unfortunately not happening at present (Lehtomäki, et al., 2020).

The situation is very similar as regards in-service professional development (PD). There is a considerable need for such PD efforts to focus on UDL, but resources are scarce. Across the profession, PD days are rare and far between (TNTP, 2015). They often become overwhelming because so much catching up is occurring and teachers are feeling exhaustion and burn out (Popova et al., 2022). There is generally, in relation to school PD, an overwhelming focus on high cost, low frequency use of keynote speakers, but few opportunities to deepen knowledge, apply competencies, or request follow-up training (Karsenty & Brodie, 2023).

It's very challenging for teachers to let go of deficit model thinking. I think it's going to be impossible for them to achieve this until they are actually exposed to the social model of disability. At present, what we see in the literature is that there is very little intentionality when it comes to introducing teachers, whether in-service or pre-service, to the social model of disability. I often introduce it during in-service professional development, when I'm called to talk about Universal Design for Learning and often these mid-career professionals have never heard of the social model. It will be very difficult to change a mindset unless we actually offer these candidates a theoretical paradigm that allows them to shift away from bio-medical perspectives or deficit model thinking, and for that we require an introduction of a social model of disability.

Navigating the Gap Between Theory and Practice

OUTCOMES AND RECOMMENDATIONS

Bridging the Gap between Policy and Practice

One of the main implications of this chapter for future research is the fact that it has highlighted a dramatic gap between theory and practice. This gap, it is argued, has been ignored or dismissed by UDL advocates and scholars alike, in an enthusiastic effort to build momentum around UDL. This gap is problematic since it indicates that key elements researched and evidenced in relation to the benefits of UDL for the inclusion of diverse learners are not effectively being understood, assimilated, or acted on by field practitioners. This is highly damaging, as it intrinsically threatens any future sustainable efforts to broaden the impact of UDL in schools.

The gap identified between theory and practice is also daunting as it highlights the fact that there is evidently a degree of denial in this area of scholarship. The literature has been quick to celebrate the successes but has not adequately evidenced the challenges. This may lead to the eventual creation of a portrayal of the school landscape that is misleading and does not allow for the accurate or realistic planning necessary to grow and develop UDL as a framework across the sector. Instead, there is a significant risk that part of the literature on UDL in Canada may currently be operating from a position of wishful thinking, rather than offering accurate benchmarks as to what is working and creating change .It is argued that it is only by confronting the harsh reality of failure or tension in UDL implementation in the K-12 sector, that researchers will come to fully grasp the complexity of UDL implementation and the multiple and varied factors that affect its success as a process of management of change. More widely, much of the literature on UDL has focused on highlighting the pedagogical benefits of its adoption for the inclusion of diverse learners. It has not sufficiently examined the process of organizational transformation itself.

Implications in Relation to Leadership for Inclusion

Both narratives in this chapter identify key concerns around leadership for inclusion. The field perspective offers a portrayal of leadership that is uneven when it comes to the implementation of UDL into the K-12 sector; the theoretical stance highlights a lack of reflective, sustainable, or structured leadership efforts that can support growth and development in the area of UDL integration. This is true of funding initiative which are, as a rule, sporadic and insufficient. There is also little reflection taking place around the resources required to support teachers long-term. This includes issues of access to PD events, coverage by substitute teachers at the time when these events take place, recognition of time invested by teachers in the redesign of teaching and assessment, acknowledgement and recognition of efforts

269

Navigating the Gap Between Theory and Practice

deployed in relation to UDL in performance review and workload assessment, and creation of mentoring positions in this specific area of teacher support.

While there is much talk of leadership for inclusion more widely in the literature, it can be argued that in many respects this remains a concept with little depth. There has been very little conceptual development carried out in relation to what this leadership for inclusion might look like. It is therefore of little surprise that the scholarship on leadership for UDL in the K-12 sector remains shallow and without nuance. There is some debate in the field as to how this issue might be addressed. Infusing a nuanced understanding of UDL amongst school leaders is a daunting task. While many school principals may be highly interested in the model when they hear about it, they often also lack a detailed understanding of the implication for them as organizational leaders and HR managers. Most school principal training currently focuses on administrative leadership rather than on pedagogical leadership. Little of this training is transformational; a transformational approach to UDL would imply a degree of inspirational modelling from administrators, possibly even the integration of the UDL principles in the interactions between leaders and school employees.

Exploring Sustainability as a Framework for UDL Implementation

The chapter highlights the lack of sustainability in current approaches to UDL implementation in the K-12 sector. At a micro-level this is evidenced by the lack of sustainable funding of UDL initiatives and pilot projects, with envelopes that are short lived, and rarely renewed or increased. In a broader context, the lack of sustainability is demonstrated by the absence of strategic planning around UDL training for teachers, in relation to teacher access to PD resources, and to the absence of planned and funded position creation around UDL mentoring and support for teachers.

Within a broader perspective still, there has been a chronic and noticeable failure to connect UDL implementation with wider sustainability efforts in the K-12 landscape. There are organic, logical, and powerful ways to connects inclusion – and UDL more generally – to the UN Sustainability Goals (United Nations, 2023). These sustainable goals already frame many K-12 initiatives and a significant volume of policy creation. While social justice is explicitly framed as a UN sustainability goal, little work has occurred to date to connect inclusion with the momentum that emerges from these UN goals in education. It is clear, however, that UDL falls squarely within the literature on sustainability, as in essence it reduces pressure on support services and on costly retrofitting practices, and instead supports the development of sustainable – and less costly or resource intensive – whole class inclusive pedagogy for all.

270

Navigating the Gap Between Theory and Practice

Examining Ecological Variables that Impact Implementation

The chapter has highlighted the lack of strategic and organizational reflection around UDL implementation in the K-12 sector as a process of management of change. It has also highlighted the fact that the representation of UDL implementation in the literature has been to date unrealistic and perhaps naïve. UDL integration should instead be positioned by the literature as a complex process of management of change and organizational transformation. This complexity is generally not sufficiently stressed because advocates and practitioners fail to fully assess the full ecological richness of the landscape within which it unfolds. UDL is not just about teachers and learners; it impacts a wide range of diverse stakeholders across educational organizations. Many of these stakeholders have not to date been acknowledged in the scholarship on UDL. Teachers' unions for example are entirely absent from the commentary, and yet represent one of the key groups that should be involved at all stages of UDL integration. Any realistic approach to UDL adoption across the sector will require a careful ecological mapping of the professionals, units and stakeholder groups involved. An ecological assessment will offer a full picture of the multitude of stakeholders who have a role to play or a say in the process. It will also examine the way these stakeholders interact with each other, as these alliances and tensions can affect UDL adoption, irrespective of the inherent pedagogical benefits of the framework itself.

Re-dynamizing the UDL Implementation Drive

After 20 years of diverse UDL initiatives across Canada, of varying scope and flavour, it is clear that the momentum for adoption is not incrementally growing. Instead, we have observed historically a process of try and error which has seen many exceptional pilot projects fail and disappear altogether. This precarity is dangerous as it leads to a phenomenon of practitioner exhaustion, and to a feeling of suspicion from those not yet familiar with the framework. This chapter has highlighted that this fragility is caused by a very specific lack of strategic and organizational reflection in relation to leadership and sustainable development. The chapter has also highlighted a lack of transparency or awareness in the literature when it comes to evidencing hurdles, challenges, points of tension, and failures. It is argued that, as long as the UDL discourse fails to take a pragmatic and realistic approach to this process of change, the momentum for implementation will remain shaky and unsustainable. There are very specific variables to identify, analyze, and address, in order to grasp the complexity of the task ahead. This chapter is therefore a call for action; it argues that a realistic, thorough, and brutally honest examination of struggles will create

Navigating the Gap Between Theory and Practice

a basis for a tangible, achievable and powerful roadmap that finally sees success in large scale UDL implementation in the K-12 sector.

CONCLUSION

This chapter is key in acknowledging and analyzing the gap and tension that exist between policy and practice when it comes to UDL implementation within the Canadian K-12 landscape. It is a gap that is rarely acknowledged, and this state of denial is hindering the growth of UDL and future implementation efforts. This chapter is precedent setting in the sense that it explicitly merges a scholar voice more focused on practice and a scholar voice that has been more theoretically focused. These two blended narratives offer an authentically broad outlook on the current state of play when it comes to the reality of UDL implementation in schools. Beyond highlighting the tension between theory and practice, it identifies specific avenues of reflection which will support future UDL advocates and the leaders who support their work. Although the chapter focuses on the current reality of the Canadian K-12 sector, it will offer the international reader broad and tangible axes for reflection on UDL integration in most jurisdictions. The themes identified are likely to have some pertinence in most educational systems, even if local and regional contexts may add further variables to the equation.

REFERENCES

Almeqdad, Q. I., Alodat, A. M., Alquraan, M. F., Mohaidat, M. A., & Al-Makhzoomy, A. K. (2023). The effectiveness of universal design for learning: A systematic review of the literature and meta-analysis. *Cogent Education*, 10(1), 2218191. Advance online publication. 10.1080/2331186X.2023.2218191

Almumen, H. A. (2020). Universal Design for Learning (UDL) Across Cultures: The Application of UDL in Kuwaiti Inclusive Classrooms. *SAGE Open*, 10(4). Advance online publication. 10.1177/2158244020969674

Arnaiz-Sánchez, P., De Haro-Rodríguez, R., Caballero, C.M., & Martínez-Abellán, R. (2023). Barriers to Educational Inclusion in Initial Teacher Training. *Societies 13, 2*(31). https://doi.org/10.3390/soc13020031

Bailey, L., & Gibson, M. (2023). School leaders of high stakes assessments during the COVID pandemic in England. *School Leadership & Management*, 43(3), 189–209. 10.1080/13632434.2023.2176482

Basma, B., & Savage, R. (2023). Teacher Professional Development and Student Reading in Middle and High School: A Systematic Review and Meta-Analysis. *Journal of Teacher Education*, 74(3), 214–228. 10.1177/00224871231153084

BCUDL. (2010) *Universal Design for Learning in BC*. Special Education Technology BC. https://curric.prn.bc.ca/wp-content/uploads/sites/37/2017/02/UDL-SET-BC.pdf

Bobongie-Harris, F., & Youse, Z. (2023). Approaches to improve the cultural capabilities of teachers engaging with culturally and linguistically diverse students and their families: A scoping review. *Frontiers in Education*, 8, 1038880. https://www.frontiersin.org/articles/10.3389/feduc.2023.1038880. 10.3389/feduc.2023.1038880

Bouakir, H. (2019) *School leadership strategies for the implementation of Universal Design for Learning*. MEd thesis. Faculty of Education, Memorial University of Newfoundland. https://research.library.mun.ca/14306/1/thesis.pdf

Cera, R. (2015). National Legislations on Inclusive Education and Special Educational Needs of People with Autism in the Perspective of Article 24 of the CRPD. In Della Fina, V., & Cera, R. (Eds.), *Protecting the Rights of People with Autism in the Fields of Education and Employment*. Springer., 10.1007/978-3-319-13791-9_4

Chaaban, Y., Al-Thani, H., & Du, X. (2021). A narrative inquiry of teacher educators' professional agency, identity renegotiations, and emotional responses amid educational disruption. *Teaching and Teacher Education*, 108, 103522. Advance online publication. 10.1016/j.tate.2021.103522

Coleman, M. B., Cramer, E. S., Park, Y., & Bell, S. M. (2015). Art educators' use of adaptations, assistive technology, and special education supports for students with physical, visual, severe and multiple disabilities. *Journal of Developmental and Physical Disabilities*, 27(5), 637–660. 10.1007/s10882-015-9440-6

Cumming, T., & Gilanyi, L. (2023). 'Our Classes Are Like Mainstream School Now': Implementing Universal Design for Learning at a Special School. *Australasian Journal of Special and Inclusive Education*, 1-15. 10.1017/jsi.2023.7

Dignath, C., Rimm-Kaufman, S., van Ewijk, R., & Kunter, M. (2022). Teachers' Beliefs About Inclusive Education and Insights on What Contributes to Those Beliefs: A Meta-analytical Study. *Educational Psychology Review*, 34(4), 2609–2660. 10.1007/s10648-022-09695-0

Disability Nottinghamshire. (2023) Social Model vs Medical Model of disability. *About Us*.https://www.disabilitynottinghamshire.org.uk/index.php/about/social -model-vs-medical-model-of-disability/

Edyburn, D. L., Rao, K., & Hariharan, P. (2017). Technological practices supporting diverse students in inclusive settings. In Hughes, M. T., & Talbott, E. (Eds.), *The Wiley handbook of diversity in special education* (pp. 357–377). Wiley., 10.1002/9781118768778.ch17

Ender, K. E., Kinney, B. J., Penrod, W. M., Bauder, D. K., & Simmons, T. (2007). Achieving systemic change with Universal Design for Learning and digital content. *Assistive Technology Outcomes and Benefits*, 4(1), 115–129. https://eric.ed.gov/?id =EJ899371

Ewe, L., & Galvin, T. (2023). Universal Design for Learning across Formal School Structures in Europe—A Systematic Review. *Education Sciences*, 13(9), 867. 10.3390/educsci13090867

Finlay, J., & dela Cruz, A. (2023). Reflexivity and Relational Spaces: Experiences of Conducting a Narrative Inquiry Study With Emerging Adult Women Living With Chronic Pain. *Global Qualitative Nursing Research*, 10, 23333936231190619. Advance online publication. 10.1177/2333393623119061937576739

Finnerty, M. S., Jackson, L. B., & Ostergren, R. (2019). Adaptations in General Education Classrooms for Students With Severe Disabilities: Access, Progress Assessment, and Sustained Use. *Research and Practice for Persons with Severe Disabilities : the Journal of TASH*, 44(2), 87–102. 10.1177/1540796919846424

Flanagan, T., Benson, F. J., & Fovet, F. (2014) A multi-perspective examination of the barriers to field-placement experiences for students with disabilities. *Collected Essays on Learning and Teaching, 7*(2) https://files.eric.ed.gov/fulltext/EJ1060220.pdf

Fovet, F. (2014) Social model as catalyst for innovation in design and pedagogical change. *Widening Participation through Curriculum Open University 2014 Conference Proceedings*, 135-139

Fovet, F. (2017) *Doing what we preach: examining the contradictions of the UDL discourse in faculties of education.* Paper presented at the 2017 AHEAD Ireland Conference, Dublin, March

Fovet, F. (2018). Making it work! Addressing teacher resistance in systemic UDL implementation across schools. In Jangira, N. K., Limaye, S., & Kapoor, S. (Eds.), *Inclusive Education: Practitioners' Perspectives.* School Inclusive Education Development Initiative.

Fovet, F. (2023) The Changing Landscape of Inclusive Education: A Shift toward Universal Design for Learning. In A. Beckett and Dr A-M. Callus (Eds.) *Handbook on Children's Rights and Disability.* Routledge https://www.taylorfrancis.com/chapters/edit/10.4324/9781003056737-37/changing-landscape-inclusive-education-frederic-fovet

Fovet, F. (2023b) *Can we do it without school principals' commitment? Exploring the complex impact of school leadership on UDL implementation.* UDL Workshop offered at the 1st International Universal Design for Learning Symposium Learning Together. Maynooth University, June.

Gauvreau, A. N., Lohmann, M. J., & Hovey, K. A. (2019). Using a Universal Design for Learning Framework to Provide Multiple Means of Representation in the Early Childhood Classroom. *The Journal of Special Education Apprenticeship*, 8(1), 3. https://scholarworks.lib.csusb.edu/josea/vol8/iss1/3. 10.58729/2167-3454.1083

Ghamrawi, N. (2022). Teachers' virtual communities of practice: A strong response in times of crisis or just another Fad? *Education and Information Technologies*, 27(5), 5889–5915. 10.1007/s10639-021-10857-w35095322

Gildlund, U. (2018). Teachers' Attitudes towards Including Students with Emotional and Behavioural Difficulties in Mainstream School: A Systematic Research Synthesis. *International Journal of Learning. Teaching and Educational Research*, 17(2), 45–63. 10.26803/ijlter.17.2.3

Griful-Freixenet, J., Struyven, K., Vantieghem, W., & Gheyssens, E. (2020). Exploring the interrelationship between Universal Design for Learning (UDL) and Differentiated Instruction (DI): A systematic review. *Educational Research Review*, 29, 100306. Advance online publication. 10.1016/j.edurev.2019.100306

Haegele, J. A., Holland, S. K., Wilson, W. J., Maher, A. J., Kirk, T. N., & Mason, A. (2023). Universal design for learning in physical education: Overview and critical reflection. *European Physical Education Review*. Advance online publication. 10.1177/1356336X231202658

Hu, H., & Huang, F. (2022). Application of Universal Design for Learning into remote English education in Australia amid COVID-19 pandemic. [IJonSE]. *International Journal on Studies in Education*, 4(1), 55–69. 10.46328/ijonse.59

Johnston, O., Wildy, H., & Shand, J. (2023). Student voices that resonate – constructing composite narratives that represent students' classroom experiences. *Qualitative Research*, 23(1), 108–124. 10.1177/14687941211016158

Kärner, T., & Schneider, G. (2023). A scoping review on the hidden curriculum in education: Mapping definitory elements for educational theory building. *PsychArchives*.https://doi.org/10.23668/psycharchives.13240

Karsenty, R., & Brodie, K. (2023). Researching "what went wrong" in professional development (PD) for mathematics teachers: What makes it so important, and so difficult? *Journal of Mathematics Teacher Education*, 26(5), 573–580. 10.1007/s10857-023-09599-y

Kelly, O., Buckley, K., Lieberman, L. J., & Arndt, K. (2022). Universal Design for Learning - A framework for inclusion in Outdoor Learning. *Journal of Outdoor and Environmental Education*, 25(1), 75–89. 10.1007/s42322-022-00096-z

Keskin, M. (2023). Discovering and Developing Research Interests: A Narrative Inquiry into Three Doctoral Students' Experiences. *Yükseköğretim Dergisi*, 13(1), 9–18. 10.2399/yod.23.1225236

Kilpatrick, J. R., Ehrlich, S., & Bartlett, M. (2021). Learning from COVID-19: Universal Design for Learning Implementation Prior to and during a pandemic. *The Journal of Applied Instructional Design*, 10(1), 1–17. https://edtechbooks.org/jaid_10_1/universal_design_forS

King-Sears, M. E., Stefanidis, A., Evmenova, A. S., Rao, K., Mergen, R. L., Sanborn Owen, L., & Strimel, M. M. (2023). Achievement of learners receiving UDL instruction: A meta-analysis. *Teaching and Teacher Education*, 122, 103956. Advance online publication. 10.1016/j.tate.2022.103956

Lambertl, R., McNiff, A., Schuck, R., Imm, K., & Zimmerman, S. (2023). "UDL is a way of thinking"; theorizing UDL teacher knowledge, beliefs, and practices. *Frontiers in Education*, 8. https://www.frontiersin.org/articles/10.3389/feduc.2023.1145293

Lehtomäki, E., Posti-Ahokas, H., Beltrán, A., Shaw, C., Edjah, H., Juma, S., Mulat, M., & Hirvonen, M. (2020) *Teacher education for inclusion: five countries across three continents*. Global Education Monitoring Report Team [1018]. UNESCO. https://unesdoc.unesco.org/ark:/48223/pf0000373804

Levey, S. (2023). Universal Design for Learning. *Journal of Education*, 203(2), 479–487. 10.1177/00220574211031954

Lohmann, M., Hovey, K. A., & Gauvreau, A. (2022) Universal Design for Learning (UDL) in Inclusive Preschool Science Classrooms. *Journal of Science Education*. https://scholarworks.rit.edu/cgi/viewcontent.cgi?article=1178&context=jsesd

Lowrey, K., Classen, A., & Sylvest, A. (2019). Exploring Ways to Support Preservice Teachers' Use of UDL in Planning and Instruction. *Journal of Educational Research and Practice*, 9(1), 261–281. 10.5590/JERAP.2019.09.1.19

Lowrey, K., Hollingshead, A., Howery, K., & Bishop, J. (2017). More than one way: Stories of UDL and inclusive classrooms. *Research and Practice for Persons with Severe Disabilities: the Journal of TASH*, 42(4), 225–242. 10.1177/1540796917711668

Lyra, O., Koullapi, K., & Kalogeropoulou, E. (2023). Fears towards disability and their impact on teaching practices in inclusive classrooms: An empirical study with teachers in Greece. *Heliyon*, 9(5), e16332. Advance online publication. 10.1016/j.heliyon.2023.e1633237305505

Mackey, M. (2019). Accessing middle school social studies content through Universal Design for Learning. *Journal of Educational Research and Practice*, 9(1), 81–88. 10.5590/JERAP.2019.09.1.06

Mahoney, K., & Harsma, E. (2021). Exploring the Connection Between Universal Design for Learning and Culturally Responsive Teaching: Community, Choice, and Support for Diverse Learners through Different Teaching Modalities. In E. Langran & D. Rutledge (Eds.), *Proceedings of SITE Interactive Conference (pp. 40-43). Online, United States: Association for the Advancement of Computing in Education (AACE)*. https://www.learntechlib.org/primary/p/220163/

Massouti, A. (2021). Pre-service teachers' perspectives on their preparation for inclusive teaching: Implications for organizational change in teacher education. *The Canadian Journal for the Scholarship of Teaching and Learning*, 12(1). Advance online publication. 10.5206/cjsotlrcacea.2021.1.10611

McKenna, J. W., Solis, M., Garwood, J., & Parenti, M. (2023). Characteristics of Individualized Education Programs for Students With Learning Disabilities: A Systematic Review. *Learning Disability Quarterly*. Advance online publication. 10.1177/07319487231182697

Miller, D., & Lang, P. (2016). Using the Universal Design for Learning Approach in Science Laboratories To Minimize Student Stress. *Journal of Chemical Education*, 93(11), 1823–1828. 10.1021/acs.jchemed.6b00108

Montero-Mesa, L., Fraga-Varela, F., Vila-Couñago, E., & Rodríguez-Groba, A. (2023). Digital Technology and Teacher Professional Development: Challenges and Contradictions in Compulsory Education. *Education Sciences*, 13(10), 1029. 10.3390/educsci13101029

Moore, C., & Nichols Hess, A. (2020) *Universal Design for Learning with (and without) Technology*. Pod Newtwork. https://podnetwork.org/universal-design-for -learning-with-and-without-technology/

Ni, H., & Wu, X. (2023). Research or teaching? That is the problem: A narrative inquiry into a Chinese college English teacher's cognitive development in the teaching-research nexus. *Frontiers in Psychology*, 14, 1018122. https://www.frontiersin.org/articles/ 10.3389/fpsyg.2023.1018122. 10.3389/fpsyg.2023.101812236818100

Novak, K. (2018, March 9) Why UDL Matters for English Language Learners. Language Magazine. https://www.languagemagazine.com/2018/03/09/why-udl -matters-for-english-language-learners/

Ok, M. W., Rao, K., Bryant, B. R., & McDougall, D. (2017). Universal Design for Learning in pre-k to grade 12 classrooms: A systematic review of research. *Exceptionality*, 25(2), 116–138. 10.1080/09362835.2016.1196450

Ontario Human Rights Commission. (2018) *Policy on accessible education for students with disabilities*. OHRC. https://www.ohrc.on.ca/en/policy-accessible -education-students-disabilities

Patfield, S., Gore, J., & Harris, J. (2023). Shifting the focus of research on effective professional development: Insights from a case study of implementation. *Journal of Educational Change*, 24(2), 345–363. 10.1007/s10833-021-09446-y

Navigating the Gap Between Theory and Practice

Popova, A., Evans, D. K., Breeding, M. E., & Arancibia, V. (2022). Teacher Professional Development around the World: The Gap between Evidence and Practice. *The World Bank Research Observer*, 37(1), 107–136. 10.1093/wbro/lkab006

Rao, K., & Meo, G. (2016). Using Universal Design for Learning to Design Standards-Based Lessons. *SAGE Open*, 6(4). Advance online publication. 10.1177/2158244016680688

Rose, D. H., Gravel, J. W., & Domings, Y. (2012). Universal design for learning "unplugged": Applications in low-tech settings. In Hall, T. E., Meyer, A., & Rose, D. H. (Eds.), *Universal design for learning in the classroom: Practical applications* (pp. 120–134). Guilford Press. https://eric.ed.gov/?id=ED568861

Rusconi, L., & Squillaci, M. (2023). Effects of a Universal Design for Learning (UDL) Training Course on the Development Teachers' Competences: A Systematic Review. *Education Sciences*, 13(5), 466. 10.3390/educsci13050466

Saia, T. (2023). Embracing Disability Culture in Schools. *Language, Speech, and Hearing Services in Schools*, 54(3), 794–798. Advance online publication. 10.1044/2023_LSHSS-22-0014237059085

Salvia, J., Ysseldyke, J. E., & Bolt, S. (2009). *Assessment in Special and Inclusive Education* (11th ed.). Houghton Mifflin Company.

Sandoval Gomez, A., & McKee, A. (2020) When Special Education and Disability Studies Intertwine: Addressing Educational Inequities Through Processes and Programming. *Frontiers in Education, 5*. https://www.frontiersin.org/articles/10.3389/feduc.2020.587045. DOI=10.3389/feduc.2020.587045

Schwartz, S. (2023, June 21) Where Teachers Say Professional Development Falls Short. *Education Week*. https://www.edweek.org/leadership/where-teachers-say -professional-development-falls-short/2023/06

Sharma, U. (2018). *Preparing to Teach in Inclusive Classrooms*. Oxford Research Encyclopedias., 10.1093/acrefore/9780190264093.013.113

Sharma, U., Furlonger, B., & Forlin, C. (2019). The Impact of Funding Models on the Education of Students With Autism Spectrum Disorder. *Australasian Journal of Special and Inclusive Education*, 43(1), 1–11. 10.1017/jsi.2019.1

Sims, S., Fletcher-Wood, H., O'Mara-Eves, A., Cottingham, S., Stansfield, C., Van Herwegen, J., & Anders, J. (2021). *What are the Characteristics of Teacher Professional Development that Increase Pupil Achievement? A systematic review and meta-analysis*. Education Endowment Foundation. https://educationendowment foundation.org.uk/education-evidence/evidence-reviews/teacherprofessional -development-characteristics

Smith, S. J., & Harvey, E. E. (2014). K-12 online lesson alignment to the principles of Universal Design for Learning: The khan academy. *Open Learning*, 29(3), 222–242. 10.1080/02680513.2014.992402

Spina, C. (2021). *Creating Inclusive Libraries by Applying Universal Design: a Guide*. Rowman & Littlefield.

Stein, L. (2016). Schools Need Leaders – Not Managers: It's Time for a Paradigm Shift. *Journal of Leadership Education*, 15(2), 21–30. Advance online publication. 10.12806/V15/I2/I3

Tafazoli, D., & Meihami, H. (2023). Narrative inquiry for CALL teacher preparation programs amidst the COVID-19 pandemic: Language teachers' technological needs and suggestions. *Journal of Computers in Education*, 10(1), 163–187. 10.1007/s40692-022-00227-x

Thoma, R., Farassopoulos, N., & Lousta, C. (2023). Teaching STEAM through universal design for learning in early years of primary education: Plugged-in and unplugged activities with emphasis on connectivism learning theory. *Teaching and Teacher Education*, 132, 104210. Advance online publication. 10.1016/j.tate.2023.104210

TNTP. (2015). The Mirage: Confronting the Hard Truth about Our Quest for Teacher Development. *The New Teacher Project*. https://files.eric.ed.gov/fulltext/ED558206.pdf

Tobin, T. J., & Behling, K. T. (2018). *Reach everyone, teach everyone: Universal Design for learning in higher education*. West Virginia University Press.

United Nations. (2023). *The 17 Goals*. https://sdgs.un.org/goals

United States Department of Education [USDofE] (2023) *The State of School Diversity in the United States*. Office of Planning, Evaluation and Policy Development. https://www2.ed.gov/rschstat/eval/resources/diversity.pdf

University of New Brunswick and Department of Education & Early Childhood Development. (2014) Universal Design for Learning Action Research. Department of Education & Early Childhood Development. https://www2.gnb.ca/content/dam/gnb/Departments/ed/pdf/UDLActionResearch.pdf

Vasilez, J. (2023) *Indigenizing Education: Universal Design for Learning and Indigenous Leadership Frameworks.* Ed.D. Dissertations in Practice, 76. University of Washington Tacoma. https://digitalcommons.tacoma.uw.edu/edd_capstones/76

Weiss, C. R., & Johnson-Koenke, R. (2023). Narrative Inquiry as a Caring and Relational Research Approach: Adopting an Evolving Paradigm. *Qualitative Health Research*, 33(5), 388–399. 10.1177/10497323231158619936803213

White, J. (2015, May 27) Teachers frustrated with inclusive classrooms, NLTA says. *CBC News.*https://www.cbc.ca/news/canada/newfoundland-labrador/teachers-frustrated-with-inclusive-classrooms-nlta-says-1.3088326

Wolbring, G., & Nguyen, A. (2023). Equity/Equality, Diversity and Inclusion, and Other EDI Phrases and EDI Policy Frameworks: A Scoping Review. *Trends in Higher Education*, 2(1), 168–237. 10.3390/higheredu2010011

Xin, W., Liu, C., Zhang, Z., & Yao, X. (2023). A person-centred examination of inclusive teachers' beliefs about teaching students with intellectual and developmental disabilities: Profiles and relations to teacher efficacy. *International Journal of Developmental Disabilities*, 1–13. Advance online publication. 10.1080/20473869.2023.2196470

KEY TERMS AND DEFINITIONS

Adaptations and Modifications: These are the terms used within Canada to describe the two main methods of providing reasonable accommodations to diverse students within the K-12 sector. Adaptations represent the measures taken to support diverse learners while they seek to reach the same objectives as the rest of the mainstream classroom and demonstrate the same learning outcomes. Modifications represent reasonable accommodations that go further and allow diverse students to access a curriculum which is different than the mainstream classroom in relation to outcomes. Modification of assessment normally involves reframing the learning outcomes so they remain achievable even for a student who may not be able to adhere to age or grade appropriate objectives.

Canadian Charter of Rights and Freedoms: This constitutional document, enshrined in 1982 during the repatriation of the Canadian Constitution, offers a canvas for the protection of individuals against recognized grounds for discrimination. It offers the key legal principles that allow schools and school districts to frame their actions and practice to support diverse learners and address possible discrimination.

K-12 UDL Implementation: UDL implementation in the K-12 sector has been slightly different than it has been in the post-secondary sector. It has been focused on providing alternatives to individual interventions for learners with disabilities. K-12 UDL implementation has been very much dependent on individual teacher initiatives, and on the emergence of communities of practice. It has therefore been mostly ad-hoc and fragmented. There is considerable evidence across Canada of UDL initiatives losing stream and disappearing before they had the opportunity to grow and become sustainable.

Leadership for Inclusion: Describes a reflection on leadership in schools that carves out a space for a specific examination of the competencies, skills, and resources required for school principals to launch, support and nurture sustainable inclusion practices in school, including UDL growth and development. While transformational leadership is often seen as compatible with current effort towards inclusion, there is a lack of specific scholarship that analyzes this possible synchronicity.

Retrofitting: Describes the act of having to adapt or modify a space, a service, a product, or an experience after the facts because it was not designed inclusively and creates barriers for persons with disabilities. Retrofitting is often required by law, once discrimination, or issues with access, have been identified. It can be costly as it can involve a significant alteration to the original design.

Social Model of Disability: The social model of disability is a theoretical paradigm which positions disability as a social construct, rather than as an inherent individual characteristic. Within this theoretical framework, disability is seen as the friction that occurs between individual embodiments and the expectations of the environment, or the features of spaces, products, and experiences that have not been designed inclusively.

Universal Design for Learning: UDL represents a set of three inclusive design principles which attempt to address learner diversity within instruction and assessment. The three UDL principles are multiple means of representation (offering optimal flexibility in the way information is presented to the learner), multiple means of action and expression (offering optimal flexibility in the way demands are made on learners for contribution, participation, and the completion of tasks), and multiple

Navigating the Gap Between Theory and Practice

means of engagement (offering optimal flexibility in the way learner engagement is conceptualized and formulated). UDL is grounded in the Social Model of Disability and focuses on the role of the educator as designer, rather than on the exceptionality of the learner. UDL operates on the basis of an analysis of barriers faced by learners; these barriers must be eliminated through a reflection on inclusive design.

Chapter 11
Aligning Teacher Competencies and Professional Standards to the UDL Framework Across Two Initial Teacher Training Contexts on the Island of Ireland

Tracy Galvin
Ulster University, Belfast, UK

Karen Buckley
https://orcid.org/0000-0002-6411-4299
Dublin City University, Ireland

Jennifer Roberts
https://orcid.org/0000-0002-5936-3047
Queen's University Belfast, UK

EXECUTIVE SUMMARY

Teacher training programs take many forms and vary in duration if it is an undergraduate or postgraduate option. In addition, there is variation in terms of the cost involved and the placement opportunities within a school setting and type. There

DOI: 10.4018/978-1-6684-4750-5.ch011

Copyright © 2024, IGI Global. Copying or distributing in print or electronic forms without written permission of IGI Global is prohibited.

Aligning Teacher Competencies and Professional Standards

is also an increase in the debate around inclusion globally, which has long been included as a core part of the lexicon of educational establishments and policy-makers. A more intentional UDL approach is discussed to a lesser degree, which does not divert away from a strategy of inclusion, but more intentionally provides a shared language across providers. In this chapter, the potential of UDL in initial teacher education is explored across the island of Ireland, which consists of both the Republic of Ireland and Northern Ireland, by mapping the UDL to both professional standards and teacher competency frameworks. It highlights how pre-service teacher training providers can embed UDL into their programs and practice and support student teachers in an ever-changing learning environment.

INTRODUCTION

Initial teacher education (ITE) curricula across the island of Ireland are closely linked to teaching competencies and professional standards, for quality assurance purposes within teacher education colleges. The island of Ireland is made up of two distinct regions: Northern Ireland (NI) and the Republic of Ireland (RoI). The two regions share an island and a long history; however, they differ from one another in terms of politics, policies, societal values, and education systems (Roulston et al., 2023). There has been a significant increase in learner diversity through immigration and the shift of inclusive education over the past ten years (Flood and Banks 2021). This new landscape has led to an increase in drawing from the Universal Design for Learning (UDL) framework across all educational sectors but especially in further (FE) and higher education (HE). Traditionally, UDL is more established in the formal school years (K-12) and within the American context where it originated over forty-five years ago and focused on tackling disability. UDL has become a key pedagogical framework which seeks to address the traditional 'one size fits all' curriculum that exists in many countries, as well as support inclusive education (Meyer et al., 2014), as well as support non-traditional students (Fovet, 2020). However, there remains a gap in the literature comparing teacher competencies and professional standards to the UDL framework, especially across the island of Ireland.

According to Smyth (et al., 2022, p. 5), NI's school system is fragmented based on "school type and religious denomination." There are a range of school categories in NI including Controlled (many of which were initially Protestant schools), Catholic Maintained, Voluntary Grammar, Integrated, Irish-Medium, and independent schools. In NI, secondary education is provided by secondary schools or grammar schools. Entry to grammar schools is through academic selection, and the results of transfer tests are used to determine places. In RoI, there are three types of schools (voluntary secondary, Education and Training Board (ETB), and community/compre-

Aligning Teacher Competencies and Professional Standards

hensive), and all schools follow the same curriculum and qualifications framework. Following recent statutory changes, secondary schools cannot assess students for entry. Second-level education comprises an initial three-year junior cycle, which has recently been reformed, followed by a two or three-year senior cycle (depending on whether students take the optional one-year Transition Year course). In urban areas, more than fifty percent of learners do not attend the school in closest proximity to their household. This suggests a substantial degree of active school selection either by the parents or the learners. The families that make more active choices tend to be more advantaged (Smyth et al., 2004).

Both regions have compulsory education known as post-primary education (secondary or high school) until 16 years, after which those who stay in education study for a further two years. In NI there are A-levels or vocational courses, whereas in the RoI schools have two options, for those within a more academic route there is the established Leaving Certificate or for vocational outcomes there is the Leaving Certificate Vocational Program or Leaving Certificate Applied in further education colleges. The intention for this chapter is to showcase the links that the UDL framework has with the already developed competency frameworks in both NI (Teaching: The Reflective Profession) and RoI (Céim: Standards for Initial Teacher Education), and how this can, in turn, provide a commonality among both jurisdictions to further support learner variability and inclusion, as well as the movement of student teachers working in both contexts.

CONTEXT

Globally, there has been a shift toward inclusive education in formal school years (Ewe and Galvin 2023; UNESCO 2017) but differ significantly across policy, theory, and practices, depending on the context, culture and values of each country and can often still be focused on disability (Ydo, 2020). The United Nations Convention on the Rights of People with Disabilities (UNESCO, 2020) and the (United Nations Convention on the Rights of the Child, 1989) highlight the importance of equitable and inclusive education. As well as the (United Nations, 2020) that promote the Sustainable Development Goals (SDG 4) to "ensure inclusive and equitable quality education and promote lifelong learning opportunities for all." Across Europe there has also been a significant rise in inclusive education across tertiary education. The Global Education Monitoring (GEM) report on inclusion and its connection to the

Aligning Teacher Competencies and Professional Standards

Sustainable Development Goals (SDG) 4 focuses on inclusive and equitable quality education and promotes lifelong learning opportunities for all (UNESCO, 2020).

UDL featured prominently in the GEM report on education equity and inclusion, in which the UDL framework was identified as particularly relevant for addressing persistent barriers to learning and maximizing accessibility (McKenzie & Dalton, 2020).

European policies on inclusive education show a general trend from a focus on disability and Special Educational Needs (SEN) towards a focus on the development of quality education for all learners (Meijer & Watkins, 2016), this has a direct consequence for teachers in the classroom and consequently for ITE providers and HEIs. The European Agency for Special and Inclusive Education has expressed the commitment of all European countries to develop more inclusive education systems, which aim to ensure that all learners of any age are provided with meaningful, high-quality educational opportunities in their local community (European Agency 2022). Although considered an essential aspect of a global human rights agenda, "ensuring education for all is a complex endeavor that is subject to the forces of globalization and the exclusionary pressures associated with migration, mobility, language, ethnicity, disability, and intergenerational poverty" (Galkienė and Monkevičienė 2022, p. ii).

The context of teacher education is ever-changing with different priorities to add to programs. Globally, education is going through various reforms where teacher educators should be a core part of (Ewe et al., 2023). The changing priorities include the advancement of new technologies, and requirement of digital skills (McCarthy et al., 2023) for employability gaps, a focus on global citizenship (Estellés & Fischman, 2021), and shifts in demographics and political parties, and parental demands and expectations of inclusive practice (Paseka & Schwab, 2020). ITE is one core way to drive change in the education sector (Abbott et al., 2019). Additionally, there is a shift toward more inclusive education systems to tackle the ever-changing diversity of learners and move away from a one size fits all approach to allow learners to reach their full learning potential (Booth & Ainscow, 2011). Indeed, as indicated by (Blanton and Pugach, 2011) in ITE, adding or infusing content on difference and diversity has proven to be ineffective. Instead, teacher education programs must "offer the opportunity to rethink difference as a feature of all learners and diversity as an opportunity for all" (European Agency 2022, p.12). Moreover, (Ewe et al., 2023, p. 17) highlight the need to prepare educators for teaching in a global society of diverse learners to build "robust teacher training programs where educators can learn and practice the skills and strategies that support productive learning environments". In contrast Sharma et al. (2019) investigated the barriers to implementing inclusive education and identified that the most significant obstacle was inadequate teacher preparation.

Inclusive pedagogy has long been included as a core part of the lexicon of educational establishments and policymakers (Florian et al., 2010). Schools and the broader education community often use a core range of strategies to differentiate learning and implement inclusion strategies. However, a more intentional UDL approach, which does not divert away from a strategy of inclusion, is discussed less often and less research across the formal school years in Europe (Ewe & Galvin, 2023). This intentional UDL focused approach, provides a meaningful action plan and context in how to ensure everyone is included where segregation and separation are minimized (Dalton et al., 2023). UDL, offers a unique framework that educators can use to design accessible and engaging learning opportunities for all students (Meyer et al., 2014)

The chapter aims to map how the UDL framework aligns with the two core professional standards and teaching competency frameworks across the island of Ireland and explore the similarities, differences, and language used in both. Also outlined are recommendations highlighting current gaps and future opportunities for ITEs to embed a more sustainable UDL ecosystem. UDL is gaining significant traction across further and higher education contexts on the island of Ireland. However, less so at a formal school level and, while gaining momentum in RoI through policy (Flood & Banks, 2021), it is developing slower in NI.

LITERATURE REVIEW

The review of literature focuses on UDL and teacher education across the island of Ireland, the differences and similarities of both contexts, and the professional competencies and standards frameworks.

UDL and Teacher Education

In the United States, where the UDL framework was founded, it is recommended to use the UDL framework in several policies such as the Higher Education Opportunity Act (2008), Every Student Succeeds Act (2015), and the National Education Technology Plan (U.S. Department of Education, Office of Educational Technology, 2016). There were also legislative actions that focused on inclusive practice, including the reauthorization of the Individuals with Disabilities Act (IDEA, 2004), the Higher Education Opportunity Act (HEOA 2008), and, most recently, the Every Student Succeeds Act (ESSA 2015) that all reference UDL.

It has been well documented that UDL was conceptualized in special education (Rose & Meyer, 2002) to support learners with disabilities, but it was quickly realized that the framework would further support general education curriculum

Aligning Teacher Competencies and Professional Standards

for all learners (Edyburn, 2013). Using UDL, teachers can design instruction that reduces barriers to learning and integrates engaging and flexible options for all learners (Meyer et al., 2014). UDL does not exist in an educational vacuum; rather, it co-exists and is intended to work with other supportive educational frameworks and approaches (Dalton, 2020), Moreover, it includes strategies that support teaching practices responsive to learner differences that are essential if inclusion in education is to benefit everyone.

UDL is a comprehensive pedagogical approach to inclusive education (Jimenez & Hudson, 2019). One possible way teacher preparation programs can "more effectively prepare general education teachers for inclusive settings is through instruction on UDL" (Vitelli, 2015, p. 167). According to Florian an inclusive education guru, "using strategies such as UDL to take account of individual differences while extending learning opportunities to all optimizes learning for diverse groups" (Florian 2021, p. vi). The iterative UDL design cycle continues with implementation: reflection on what worked and what required change to increase access further, and lesson revisions as needed (Rao & Meo, 2016).

The power that educators hold is well documented through the "design, goals set, learning experiences, activities are chosen, power to inspire and celebrate learner's voice" (Chardin & Novak, 2020, p.6). They go on to say that to connect social justice and UDL, we must use this "power to dismantle inequalities so all students have equal opportunities to learn, where we need to identify barriers, embrace variability, reflect on our biases, expect discomfort, amplify student voice and take action" (ibid, p.10). Teacher educators, academic developers, and professional services can use the UDL framework to facilitate inclusion by enabling educators and teacher educators to reduce barriers to learning while maintaining high expectations for all learners. This is achieved by intentionally considering learner differences, preferences, interests, and needs from the learning design and planning phase. Rather than a one size fits all approach or single pathway of learning, e.g., passive learning, taking notes, or reading a text, educators should draw from a flexible and accessible approach and offer choices to engage all learners. The authors aim to highlight how intentionally and meaningfully embedding the UDL into curriculum design, planning, development, and assessment "meets the needs of the widest range of learners, which reduces the need for individualization" (Israel, 2014, p. 5). However, we acknowledge that some learners will always require additional support, such as assistive technology, specialized support through one-to-one instruction, or a specialized school.

The UDL guidelines suggest that teachers consider how their curriculum can provide learners with options to engage in their learning. According to Hartman (2015), to support each student to become a resourceful and knowledgeable learner, the UDL guidelines provide guidance on equipping learners with multiple means of representation to foster a deeper understanding of concepts. Lastly, the UDL guidelines suggest ways in which curriculum can provide learners with options to act on and show what they know, thus moving them forward in their journey to becoming a strategic and goal-directed learner.

Teacher training programs take many forms globally and vary in duration, undergraduate (UG) and postgraduate (PG) options, and the cost and placement opportunities within a school setting. Strategically, there has been a significant shift in the promotion of UDL across higher education institutions (HEIs) from administrations, libraries, support, and professional services, and particularly in academic practice through building communities of practice (Galvin & Geron, 2021). Teacher education is an area we have less knowledge of in terms of uptake and implementation of UDL. However, the implementation of UDL has gained significant interest in HE across various contexts and disciplines (CAST, 2019).

According to Darling-Hammond et al. (2020), knowledge rapidly expands in the twenty-first century. Today's ability to find, analyze, synthesize, and apply knowledge to novel situations is essential. Developing such skills requires a different kind of teaching and learning in which the learning reveals itself as something else than the mere reception of facts and teaching or the transmission of information. This is timely as there is a shift toward a more flexible and inclusive approach to teaching and learning, where learners are expected to self-regulate and be more responsible for their learning, in addition to becoming problem solvers and critical thinkers, and to being reflexive in their approach.

There is a plethora of research to indicate the benefits of UDL, if it is embraced, it can be viewed as a "transformative powerful driver of inclusive learning" (Gentile & Budzilowicz, 2022, p.39), and it is the only framework positioned around inclusion that aligns itself with principles of sustainability (Fovet, 2017). However, there is still a lack of uptake within teacher education programs. Even in the USA, a "review of the literature suggests that UDL is not widely incorporated into general education teacher preparation programs" (Vitelli, 2015, p.167). Lanterman and Applequist (2018) call for teacher preparation programs to consider the value of training in UDL as a more substantial element of their curricula.

Teacher Training Programs

The two teacher training programs discussed throughout the chapter are from on-campus ITE providers based in Dublin and Belfast. Dublin City University (DCU) offers UG and PG programs. RoI has 17 ITE providers for primary (elementary) and post-primary (secondary) education. With effect from September 2014, PG programs of ITE accredited by the Teaching Council were extended to two years of full-time study or 120 ECTS credits. 10 Credits are equivalent to 200-250 hours of study on campus or self-directed learning, including class contact time and assessments. In

Aligning Teacher Competencies and Professional Standards

the RoI, post-primary ITE is provided through programs of a consecutive learning (PG, two year) to a Professional Master of Education (post-primary), which is the most common route or a concurrent (UG, four year) leading to a Bachelor of Education or Science course depending on the subject(s) chosen. The concurrent application is made through the Central Applications Office (CAO), and selection is based on the points system from the leaving certificate examinations. With both routes, students must register with the Teaching Council to be suitable for teaching at the post-primary level, and to teach at least one curricular subject to the highest level within the post-primary schools' curriculum. If one intends to teach at the post-primary level, one must ensure that the subjects chosen at the UG level are recognized for teaching purposes.

In the 1990s, teacher education in the RoI lacked external review and a clear vision for the future. An Organization for Economic Co-operation and Development (OECD) review identified the need for a comprehensive policy and a national council to oversee teaching professionalism. This led to the Education Act (1998), which emphasized ongoing teacher development. The Teaching Council Act (2001) established a framework for reviewing and accrediting teacher education programs and ensuring teachers' induction, probation, and continuous professional development (CPD). The establishment of the Teaching Council in 2006 significantly changed teacher education and professional development across RoI, where teachers must register with the Council, adhere to professional values, and conduct, and engage in lifelong professional development. The Teaching Council (TC) is responsible for maintaining the quality of ITE programs in RoI. The TC recognized the need to enhance teacher education and promote lifelong learning. As of 2023, The Institute of Education at DCU has 4,061 students, comprising 2727 UG students, 1157 taught PG students, and 177 PG doctoral students. These are in the areas of Early Childhood Education, Primary Education, Post-Primary Education, and Further Education and Training, who attend a range of taught UG and research-based PG programs at doctoral, masters, diploma, and certificate levels.

In NI, there are a total of 4 ITE providers. As noted earlier, the education system in NI is segregated on several lines, which is reflected in ITE providers (Montgomery & Smith, 2006). The length of each program is significantly different depending on whether it is an UG (4 years) or PG (1 year) course. Some providers cover primary and secondary initial teacher education, and some only train teachers for one phase of education. However, it is essential to note that the competency framework and the accompanying examples are the same for all phases. Settings provide a range of UG and PG routes into teaching. These are mainly four-year Bachelor of Education programs and one-year Postgraduate Certificate of Education (PGCE) programs. In 22/23, 580 students were admitted to ITE courses in NI PGCE programs in Queen's

University Belfast (QUB) are one year in duration. QUB trains around 130 teachers yearly in its one-year PGCE program across seven subjects.

ITE courses in NI remain oversubscribed, and teaching has remained a well-regarded graduate profession (Moran, 2012; Hagan & Eaton, 2020). As a result, ITE students are more likely to have attended a grammar school (Moran, 2008) and have high-level entry qualifications. This is reflected in the NI teacher workforce. ITE and educational administration in NI has been influenced heavily by the "deep-seated and complex macro-social, political and cultural issues underpinning the governance of NI" (Hagan & Eaton, 2020, p.263). The professional licensing of teachers in NI has historically been the responsibility of The General Teaching Council Northern Ireland. Following an effectiveness review in December 2021, the GTCNI was disbanded immediately after that, which led to some uncertainty in NI surrounding the process; however, the competency framework is still in effect.

While the authors are discussing two different jurisdictions and education systems separately, it is important to highlight several cross-border collaborations between NI and RoI in the teacher education and formal education sectors. One such teacher education initiative is SCoTENs (Standing Conference on Teacher Education, North and South), which funds research and projects where stakeholders from both NI and RoI pair up and disseminate and share best practice each year at the annual conference across the island (Smith et al., 2022). However, the report highlighted the barriers and challenges of such cross-border links in terms of resources, funding, and time, especially after Brexit; it also showcased how these partnerships were meaningful in terms of consultation, resources, professional development, apprenticeships, and systemic change. Evmenova (2018, p. 148) states, "today's classrooms are characterized by ever-growing diversity. In one instructional setting, students with disabilities, gifted students, English language learners, and culturally and linguistically diverse students learn side-by-side". This is very pertinent for our Irish and Northern Irish settings as both contexts are much more multicultural than even ten years ago, with the increasing number of asylum seekers and refugees, especially under the current climate of the Ukraine invasion, where Ireland has already received over 25,000 refugees, with approximately 10,000 school-age children.

Changing School Contexts Across the Island of Ireland

According to (Roulston et al., 2023) there has been a long and shared history of education, once having a universal and free primary education system until the partition of the island, that became the RoI and the formation of NI. The authors outline the different school types that have emerged, church-state relationships, monitoring systems and educational approaches. In terms of statistics, the RoI has 3,241 primary schools serving 560,000 students, aged 5 to 12 years, and 730

Aligning Teacher Competencies and Professional Standards

secondary schools catering to 380,000 students, between 12 and 19 years of age (Education Statistics, 2021). There are 1,029 schools in NI, including 784 primary schools serving 172,323 students, and 192 secondary schools serving 151,908 students, that includes 39 special schools serving 6653 students and 14 independent schools (Dept of Education, 2021).

Over the past 20 years schools across the island of Ireland have changed, and today's schools (mainly in urban areas) are host to various ethnicities, nationalities, religions, and cultural backgrounds among learners. This indicates an ever-increasing diversity that now constitutes a diverse learner population. To showcase the extent in NI, the number of newcomer (requires additional English language support) pupils welcomed into primary and post-primary schools has "increased from just over 1,000 in 2001/2002 to over 19,000 in 2022/2023, a rise of 1,306%, representing 5.5% of the pupil population" (Independant Review of Education, 2023, 73). However, pre-service teachers feel under-prepared to deal with this diversity in the classroom, nonetheless, recognizing its importance (Montgomery and McGlynn, 2009).

Within initial teacher education, responsibility concerning diversity presupposes an engagement in the inter-relationship between education and diversity in all its forms and on the pedagogical implications of cultural diversity, poverty, social exclusion, and special educational needs. The ITE curriculum can often lag the realities of learners and their communities. Responding appropriately to learners' diverse and varied needs in classrooms forms one of the most significant challenges facing teachers, schools, and education systems (Humphrey et al., 2006). As pointed out by Florian (2021, p. xi), one way to counteract this is to use strategies that support teaching practices that are "responsive to learner differences are essential if inclusion in education is to benefit everyone. Using strategies such as UDL to take account of individual differences while extending learning opportunities to all optimizes learning for diverse groups".

A study of student teachers, in a concurrent four-year UG program, found that they were likely to have had little contact with people from diverse backgrounds and that, except for those that had lived outside the country, they had little understanding of the impact of diversity or the experience of discrimination (Leavy, 2005). Several issues concerning diversity have been identified in relation to teacher education in western societies that are directly relevant to ITE programs across the Island of Ireland.

An RoI study shows that over 90% of Irish pre-service teachers are white, settled (non-traveling community), middle-class females (Keane & Heinz, 2016), whereas (McDaid & Nowlan, 2021) indicate that the teaching workforce has tended to remain monoethnic. A similar context can be observed in the NI context, which is not always representative to learners in the classroom. The student-teacher population is relatively homogeneous regarding socio-cultural background (Hagan & McGlynn, 2004; Leavy, 2005; Lenski et al., 2005; Mills, 2008; Sleeter, 2008). One such response to this homogeneity by the Department of Education in partnership with Maynooth University was through a Programme for Access to High Education (PATH), which encouraged potential teachers from lower class backgrounds to get into teaching.

A more recent research study of diversity in initial teacher education in the RoI – the DITE project – reported similar findings, despite significant changes in the cultural demographics of Ireland since the Leavy study (Keane & Heinz, 2015). This can challenge teacher educators regarding student teachers' perceptions and lay theories (Hagan & McGlynn, 2004; Clarke & Drudy, 2007). These findings suggest that despite Ireland's evolving cultural landscape, perceptions and biases among student teachers remain a challenge. This emphasizes the importance of integrating diversity education not only in elective courses, which have shown limited impact, but instead become a mandatory part of teacher training. Such integration ensures that all student teachers, regardless of their chosen specializations, receive comprehensive exposure to inclusion, diversity and social justice issues. This exposure is crucial for preparing future teachers to effectively navigate and contribute to increasingly diverse educational environments.

Moreover, while exposure to diversity and social justice issues in the context of student teaching placements has been associated with a higher commitment on the part of student teachers to engage with issues of diversity (Clarke & Drudy, 2007), research suggests the limited impact of elective courses (Dillon & O'Shea, 2009). It underlines the need for mandatory provision of diversity-related courses and placement experiences in different kinds of schools for all learners.

Pearson (2015) points out that, while student teachers need to understand the impact of diversity on syllabus content and pedagogy, more than such an understanding is needed for developing an intercultural and inclusive practice. Mills (2008) identified dispositional factors, including openness and receptiveness to diversity, self-awareness, and commitment to social justice, as essential elements in a teacher's capacity to engage with diversity issues. It is also evident that support and continuing professional development are essential as beginning teachers need to develop a critical understanding of the social and political contexts of education and the cross-cutting nature of categories such as race, ethnicity, class, age, religion, dis/ability, sexual orientation, and gender (Howard & Aleman, 2008; Leavy, 2005; Kenny & McLaughlin, 2004). Likewise, Flood & Banks (2021, p. 9) highlight that "the exploration of recent curriculum developments in Ireland indicates a shift in mindset towards UDL as a framework for inclusive education in Irish schools," that highlights both teachers and student teachers alike are making connections on engagement, choice, and flexibility.

Aligning Teacher Competencies and Professional Standards

Interconnectivity of Programs

An international study carried out by Darling-Hammond (2017) examines best practice, with a focus on the well-established induction models within teacher education to support new teachers. Within this study the author also refers to continuous and targeted professional development to effect change in the classroom, the use of professional standards on learning and evaluation of critical knowledge, integrating skills and embedding reflective practice. Both ITE programs across the island draw from a similar process, and both have a long history of school partnerships, reform policies, professional standards, change in learner demographics and teacher induction processes. Both programs draw on a broad range of theories of knowledge and learning, primarily sociocultural, constructivist, cognitive, and critical theory, while recognizing the contribution of learning theories grounded in the behaviorist paradigm (Kirschner, 2016). ITE programs incorporate a range of diverse teaching approaches, including plenary lectures, seminars and workshops, inquiry-based teaching in the laboratory and practical modules, group work, reflective diaries, e-portfolios, case studies, critical incident analysis, and role play. Structured workshop tasks and discussions help to build communities of inquiry and practice (Wenger, 1998). However, there remains a gap in research regarding the implementation and impact of UDL in ITE (Benton-Borghi, 2016), which is very evident across Ireland. One of the key objectives of this chapter is to explore this gap, by looking at how these programs have changed and adapted thanks to this approach.

Both programs are formalized through the standardization, competencies, and professional standards required for such ITE programs. Each of the programs has its own set of unique contextual factors. Across the programs, design is increasingly informed by UDL principles where ITE providers actively and intentionally embed UDL into their practice and encourage student teachers to do so. Assessment is also informed by UDL principles incorporating authentic and challenge-based assessments, such as interactive orals and projects focused on creating resources such as wikis and websites, a balance of individual and group tasks, and a strong focus on self and peer assessment. This allows for multiple means of representation and multiple means of assessment, both key principles of a UDL approach, although only sometimes formally named as such. In NI UDL training for staff in ITE is limited and not compulsory. Embedding this approach in ITE programs depends on the individual and is often ad-hoc. While UDL presents an array of options that teachers can use as part of their instructional planning to address learner variability in the classroom without prescribing how they should be used (Rao & Okolo, 2018), it is certainly more descriptive than the current competency frameworks. According to Israel et al. (2014, p.20), teachers can use the guidelines and the essential elements of UDL

295

"to improve planning and the subsequent instructional experiences of students. The checkpoints guide teachers through understanding the principles and guidelines that extend beyond a definition to support the implementation of UDL. For example, the National Center on Universal Design for Learning defines the checkpoints; explains the potential barriers and how the principles and guidelines address content and instructional limitations; and offers examples and links to resources, giving teachers solutions and tools for subsequent implementation".

Professional Standard and Competency Frameworks

Education is defined as one of the most powerful and proven vehicles for sustainable development by the United Nations (2020). For this idea to become a reality, however, learners must have access to an educational system that prioritizes competencies over content, understanding over memorization, and thinking over repetition (Bilbao et al., 2021, p.12). Frameworks for teacher competencies need to rely on key partners agreement as to what shapes quality teachers—which competencies they require and how these are understood and described (European Commission, 2013). It is also important to consider where it sits in the wider context of an individual's identity as a teacher, school values, the local community and availability of professional networks (OECD, 2009). The continuum approach to ITE policy must link ITE, selection, recruitment, induction, and professional development with clear roles and responsibilities for support and quality assurance (European Commission 2014). ITE has long been associated with education policy and competency frameworks that require a clear reference framework for teachers' competencies to provide common ground between different teaching/learning settings, such as induction, to CPD once qualified and throughout their career (European Commission 2013a).

When outlining competency frameworks, statements are often outlined which refer to what teachers should know and be able to do. While very different globally, their value, use, and recognition vary widely, as do the roles of stakeholders (Eurydice, 2013). Competency frameworks are primarily a set of broad statements, thematic strands, or structured lists that outline lifelong learning, assessment practices, pedagogical knowledge, social and interpersonal skills, the inclusion of equity-deserving groups, and research skills. According to Koster and Dengerink (2008), teacher competencies include knowledge, skills, attitudes, values, and personal characteristics that allow teachers to act professionally and effectively, particularly in teaching and learning situations. Spratt and Florian (2015) see the inclusive teacher's relevant competency as the ability to support everyone in the context of 'everybody.'

Aligning Teacher Competencies and Professional Standards

While competencies and standards have immense value across formal education, there is a need to move away from a one size fits all approach to avoid an exclusionary mindset and an inequitable system where there is only one way to do something and one outcome to achieve, or one way to demonstrate learner knowledge or one way to instruct or share knowledge. Thus, UDL can be viewed as a comprehensive pedagogical approach to inclusive education (Jimenez & Hudson, 2019). UDL is an inclusive framework for meeting learner needs (CAST, 2018). The competency framework being discussed have been set forth by The General Teaching Council Northern Ireland (GTCNI) and The General Teaching Council Ireland (GTCI) these organizations are responsible for the registration of teachers and the competency statements are the minimum standards for beginning teachers. A close reading of the standards and the areas within the UDL framework show some key areas of similarity. Beginning teachers are required to have an approach that best meets learner needs. More thoroughly mapping these frameworks allows us to see precisely how aligned the framework for beginning teacher practice is expected to be. The Teacher Education Partnership Handbook (DENI 2010, p. 36) identifies the critical importance placed in extended school placements and states that:

The foundation for the partnerships between schools and HEIs rests on the fact that some competencies can best be developed and extended during the school-based aspect of the course. It is crucial, therefore, that there should be the closest possible partnership between schools and HEIs.

ITE Competency and UDL

ITE in both NI and RoI are competency-driven, professional courses. Students leave their ITE programs with the opportunity to apply for registrations from the General Teaching Council Northern Ireland (QUB student teachers) and the Teaching Council of Ireland (DCU student teachers) which allows them to secure a professional teaching role. A commitment to learners and an ITE curriculum that prepares teachers for diverse settings are central to the curriculum; however, what remains to be seen is how the UDL framework fits with the core aims of the competency framework. As discussed earlier in the chapter, UDL in ITE is gaining traction, but it is unknown how this is reflected in the competency framework which underpins ITE achievement and entry to the profession.

Several ITE providers in NI aim to train beginning teachers to achieve the standards set out in 'The Reflective Practitioner' (GTCNI, 2011). There are 27 key competencies, divided into five key areas. These are accompanied by phase exemplars outlining the threshold teachers must meet at different phases of their career: Initial Teacher Education, Induction, Early Professional Development, and Continuing Professional Development. The key areas are: Professional Values and Practice (1 competency); Professional Knowledge and Understanding (12 competencies); Professional Skills and Application; Planning and Leading (5 competencies) and Teaching and Learning (5 competencies) and Assessment (4 competencies)

Post-primary ITE is provided through programs of a consecutive or concurrent nature in RoI. The most common route to qualification is the consecutive route, which comprises a suitable degree and teacher education qualification. There are 14 ITE qualification providers in RoI, incorporating three specific elements outlined by Céim: Standards for Initial Teacher Education In accordance with Section 38 of the Teaching Council Acts (2001-2015): Foundation Studies; and Professional Studies and School Placement

The Teaching Council determines the Graduate Teacher Standards which outline the skills, knowledge, understanding, and professional values expected of newly qualified teachers. In this respect, student teachers are expected to use these standards as a tool to support their ongoing development, including reflective practice and inquiry pedagogies. Teacher educators use the Graduate Teacher Standards to support program design and accreditation. A range of learning outcomes are set out under three broad headings: professional Values (2 elements - 11 competencies); Professional Skills and Practice (4 elements - 32 competencies); and Professional Knowledge and Understanding (4 elements - 25 competencies)

Table 1 looks at the GTCNI competency framework and links the current competency framework and the principles of UDL. Table Two looks at the Céim standards in RoI. Each competency statement has been examined and, where links have been visible, organized into the UDL framework.

Aligning Teacher Competencies and Professional Standards

Table 1. Where the NI teacher competencies align with the UDL framework

Engagement	Representation	Action and Expression
Recruiting Interest (7) 3: Teachers will have developed a knowledge and understanding of the learning area/subject(s) they teach, including the centrality of strategies and initiatives to improve, literacy, numeracy and thinking skills, keeping curricular, subject and pedagogical knowledge up-to-date through reflection, self-study and collaboration with colleagues. 7: An understanding of the significance of pupil voice. A knowledge and understanding of a range of strategies to establish an effective learning environment. 19: Create and maintain a learning environment, with appropriate clarity of purpose for activities. 20: Use a range of resources that enable learning to take place. Use a range of teaching strategies and resources that maintain pace within lessons and over time.	**Perception (1)** 19: Create and maintain a learning environment, with appropriate clarity of purpose for activities. 20: Use a range of teaching strategies that enable learning to take place. Use a range of resources that enable learning to take place. Use a range of teaching strategies and resources that maintain pace within lessons and over time. 21: Develop multi-sensory strategies that meet the needs of pupils who are not learning in their first language	**Physical Action (4)** 11: Teachers will have developed a knowledge and understanding of how to use technology effectively, both to aid pupil learning and to support their professional role, and how this competence embeds across all competences. 19: Create and maintain a learning environment, with appropriate clarity of purpose for activities. 20: Use a range of teaching strategies and resources that maintain pace within lessons and over time.
Sustaining Effort & Persistence (8) 14: Teachers will set appropriate learning objectives/outcomes/ intentions, taking account of what pupils know, understand and can do, and the demands of the Northern Ireland Curriculum* in terms of knowledge, skills acquisition and progression. 15: Teachers will plan and evaluate lessons that enable all pupils, including those with special educational needs, to meet learning objectives/outcomes/ intentions, showing high expectations and an awareness of potential areas of difficulty.	**Language & Symbols (2)** 10: Teachers will have developed a knowledge and understanding of strategies for communicating effectively with pupils, parents, colleagues and personnel from relevant child and school support agencies. 20: Use a range of teaching strategies that enable learning to take place. 21: Develop multi-sensory strategies that meet the needs of pupils who are not learning in their first language	**Expression & Communication (5)** 10: Teachers will have developed a knowledge and understanding of strategies for communicating effectively with pupils, parents, colleagues and personnel from relevant child and school support agencies. 11: Teachers will have developed a knowledge and understanding of how to use technology effectively, both to aid pupil learning and to support their professional role, and how this competence embeds across all competences. 20: Use a range of resources that enable learning to take place.

continued on following page

Aligning Teacher Competencies and Professional Standards

Table 1. Continued

Engagement	Representation	Action and Expression
Self-Regulation (9) 7: A knowledge and understanding of a range of strategies to promote and maintain positive behaviour. 19: Create and maintain a safe, interactive and challenging learning environment. 21: Employ strategies that motivate and meet the needs of pupils with special and additional educational needs. 24: Help pupils reflect on and improve their learning.	**Comprehension (3)** 3: Teachers will have developed a knowledge and understanding of the learning area/subject(s) they teach, including the centrality of strategies and initiatives to improve, literacy, numeracy and thinking skills, keeping curricular, subject and pedagogical knowledge up-to-date through reflection, self-study and collaboration with colleagues. 14: Teachers will set appropriate learning objectives/outcomes/ intentions, taking account of what pupils know, understand and can do, and the demands of the Northern Ireland Curriculum* in terms of knowledge, skills acquisition and progression. 15: Teachers will plan and evaluate lessons that enable all pupils, including those with special educational needs, to meet learning objectives/outcomes/ intentions, showing high expectations and an awareness of potential areas of difficulty. 20: Use a range of teaching strategies that enable learning to take place. 21: Develop multi-sensory strategies that meet the needs of pupils who are not learning in their first language	**Executive Functions (6)** 7: A knowledge and understanding of a range of strategies to establish an effective learning environment. An understanding of the significance of pupil voice. 19: Create and maintain a safe, interactive and challenging learning environment. 21: Employ strategies that motivate and meet the needs of pupils with special and additional educational needs. 24: Monitor pupils' progress. Help pupils reflect on and improve their learning. Help pupils reflect on and improve their learning.

Overarching - Teachers will have developed a knowledge and understanding of contemporary debates about the nature and purposes of education and the social and policy contexts in which the aims of education are defined and implemented. Teachers will have developed a knowledge and understanding of their responsibilities under the Special Educational Needs Code of Practice and know the features of the most common special needs and appropriate strategies to address these.

Table 2 looks at the Céim Standards for Initial Teacher Education and links the current competency framework and the principles of UDL. The Céim Standards for ITE sets out the requirements that all programs of qualification for teaching in Ireland must meet to gain accreditation from the Teaching Council in the Republic of Ireland. The Programme Standards outlined above are the review and accreditation process benchmarks. The Graduate Teacher Standards outline the skills, knowledge, understanding, and professional values expected of newly qualified teachers. In this respect, student teachers must use the Céim standards to support their ongoing development, including reflective practice and inquiry pedagogies. A range of learning outcomes are set out under three broad headings; 2.1 Professional Values; 2.2 Professional Skills and Practice; 2.3 Professional Knowledge and Understanding

Aligning Teacher Competencies and Professional Standards

Table 2. Where the RoI professional standards align with the UDL framework

Engagement	Representation	Action and Expression
Recruiting Interest (7) 1: Use appropriate class management and organisation skills to cater for a range of classroom situations 3; Establish classroom management strategies that support suitable and effective learning for all pupils 4: Create and maintain a safe, interactive and challenging environment using strategies that promote and maintain positive behaviour, according to school policy. 9: Access, develop, adapt and use a variety of curriculum resources and materials for learning and teaching to support and challenge all pupils 10: Set clear, challenging and achievable expectations for all pupils in line with the curriculum 11: Motivate, inspire, acknowledge and celebrate effort and success	**Perception (1)** 3: Establish classroom management strategies that support suitable and effective learning for all pupils 8: Enable pupils to resolve conflict.	**Physical Action (4)** 14: Engage with pupils to develop effective, creative and imaginative strategies that promote individual and shared learning 15: Assess the achievement of curriculum objectives and adapt their teaching accordingly 16. apply his/her knowledge of pupils' holistic development to their teaching and promote social responsibility 17: Employ relevant technical knowledge and skills of a range of digital technologies including multi-media resources, effectively to facilitate teaching and assessment practices and to aid pupil learning 10: Pupils as active agents in their own learning
Sustaining Effort & Persistence (8) 20: Conduct a systematic, holistic assessment of pupil needs 21: Implement a range of methodologies to achieve planned outcomes 22: Evaluate pupil progress towards those outcomes 14: Engage with pupils in order to develop effective, creative and imaginative strategies that promote individual and shared learning	**Language & Symbols (2)** 7: Communicate effectively with pupils, parents, colleagues, the school principal, school management, co-professionals, colleagues, and the wider community by using appropriate skills (including digital skills), styles and systems to suit the given situation and setting 28: Engage in various forms of data gathering and critically analyse and evaluate relevant knowledge and research	**Expression & Communication (5)** 1: Demonstrate knowledge and understanding of the unique role of the teacher as professional in providing for the holistic development of students, and the complex and intricate nature of teaching, as explicated in the Code of Professional Conduct for Teachers 5: Develop positive relationships and communicate effectively with pupils, parents, colleagues, student teachers, the school principal, school management, co-professionals and the wider community 6: Foster good relationships with and among pupils based on mutual respect, trust and meaningful interactions

continued on following page

Table 2. Continued

Engagement	Representation	Action and Expression
Self-Regulation (9) 27: Reflect critically on the effectiveness of practice on an ongoing basis to inform and adjust his/her practice. 6: The factors that promote and hinder effective learning, the impact of pupils' backgrounds and identities on learning and the need to provide for the holistic development of the pupil, particularly through differentiated approaches 8: Current thinking on human development and learning 9: The role of teachers as leaders of teaching and learning, who contribute to creating and sustaining learning communities in their classrooms, in their schools and through their professional networks 10: Pupils as active agents in their own learning	**Comprehension (3)** 9: Access, develop, adapt and use a variety of curriculum resources and materials for learning and teaching to support and challenge all pupils 10: Set clear, challenging and achievable expectations for all pupils in line with the curriculum 12: Apply knowledge of the individual potential of pupils, dispositions towards learning, varying backgrounds, identities, experiences and learning styles to planning for teaching, learning and assessment 13: Use a range of strategies to support, monitor and assess pupils' approach to learning and their progress – including effective feedback strategies 15: Assess the achievement of curriculum objectives and adapt their teaching accordingly 14: Models of planning coherent, differentiated and integrated teaching programmes which are informed by ongoing reflection on professional practice.	**Executive Functions (6)** 4: Create and maintain a safe, interactive and challenging environment using strategies that promote and maintain positive behaviour, according to school policy. 26: Individually, and in collaboration with colleagues, reflect on his/her attitudes, and beliefs about teaching and learning which inform and guide his/her professional practice 27: Reflect critically on the effectiveness his/her practice on an ongoing basis to inform and adjust his/her practice. 28: Engage in various forms of data gathering and critically analyse and evaluate relevant knowledge and research 29: Think critically, analyse, and solve problems, as an individual and a member of a team 31: Demonstrate a professional commitment to seeking, accepting and acting upon constructive advice 32: Actively participate in professional learning communities which engage in group reflection, learning and practice

Overarching: By the end of the programme of initial teacher education, the student teacher will be able to understand the nature and purposes of education and the social and policy contexts in which the aims of education are defined and implemented. The origins and development of the statutory and policy-making framework pertaining to education, his/her specific role and responsibilities emanating from that framework, together with the roles and responsibilities of all stakeholders, including parents. The rights of children and young people, including their right to a voice in various matters that relate to their lives. The sector in which he/she will be teaching and his/her professional responsibilities within it educational research and its contribution to teaching, learning and assessment & the importance of teachers' intergenerational responsibility to support student teachers.

As can be seen from Table 1, which represents the QUB context, here are possible comparisons between the ITE competency framework in NI and the UDL framework. However, there are very few explicit links between the two. UDL has yet to be considered when creating the formal standards which beginning teachers need to achieve upon entry into the profession. Instead, we see elements of practice that are aligned. This alignment is unlikely to be intentional and is likely due to similar evidence bases or scoping exercises where each document has considered the key debates and arguments in the field during its creation. The framework provides much more detail about what it means to implement this type of practice in a class-

Aligning Teacher Competencies and Professional Standards

room. The competency statements are much broader and more general. The table also shows how some statements fit into multiple areas of the UDL framework. Of the 27 competency statements, 12 have links with the UDL principles. Of these 12 statements with alignment, 10 appear in more than one column.

To summarize, there are some common elements throughout both tables one and two when examined with a lens that includes broader education theory and inclusion in general. Gardner's (1993) brain-based theory of Multiple Intelligences is evident where learners do not have one global learning capacity but many mul-tifaceted learning capacities unique to the individual and not dependent on each other. Continuing the theme of neuroscience and inclusive education, Vygotsky's (1962 and 1978) theory of the Zone of Proximal Development (ZPD) and socio-cultural theory outline the principles of learning to learn (metacognition). This is closely linked to UDL regarding self-regulation and executive functioning skills, where learners become expert learners through their own experiences and ability to apply that learning in different contexts (Meyer et al., 2014). In addition, the theory of the bioecological model developed by Bronfenbrenner and Ceci (1994) and Bronfenbrenner's ecological systems theory, which describes the impacts of environmental interactions on a developing child (Guy-Evans, 2020), which further supports the concept of UDL.

This theory emphasizes the impact of proximal processes and the environment on human development and its relationship with the social and cultural processes it is surrounded and influenced by in this case, its perception, adoption, and creation. Nonetheless, there is a difference between these established learning theories which have prevailed that are routinely taught in ITE programs and the informal UDL mapping that may take place.

Working towards the implementation of quality inclusive education, by means of a mapping of the competencies, all 9 of the UDL checkpoints were incorporated in some way. However, there are some common themes and areas of interest which emerge from this mapping and analysis. The first commonality is individuality. The competency and UDL frameworks emphasize the importance of child-centered and child-led pedagogy to aid pupil learning. This notion of individual development and learning is linked to theories of learning, work on constructivism and scaffolding information. Another common thread that is explicitly addressed in both is commu-nication. Both specify the importance of communication and highlight the need for various communication techniques to promote successful learning. A third common thread is variety. This is rather broad, but a variety of teaching strategies to deliver information in several ways is highlighted as a key element of good practice and is linked to motivation and understanding.

303

What is important to note is the ambiguous nature of the language used in the competency statements. Language such as 'contemporary debates' has been taken here to include UDL; however, another provider may interpret this differently. There are connections and crossovers between both frameworks, but UDL is not explicitly mentioned in relation to teacher training provision, and UDL does not specifically target initial teacher education. It is important to examine the strength of these identified links, as they may be tenuous in nature, accidental or based on other literature. Two institutions or indeed individuals could (and likely do) interpret the varied and broad statements from the competencies to fit their view of education and what it means to be a 'good' teacher.

UDL could be embedded in ITE more readily and might bring many benefits. However, it is clear from the mapping exercise that the two frameworks of competency which have been examined do not make explicit links with UDL. The links which exist are created at the institutional or lecturer level rather than any specific links or parallels at a design or program level. Beginning teachers often work across schools and are uniquely positioned to learn from various professional voices. How exposed they are to UDL as a concept, or its principles, depends entirely on their institution. There are multiple ways to interpret the statements of competency, and UDL is only one approach. As well as the teacher competencies, each program must align with professional values. Mapping is a valuable tool, but it is important to consider how to strengthen connections and impact professional practice. Teachers often feel overburdened and may be reluctant to embed a UDL framework in their classroom; however, 'good practice' in its current form is not misaligned with the framework.

Professional Values

Across Europe, competency frameworks take different approaches in ITE. Some have thematic strands with broad statements, e.g., assessment. Others, on the other hand, can be detailed, e.g., structured lists of knowledge, skills, and attitudes, with indicators or can-do statements distinguished by school level (European Commission 2014). This is the case across the island of Ireland. Throughout both frameworks in use on the island of Ireland (ROI and NI), a set of values are in place which ITE providers to follow and implement throughout the undergraduate or post graduate course to ensure students are embodying the professional values and skills deemed necessary to be an effective teacher. Table three showcases the values of NI and the RoI.

Aligning Teacher Competencies and Professional Standards

Table 3. Professional values in ITE across the island of Ireland

Northern Ireland	Republic of Ireland
Respect Integrity Trust Fairness Equality Tolerance Fairness Service Dignity Honesty Commitment Excellence	Respect Integrity Trust Care Ethical Standards and Professional Behaviour Professional and Ethical Teaching

As summarized in Table 3, the first three values are the same. While the values are not explicitly discussed concerning a UDL approach, one can see the links between the two frameworks being discussed. To meet the needs of the individual students in the classroom, there needs to be mutual respect and trust that will be met. However, RoI has *Care*, and NI has an additional five values outlined, with some overlap with care (trust, fairness, equality, tolerance, fairness, service, dignity, honesty, commitment, and excellence). The Code of Conduct for Teachers asserts the professional values outlined that are embedded across both the ITE programs and are particularly targeted in School Placement modules in each year of the program. In both contexts, these school-based placement modules allow student teachers to directly address and cultivate their own personal and professional identity in the classroom, including understanding their legal and professional responsibilities towards students and the school community and appropriate engagement with parents and other key stakeholders and partners in education. School placement provides a site for constructing ethical practices. A key element of the wider school placement experience is the exposure of student teachers to the role of other stakeholders in pupils' education, with a focus on parents' roles. In Ireland, the creation of students' identities as language speakers will be developed through language modules, school placement experiences in schools, Gaeltacht (Irish speaking) internships, Erasmus mobility to other countries through engagement with staff, other students, and language events. One such framework for student teachers to consider during school placement is the UDL framework that moves away from a one size fits all approach, to represent a paradigm shift in how educators look and support learner differences through curriculum change in design and planning, accommodations and differentiation (Reynor 2021).

KEY DISCUSSION THEMES

Several themes have arisen throughout the document analysis by aligning the UDL framework to both ITE programs. The overarching themes are (a) the value of UDL for all learners; (b) the importance of intentional design, implementation, and reflection, (c) policy and systemic change, and (d) the need for more professional development for all teachers and ITE providers.

The Value of UDL for All Learners

Every educator can identify with the administrative role accommodations require, often with little or any advance notice. It is often one occurrence for one person and without any discussion or expertise in a specific area required by educators. The additional time required due to exceptional circumstances is very much based on retrofitting content and focused on the medical approach that is not sustainable with the ever-increasing number of learners registering with disability services. While individual accommodations will never be eradicated, there also exists a duty of care and legal obligation to support and provide accommodations for learners with disabilities, individual learning needs and differences, and neurodiverse learners, while more and more learners face mental health and wellbeing challenges. Moreover, with the increase in access to university and further education, a rapidly increasing number of learners are coming from diverse backgrounds; they may be mature students, parents, asylum seekers, refugees, and international students for whom English may be an additional language. However, rather than thinking about differentiation and individual accommodations, the focus should be on an intentional design that "reduces the need to make those individual-support accommodations in the first place and maximizes everyone's learning opportunities… this way, learners can feel "a part of" rather than "apart from" their learning" (SOLAS 2021, p.3.). In addition, as indicated by Florian 2021, p. vi) "using strategies such as UDL to take account of individual differences while extending learning opportunities to all optimizes learning for diverse groups". Florian (2019) also claims that the problem of focusing on 'some' learners leads to the exclusion of others. This can be solved by seeing the uniqueness of every individual as a basis for the diversity of people and the evolution of humankind.

In both contexts, university-based teaching blocks usually take place between more extended school placements. If beginning teachers are being taught UDL pedagogy and perceived as agents of change, one must consider their limited power in a department and school (Mkandawire et al, 2016). Very often, student teachers are asked to adhere to school values and ethos and 'fit in' with the prevailing methods of instruction. This lack of power may be formal (i.e., by being a student)

Aligning Teacher Competencies and Professional Standards

and informal (i.e., due to their social identities and relationships with supervisors). Interestingly, an Irish study on UDL in ITE found that student teachers were often confused by the principles of UDL and found the large amounts of material difficult to understand (Smith et al., 2017). This was further supported by a study where Lowry et al. (2019, p.261-2) highlighted that although [UDL] is seen as an important educational framework for implementation in instructional design, to date, "no research-based pre-service professional development model is available to support teacher candidates to adequately understand, implement, and evaluate the UDL framework in authentic school settings." Thus, UDL must be at the core of instruction with student teachers to enable them to link content to applications and reflect on what is happening. This approach allows student teachers to take on the role of an 'expert learner' and, in turn, support their own 'expert learners' in their classrooms. This becomes difficult if ITE providers struggle with UDL implementation and application.

Intentional Design, Implementation, and Reflection

The UDL framework is directly tied to effective curriculum design and instruction, appropriate for all content areas, assessment, and accessibility, and leads to improved outcomes for all students (CAST, 2011). It is linked to a comprehensive definition of learner diversity, as highlighted by Fovet (2021, p.34), who states that educators need to work towards inclusive provisions for 'all diverse learners. Notably, these include international students, culturally diverse learners, racialized students, Indigenous students, LGBTQ2S+ students, and first-generation students who must all be considered by teachers, instead of focusing solely on students with disabilities. According to Ewe (et al., p.19) UDL is a "valuable tool to guide the preparation of teachers to design and develop more inclusive learning environments for the diversity of students in classrooms". Therefore, outlining the importance of implementing inclusive education and putting into effect the UDL principles to guide that process as teachers significantly impact students' learning (Waitoller & Artiles, 2013) which can be achieved by ensuring educators are flexible in constructing learning environments for all students Lakkala & Kyrö-Ämmälä (2021). This is consistent with Vitelli's assertions (2015), who outlined that, even when UDL is incorporated into the teacher education curriculum, a lack of faculty awareness and confidence can be a barrier to the overall impact of these practices for teacher candidates.

Israel et al. (2014) developed a framework to support student teachers' basic understanding of UDL by considering learner variability and the barriers to learning; in such teacher training, the focus would be on design, curriculum evaluation, learner progression, and modeling. Good teaching practices are key to learning and assessment. It is also fundamental to embed reflective practice throughout the

Aligning Teacher Competencies and Professional Standards

process of learning about the UDL framework and attempting to implement it into practice. Such windows of reflective practice support change of mindsets toward a more inclusive education. Nonetheless, due to the growing complexity and diversity in classrooms, it is more important than ever that teacher training and the ongoing teacher professional development supports inclusive learning environments to tackle such need and challenges (Ewe et al., 2023)

UDL policy is making its way into HE in terms of academic practice (Galvin & Geron, 2021; O'Neill & Maguire 2019) across the island of Ireland, but ITE programs are integrating UDL at a slower pace than institutional policy requires. UDL implementation (intentional or ad hoc) has been occurring in academic practice. However, intentional change at the policy level is less evident. The chapter has well documented the importance of reflective practice in ITE, and for educators in general.

Policy and Systemic Change

It is important to acknowledge that policy standards exist across both NI and RoI. While similar, there are distinct differences in both the teaching standards and their implementation. When looking at the standards, the length may be the first logical comparison. NI's 27 competencies pale when compared with Ireland's 68. Both frameworks focus on the teacher and what they need to do, a distinct difference with the UDL framework which is entirely learner focused.

Both regions have an under-representation of minority groups and a lack of diversity in the teacher demographics. There needs to be a drive across the island of Ireland to widen participation, retain staff, and support those from under-represented groups; these efforts should include peer support, to increase a sense of belonging, as highlighted by Wilkins and Lall (2011).

Increasing numbers of student teachers from lower socio-economic groups, as well as ethnic minorities, can lead to entry into the profession of more relatable and inclusive teachers, and the emergence of a landscape where learners see representation. However, it is argued that this can often lead to teachers from marginalized groups becoming overburdened due to their positionality and lived experience (Keane 2020). While representation is important, Keane et al. (2023b) argue that system transformation, including institutional change, is simultaneously required, to achieve a more diverse, equitable, and inclusive teaching profession (Heinz et al., 2023).

Student teachers face a range of issues throughout their ITE course, which may impact their ability to implement UDL immediately and during the initial years after graduation, such as the lack of confidence and the experiencing of time pressures (Perryman and Calvert, 2020). Implementing this type of approach may seem daunting and students may be reluctant to integrate UDL given their workload (Sellen, 2016). However, being a student teacher is a unique position within a school and

308

Aligning Teacher Competencies and Professional Standards

Backhouse (2016) found that, while some students did become integrated and part of the department and school, they were working induring their placement, not all did. This idea of gaining experience and becoming a part of the group in this way is often called legitimate peripheral participation and is an important concept to consider when thinking of student teachers' ability to integrate and schools as communities of practice, where student teachers are joining an already established way of working. For student teachers this can provide a barrier to their UDL practice.

A further systemic barrier to implementation is the policies which prevail. This chapter has focused on teacher competency frameworks, but these are linked to education policies. In NI the SEND Code of Practice has been under review for an extended period. A new Code of Practice, which outlines how the profession should best deal with individual needs in classrooms, has been proposed but there are delays in implementation. This is coupled with other issues as identified by Purdy (2020) where individuality often prevails and the misuse of the term special educational needs. He argues that there are those 'who fail to see how the identification of individual needs is the first step towards the provision of appropriate support' (Purdy, 2020 pg.17). Similarly, RoI has moved from 'a deficit model of resource allocation to one requiring a social, collective response from schools' (Fitzgerald & Radford, 2017). Both areas adopt the notion of movement toward an inclusive pedagogy, and one could argue that the movement is towards an approach which strives to identify and meet the needs of an individual, as shown in the UDL framework. In addition, Flood and Banks (2021, p. 9) highlight how a "greater understanding of UDL at ITE is required to establish the effect of UDL on student teachers' knowledge, skills, and practice in the classroom.

RECOMMENDATIONS

Earlier in this chapter, the overlap between the two competency standards and UDL were discussed. One such area of overlap was around meeting individual needs. This is linked to the previous discussion on diversity and inclusion, and some of the arguments around inclusive pedagogy. As pointed out by Healy et al., (2023), UDL is a sustainable response that focuses largely on applying differentiated accommodations to ever-increasing numbers of learners.

This diagnosis-led approach is somewhat at odds with the child-centered, learning needs approach embodied in UDL. The chapter has identified that child-centered practice is a core theme running through standards. However, it is difficult to pinpoint what this means in practice, or if all those involved in ITE have a shared understanding of this as classroom practice. One of the key tenets of UDL is the assumption of diversity, i.e., programs often work on a medical-based model which perpetuates difference, where the learner is identified as the issue and not the structures or systemic barriers. A model which assumes diversity can allow learners to understand the principles of inclusive pedagogy in a real and practical sense, as well as have a shared language across the island of Ireland.

It is well documented that underrepresented groups are a minority in the teaching profession across the Island of Ireland. Institutions need to ensure student teachers are culturally and ethnically diverse, come from different socio-economic backgrounds: mature students, refugees, asylum seekers, the traveling community, those from the LGBTQ+, and students with disabilities (Flood and Banks 2021). To ensure access to HE, institutions must provide funding or incentives toward widening access to study. One such attempt to increase numbers in RoI is through a scheme called the Turn to Teaching program that operates across six centers to support under-represented groups logistically, financially, academically, and socially through an ITE program.

While most teachers strive towards inclusive education through transformative pedagogies, as stated by Lakkala and Kyrö-Ämmälä (2017), it has become very clear that inclusive education cannot be carried out by single teachers. Instead, it requires an institutional approach. This is also highlighted by Fovet (2020) who encourages a cross pollination of shared national and international approaches, as this would certainly add value and sustainability to systemic change. ITE needs to both discuss, exemplify, and reflect on best practice of implementing UDL. UDL is not embedded into either the competency or professional standard frameworks, so there is a lack of consistency in the messages HE providers are sending.

CONCLUSION

The chapter highlights how the UDL framework was mapped across two institutions on the island of Ireland that are subject to different competency and professional standard frameworks. The authors identify the various intersections and alignment with the two frameworks, as well as the differences that exist and what still needs to be achieved to be fully inclusive with all learners. However, this is a starting point to identify how ITE providers can embed UDL further into their programs by revisiting the language of the teacher competencies and standards, by supporting and mentoring student teachers to work with diverse learners in the formal education systems, and by providing a clear pathway to achieve that as they become expert teachers.

While small steps are being made in both contexts, they are further developed in RoI through various PATH 4 Phase 1 Universal Design Fund funding streams, the support of AHEAD, and collaborative approach across tertiary education, as well as funding from the Minister of Education. Moreover, UDL has been noted as an

Aligning Teacher Competencies and Professional Standards

appropriate framework for inclusive education in the Standards for Initial Teacher Education (Teaching Council, 2020). Nonetheless, while there is a significant increase in UDL awareness, institutional support remains underdeveloped (Healy et al., 2023) and is more common in HE, than in primary and secondary education (Flood & Banks 2021). Not only can NI and RoI learn much from one another; they can also incorporate a cross-pollination approach as coined by Fovet (2020), where universities, through sharing their UDL journey and research, can learn from one another.

While teacher competency frameworks and professional standard frameworks can be powerful tools, they need to take into consideration both new and established teachers as lifelong learners through continuous professional development, offering an abundance of support at the beginning of their career (Mohamed et al., 2017; Liston et al., 2006 and Ewe et al., 2023). However, as indicated by Edyburn (2020), without clear policy and messaging across the island that supports effective professional learning for all teachers, there are concerns that UDL may become another 'educational fad' associated solely with special education or something that is not properly resourced.

Schools need to be resourced and funded, or this can result in negative effects on the learner, such as exclusion, removal from class, disciplinary measures, school refusal, suspension, or even expulsion (Busby, 2018). UDL is "an approach to teaching and learning that can help educators reach all learners, including those diagnosed with disabilities. UDL enables students to achieve their full potential, which contrasts with the design of a more traditional reactive approach where adaptations only occur after needs have been identified (Navaitienė and Stasiūnaitienė, 2021). As such, this framework can play an important role in supporting inclusive educational environments, and more broadly, in "fostering improved outcomes for students with disabilities" (Vitelli 2015, p. 176) as well as the diversity of all learners.

The intention of this chapter was to start that process or at least start to identify how policy already developed through the teacher competency frameworks and professional standards showcase how UDL is already intertwined into what future and current teachers should be aware of and supported to practice. As highlighted by (Galkienė and Monkevičienė, p6), university educators engaged in teacher training need to have a knowledge and awareness of UDL where the "interaction might create conditions to continuously improve their inclusive education and UDL skills. Together, these components would lead to enhanced sustainability of inclusive education". Considering UDL and learner diversity enables educators to provide more inclusive learning opportunities where all learners can thrive and have an equitable learning experience.

REFERENCES

Aleman, T. C. H., & Glenda, R. (2008). Teacher capacity for diverse learners: What do teachers need to know? In *Handbook of Research on Teacher Education* (3rd ed.). Routledge.

Backhouse, A. (2020). 'Stepping on the teacher's toes': Student teachers' experience of a one-year postgraduate teacher training programme. *European Journal of Teacher Education*, 45(5), 1–20. 10.1080/02619768.2020.1860005

Benton-Borghi, B. H. (2013). A Universally Designed for Learning (UDL) Infused Technological Pedagogical Content Knowledge (TPACK) Practitioners' Model Essential for Teacher Preparation in the 21st Century. *Journal of Educational Computing Research*, 48(2), 245–265. 10.2190/EC.48.2.g

Bilbao, N., Garay, U., Romero, A., & López de la Serna, A. (2021). The European Competency and the Teaching for Understanding Frameworks: Creating Synergies in the Context of Initial Teacher Training in Higher Education. *Sustainability (Basel)*, 13(4), 1–14. 10.3390/su13041810

Booth, T., & Ainscow, M. (2011). *Index for Inclusion: Developing Learning and Participation in Schools*. Centre for Studies on Inclusive Education. https://books .google.ie/books?id=FprJMwEACAAJ

Bronfenbrenner, U., & Ceci, S. J. (1994). Nature-nuture reconceptualized in developmental perspective: A bioecological model. *Psychological Review*, 101(4), 568–586. 10.1037/0033-295X.101.4.5687984707

Bruner, J. S. (1965). *Thought and Language*. The MIT Press. https://mitpress.mit .edu/9780262720014/thought-and-language/

Busby, E. (2018, July). Headteachers blame funding cuts as schools expel 40 pupils each day. *Independant: UK Edition*: https://www.independent.co.uk/news/education/ education-news/school-exclusions-children-rise-england-funding-cuts-headteachers -behaviour-a8454516.html

Canter, L. L. S., King, L. H., Williams, J. B., Metcalf, D., & Potts, K. R. M. (2017). Evaluating Pedagogy and Practice of Universal Design for Learning in Public Schools. *Exceptionality Education International*, 27(1), 1. Advance online publication. 10.5206/eei.v27i1.7743

CAST. (2011). *Universal design for learning guidelines version 2.0*. Wakefield, MA. https://udlguidelines.cast.org/binaries/content/assets/udlguidelines/udlg-v2 -0/udlg_graphicorganizer_v2-0.pdf

Aligning Teacher Competencies and Professional Standards

CAST. (2019). *UDL On Campus: Postsecondary Institutions with UDL Initiatives.* http://udloncampus.cast.org/page/udl_institutions

Chardin, M., & Novak, K. R. (2020). *Equity by Design: Delivering on the Power and Promise of UDL.* Corwin Press. https://ebookcentral.proquest.com/lib/dcu/detail.action?docID=6331818

Clarke, L., & O'Doherty, T. (2021). The professional place of teachers on the island of Ireland: Truth flourishes where the student's lamp has shone. *European Journal of Teacher Education,* 44(1), 62–79. 10.1080/02619768.2020.1844660

Clarke, M., & Drudy, S. (2007). Social justice in initial teacher education: Student Teachers Reflections on Praxis. In Gaine, C., Bhatti, G., Leeman, Y., & Gobbo, F. (Eds.), *Social Justice and Intercultural Education: An open ended Dialogue: Trentham.*

Craig, S. L., Smith, S. J., & Frey, B. B. (2022). Professional development with universal design for learning: Supporting teachers as learners to increase the implementation of UDL. *Professional Development in Education,* 48(1), 22–37. 10.1080/19415257.2019.1685563

Dalton, E. M. (2020). UDL and connected laws, theories, and frameworks. In Gronseth, S. L., & Dalton, E. M. (Eds.), *Universal access through inclusive instructional design: International perspectives on UDL* (pp. 3–16). Routledge.

Darling-Hammond, L. (2017). Teacher education around the world: What can we learn from international practice? *European Journal of Teacher Education,* 40(3), 291–309. 10.1080/02619768.2017.1315399

Department of Education. (2021, December 8). *School enrolments—2021-22 provisional statistical bulletins datafiles.* Education. https://www.education-ni.gov.uk/publications/school-enrolments-2021-22-provisional-statistical-bulletins-datafiles

Dillon, S., & O'Shea, K. (2009). *From the College to the Classroom: The Impact of DICE Courses on the Inclusion of Development Education and Intercultural Education in the Primary Classroom* (p. 79). DICE project. https://developmenteducation.ie/resource/from-the-college-to-the-classroom-the-impact-of-dice-courses-on-the-inclusion-of-development-education-and-intercultural-education-in-the-primary-classroom/

Edyburn, D. L. (2013). Critical Issues in Advancing the Special Education Technology Evidence Base. *Exceptional Children,* 80(1), 7–24. 10.1177/001440291308000107

Estellés, M., & Fischman, G. E. (2021). Who Needs Global Citizenship Education? A Review of the Literature on Teacher Education. *Journal of Teacher Education,* 2(72), 223–236. 10.1177/0022487120920254

European Agency for Special Needs and Inclusive Education. (2022). *Agency Position on Inclusive Education Systems* (2nd ed.).

European Commission. (2013). *Supporting teacher competence development for better learning outcomes.* https://www.academia.edu/6623391/Supporting_teacher_competence_development_for_better_learning_outcomes

European Education and Culture Executive Agency. (2015). *The structure of the European education systems 2013/14: Schematic diagrams.* Eurydice., 10.2797/206797

Evmenova, A. (2018). Preparing Teachers to Use Universal Design for Learning to Support Diverse Learners. *Journal of Online Learning Research*, 4(2), 147–171.

Ewe, L. P., Dalton, E. M., Bhan, S., Gronseth, S. L., & Dahlberg, G. (2023). Inclusive Education and UDL Professional Development for Teachers in Sweden and India. In Koreeda, K., Tsuge, M., Ikuta, S., Dalton, E., & Ewe, L. (Eds.), *Developing Inclusive Environments in Education: Global Practices and Curricula* (pp. 14–33). IGI Global., 10.4018/979-8-3693-0664-2.ch002

Ewe, L. P., & Galvin, T. (2023). Universal Design for Learning across Formal School Structures in Europe: A Systematic Review. *Education Sciences*, 13(9), 867. 10.3390/educsci13090867

Faas, D., Smith, A., & Darmody, M. (2018). Between ethos and practice: Are Ireland's new multi- denominational primary schools equal and inclusive? *Compare: A Journal of Comparative Education*, 49(4), 602–618. 10.1080/03057925.2018.1441704

Fitzgerald, J., & Radford, J. (2017). The SENCO role in post-primary schools in Ireland: Victims or agents of change? *European Journal of Special Needs Education*, 32(3), 452–466. 10.1080/08856257.2017.1295639

Flood, M., & Banks, J. (2021). Universal Design for Learning: Is It Gaining Momentum in Irish Education? *Education Sciences*, 11(7), 341. 10.3390/educsci11070341

Florian, L. (2019). On the necessary co-existence of special and inclusive education. *International Journal of Inclusive Education*, 23(7–8), 691–704. 10.1080/13603116.2019.1622801

Florian, L. (2021). Series Editor's Preface. In *Improving Inclusive Education through Universal Design for Learning* (Vol. 5). Springer International Publishing., 10.1007/978-3-030-80658-3

Aligning Teacher Competencies and Professional Standards

Florian, L., Young, K., & Rouse, M. (2010). Preparing teachers for inclusive and diverse educational environments: Studying curricular reform in an initial teacher education course. *International Journal of Inclusive Education*, 14(7), 709–722. 10.1080/13603111003778536

Fovet, F. (2017). Access, Universal Design and the Sustainability of Teaching Practices: A Powerful Synchronicity of Concepts at a Crucial Conjuncture for Higher Education. *Indonesian Journal of Disability Studies*, 4(2), 2.

Fovet, F. (2020). Universal Design for Learning as a Tool for Inclusion in the Higher Education Classroom: Tips for the Next Decade of Implementation. *Education Journal*, 9(6), 6. Advance online publication. 10.11648/j.edu.20200906.13

Fritzgerald, A., & Rice, S. (2020). *Antiracism and Universal Design for Learning: Building Expressways to Success*. CAST, Incorporated. https://books.google.ie/books?id=vF_HzQEACAAJ

Galkienė, A., & Monkevičienė, O. (Eds.). (2021). *Improving Inclusive Education through Universal Design for Learning* (Vol. 5). Springer International Publishing., 10.1007/978-3-030-80658-3

Galkiene, A., & Monkeviciene, O. (2021). *The Model of UDL Implementation Enabling the Development of Inclusive Education in Different Educational Contexts: Conclusions* (pp. 313–323). https://doi.org/10.1007/978-3-030-80658-3_12

Galvin, T., & Geron, M. (2021). Building a community of practice across an institution: How to embed UDL through the Plus One Approach between an academic developer and instructor in STEM. In Fovet, F. (Ed.), *Handbook of Research on Applying Universal Design for Learning Across Disciplines: Concepts, Case Studies, and Practical Implementation* (pp. 323–344). IGI Global. 10.4018/978-1-7998-7106-4.ch017

Gardner, H. (1993). *Multiple intelligences: The theory in practice* (pp. xvi, 304). Basic Books/Hachette Book Group.

General Teaching Council for Northern Ireland. (2011). *Teaching: The Reflective Profession*.

General Teaching Council for Northern Ireland. (2015). *Teacher Education Partnership Handbook | Department of Education*. https://www.education-ni.gov.uk/publications/teacher-education-partnership-handbook

Gentile, A. L., & Budzilowicz, M. (2022). Empowering college students: UDL, culturally responsive pedagogy, and mindset as an instructional approach. *New Directions for Teaching and Learning*, 2022(172), 33–42. 10.1002/tl.20524

Government of Ireland. (2019, October 16). *Education statistics*. https://www.gov.ie/en/publication/055810-education-statistics/

Griful-Freixenet, J., Struyven, K., Vantieghem, W., & Gheyssens, E. (2020). Exploring the interrelationship between Universal Design for Learning (UDL) and Differentiated Instruction (DI): A systematic review. *Educational Research Review*, 29, 100306. 10.1016/j.edurev.2019.100306

Hagan, M., & Eaton, P. (2020). Teacher education in Northern Ireland: Reasons to be cheerful or a 'Wicked Problem'? *Teacher Development*, 24(2), 258–273. 10.1080/13664530.2020.1751260

Hagan, M., & McGlynn, C. (2004). Moving barriers: Promoting learning for diversity in initial teacher education. *Intercultural Education*, 15(3), 243–252. 10.1080/1467598042000262545

Hamdan, A. R., Anuar, M. K., & Khan, A. (2016). Implementation of Co-Teaching Approach in an Inclusive Classroom: Overview of the Challenges, Readiness, and Role of Special Education Teacher. *Asia Pacific Education Review*, 17(2), 289–298. 10.1007/s12564-016-9419-8

Hartmann, E. (2015). Universal Design for Learning (UDL) and Learners with Severe Support Needs. *International Journal of Whole Schooling*, 11(1), 54–67.

Heelan, A., & Tobin, T. J. (2021). *UDL for FET Practitioners Guidance for Implementing Universal Design for Learning in Irish Further Education and Training*. https://www.solas.ie/f/70398/x/81044b80ce/fet_practitioners-main.pdf

Humphrey, N., Bartolo, P., Ale, P., Calleja, C., Hofsaess, T., Janikova, V., Lous, A. M., Vilkiene, V., & Wetso, G. (2006). Understanding and responding to diversity in the primary classroom: An international study. *European Journal of Teacher Education*, 29(3), 305–318. 10.1080/02619760600795122

Independant Education Review. (2023). *Investing in a better future: The independent review of education in Northern Ireland (Volume 2)*.https://www.independentreviewofeducation.org.uk/files/independentreviewofeducation/2024-01/Investing%20in%20a%20Better%20Future%20-%20Volume%202.pdf

Individuals with Disabilities Education Act (IDEA). (1975). https://sites.ed.gov/idea/

Jimenez, B. A., & Hudson, M. E. (2019). Including students with severe disabilities in general education and the potential of universal design for learning for all children. *The SAGE Handbook of Inclusion and Diversity in Education*, 288–306. https://dialnet.unirioja.es/servlet/articulo?codigo=7146989

Keane, E., & Heinz, M. (2015). Diversity in initial teacher education in Ireland: The socio-demographic backgrounds of postgraduate post-primary entrants in 2013 and 2014. *Irish Educational Studies*, 34(3), 281–301. 10.1080/03323315.2015.1067637

Keane, E., & Heinz, M. (2016). Excavating an injustice?: Nationality/ies, ethnicity/ies and experiences with diversity of initial teacher education applicants and entrants in Ireland in 2014. *European Journal of Teacher Education*, 39(4), 507–527. 10.1080/02619768.2016.1194392

Kirshner, D. (2016). *Configuring Learning Theory to Support Teaching*.

Koster, B., & Dengerink, J. J. (2008). Professional standards for teacher educators: How to deal with complexity, ownership and function. Experiences from the Netherlands. *European Journal of Teacher Education*, 31(2), 135–149. 10.1080/02619760802000115

Lakkala, S., & Kyrö-Ämmälä, O. (2021). Teaching for Diversity with UDL: Analysing Teacher Competence. In Galkienė, A., & Monkevičienė, O. (Eds.), *Improving Inclusive Education through Universal Design for Learning* (Vol. 5, pp. 241–277). Springer., 10.1007/978-3-030-80658-3_10

Lakkala, S. P., & Kyrö-Ämmälä, O. (2017). The Finnish School Case. In A. Galkienė (Ed.), *Inclusion in socio-educational frames* (pp. 267–309). The publishing house of the Lithuanian University of Educational Sciences.

Lanterman, C. S., & Applequist, K. (2018). Pre-service Teachers' Beliefs: Impact of Training in Universal Design for Learning. *Exceptionality Education International*, 28(3). Advance online publication. 10.5206/eei.v28i3.7774

Leavy, A. (2005). 'When I meet them I talk to them': The challenges of diversity for preservice teacher education. *Irish Educational Studies*, 24(2–3), 159–177. 10.1080/03323310500435422

Lenski, S. D., Crawford, K., Crumpler, T., & Stallworth, C. (2005). Preparing Preservice Teachers in a Diverse World. *Action in Teacher Education*, 27(3), 3–12. 10.1080/01626620.2005.10463386

Liston, D., Whitcomb, J., & Borko, H. (2006). Too Little or Too Much: Teacher Preparation and the First Years of Teaching. *Journal of Teacher Education*, 57(4), 351–358. 10.1177/0022487106291976

Lowrey, K. A., Classen, A., & Sylvest, A. (2019). Exploring Ways to Support Preservice Teachers' Use of UDL In Planning and Instruction. *Journal of Educational Research & Practice*, 9(1), 261–281. 10.5590/JERAP.2019.09.1.19

ΜχΚενζιε, ϑ., & Δαλτον, Ε. (2020). Υνιϖερσαλ δεσιγν φορ λεαρνιγ ιν ινχλυσιϖε εδυχατιον πολιχψ ιν Σουτη Αφριχα. *Αφριχαν ϑουρναλ οφ Δισαβιλιτψ, 9*, 1–8. ηττπσ://δοι.οργ/ ΠΜΙΔ:3339206210.4102/αφοδ.ϖ9ι0.776

McCarthy, A. M., Maor, D., McConney, A., & Cavanaugh, C. (2023). Digital transformation in education: Critical components for leaders of system change. *Social Sciences & Humanities Open*, 8(1), 1–15. 10.1016/j.ssaho.2023.100479

McDaid, R., & Nowlan, E. (2021). Barriers to recognition for migrant teachers in Ireland'. *European Educational Research Journal*, 21(2), 247–264. 10.1177/14749041211031724

McLaughlin, H., & Kenny, M. (2004). *Diversity in Early Years Education North and South—Implications for Teacher Education* [Report for the Centre for Cross Border Studies and the Standing Conference on Teacher Education, North and South].

Meijer, C., & Watkins, A. (2016). Changing Conceptions of Inclusion Underpinning Education Policy. In *Implementing Inclusive Education: Issues in Bridging the Policy-Practice Gap* (Vol. 8, pp. 1–16). Emerald Group Publishing Limited. https://doi.org/10.1108/S1479-363620160000008001

Meyer, A., Rose, D. H., & Gordon, D. (2014). *Universal Design for Learning: Theory & Practice*. Wakefield, MA. https://www.cast.org/products-services/resources/2014/universal-design-learning-theory-practice-udl-meyer

Mills, C. (2008). Reproduction and transformation of inequalities in schooling: The transformative potential of the theoretical constructs of Bourdieu. *British Journal of Sociology of Education*, 29(1), 79–89. 10.1080/01425690701737481

Mkandawire, M. T., Mwanjejele, J., Luo, Z., & Ruzagirizad, A. U. (2016). What Mismatch Challenges are there between What Teacher Education Institutions Teach and What is Expected at Work Place? Retrospective Views of Secondary School Teachers from Tanzania and Malawi Studying in China. *American Scientific Research Journal for Engineering, Technology, and Sciences*, 22, 39–49.

Mohamed, Z., Valcke, M., & De Wever, B. (2017). Are they ready to teach? Student teachers' readiness for the job with reference to teacher competence frameworks. *Journal of Education for Teaching*, 43(2), 151–170. 10.1080/02607476.2016.1257509

Montgomery, A., & Smith, A. (2006). Teacher Education in Northern Ireland: Policy Variations Since Devolution. *Scottish Educational Review*, 37(3), 46–58. 10.1163/27730840-03703005

Moran, A. (2008). Challenges surrounding widening participation and fair access to initial teacher education: Can it be achieved? *Journal of Education for Teaching*, 34(1), 63–77. 10.1080/02607470701773481

Moran, A. (2012). Crises as catalysts for change: Re-energising teacher education in Northern Ireland. *Educational Research*, 54(2), 137–147. 10.1080/00131881.2012.680039

National Forum. (2020). *INDEx Survey: Final Summary Report*. https://hub.teachingandlearning.ie/wp-content/uploads/2021/06/INDEx-Survey-Final-Report-15-April-2021.pdf

Navaitienė, J., & Stasiūnaitienė, E. (2023). The Goal of the Universal Design for Learning: Development of All to Expert Learners. In A. Galkienė, & O, Monkevičienė (Eds). *Improving Inclusive Education through Universal Design for Learning (pp. 23–57)*. Springer. https://link.springer.com/content/pdf/10.1007/978-3-030-80658-3.pdf

O'Neill, G., & Maguire, T. (2019). Developing assessment and feedback approaches to empower and engage students: A sectoral approach in Ireland. In *Transforming Higher Education Through Universal Design for Learning*. Routledge. 10.4324/9781351132077-17

OECD. (2009). *Creating effective teaching and learning environments: First results from TALIS*. OECD.

Paseka, A., & Schwab, S. (2020). Parents' attitudes towards inclusive education and their perceptions of inclusive teaching practices and resources. *European Journal of Special Needs Education*, 35(2), 254–272. 10.1080/08856257.2019.1665232

Pearson, M. (2015). Modeling Universal Design for Learning Techniques to Support Multicultural Education for Pre-Service Secondary Educators. *Multicultural Education*.

Perryman, J., & Calvert, G. (2020). What Motivates People to Teach, and Why Do They Leave? Accountability, Performativity and Teacher Retention. *British Journal of Educational Studies*, 68(1), 3–23. 10.1080/00071005.2019.1589417

Purdy, N., Hunter, J., & Totton, L. (2020). Examining the legacy of the Warnock Report in Northern Ireland: A Foucauldian genealogical approach. *British Educational Research Journal*, 46(3), 706–723. 10.1002/berj.3604

Rao, K., & Meo, G. (2016). Using Universal Design for Learning to Design Standards-Based Lessons. *SAGE Open*, 6(4), 2158244016680688. 10.1177/2158244016680688

Rao, K., & Okolo, C. (n.d.). *Teacher Education and Professional Development on UDL.*

Reinhardt, K. S., Robertson, P. M., & Johnson, R. D. (2021). Connecting inquiry and Universal Design for Learning (UDL) to teacher candidates' emerging practice: Development of a signature pedagogy. *Educational Action Research*, 0(0), 1–18. 10.1080/09650792.2021.1978303

Reynor, E. (2021). From student teachers to educators: Walking the talk with universal design for learning. *A review of inclusive education and employment practices*, 2(12). https://www.ahead.ie/journal/From-student-teachers-to-Educators-Walking -the-Talk-with-Universal-Design-for-Learning

Root, J. R., Jimenez, B., & Saunders, A. (2022). Leveraging the UDL Framework to Plan Grade-Aligned Mathematics in Inclusive Settings. *In Practice*, 1(1), 13–22. 10.1177/2732474521990028

Rose, D. (2001). Universal Design for Learning. *Journal of Special Education Technology*, 16(2), 66–67. 10.1177/016264340101600208

Rose, D., & Meyer, A. (2006). *A Practical Reader in Universal Design for Learning.*

Roulston, S., Brown, M., Taggart, S., & Eivers, E. (2023). A Century of Growing Apart and Challenges of Coming Together: Education Across the Island of Ireland. *Irish Studies in International Affairs, 34*(2), 78-121. https://doi.org/10.1353/isia .2023.a899832

Sellen, P. (2016, October). *Teacher workload and professional development in England's secondary schools: Insights from TALIS: 10 October 2016.* Education Policy Institute. https://dera.ioe.ac.uk/27930/1/TeacherWorkload_EPI.pdf

Sharma, U., Armstrong, A. C., Merumeru, L., Simi, J., & Yared, H. (2019). Addressing barriers to implementing inclusive education in the Pacific. *International Journal of Inclusive Education*, 23(1), 65–78. 10.1080/13603116.2018.1514751

Simpson, M., & Anderson, B. (2009). Redesigning Initial Teacher Education. In *Effective Blended Learning Practices: Evidence-Based Perspectives in ICT-Facilitated Education* (pp. 62–78). IGI Global. 10.4018/978-1-60566-296-1.ch004

Sleeter, C. (2008). An Invitation To Support Diverse Students Through Teacher Education. *Journal of Teacher Education*, 59(3), 212–219. 10.1177/0022487108317019

Smyth, E., Devlin, A., Bergin, A., & McGuinness, S. (2022). *A North-South comparison of education and training systems: Lessons for policy* [Report]. ESRI. 10.26504/rs138

Aligning Teacher Competencies and Professional Standards

Spratt, J., & Florian, L. (2015). Inclusive pedagogy: From learning to action. Supporting each individual in the context of 'everybody.' *Teaching and Teacher Education*, 49, 89–96. 10.1016/j.tate.2015.03.006

Text of H.R. 4137 (110th): Higher Education Opportunity Act (Passed Congress version)—GovTrack.us. Retrieved June 16, 2023, from https://www.govtrack.us/congress/bills/110/hr4137/text

The Teaching Council Act—Teaching Council. (2001). https://www.teachingcouncil.ie/en/about-us1/relevant-legislation/the-teaching-council-act/

UNESCO. (1994). *The Salamanca Statement and Framework for Action on Special Needs Education.* Retrieved from the United Nations Educational, Scientific, and Cultural Organization website: https://unesdoc.unesco.org/ark:/48223/pf0000098427

UNESCO. (2017). *A Guide for Ensuring Inclusion and Equity in Education.* Retrieved from the United Nations Educational, Scientific, and Cultural Organization website: https://unesdoc.unesco.org/ark:/48223/pf0000248254

UNESCO. (2020a). *Towards inclusion in education: Status, trends and challenges.* The UNESCO Salamanca Statement 25 years on. Retrieved from the United Nations Educational, Scientific, and Cultural Organization website: https://unesdoc.unesco.org/ark:/48223/pf0000374246

UNESCO. (2020b). *Inclusion and education: all means all.* Global education monitoring *report.* Retrieved from the United Nations Educational, Scientific, and Cultural Organization website: https://unesdoc.unesco.org/ark:/48223/pf0000373718

United Nations. (2020a). *Decade of Action. Ten Years to Transform Our World.* Retrieved from the United Nations Educational, Scientific, and Cultural Organization website: https://www.un.org/sustainabledevelopment/decade-of-action

United Nations. (2020b). *The sustainable development goal report—SDG Indicators.* Retrieved from the United Nations Educational, Scientific, and Cultural Organization website: https://unstats.un.org/sdgs/report/2020/

Vitelli, E. M. (2015). Universal Design for Learning: Are We Teaching It to Preservice General Education Teachers? *Journal of Special Education Technology*, 30(3), 166–178. 10.1177/0162643415618931

Vygotsky, L. (1962). *Thought and language.* MIT Press. 10.1037/11193-000

Vygotsky, L. S. (1980). *Mind in Society: Development of Higher Psychological Processes* (Cole, M., John-Steiner, V., Scribner, S., & Souberman, E., Eds.). Harvard University Press.

Waitoller, F. R., & Artiles, A. J. (2013). A Decade of Professional Development Research for Inclusive Education: A Critical Review and Notes for a Research Program. *Review of Educational Research*, 83(3), 319–356. 10.3102/0034654313483905

Whitehead, I. A. (2019). *The Transformation of Initial Teacher Education: The Changing Nature of Teacher Training*. Routledge. 10.4324/9780429424564

Wilkins, C., & Lall, R. (2011). 'You've got to be tough and I'm trying': Black and minority ethnic student teachers' experiences of initial teacher education. *Race, Ethnicity and Education*, 14(3), 365–386. 10.1080/13613324.2010.543390

Ydo, Y. (2020). Inclusive education: Global priority, collective responsibility. *Prospects*, 49(3), 97–101. 10.1007/s11125-020-09520-y

Compilation of References

Abbott, P., & Connors, E. (2020). Braille and other tactile forms of communication. In Lee, H., & Ottowitz, J. (Eds.), *Foundations of Vision Rehabilitation Therapy* (4th ed., pp. 199–243). APH Press.

Abes, E. S., & Zahneis, M. E. (2020). A Duoethnographic Exploration of Disability Ally Development. *Disability Studies Quarterly*, 40(3). Advance online publication. 10.18061/dsq.v40i3.7038

AccessATCanada. (2019). *AccessATCanada: Find out which government and charity programs offer assistive technology funding and services in Canada and its provinces and territories*. Retrieved November 12 from https://www.accessassistivetech.ca/programs

Ackland, P., Resnikoff, S., & Bourne, R. (2017). World blindness and visual impairment: Despite many successes, the problem is growing. *Community Eye Health*, 30(100), 71–73. https://www.ncbi.nlm.nih.gov/pmc/articles/PMC5820628/29483748

Adamec, P. (2023). Teaching Vocational Subjects in Secondary School: A New Career or a Backup Plan? *International Journal of Engineering Pedagogy*, 13(5), 142–160. 10.3991/ijep.v13i5.37555

Aguilar-de Borja, J. M. (2018). Teacher action research: Its difficulties and implications. *Humanities and Social Sciences Reviews*, 6(1), 29–35. 10.18510/hssr.2018.616

AHEAD. (2023). CPD - the Digital Badge for Universal Design in Teaching & Learning. *Training*. https://www.ahead.ie/udl-digitalbadge

Ajaj, R. (2020). Navigating the World of Higher Education as a Blind or Visually Impaired Student: Unequal Opportunities for Academic Success.

Aktay, A., Bavadekar, S., Cossoul, G., Davis, J., Desfontaines, D., Fabrikant, A., Gabrilovich, E., Gadepalli, K., Gipson, B., Guevara, B., Kamath, C., Kansal, M., Lange, A., Mandayam, C., Oplinger, A., Pluntke, C., Roessler, T., Schlosberg, A., Shekel, T., . . . Wilson, R. J. (2020). *Google COVID-19 community mobility reports: Anonymization process description* (version 1.1). https://arxiv.org/abs/2004.04145

Aleman, T. C. H., & Glenda, R. (2008). Teacher capacity for diverse learners: What do teachers need to know? In *Handbook of Research on Teacher Education* (3rd ed.). Routledge.

Almeqdad, Q., Alodat, A. M., Alquraan, M. F., Mohaidat, M. A., & Al-Makhzoomy, A. K. (2023). The effectiveness of universal design for learning: A systematic review of the literature and meta-analysis. *Cogent Education*, 10(1), 2218191. Advance online publication. 10.1080/2331186X.2023.2218191

Almumen, H. A. (2020). Universal Design for Learning (UDL) Across Cultures: The Application of UDL in Kuwaiti Inclusive Classrooms. *SAGE Open*, 10(4). Advance online publication. 10.1177/2158244020969674

AlRawi, J. M., & AlKahtani, M. A. (2021). Universal design for learning for educating students with intellectual disabilities: A systematic review. *International Journal of Developmental Disabilities*, 68(6), 800–808. 10.1080/20473869.2021.190050536568615

Amado-Alonso, D., León-del-Barco, B., Mendo-Lázaro, S., Sánchez-Miguel, P. A., & Iglesias Gallego, D. (2019). Emotional intelligence and the practice of organized physical-sport activity in children. *Sustainability (Basel)*, 11(6), 1615. 10.3390/su11061615

American Printing House for the Blind. (n.d.). *APH Museum: A museum dedicated to ordinary people doing extraordinary things*. Retrieved November 12 from https://aphmuseum.org/

Anastasiou, D., & Kauffman, J. M. (2013). The social model of disability: Dichotomy between impairment and disability. *The Journal of Medicine and Philosophy*, 38(4), 441–459. 10.1093/jmp/jht02623856481

Anya, U. (2017). *Racialized identities in second language learning: Speaking blackness in Brazil*. Routledge.

Apple Inc. (n.d.). *Apple VoiceOver Guide - Chapter 10 - Using braille displays*. Apple Inc. Retrieved November 3 from https://www.apple.com/voiceover/info/guide/_1129.html

Aravossitas, T., & Oikonomakou, M. (2020). New directions for Greek education in the diaspora: teaching heritage language learners in Canada. In *Language diversity in Greece – Local challenges with international implications* (pp. 235-253). Springer. 10.1007/978-3-030-28396-4_18

Arias-Flores, H., Sanchez-Gordon, S., & Calle-Jimenez, T. (2021). Analysis of the Level of Accessibility of Scientific Online Conferences for Blind Participants. International Conference on Applied Human Factors and Ergonomics.

Arigita-García, A., Sánchez-Cabrero, R., Barrientos-Fernández, A., Mañoso-Pacheco, L., & Pericacho-Gómez, F. J. (2021). Pre-eminence of determining factors in second language learning: An educator's perspective from Spain. *Heliyon*, 7(2), e06282. 10.1016/j.heliyon.2021.e0628233665442

Arnaiz-Sánchez, P., De Haro-Rodríguez, R., Caballero, C.M., & Martínez-Abellán, R. (2023). Barriers to Educational Inclusion in Initial Teacher Training. *Societies 13, 2*(31). https://doi.org/10.3390/soc13020031

Compilation of References

Arnett, K. & Mady, C. (2018). The influence of classroom experience on teacher belief systems: New French second language teachers' beliefs about program options for English language learners and students with learning difficulties. *McGill Journal of Education / Revue des sciences de l'éducation de McGill, 53*(3). 10.7202/1058418ar

Arnett, K., & Mady, C. (2017). Core or immersion? Canadian French-second-language teacher candidates' perceptions and experiences of the best and worst program options for students with learning difficulties and for English language learners. *Exceptionality Education International,* 27(1), 17–37. 10.5206/eei.v27i1.7744

Arnott, S., Masson, M., & Lapkin, S. (2019). Exploring Trends in 21st Century Canadian K-12 French as Second Language Research: A Research Synthesis. *Canadian Journal of Applied Linguistics. Canadian Journal of Applied Linguistics*, 22(1). Advance online publication. 10.7202/1060906ar

Arnou, C., Cornelis, G., Jan Heymans, P., Howard, S. K., Leemans, G., Nuyens, I., Tondeur, J., Vaesen, J., Van Den Driessche, M., Elen, J., & Valcke, M. (2020). *COVID-19 and educational spaces: Creating a powerful and social inclusive learning environment at home.*https://www.academia.edu/download/63264421/20200507_EN_create_a_learning_environment_at_home20200510-115155-1l3v4pe.pdf

Asadifard, A., & Koosha, M. (2013). EFL Instructors and Student Writers' Perceptions on Academic Writing Reluctance. *Theory and Practice in Language Studies*, 3(9), 1572–1578. 10.4304/tpls.3.9.1572-1578

Asfeldt, M., Purc-Stephenson, R., & Zimmerman, T. (2022). Outdoor education in Canadian public schools: Connecting children and youth to people, place, and environment. *Environmental Education Research*, 28(10), 1510–1526. 10.1080/13504622.2022.2061919

Ashkenas, R. N. (1994). Beyond fads: How leaders drive change with results. *People and Strategy*, 17(2), 25.

Association of Experiential Learning. (2023). *What is Experiential Education? AEL*https://www.aee.org/what-is-experiential-education

Atlantic Technological University. (2023). Postgraduate Certificate in Universal Design for Learning (Online). Courses. *Faculty of Business and Social Sciences.* https://www.itsligo.ie/courses/postgraduate-certificate-in-universal-design-for-learning-online-2/#:~:text=Based%20in%20cognitive%20neurosciences%2C%20UDL,designing%20capacity%20building%20learning%20experiences

AuCoin, A., Porter, G. L., & Baker-Korotkov, K. (2020). *New Brunswick's Journey to Inclusive Education.*https://inclusiveeducation.ca/wp-content/uploads/sites/3/2020/09/FINAL-UNESCO-Article-NB-Inclusion-Sept-2020-AuCoin-Porter-Korotkov.pdf

Auxier, B. E., Buntain, C. L., Jaeger, P., Golbeck, J., & Kacorri, H. (2019). # HandsOffMyADA: A Twitter Response to the ADA Education and Reform Act. Proceedings of the 2019 CHI Conference on Human Factors in Computing Systems.

Backhouse, A. (2020). 'Stepping on the teacher's toes': Student teachers' experience of a one-year postgraduate teacher training programme. *European Journal of Teacher Education*, 45(5), 1–20. 10.1080/02619768.2020.1860005

Badil, D. D. M., Zeenaf Aslam, Z. A., Kashif Khan, K. K., Anny Ashiq, A. A., & Uzma Bibi, U. B. (2023). The Phenomenology Qualitative Research Inquiry: A Review Paper: Phenomenology Qualitative Research Inquiry. *Pakistan Journal of Health Sciences, 4*(3), 9–13. 10.54393/pjhs. v4i03.626

Baglieri, S. (2020). Toward Inclusive Education? Focusing a Critical Lens on Universal Design for Learning. *Canadian Journal of Disability Studies*, 9(5), 42–74. 10.15353/cjds.v9i5.690

Baglieri, S., Valle, J. W., Connor, D. J., & Gallagher, D. J. (2011). Disability studies in education: The need for a plurality of perspectives on disability. *Remedial and Special Education*, 32(4), 267–278. 10.1177/0741932510362200

Bailey, L., & Gibson, M. (2023). School leaders of high stakes assessments during the COVID pandemic in England. *School Leadership & Management*, 43(3), 189–209. 10.1080/13632434.2023.2176482

Banks, J., & McCoy, S. (2011). A Study on the Prevalence of Special Educational Needs. In *National Council for Special Education*. https://www.esri.ie/publications/a-study-on-the-prevalence -of-special-educational-needs

Barac, R., Bialystok, E., Castro, D. C., & Sanchez, M. (2014). The Cognitive Development of Young Dual Language Learners: A Critical Review. *Early Childhood Research Quarterly*, 29(4), 699–714. 10.1016/j.ecresq.2014.02.00325284958

Baran, J., Cierpiałowska, T., & Dyduch, E. (2021). Transformations of the Teaching–Learning Process Towards Inclusive Education as a Result of the UDL Approach Implementation. In *Improving Inclusive Education through Universal Design for Learning* (pp. 95–118). Springer. 10.1007/978-3-030-80658-3_5

Barnes, C. (2020). Understanding the social model of disability: Past, present and future. In N. Watson & S. Vehmas (Eds.), *Routledge Handbook of Disability Studies* (pp. 14–31). Routledge.

Barrett DeWiele, C. E., & Edgerton, J. D. (2021). Opportunity or inequality? The paradox of French immersion education in Canada. *Journal of Multilingual and Multicultural Development*. Advance online publication. 10.1080/01434632.2020.1865988

Basham, J. D., & Blackorby, J. (2020). UDL next: The future of the framework. In Lowrey, K. A. (Ed.), *Critical issues in universal design for learning*. Knowledge by Design.

Basham, J. D., Blackorby, J., & Marino, M. T. (2020). Opportunity in crisis: The role of Universal Design for Learning in educational redesign. *Learning Disabilities (Weston, Mass.)*, 18(1), 71–91.

Basham, J. D., Blackorby, J., & Marino, M. T. (2020). Opportunity in Crisis: The Role of Universal Design for Learning in Educational Redesign. *Learning Disabilities (Weston, Mass.)*, 18, 71–91. https://files.eric.ed.gov/fulltext/EJ1264277.pdf

Compilation of References

Basham, J. D., Blackorby, J., Stahl, S., & Zhang, L. (2018). Universal design for learning: Because students are (the) variable. In Kennedy, K., & Ferdig, R. E. (Eds.), *Handbook of research on K-12 online and blended learning* (2nd ed., pp. 477–507). ETC Press.

Basma, B., & Savage, R. (2023). Teacher Professional Development and Student Reading in Middle and High School: A Systematic Review and Meta-Analysis. *Journal of Teacher Education*, 74(3), 214–228. 10.1177/00224871231153084

Batorowicz, B., Missiuna, C. A., & Pollock, N. A. (2012). Technology supporting written productivity in children with learning disabilities: A critical review. *Canadian Journal of Occupational Therapy*, 79(4), 211–224. 10.2182/cjot.2012.79.4.323210371

BCUDL. (2010) *Universal Design for Learning in BC*. Special Education Technology BC. https://curric.prn.bc.ca/wp-content/uploads/sites/37/2017/02/UDL-SET-BC.pdf

Benetech. (2022). *Born Accessible: A Benetch Initiative*. Retrieved November 12 from https://bornaccessible.benetech.org/

Benton-Borghi, B. H. (2013). A Universally Designed for Learning (UDL) Infused Technological Pedagogical Content Knowledge (TPACK) Practitioners' Model Essential for Teacher Preparation in the 21st Century. *Journal of Educational Computing Research*, 48(2), 245–265. 10.2190/EC.48.2.g

Bergmark, U. (2023). Teachers' professional learning when building a research-based education: Context-specific, collaborative and teacher-driven professional development. *Professional Development in Education*, 49(2), 210–224. 10.1080/19415257.2020.1827011

Berquist, E. (2017). *UDL: Moving from exploration to integration*. CAST Professional Publishing.

Bialystok, E. (2018). Bilingual education for young children: Review of the effects and consequences. *International Journal of Bilingual Education and Bilingualism*, 21(6), 666–679. 10.1080/13670050.2016.120385930288137

Bilbao, N., Garay, U., Romero, A., & López de la Serna, A. (2021). The European Competency and the Teaching for Understanding Frameworks: Creating Synergies in the Context of Initial Teacher Training in Higher Education. *Sustainability (Basel)*, 13(4), 1–14. 10.3390/su13041810

Bobongie-Harris, F., & Youse, Z. (2023). Approaches to improve the cultural capabilities of teachers engaging with culturally and linguistically diverse students and their families: A scoping review. *Frontiers in Education*, 8, 1038880. https://www.frontiersin.org/articles/10.3389/feduc.2023.1038880. 10.3389/feduc.2023.1038880

Bonyadi, A. (2023). Phenomenology as a research methodology in teaching English as a foreign language. *Asian Journal of Second and Foreign Language Education*, 8(1), 11. 10.1186/s40862-022-00184-z

Booth, T., & Ainscow, M. (2011). *Index for Inclusion: Developing Learning and Participation in Schools*. Centre for Studies on Inclusive Education. https://books.google.ie/books?id=FprJMwEACAAJ

Borsch, A. S., Skovdal, M., & Smith Jervelund, S. (2021). How a School Setting Can Generate Social Capital for Young Refugees: Qualitative Insights from a Folk High School in Denmark. *Journal of Refugee Studies*, 34(1), 718–740. 10.1093/jrs/fez003

Bouakir, H. (2019) *School leadership strategies for the implementation of Universal Design for Learning*. MEd thesis. Faculty of Education, Memorial University of Newfoundland. https://research.library.mun.ca/14306/1/thesis.pdf

Bourgoin, R. (2014). Inclusionary practices in French immersion: A need to link research to practice. *Canadian Journal for New Scholars in Education*, 5(1), 1–11.

Bourgoin, R. (2016). French immersion "So why would you do something like that to a child?" Issues of advocacy, accessibility, and inclusion. *International Journal of Bias, Identity and Diversities in Education*, 1(1), 42–58. 10.4018/IJBIDE.2016010104

Bowers, S. (2023, August 29). 'Gamechanger' programme allows students to attain third-level degree outside CAO points race. *Irish Times*. https://www.irishtimes.com/ireland/education/2023/08/29/alternative-pathways-to-further-education/

Bowling, E. (2015). What's the value of eye care? *Optometry Times, 7*(1), 3. https://www.proquest.com/openview/32cd8c656e0e087bea741d2e4c4d4a84/1?pq-origsite=gscholar&cbl=2029739

Bray, A., Devitt, A., Banks, J., Sanchez Fuentes, S., Sandoval, M., Riviou, K., Byrne, D., Flood, M., Reale, J., & Terrenzio, S. (2023). What next for Universal Design for Learning? A systematic literature review of technology in UDL implementations at second level. *British Journal of Educational Technology*, 1–26. 10.1111/bjet.13328

Brazant, K. J. (2023). Disrupting the discourse: Applying critical race theory as a conceptual framework for reflecting on learning and teaching in higher education. *Equity in Education & Society*. Advance online publication. 10.1177/27526461231163325

Brillante, P., & Nemeth, K. (2022). *Universal Design for Learning in the Early Childhood Classroom: Teaching Children of all Languages, Cultures, and Abilities, Birth – 8 Years* (2nd ed.). Routledge. 10.4324/9781003148432

Bronfenbrenner, U. (1993). Ecological models of human development. In Gauvain, M., & Cole, M. (Eds.), *Readings on the development of children* (2nd ed., pp. 37–43). Freeman.

Bronfenbrenner, U., & Ceci, S. J. (1994). Nature-nuture reconceptualized in developmental perspective: A bioecological model. *Psychological Review*, 101(4), 568–586. 10.1037/0033-295X.101.4.5687984707

Brown, M. (2023). *Warrior Woman*. https://warrriorwomen.ca/

Brown, N., & Leigh, J. (2018). Ableism in academia: Where are the disabled and ill academics? *Disability & Society*, 33(6), 985–989. 10.1080/09687599.2018.1455627

Bruner, J. S. (1965). *Thought and Language*. The MIT Press. https://mitpress.mit.edu/9780262720014/thought-and-language/

Compilation of References

Burns, A., & Westmacott, A. (2018). Teacher to researcher: Reflections on a new action research program for University EFL teachers. *Profile: Issues in Teachers'. Professional Development (Philadelphia, Pa.)*, 20(1), 15–23. 10.15446/profile.v20n1.66236

Busby, E. (2018, July). Headteachers blame funding cuts as schools expel 40 pupils each day. *Independant: UK Edition*: https://www.independent.co.uk/news/education/education-news/school-exclusions-children-rise-england-funding-cuts-headteachers-behaviour-a8454516.html

Canadian Council of the Blind. (n.d.). *Get Together With Technology (GTT)*. Retrieved November 12 from https://ccbnational.net/shaggy/get-together-with-technology/

Canadian Institute for Health Information. (2022). *Child and youth mental health in Canada — Infographic*. https://www.cihi.ca/en/child-and-youth-mental-health-in-canada-infographic

Canadian Institutes of Health Research. (2022). *Resources: Accessibility and eliminating systemic ableism*. CIHR. Retrieved November 13 from https://cihr-irsc.gc.ca/e/52842.html

Canadian Parents for French. (2013). *An Overview of French Second Language Education in Canada*. CPF. https://sencanada.ca/content/sen/committee/412/OLLO/Briefs/2013-11-22CPFBrief_Addendum_e.pdf

Candela, A. (2006). Legends and pioneers of blindness assistive technology, Part 2. *AccessWorld*, 7(5). https://www.afb.org/aw/7/5/14437

Capp, M. (2017). The effectiveness of universal design for learning: A meta-analysis of literature between 2013 and 2016. *International Journal of Inclusive Education*, 21(8), 791–807. 10.1080/13603116.2017.1325074

Carlson, S., Gerhards, J., & Hans, S. (2017). Educating Children in Times of Globalisation: Class-specific Child-rearing Practices and the Acquisition of Transnational Cultural Capital. *Sociology*, 51(4), 749–765. 10.1177/0038038515618601

Carnahan, C. R., & Lowrey, K. A. (2018). *Facilitating Evidence-Based Practice for Students with ASD: A Classroom Observation Tool for Building Quality Education* (1st ed.). Paul H. Brookes Publishing.

Carver, L., & Rowe, A. (2021). Students with disabilities and online learning in a pandemic. *Interdisciplinary Insights: The Journal of Saint Leo University's College of Education and Social Services*, 3(1), 59–73.

Casebolt, T., & Humphrey, T. (2023). Use of Universal Design for Learning Principles in a Public Health Course. *Annals of Global Health*, 89(1), 48. 10.5334/aogh.404537484884

CAST. (2011). *Universal design for learning guidelines version 2.0*. Wakefield, MA. https://udlguidelines.cast.org/binaries/content/assets/udlguidelines/udlg-v2-0/udlg_graphicorganizer_v2-0.pdf

CAST. (2018). *The Universal Design for Learning Guidelines Graphic Organizer*. https://udlguidelines.cast.org/more/downloads

329

CAST. (2018). *UDL and the learning brain.* CAST Publishing. https://www.cast.org/our-work/publications/2018/udl-learning-brain-neuroscience.html

CAST. (2018). Universal Design for Learning Guidelines version 2.2. Retrieved from http://udlguidelines.cast.org

CAST. (2019). *UDL On Campus: Postsecondary Institutions with UDL Initiatives.* http://udloncampus.cast.org/page/udl_institutions

CAST. (2020). *Universal Design for Learning Guidelines.* https://udlguidelines.cast.org/

CAST. (2022). The Goal of UDL: Becoming Expert Learners. *Home.* https://www.learningdesigned.org/resource/goal-udl-becoming-expert-learners

CAST. (2022). *The Universal Design for Learning guidelines.* https://udlguidelines.cast.org/

CAST. (2023) *Add Universal Design for Learning to Your CTE State Plan.* Home. https://www.cast.org/news/2023/universal-design-for-learning-udl-cte-state-plan

CAST. (2023). About Universal Design for Learning. *Our Impact.* https://www.cast.org/impact/universal-design-for-learning-udl

CAST. (n.d.). *National Center on Accessible Educational Materials.* CAST. Retrieved November 13 from https://aem.cast.org/

Celik, I., Dindar, M., Muukkonen, H., & Järvelä, S. (2022). The promises and challenges of artificial intelligence for teachers: A systematic review of research. *TechTrends, 66*(4), 616–630. 10.1007/s11528-022-00715-y

Cera, R. (2015). National Legislations on Inclusive Education and Special Educational Needs of People with Autism in the Perspective of Article 24 of the CRPD. In Della Fina, V., & Cera, R. (Eds.), *Protecting the Rights of People with Autism in the Fields of Education and Employment.* Springer., 10.1007/978-3-319-13791-9_4

Ceylan, O. N. (2019). Student Perceptions of Difficulties in Second Language Writing. *Journal of Language and Linguistic Studies, 15*(1), 151–157. 10.17263/jlls.547683

Chaaban, Y., Al-Thani, H., & Du, X. (2021). A narrative inquiry of teacher educators' professional agency, identity renegotiations, and emotional responses amid educational disruption. *Teaching and Teacher Education, 108,* 103522. Advance online publication. 10.1016/j.tate.2021.103522

Chardin, M., & Novak, K. R. (2020). *Equity by Design: Delivering on the Power and Promise of UDL.* Corwin Press. https://ebookcentral.proquest.com/lib/dcu/detail.action?docID=6331818

Chardin, M., & Novak, K. (2020). *Equity by design: Delivering on the power and promise of UDL.* Corwin Press.

Cheadle, B. (2007). A parent's guide to the slate and stylus. *Future Reflections, 26*(1). https://nfb.org/images/nfb/publications/fr/fr25/fr07spr18.htm

Compilation of References

Chen, J. C. (2017). Nontraditional Adult Learners: The Neglected Diversity in Postsecondary Education. *SAGE Open*, 7(1). Advance online publication. 10.1177/2158244017697161

Chita-Tegmark, M., Gravel, J. W., Serpa, M. D. L. B., Domings, Y., & Rose, D. H. (2012). Using the universal design for learning framework to support culturally diverse learners. *Journal of Education*, 192(1), 17–22. 10.1177/002205741219200104

Choy, S., & Hodge, S. (2017). Teaching practice in Australian vocational education and training: A practice theory analysis. In *Practice Theory Perspectives on Pedagogy and Education* (pp. 157–173). Springer. 10.1007/978-981-10-3130-4_8

Christle, C. A., & Yell, M. L. (2010). Individualized Education Programs: Legal Requirements and Research Findings. *Exceptionality*, 18(3), 109–123. 10.1080/09362835.2010.491740

Cioe-Pena, M. (2017). Bilingualism, Disability and What it Means to Be Normal. *Journal of Bilingual Education Research & Instruction*, 19(1).

Cioè-Peña, M. (2020). Bilingualism for students with disabilities, deficit or advantage? Perspectives of Latinx mothers. *Bilingual Research Journal*, 43(3), 253–266. 10.1080/15235882.2020.1799884

Clandinin, D. J. (2013). *Engaging in Narrative Inquiry*. Routledge., 10.4324/9781315429618

Clarke, L., & O'Doherty, T. (2021). The professional place of teachers on the island of Ireland: Truth flourishes where the student's lamp has shone. *European Journal of Teacher Education*, 44(1), 62–79. 10.1080/02619768.2020.1844660

Clarke, M., & Drudy, S. (2007). Social justice in initial teacher education: Student Teachers Reflections on Praxis. In Gaine, C., Bhatti, G., Leeman, Y., & Gobbo, F. (Eds.), *Social Justice and Intercultural Education: An open ended Dialogue: Trentham.*

Coe, C., & Shani, S. (2015). Cultural capital and transnational parenting. *Harvard Educational Review*, 85(4), 562–586. 10.17763/0017-8055.85.4.562

Cohen, L., Manion, L., & Morrison, K. (2011). *Research Methods in Education* (7th ed.). Routledge.

Coleman, M. B., Cramer, E. S., Park, Y., & Bell, S. M. (2015). Art educators' use of adaptations, assistive technology, and special education supports for students with physical, visual, severe and multiple disabilities. *Journal of Developmental and Physical Disabilities*, 27(5), 637–660. 10.1007/s10882-015-9440-6

Coley, R. L., Lynch, A. D., & Kull, M. (2015). Early exposure to environmental chaos and children's physical and mental health. *Early Childhood Research Quarterly*, 32, 94–104. 10.1016/j.ecresq.2015.03.00125844016

Collins, B. A., Toppelberg, C. O., Suárez-Orozco, C., O'Connor, E., & Nieto-Castañon, A. (2011). Cross-Sectional Associations of Spanish and English Competence and Well-Being in Latino Children of Immigrants in Kindergarden. *International Journal of the Sociology of Language*, 208, 5–23.

Collums, D. (2023). *Exploring Transformational Leadership in a School Implementing Universal Design for Learning: A Case Study*. EdD Thesis, Southern Nazarene University. https://www.proquest.com/openview/756e9a6630490eae3802fd894dd60a33/1?pq-origsite=gscholar&cbl=18750&diss=y

Cook, S. C., & Rao, K. (2018). Systematically applying UDL to effective practices for students with learning disabilities. *Learning Disability Quarterly*, 41(3), 179–191. 10.1177/0731948717749936

Corn, A. L., & Erin, J. N. (2010). *Foundations of low vision: Clinical and functional perspectives*. American Foundation for the Blind.

Coronavirus disease (COVID-19). (2022). *COVID-19 resources for parents and children*. https://www.canada.ca/en/public-health/services/diseases/coronavirus-disease-covid-19/resources-parents-children.html

Courey, S. J., Tappe, P., Siker, J., & LePage, P. (2013). Improved lesson planning with universal design for learning (UDL). *Teacher Education and Special Education*, 36(1), 7–27. 10.1177/0888406412446178

Courts, R., Chatoor, K., Pichette, J., Okojie, O., & Tishcoff, R. (2023). *HEQCO's Dialogues on Universal Design for Learning: Finding Common Ground and Key Recommendations from the Sector*. Higher Education Quality Council of Ontario. https://heqco.ca/wp-content/uploads/2023/04/HEQCOs-Dialogues-on-Universal-Design-for-Learning-UDL-2.pdf

Craig, S. L., Smith, S. J., & Frey, B. B. (2019). Professional Development with Universal Design for Learning: Supporting Teachers as Learners to Increase the Implementation of UDL. *Professional Development in Education*. Advance online publication. 10.1080/19415257.2019.1685563

Crosby, C., & Aguilar, F. (2022). Navigating the Abyss: Early childhood educator perspectives on the impact of remote learning during a 21st century pandemic. In *Handbook of Research on Adapting Remote Learning Practices for Early Childhood and Elementary School Classrooms* (pp. 352-357). IGI Global.

Crotty, M. J. (1998). *The Foundations of Social Research: Meaning and Perspective in the Research Process*. SAGE Publications, Limited. https://ebookcentral.proquest.com/lib/trinitycollege/detail.action?docID=6417765

Cryer, H., & Home, S. (2011). *Use of braille displays* (RNIB Centre for Accessible Information, Issue. Davis, L. J. (1997). Constructing normalcy. *The disability studies reader, 3*, 3-19.

Cuiccio, C., & Husby-Slater, M. (2018). *Needs Assessment Guidebook. American Institutes for Research* under U.S. Department of Education.https://oese.ed.gov/files/2020/10/needsassessmentguidebook-508_003.pdf

Cumming, T., & Gilanyi, L. (2023). 'Our Classes Are Like Mainstream School Now': Implementing Universal Design for Learning at a Special School. *Australasian Journal of Special and Inclusive Education*, 1-15. 10.1017/jsi.2023.7

Compilation of References

Cumming, T. M., & Rose, M. C. (2022). Exploring universal design for learning as an accessibility tool in higher education: A review of the current literature. *Australian Educational Researcher*, 49(5), 1025–1043. 10.1007/s13384-021-00471-7

Dalton, E. M. (2020). UDL and connected laws, theories, and frameworks. In Gronseth, S. L., & Dalton, E. M. (Eds.), *Universal access through inclusive instructional design: International perspectives on UDL* (pp. 3–16). Routledge.

Dalton, L., Rapa, E., & Stein, A. (2020). Protecting the psychological health of children through effective communication about COVID-19. *The Lancet. Child & Adolescent Health*, 4(5), 346–347. 10.1016/S2352-4642(20)30097-332243784

Darling-Hammond, L. (2017). Teacher education around the world: What can we learn from international practice? *European Journal of Teacher Education*, 40(3), 291–309. 10.1080/02619768.2017.1315399

David, L., & Weinstein, N. (2023). A Gamified Experiential Learning Intervention for Engaging Students Through Satisfying Needs. *Journal of Educational Technology Systems*, 52(1), 52–72. 10.1177/00472395231174614

Davis, S., Ballinger, S., & Sarkar, M. (2019). The Suitability of French Immersion for Allophone Students in Saskatchewan: Exploring Diverse Perspectives on Language Learning and Inclusion. *Canadian Journal of Applied Linguistics. Canadian Journal of Applied Linguistics*, 22(2), 27–63. 10.7202/1063773ar

Debreli, E., Ishanova, I., & Sheppard, C. (2019). Foreign language classroom management: Types of student misbehaviour and strategies adapted by the teachers in handling disruptive behaviour. *Cogent Education, 6*(1). 10.1080/2331186X.2019.1648629

Delcourt, L. (2018) Elitist, Inequitable And Exclusionary Practices: A Problem Within Ontario French Immersion Programs? A Literature Review. *Actes du Jean-Paul Dionne Symposium Proceedings.* 10.18192/jpds-sjpd.v2i1.3152

Della Líbera, B., & Jurberg, C. (2020). Communities of practice on WhatsApp: A tool for promoting citizenship among students with visual impairments. *British Journal of Visual Impairment*, 38(1), 58–78. 10.1177/0264619619874836

Department of Education and Skills. (2015). A Framework for the Junior Cycle. In *National Council for Curriculum and Assessment*. https://ncca.ie/en/resources/framework-for-junior-cycle-2015-2

Department of Education. (1993). *Report of the Special Education Review Committee.* SERC.

Department of Education. (2021, December 8). *School enrolments—2021-22 provisional statistical bulletins datafiles.* Education. https://www.education-ni.gov.uk/publications/school-enrolments -2021-22-provisional-statistical-bulletins-datafiles

Department of Education. (2022). *Consultation Paper on the Review of the Education for Persons with Special Educational Needs Act 2004.* https://assets.gov.ie/287121/5a418b66-affe-4a47 -bd31-2f8f3a858a25.pdf

Diaz-Vega, M., Moreno-Rodriguez, R., & Lopez-Bastias, J. L. (2020). Educational Inclusion through the Universal Design for Learning: Alternatives to Teacher Training. *Education Sciences*, 10(11), 303. 10.3390/educsci10110303

Dickinson, K. J., & Gronseth, S. L. (2020). Application of universal design for learning (UDL) principles to surgical education during the COVID-19 pandemic. *Journal of Surgical Education*, 77(5), 1008–1012. 10.1016/j.jsurg.2020.06.00532576451

Dicks, J., & Genesee, F. (2017). Bilingual Education in Canada. In García, O., Lin, A., & May, S. (Eds.), *Bilingual and Multilingual Education. Encyclopedia of Language and Education* (3rd ed.). Springer. 10.1007/978-3-319-02258-1_32

Dignath, C., Rimm-Kaufman, S., van Ewijk, R., & Kunter, M. (2022). Teachers' Beliefs About Inclusive Education and Insights on What Contributes to Those Beliefs: A Meta-analytical Study. *Educational Psychology Review*, 34(4), 2609–2660. 10.1007/s10648-022-09695-0

Dillon, S., & O'Shea, K. (2009). *From the College to the Classroom: The Impact of DICE Courses on the Inclusion of Development Education and Intercultural Education in the Primary Classroom* (p. 79). DICE project. https://developmenteducation.ie/resource/from-the-college -to-the-classroom-the-impact-of-dice-courses-on-the-inclusion-of-development-education-and -intercultural-education-in-the-primary-classroom/

Disability Nottinghamshire. (2023) Social Model vs Medical Model of disability. *About Us*. https:// www.disabilitynottinghamshire.org.uk/index.php/about/social-model-vs-medical-model-of -disability/

Dixon, J. (Ed.). (2000). *Braille into the next milennium*. National Library Service for the Blind and Physically Handicapped.

Dodgson, J. E. (2023). Phenomenology: Researching the Lived Experience. *Journal of Human Lactation*, 39(3), 385–396. 10.1177/08903344231176453337278304

Dos Santos, L. M. (2020). The Discussion of Communicative Language Teaching Approach in Language Classrooms. *Journal of Education and e-learning Research*, 7(2), 104–109. 10.20448/ journal.509.2020.72.104.109

Dudley-Marling, C., & Paugh, P. (2010). Confronting the Discourse of Deficiencies. *Disability Studies Quarterly*, 30(2). Advance online publication. 10.18061/dsq.v30i2.1241

Dumont, H., & Ready, D. D. (2023). On the promise of personalized learning for educational equity. *NPJ Science of Learning*, 8(1), 26. 10.1038/s41539-023-00174-x37542046

Early, M., Dagenais, D., & Carr, W. (2017). Second and Foreign Language Education in Canada. In Van Deusen-Scholl, N., & May, S. (Eds.), *Encyclopedia of Language and Education, 4* (pp. 197–208). Springer.

Ebneyamini, S., & Moghadam, M. R. (2018). Toward developing a framework for conducting case study research. *International Journal of Qualitative Methods*, 17(1), 1–11. 10.1177/1609406918817954

Compilation of References

Edyburn, D. L. (2005). Universal Design for Learning. *Special Education Technology Practice,* *7*(5), 16–22. https://elib.tcd.ie/login?url=https://search.ebscohost.com/login.aspx?direct=true &db=edo&AN=34232842

Edyburn, D. L. (2013). Critical Issues in Advancing the Special Education Technology Evidence Base. *Exceptional Children*, 80(1), 7–24. 10.1177/001440291308000107

Edyburn, D. L., Rao, K., & Hariharan, P. (2017). Technological practices supporting diverse students in inclusive settings. In Hughes, M. T., & Talbott, E. (Eds.), *The Wiley handbook of diversity in special education* (pp. 357–377). Wiley., 10.1002/9781118768778.ch17

Elder, B. C. (2020). Necessary first steps: Using professional development schools (pds) to support more students with disability labels in inclusive classrooms. *School-University Partnerships,* *13*(1), 32–43. https://eric.ed.gov/?id=EJ1249469

Elder, B. C., Givens, L., LoCastro, A., & Rencher, L. (2021). Using Disability Studies in Education (dse) and Professional Development Schools (pds) to Implement Inclusive Practices. *Journal of Disability Studies in Education.* 10.1163/25888803-bja10010

Emiliussen, J., Engelsen, S., Christiansen, R., & Klausen, S. H. (2021). We are all in it!: Phenomenological Qualitative Research and Embeddedness. *International Journal of Qualitative Methods*, 20. Advance online publication. 10.1177/1609406921995304

Ender, K. E., Kinney, B. J., Penrod, W. M., Bauder, D. K., & Simmons, T. (2007). Achieving systemic change with Universal Design for Learning and digital content. *Assistive Technology Outcomes and Benefits*, 4(1), 115–129. https://eric.ed.gov/?id=EJ899371

Engleman, M., & Schmidt, M. (2007). Testing an experimental universally designed learning unit in a graduate level online teacher education course. *Journal of Online Learning and Teaching*, 3(2), 112–132.

Espada-Chavarria, R., González-Montesino, R. H., López-Bastías, J. L., & Díaz-Vega, M. (2023). Universal Design for Learning and Instruction: Effective Strategies for Inclusive Higher Education. *Education Sciences*, 13(6), 620. 10.3390/educsci13060620

Estellés, M., & Fischman, G. E. (2021). Who Needs Global Citizenship Education? A Review of the Literature on Teacher Education. *Journal of Teacher Education*, 2(72), 223–236. 10.1177/0022487120920254

European Agency for Special Needs and Inclusive Education. (2022). *Agency Position on Inclusive Education Systems* (2nd ed.).

European Commission. (2013). *Supporting teacher competence development for better learning outcomes.* https://www.academia.edu/6623391/Supporting_teacher_competence_development _for_better_learning_outcomes

European Education and Culture Executive Agency. (2015). *The structure of the European education systems 2013/14: Schematic diagrams.* Eurydice., 10.2797/206797

Eurydice. (2023). *National reforms in further education and training and adult learning*. National Education Systems. European Commission. https://eurydice.eacea.ec.europa.eu/national-education-systems/ireland/national-reforms-further-education-and-training-and-adult

Evans, C., Williams, J. B., King, L., & Metcalf, D. (2010). Modeling, guided instruction, and application of UDL in a rural special education teacher preparation program. *Rural Special Education Quarterly*, 29(4), 41–48. 10.1177/875687051002900409

Every, S. S. A. 20 U.S.C. § 6301 (2015). https://www.congress.gov/bill/114th-congress/senate-bill/1177

Evmenova, A. (2018). Preparing Teachers to Use Universal Design for Learning to Support Diverse Learners. *Journal of Online Learning Research*, 4(2), 147–171.

Ewe, L. P., Dalton, E. M., Bhan, S., Gronseth, S. L., & Dahlberg, G. (2023). Inclusive Education and UDL Professional Development for Teachers in Sweden and India. In Koreeda, K., Tsuge, M., Ikuta, S., Dalton, E., & Ewe, L. (Eds.), *Developing Inclusive Environments in Education: Global Practices and Curricula* (pp. 14–33). IGI Global., 10.4018/979-8-3693-0664-2.ch002

Ewe, L., & Galvin, T. (2023). Universal Design for Learning across Formal School Structures in Europe—A Systematic Review. *Education Sciences*, 13(9), 867. 10.3390/educsci13090867

Faas, D., Smith, A., & Darmody, M. (2018). Between ethos and practice: Are Ireland's new multi- denominational primary schools equal and inclusive? *Compare: A Journal of Comparative Education*, 49(4), 602–618. 10.1080/03057925.2018.1441704

Fareed, M., Ashraf, A., & Bilal, M. (2016). ESL Learners' Writing Skills: Problems, Factors and Suggestions. *Journal of Education and Social Sciences*, 4(2), 81–92. 10.20547/jess0421604201

Farley-Ripple, E., May, H., Karpyn, A., Tilley, K., & McDonough, K. (2018). Rethinking Connections Between Research and Practice in Education: A Conceptual Framework. *Educational Researcher*, 47(4), 235–245. 10.3102/0013189X18761042

Faubert, J., & Overbury, O. (1987). Active-passigm paradigm in assessing CCTV-aided reading. *Optometry and Vision Science*, 64(1), 23–28. 10.1097/00006324-198701000-000043826273

Ferguson, B. T. (2019). Balancing requirements, options and choice in UDL:Smorgasbord or nutritious diet? In Gronseth, S. L., & Dalton, E. M. (Eds.), *Universal Access Through Inclusive Instructional Design: International Perspectives on UDL* (pp. 96–102). Routledge. 10.4324/9780429435515-12

Fernández-Villardón, A., Valls-Carol, R., Melgar Alcantud, P., & Tellado, I. (2021) Enhancing Literacy and Communicative Skills of Students With Disabilities in Special Schools Through Dialogic Literary Gatherings. *Frontiers in Psychology, 12*, 1275. 10.3389/fpsyg.2021.662639

Fichten, C. S., Asuncion, J. V., & Scapin, R. (2014). Digital technology, learning, and postsecondary students with disabilities: Where we've been and where we're going. *Journal of Postsecondary Education and Disability*, 27(4), 369–379.

Compilation of References

Fichten, C. S., Asuncion, J. V., Wolforth, J., Barile, M., Budd, J., Martiniello, N., & Amsel, R. (2012). Information and communication technology related needs of college and university students with disabilities. *Research in Learning Technology*, 20, 20. 10.3402/rlt.v20i0.18646

Fichten, C. S., Nguyen, M. N., Asuncion, J. V., Martiniello, N., Jorgensen, M., Budd, J., Amsel, R., & Libman, E. (2016). An exploratory study of college and university students with visual impairment in Canada: Grades and graduation. *British Journal of Visual Impairment*, 34(1), 91–100. 10.1177/0264619615616259

Finlay, J., & Dela Cruz, A. (2023). Reflexivity and Relational Spaces: Experiences of Conducting a Narrative Inquiry Study With Emerging Adult Women Living With Chronic Pain. *Global Qualitative Nursing Research*, 10. Advance online publication. 10.1177/23333936231190619 37576739

Finnerty, M. S., Jackson, L. B., & Ostergren, R. (2019). Adaptations in General Education Classrooms for Students With Severe Disabilities: Access, Progress Assessment, and Sustained Use. *Research and Practice for Persons with Severe Disabilities : the Journal of TASH*, 44(2), 87–102. 10.1177/1540796919846424

Fitzgerald, J., & Radford, J. (2017). The SENCO role in post-primary schools in Ireland: Victims or agents of change? *European Journal of Special Needs Education*, 32(3), 452–466. 10.1080/08856257.2017.1295639

Flanagan, T., Benson, F. J., & Fovet, F. (2014) A multi-perspective examination of the barriers to field-placement experiences for students with disabilities. *Collected Essays on Learning and Teaching, 7*(2) https://files.eric.ed.gov/fulltext/EJ1060220.pdf

Flanagan, T., Benson, F. J., & Fovet, F. (2014). A multi-perspective examination of the barriers to field-placement experiences for students with disabilities. *Collected Essays on Learning and Teaching*, 7(2), n2. 10.22329/celt.v7i2.3993

Flood, M., & Banks, J. (2021). Universal design for learning: Is it gaining momentum in Irish education? *Education Sciences*, 11(7), 341. Advance online publication. 10.3390/educsci11070341

Florian, L. (2019). On the necessary co-existence of special and inclusive education. *International Journal of Inclusive Education*, 23(7–8), 691–704. 10.1080/13603116.2019.1622801

Florian, L., Young, K., & Rouse, M. (2010). Preparing teachers for inclusive and diverse educational environments: Studying curricular reform in an initial teacher education course. *International Journal of Inclusive Education*, 14(7), 709–722. 10.1080/13603111003778536

Fornauf, B. S., & Dangora Erickson, J. (2020). Toward an Inclusive Pedagogy Through Universal Design for Learning in Higher Education: A Review of the Literature. *Journal of Postsecondary Education and Disability*, 33(2), 183.

Fovet, F. (2014) Social model as catalyst for innovation in design and pedagogical change. *Widening Participation through Curriculum Open University 2014 Conference Proceedings*, 135-139

Fovet, F. (2014) Social model as catalyst for innovation in design and pedagogical change. *Widening Participation through Curriculum Open University 2014 Conference Proceedings*, 135-139.

Fovet, F. (2017) *Doing what we preach: examining the contradictions of the UDL discourse in faculties of education.* Paper presented at the 2017 AHEAD Ireland Conference, Dublin, March

Fovet, F. (2018) Exploring the Student Voice within Universal Design for Learning Work. *The AHEAD Journal, 8.* https://www.ahead.ie/journal/Exploring-the-Student-Voice-within-Universal -Design-for-Learning-Work

Fovet, F. (2020) Universal Design for Learning as a Tool for Inclusion in the Higher Education Classroom: Tips for the Next Decade of Implementation. Education Journal. *Special Issue: Effective Teaching Practices for Addressing Diverse Students' Needs for Academic Success in Universities, 9*(6), 163-172. http://www.sciencepublishinggroup.com/journal/paperinfo?journalid =196&doi=10.11648/j.edu.20200906.13

Fovet, F. (2020b). Universal Design for Learning as a Tool for Inclusion in the Higher Education Classroom: Tips for the Next Decade of Implementation. *Education Journal, 9*(6), 163-172. http://www.sciencepublishinggroup.com/journal/paperinfo?journalid=196&doi=10.11648/j .edu.20200906.13

Fovet, F. (2023) The Changing Landscape of Inclusive Education: A Shift toward Universal Design for Learning. In A. Beckett and Dr A-M. Callus (Eds.) *Handbook on Children's Rights and Disability.* Routledge https://www.taylorfrancis.com/chapters/edit/10.4324/9781003056737 -37/changing-landscape-inclusive-education-frederic-fovet

Fovet, F. (2023b) *Can we do it without school principals' commitment? Exploring the complex impact of school leadership on UDL implementation.* UDL Workshop offered at the 1st International Universal Design for Learning Symposium Learning Together. Maynooth University, June.

Fovet, F. (2017). Access, Universal Design and the Sustainability of Teaching Practices: A Powerful Synchronicity of Concepts at a Crucial Conjuncture for Higher Education. *Indonesian Journal of Disability Studies*, 4(2), 2.

Fovet, F. (2018). Exploring the student voice within Universal Design for Learning work. *The Ahfad Journal*, (8), 1–6.

Fovet, F. (2018). Making it work! Addressing teacher resistance in systemic UDL implementation across schools. In Jangira, N. K., Limaye, S., & Kapoor, S. (Eds.), *Inclusive Education: Practitioners' Perspectives*. School Inclusive Education Development Initiative.

Fovet, F. (2019). Not just about disability: Getting traction for UDL implementation with International Students. In Novak, K., & Bracken, S. (Eds.), *Transforming Higher Education through Universal Design for Learning: An International Perspective*. Routledge. 10.4324/9781351132077-11

Fovet, F. (2020). Integrating Universal Design for Learning in Schools: Implications for Teacher Training, Leadership and Professional Development. In Al Mahdi, O. (Ed.), *Innovations in Educational Leadership and Continuous Teachers' Professional Development*. CSMFL Publications. 10.46679/isbn978819484832513

Compilation of References

Fovet, F. (2020). Universal Design for Learning as a Tool for Inclusion in the Higher Education Classroom: Tips for the Next Decade of Implementation. *Education Journal*, 9(6), 6. Advance online publication. 10.11648/j.edu.20200906.13

Fovet, F. (2020b). Beyond Novelty – "Innovative" Accessible Teaching as a Return to Fundamental Questions Around Social Justice and Reflective Pedagogy. In Palahicky, S. (Ed.), *Enhancing Learning Design for Innovative Teaching in Higher Education*. IGI Global. 10.4018/978-1-7998-2943-0.ch002

Fovet, F. (2021). Developing an Ecological Approach to Strategic UDL Implementation in Higher Education. *Journal of Education and Learning*, 10(4), 27. 10.5539/jel.v10n4p27

Fritzgerald, A., & Rice, S. (2020). *Antiracism and Universal Design for Learning: Building Expressways to Success*. CAST, Incorporated. https://books.google.ie/books?id=vF_HzQEACAAJ

Frumos, L. (2020). Inclusive education in remote instruction with universal design for learning. *Revista Românească pentru Educaţie Multidimensională, 12*(2supl1), 138-142.

Fuhrer, M. J. (2001, July). Assistive technology outcomes research: Challenges met and yet unmet. *American Journal of Physical Medicine & Rehabilitation*, 80(7), 528–535. 10.1097/0000206 0-200107000-0001311421522

GAAD Foundation. (n.d.). *Global Accessibility Awareness Day*. GAAD Foundation. Retrieved November 12 from https://accessibility.day

Galkiene, A., & Monkeviciene, O. (2021). *The Model of UDL Implementation Enabling the Development of Inclusive Education in Different Educational Contexts: Conclusions* (pp. 313–323). https://doi.org/10.1007/978-3-030-80658-3_12

Gallagher-MacKay, K., Srivastava, P., Underwood, K., Dhuey, E., McCready, L., Born, K.B., Maltsev, A., Perkhun, A., Steiner, R., Barrett, K., & Sander, B. (2021) COVID-19 and education disruption in Ontario: emerging evidence on impacts. *Science Briefs of the Ontario COVID-19 Science Advisory Table, 2*(34). 10.47326/ocsat.2021.02.34.1.0

Galvin, T., & Geron, M. (2021). Building a community of practice across an institution: How to embed UDL through the Plus One Approach between an academic developer and instructor in STEM. In Fovet, F. (Ed.), *Handbook of Research on Applying Universal Design for Learning Across Disciplines: Concepts, Case Studies, and Practical Implementation* (pp. 323–344). IGI Global. 10.4018/978-1-7998-7106-4.ch017

Ganias, M., & Novak, K. (2019). A perfect pairing: UDL and PLCs. *eSchool News*. https://www.eschoolnews.com/2019/11/06/a-perfect-pairing-udl-and-plcs/

Ganley, P., & Ralabate, P. K. (2013). UDL implementation: A tale of four districts. CAST (https://www.cast.org/products-services/resources/2013/udl-implementation-tale-four-districts)

Gardner, H. (1993). *Multiple intelligences: The theory in practice* (pp. xvi, 304). Basic Books/Hachette Book Group.

Gauvreau, A. N., Lohmann, M. J., & Hovey, K. A. (2019). Using a Universal Design for Learning Framework to Provide Multiple Means of Representation in the Early Childhood Classroom. *The Journal of Special Education Apprenticeship*, 8(1), 3. https://scholarworks.lib.csusb.edu/josea/vol8/iss1/3. 10.58729/2167-3454.1083

Gelpieryn, A. (2023, October 7) Substitute teachers are in short supply, but many schools still don't pay them a living wage. *CBS News*. https://www.cbsnews.com/news/substitute-teacher-shortage-living-wage/

General Teaching Council for Northern Ireland. (2011). *Teaching: The Reflective Profession.*

General Teaching Council for Northern Ireland. (2015). *Teacher Education Partnership Handbook | Department of Education.* https://www.education-ni.gov.uk/publications/teacher-education-partnership-handbook

Gentile, A. L., & Budzilowicz, M. (2022). Empowering college students: UDL, culturally responsive pedagogy, and mindset as an instructional approach. *New Directions for Teaching and Learning*, 2022(172), 33–42. 10.1002/tl.20524

Ghamrawi, N. (2022). Teachers' virtual communities of practice: A strong response in times of crisis or just another Fad? *Education and Information Technologies*, 27(5), 5889–5915. 10.1007/s10639-021-10857-w35095322

Gildlund, U. (2018). Teachers' Attitudes towards Including Students with Emotional and Behavioural Difficulties in Mainstream School: A Systematic Research Synthesis. *International Journal of Learning. Teaching and Educational Research*, 17(2), 45–63. 10.26803/ijlter.17.2.3

Girma, H. (2019). *Haben* [Audio Recording]. Hachette Audio. https://www.audible.ca/pd/Haben-Audiobook/B07VWKKNMT?language=en_CA

Gitlin, L. N. (1995). Why older people accept or reject assistive technology. *Generations (San Francisco, Calif.)*, 19, 41–46.

Gleason, C., Valencia, S., Kirabo, L., Wu, J., Guo, A., Jeanne Carter, E., Bigham, J., Bennett, C., & Pavel, A. (2020). Disability and the COVID-19 pandemic: Using Twitter to understand accessibility during rapid societal transition. The 22nd International ACM SIGACCESS Conference on Computers and Accessibility.

Golberstein, E., Wen, H., & Miller, B. F. (2020). Coronavirus disease 2019 (COVID-19) and mental health for children and adolescents. *JAMA Pediatrics*, 174(9), 819–820. 10.1001/jamapediatrics.2020.145632286618

Google. (2022). *Android developer documentation: Build accessible apps.* Google. Retrieved November 12 from https://developer.android.com/guide/topics/ui/accessibility

Government of Ireland. (1998). *Education Act* (Issue 51). https://www.irishstatutebook.ie/eli/1998/act/51/enacted/en/html?q=education

Compilation of References

Government of Ireland. (2004). *Education for Persons with Special Educational Needs Act (EPSEN)*. https://www.oireachtas.ie/en/bills/bill/2003/34/

Government of Ireland. (2019, October 16). *Education statistics*. https://www.gov.ie/en/publication/055810-education-statistics/

Graham, M., Wright, M., Azevedo, L. B., Macpherson, T., Jones, D., & Innerd, A. (2021). The school playground environment as a driver of primary school children's physical activity behaviour: A direct observation case study. *Journal of Sports Sciences*, 39(20), 2266–2278. 10.1080/02640414.2021.192842334080956

Grapin, S. E., Llosa, L., Haas, A., & Lee, O. (2021). Rethinking instructional strategies with English learners in the content areas. *TESOL Journal*, 12(2), e557. Advance online publication. 10.1002/tesj.557

Grasmane, D., & Grasmane, S. (2011). Foreign language skills for employability in the EU labour market. *European Journal of Higher Education*. 10.1080/21568235.2011.629487

Gravel, B. E., & Puckett, C. (2023). What shapes implementation of a school-based makerspace? Teachers as multilevel actors in STEM reforms. *International Journal of STEM Education*, 10(7), 7. Advance online publication. 10.1186/s40594-023-00395-x

Greene, J. C., Kreider, H., & Mayer, E. (2005). Combining qualitative and quantitative methods in social inquiry. *Research Methods in the Social Sciences, 1*, 275-282.

Griful-Freixenet, J., Struyven, K., Vantieghem, W., & Gheyssens, E. (2020). Exploring the inter-relationship between Universal Design for Learning (UDL) and Differentiated Instruction (DI): A systematic review. *Educational Research Review*, 29, 100306. Advance online publication. 10.1016/j.edurev.2019.100306

Griggs, N., & Moore, R. (2023). Removing Systemic Barriers for Learners with Diverse Identities: Antiracism, Universal Design for Learning, and Edpuzzle. *Journal of Special Education Technology*, 38(1), 15–22. 10.1177/01626434221143501

Grillo, M. (2022). The Administrator's Role in Universal Design for Learning's Successful Implementation. *Teaching Exceptional Children*, 54(5), 372–379. 10.1177/00400599211022030

Guo, D., & Wang, A. (2020). Is vocational education a good alternative to low-performing students in China. *International Journal of Educational Development*, 75, 102187. Advance online publication. 10.1016/j.ijedudev.2020.102187

Haegele, J. A., Holland, S. K., Wilson, W. J., Maher, A. J., Kirk, T. N., & Mason, A. (2023). Universal design for learning in physical education: Overview and critical reflection. *European Physical Education Review*. Advance online publication. 10.1177/1356336X231202658

Haft, S. L., Greiner de Magalhães, C., & Hoeft, F. (2023). A Systematic Review of the Consequences of Stigma and Stereotype Threat for Individuals With Specific Learning Disabilities. *Journal of Learning Disabilities*, 56(3), 193–209. 10.1177/00222194221087383355499115

Hagan, M., & Eaton, P. (2020). Teacher education in Northern Ireland: Reasons to be cheerful or a 'Wicked Problem'? *Teacher Development*, 24(2), 258–273. 10.1080/13664530.2020.1751260

Hagan, M., & McGlynn, C. (2004). Moving barriers: Promoting learning for diversity in initial teacher education. *Intercultural Education*, 15(3), 243–252. 10.1080/1467598042000262545

Hall, T. E., Cohen, N., Vue, G., & Ganley, P. (2015). Addressing learning disabilities with UDL and technology: Strategic reader. *Learning Disability Quarterly*, 38(2), 72–83. 10.1177/0731948714544375

Hamdan, A. R., Anuar, M. K., & Khan, A. (2016). Implementation of Co-Teaching Approach in an Inclusive Classroom: Overview of the Challenges, Readiness, and Role of Special Education Teacher. *Asia Pacific Education Review*, 17(2), 289–298. 10.1007/s12564-016-9419-8

Hannan, C. K. (2006). Review of research: Neuroscience and the impact of brain plasticity on braille reading. *Journal of Visual Impairment & Blindness*, 100(7), 397–413. 10.1177/0145482X0610000704

Hargreaves, A. (2014). *Handbook of professional development in education: Successful models and practices, PreK-12*. Guilford Publications.

Harris, L., Yearta, L., & Chapman, H. (2018). The intersection of the UDL and TPACK frameworks: An investigation into teacher candidates' use of technology during internship. In *Society for Information Technology & Teacher Education International Conference* (pp. 2175-2180). Association for the Advancement of Computing in Education (AACE).

Harte, H. A. (2013). Universal design and outdoor learning. *Dimensions of Early Childhood*, 41(3), 18–22.

Hartmann, E. (2015). Universal Design for Learning (UDL) and Learners with Severe Support Needs. *International Journal of Whole Schooling*, 11(1), 54–67.

Hartmann, E. (2015). Universal design for learning (UDL) and learners with severe support needs. *International Journal of Whole Schooling*, 11(1), 54–67. https://eric.ed.gov/?id=EJ1061020

Havens, G. (2020). Universal design in the age of COVID-19. *Planning for Higher Education*, 48(4), 14–24.

Hawke, L. D., Barbic, S. P., Voineskos, A., Szatmari, P., Cleverley, K., Hayes, E., Relihan, J., Daley, M., Courtney, D., Cheung, A., Darnay, K., & Henderson, J. L. (2020). Impacts of COVID-19 on youth mental health, Substance Use, and well-being: A rapid survey of clinical and community samples: Répercussions de la COVID-19 sur la santé mentale, l'utilisation de substances et le bien-être des adolescents: Un sondage rapide d'échantillons cliniques et communautaires. *Canadian Journal of Psychiatry*, 65(10), 701–709. 10.1177/0706743720940562326662303

Hayday, M. (2015). *So they want us to learn French: Promoting and opposing bilingualism in English-speaking Canada*. UBC Press. 10.59962/9780774830065

342

Compilation of References

Head, G. (2020). Ethics in educational research: Review boards, ethical issues and researcher development. *European Educational Research Journal*, 19(1), 72–83. 10.1177/1474904118796315

Heelan, A., & Tobin, T. J. (2021). *UDL for FET Practitioners Guidance for Implementing Universal Design for Learning in Irish Further Education and Training*. https://www.solas.ie/f/70398/x/81044b80ce/fet_practitioners-main.pdf

Hefferman, P. J. (2011). Second-language (L2) teacher preparation and ongoing professional development in a world in need of social justice. *Journal of Interdisciplinary Education*, 10(1), 142–155.

Higher Education Opportunity Act of 2008, Pub. L. No. 110-135, 122 Stat.3078 (2008) https://www.govinfo.gov/content/pkg/PLAW-110publ315/pdf/PLAW-110publ315.pdf

Hills, M., Overend, A., & Hildebrandt, S. (2022). Faculty Perspectives on UDL: Exploring Bridges and Barriers for Broader Adoption in Higher Education. *The Canadian Journal for the Scholarship of Teaching and Learning*, 13(1). Advance online publication. 10.5206/cjsotlrcacea.2022.1.13588

Hoban, G., & Hastings, G. (2006). Developing different forms of student feedback to promote teacher reflection: A 10-year collaboration. *Teaching and Teacher Education*, 22(8), 1006–1019. 10.1016/j.tate.2006.04.006

Hoekstra, A., & Newton, P. (2017). Departmental leadership for learning in vocational and professional education. *Empirical Research in Vocational Education and Training*, 9(1), 12. 10.1186/s40461-017-0057-0

Holbrook, M. C., & Koenig, A. J. (1992). Teaching Braille Reading to Students with Low Vision. *Journal of Visual Impairment & Blindness*, 86(1), 44–48. 10.1177/0145482X9208600119

Hoover, J. J., Erickson, J. R., Patton, J. R., Sacco, D. M., & Tran, L. M. (2018). Examining IEPs of English Learners with learning disabilities for cultural and linguistic responsiveness. *Learning Disabilities Research & Practice*, 34(1), 14–22. 10.1111/ldrp.12183

Horn, E. M., Palmer, S. B., Butera, G. D., & Lieber, J. (2016). *Six steps to inclusive preschool curriculum: A UDL-based framework for children's school success*. Brookes Publishing Company.

Hromalik, C. D., Myhill, W. M., Ohrazda, C. A., Carr, N. R., & Zumbuhl, S. A. (2021). Increasing Universal Design for Learning knowledge and application at a community college: The Universal Design for Learning Academy. *International Journal of Inclusive Education*. Advance online publication. 10.1080/13603116.2021.1931719

Hu, H., & Huang, F. (2022). Application of Universal Design for Learning into remote English education in Australia amid COVID-19 pandemic. [IJonSE]. *International Journal on Studies in Education*, 4(1), 55–69. 10.46328/ijonse.59

Humphrey, N., Bartolo, P., Ale, P., Calleja, C., Hofsaess, T., Janikova, V., Lous, A. M., Vilkiene, V., & Wetso, G. (2006). Understanding and responding to diversity in the primary classroom: An international study. *European Journal of Teacher Education*, 29(3), 305–318. 10.1080/02619760600795122

Independant Education Review. (2023). *Investing in a better future: The independent review of education in Northern Ireland (Volume 2)*.https://www.independentreviewofeducation.org.uk/files/independentreviewofeducation/2024-01/Investing%20in%20a%20Better%20Future%20-%20Volume%202.pdf

Individuals with Disabilities Education Act (IDEA). (1975). https://sites.ed.gov/idea/

Israel, M., Ribuffo, C., & Smith, S. J. (2014). *Universal design for learning innovation configuration: recommendations for pre-service teacher preparation and in-service professional development*.https://kuscholarworks.ku.edu/bitstream/handle/1808/18509/10%20Universal%20Design%20for%20Learning-1.pdf;sequence=1

Ivančević-Otanjac, M. (2016). Students with language learning disabilities and difficulties in a foreign language classroom. *Specijalna edukacija i rehabilitacija, 15*(4), 461-474.

Jack, D., & Nyman, J. (2019). Meeting Labour Market Needs for French as a Second Language Instruction in Ontario. *American Journal of Educational Research*, 7(7), 428–438. 10.12691/education-7-7-1

Jaime, K., & Knowlton, E. (2007). Visual supports for students with behavior and cognitive challenges. *Intervention in School and Clinic*, 42(5), 259–270. 10.1177/10534512070420050101

Jaiswal, A., Aldersey, H., Wittich, W., Mirza, M., & Finlayson, M. (2018). Participation experiences of people with deafblindness or dual sensory loss: A scoping review of global deafblind literature. *PLoS One*, 13(9), e0203772. 10.1371/journal.pone.020377230212504

Jan, G. (2015). The problem of the supercrip: Representation and misrepresentation of disability. In *Disability Research Today* (pp. 204–218). Routledge.

Jenson, K. (2018). Discourses of disability and inclusive education. *He Kupu, Special Edition, 5*(4). https://www.hekupu.ac.nz/article/discourses-disability-and-inclusive-education

Jimenez, B. A., & Hudson, M. E. (2019). Including students with severe disabilities in general education and the potential of universal design for learning for all children. *The SAGE Handbook of Inclusion and Diversity in Education*, 288–306. https://dialnet.unirioja.es/servlet/articulo?codigo=7146989

Johnson, A. P. (2012). *A short guide to action research* (4th ed.). Pearson.

Johnston, S. (2020). *Universal design for learning to support remote learning*. EDUCAUSE. https://events.educause.edu/-/media/files/events/webinar/2020/eliweb2004/transcript.pdf

Johnston, O., Wildy, H., & Shand, J. (2023). Student voices that resonate – constructing composite narratives that represent students' classroom experiences. *Qualitative Research*, 23(1), 108–124. 10.1177/14687941211016158

Joyce, K. E., & Cartwright, N. (2020). Bridging the gap between research and practice: Predicting what will work locally. *American Educational Research Journal*, 57(3), 1045–1082. 10.3102/0002831219866687

Compilation of References

Kamei-Hannan, C., Lee, D. B., & Presley, I. (2017). Assistive Technology. In C. K. Hannan, C. Holbrook, & T. McCarthy (Eds.), *Foundations of Education: Volume II: Instructional Strategies for Teaching Children and Youths with Visual Impairments* (3rd ed.). APH Press.

Kane, T. J., Gehlbach, H., Greenberg, M., Quinn, D., & Thal, D. (2016). The Best Foot Forward Project: Substituting Teacher-Collected Video. https://cepr.harvard.edu/files/cepr/files/l4a_best_foot_forward_research_brief1.pdf

Karisa, A. (2023). Universal design for learning: Not another slogan on the street of inclusive education. *Disability & Society*, 38(1), 194–200. 10.1080/09687599.2022.2125792

Kärner, T., & Schneider, G. (2023). A scoping review on the hidden curriculum in education: Mapping definitory elements for educational theory building. *PsychArchives.*https://doi.org/10.23668/psycharchives.13240

Karsenty, R., & Brodie, K. (2023). Researching "what went wrong" in professional development (PD) for mathematics teachers: What makes it so important, and so difficult? *Journal of Mathematics Teacher Education*, 26(5), 573–580. 10.1007/s10857-023-09599-y

Kasch, H. (2018). New multimodal designs for foreign language learning. Learning Tech–Tidsskrift for læremidler, didaktik og teknologi, 5, 28–59. 10.7146/lt.v4i5.111561

Kasch, H. (2019). Experimental Studies of the affordances of assistive multimodal learning designs: Universal Design for Learning in modern language classrooms. *JISTE*, 23(2), 93.

Kasprisin, L. (2015). Challenging the Deficit Model and the Pathologizing of Children: Envisioning Alternative Models. *Journal of Educational Controversy*, 9(1), 1. https://cedar.wwu.edu/jec/vol9/iss1/1

Katz, J. (2013). The three block model of universal design for learning (UDL): Engaging students in inclusive education. *Canadian Journal of Education*, 36(1), 153–194.

Katz, J. (2015). Implementing the Three Block Model of Universal Design for Learning: Effects on teachers' self-efficacy, stress, and job satisfaction in inclusive classrooms K-12. *International Journal of Inclusive Education*, 19(1), 1–20. 10.1080/13603116.2014.881569

Kazmi, A. B., Kamran, M., & Siddiqui, S. (2023) The effect of teacher's attitudes in supporting inclusive education by catering to diverse learners. *Frontiers in Education, 8.*10.3389/feduc.2023.1083963

Keane, E., & Heinz, M. (2015). Diversity in initial teacher education in Ireland: The socio-demographic backgrounds of postgraduate post-primary entrants in 2013 and 2014. *Irish Educational Studies*, 34(3), 281–301. 10.1080/03323315.2015.1067637

Keane, E., & Heinz, M. (2016). Excavating an injustice?: Nationality/ies, ethnicity/ies and experiences with diversity of initial teacher education applicants and entrants in Ireland in 2014. *European Journal of Teacher Education*, 39(4), 507–527. 10.1080/02619768.2016.1194392

Kelly, O., Buckley, K., Lieberman, L. J., & Arndt, K. (2022). Universal Design for Learning - A framework for inclusion in Outdoor Learning. *Journal of Outdoor and Environmental Education*, 25(1), 75–89. 10.1007/s42322-022-00096-z

Kent, C., du Boulay, B., & Cukurova, M. (2022). Keeping the Parents outside the School Gate—A Critical Review. *Education Sciences*, 12(10), 683. 10.3390/educsci12100683

Keskin, M. (2023). Discovering and Developing Research Interests: A Narrative Inquiry into Three Doctoral Students' Experiences. *Yükseköğretim Dergisi*, 13(1), 9–18. 10.2399/yod.23.1225236

Khan, I. (2022). Remote learning in early childhood and elementary schools: An unprecedented shift. In *Handbook of Research on Adapting Remote Learning Practices for Early Childhood and Elementary School Classrooms* (pp. 482–505). IGI Global. 10.4018/978-1-7998-8405-7.ch028

Khatib, M., & Tootkaboni, A. A. (2019). Attitudes toward communicative language teaching: The case of efl learners and teachers. *Íkala. Revista de Lenguaje y Cultura*, 24(3), 471–485. Advance online publication. 10.17533/udea.ikala.v24n03a04

Kheirabadi, R., & Alavi Moghaddam, S. B. (2014). New horizons in teaching English in Iran: A transition from reading-based methods to communicative ones by 'English for schools' series. *International Journal of Language Learning and Applied Linguistics World*, 5(4), 225–232.

Khlaif, Z. N., & Salha, S. (2020). The unanticipated educational challenges of developing countries in Covid-19 crisis: A brief report. *Interdisciplinary Journal of Virtual Learning in Medical Sciences*, 11(2), 130–134. 10.30476/IJVLMS.2020.86119.1034

Khosravi, H., Shum, S. B., Chen, G., Conati, C., Tsai, Y.-S., Kay, J., Knight, S., Martinez-Maldonado, R., Sadiq, S., & Gašević, D. (2022). Explainable artificial intelligence in education. *Computers and Education: Artificial Intelligence*, 3, 100074. Advance online publication. 10.1016/j.caeai.2022.100074

Kieran, L., & Anderson, C. (2019). Connecting Universal Design for Learning With Culturally Responsive Teaching. *Education and Urban Society*, 51(9), 1202–1216. 10.1177/0013124518785012

Kilpatrick, J. R., Ehrlich, S., & Bartlett, M. (2021). Learning from COVID-19: Universal Design for Learning Implementation Prior to and during a pandemic. *The Journal of Applied Instructional Design*, 10(1), 1–17. https://edtechbooks.org/jaid_10_1/universal_design_forS

Kim, R. (2023). Under the Law: CTE: A checkered legal history. *Phi Delta Kappan*, 104(6), 58–60. 10.1177/00317217231161544

King-Sears, M. E., Stefanidis, A., Evmenova, A. S., Rao, K., Mergen, R. L., Sanborn Owen, L., & Strimel, M. M. (2023). Achievement of learners receiving UDL instruction: A meta-analysis. *Teaching and Teacher Education*, 122, 103956. Advance online publication. 10.1016/j.tate.2022.103956

Kirshner, D. (2016). *Configuring Learning Theory to Support Teaching*.

Kline-Martin, E. (2018) *Yes Oui Can: Addressing British Columbia's Shortage of French Immersion Teachers*. Master's thesis. School of Public Policy, Simon Fraser University.

Compilation of References

Koestler, F. A. (2004). *The Unseen Minority: A Social History of Blindness in the United States.* https://www.afb.org/unseen/book.asp?ch=Koe-00toc

Konakli, T., & Akdeniz, R. K. (2023). The Emergence, Reasons and Results of Resistance to Change in Teachers. *International Journal on Lifelong Education and Leadership*, 8(1), 49–67. Advance online publication. 10.25233/ijlel.1107137

Koster, B., & Dengerink, J. J. (2008). Professional standards for teacher educators: How to deal with complexity, ownership and function. Experiences from the Netherlands. *European Journal of Teacher Education*, 31(2), 135–149. 10.1080/02619760802000115

Krausneker, V., Becker, C., Audeoud, M., & Tarcsiová, D. (2017). Bimodal Bilingual School Practice in Europe. In K. Reuter (Ed.), *UNCRPD Implementation in Europe - A Deaf Perspective*. EUD

Krausneker, V., Becker, C., Audeoud, M., & Tarcsiová, D. (2020). Bilingual school education with spoken and signed languages in Europe. *International Journal of Bilingual Education and Bilingualism*. Advance online publication. 10.1080/13670050.2020.1799325

Kreisman, D., & Stange, K. (2020). Vocational and Career Tech Education in American High Schools: The Value of Depth Over Breadth. *Education Finance and Policy*, 15(1), 11–44. 10.1162/edfp_a_00266

Krusenvik, L. (2016). *Using case studies as a scientific method: Advantages and disadvantages.* http://www.diva-portal.org/smash/record.jsf?dswid=5853&pid=diva2%3A1054643

Kupers, E., de Boer, A., Loopers, J., Bakker, A., & Minnaert, A. (2023). Differentiation and Students with Special Educational Needs: Teachers' Intentions and Classroom Interactions. In Maulana, R., Helms-Lorenz, M., & Klassen, R. M. (Eds.), *Effective Teaching Around the World*. Springer. 10.1007/978-3-031-31678-4_36

Kurniasari, K., Masitoh, S., & Bachri, B. S. (2021). Learning planning development of Universal Design for Learning for autism in elementary school. *Budapest International Research and Critics in Linguistics and Education (BirLE). Journal*, 4(4), 1339–1350.

Kurzweil Education. (n.d.). *The history of text-to-speech technology*. Retrieved October 30 from https://www.kurzweiledu.com/about-kurzweil/history-of-text-to-speech.html

Lai, C., & Gu, M. (2011). Self-regulated out-of-class language learning with technology. *Computer Assisted Language Learning*, 24(4), 317–335. 10.1080/09588221.2011.568417

Lakkala, S. P., & Kyrö-Ämmälä, O. (2017). The Finnish School Case. In A. Galkienė (Ed.), *Inclusion in socio-educational frames* (pp. 267–309). The publishing house of the Lithuanian University of Educational Sciences.

Lambertl, R., McNiff, A., Schuck, R., Imm, K., & Zimmerman, S. (2023). "UDL is a way of thinking"; theorizing UDL teacher knowledge, beliefs, and practices. *Frontiers in Education*, 8. https://www.frontiersin.org/articles/10.3389/feduc.2023.1145293

Lambert, R., McNiff, A., Schuck, A., Kara, I., & Zimmerman, S. (2023). 'UDL is a way of thinking'; Theorizing UDL teacher knowledge, beliefs, and practices. *Frontiers in Education*, 8, 1145293. 10.3389/feduc.2023.1145293

Lanca, C., & Saw, S. M. (2020). The association between digital screen time and myopia: A systematic review. *Ophthalmic & Physiological Optics*, 40(2), 216–229. 10.1111/opo.1265731943280

Lanterman, C. S., & Applequist, K. (2018). Pre-service Teachers' Beliefs: Impact of Training in Universal Design for Learning. *Exceptionality Education International*, 28(3). Advance online publication. 10.5206/eei.v28i3.7774

LaRon, A. S. (2018). Barriers With Implementing a Universal Design for Learning Framework. *Inclusion (Washington, D.C.)*, 6(4), 274–286. 10.1352/2326-6988-6.4.274

Larsen-Freeman, D. (2018). Looking ahead: Future directions in, and future research into, second language acquisition. *Foreign Language Annals*, 51(1), 55–72. 10.1111/flan.12314

Laureano, B. I., & Turman, A. (2020). *Crimp Camp Curriculum*. Netflix. Retrieved November 12 from https://cripcamp.com/curriculum/

Lawson, A., & Beckett, A. E. (2021) The social and human rights models of disability: towards a complementarity thesis, *The International Journal of Human Rights, 25*(2), 348-379. 10.1080/13642987.2020.1783533

Leavy, A. (2005). 'When I meet them I talk to them': The challenges of diversity for preservice teacher education. *Irish Educational Studies*, 24(2–3), 159–177. 10.1080/03323310500435422

Lehtomäki, E., Posti-Ahokas, H., Beltrán, A., Shaw, C., Edjah, H., Juma, S., Mulat, M., & Hirvonen, M. (2020) *Teacher education for inclusion: five countries across three continents.* Global Education Monitoring Report Team [1018]. UNESCO. https://unesdoc.unesco.org/ark:/48223/pf0000373804

Lenski, S. D., Crawford, K., Crumpler, T., & Stallworth, C. (2005). Preparing Preservice Teachers in a Diverse World. *Action in Teacher Education*, 27(3), 3–12. 10.1080/01626620.2005.10463386

Leonardo, M. D. F., & Cha, J. (2021). Filipino Science Teachers' Evaluation on Webinars' Alignments to Universal Design for Learning and Their Relation to Self-Efficacy amidst the Challenges of the COVID-19 Pandemic. *Asia-Pacific Science Education*, 7(2), 421–451. 10.1163/23641177-bja10035

Levey, S. (2023). Universal Design for Learning. *Journal of Education*, 203(2), 479–487. 10.1177/00220574211031954

Lewis, S. (2018). Universal Design for Learning: A Support for Changing Teacher Practice. *BU Journal of Graduate Studies in Education*, 10(1), 40–43.

Li, P., & Jeong, H. (2020) The social brain of language: grounding second language learning in social interaction. *NPJ Science of Learning, 5*, 8. 10.1038/s41539-020-0068-7

Compilation of References

Lindholm-Leary, K., & Genesee, F. (2014). Student outcomes in one-way, two-way, and indigenous language immersion education. *Journal of Immersion and Content Based Language Education*, 2(2), 165–180. 10.1075/jicb.2.2.01lin

Liston, D., Whitcomb, J., & Borko, H. (2006). Too Little or Too Much: Teacher Preparation and the First Years of Teaching. *Journal of Teacher Education*, 57(4), 351–358. 10.1177/0022487106291976

Liu, L., Li, W., & Dini, D. (2017). Accessibility of teacher education online courses: Design and assessment with a UDL infused technology integration model. In *Society for Information Technology & Teacher Education International Conference* (pp. 2521-2528). Association for the Advancement of Computing in Education (AACE).

Li, Y.-F., Zhang, D., Dulas, H. M., & Whirley, M. L. (2023). The Impact of COVID-19 and Remote Learning on Education: Perspectives from University Students With Disabilities. *Journal of Disability Policy Studies*. Advance online publication. 10.1177/10442073231185264

Lohmann, M., Hovey, K. A., & Gauvreau, A. (2022) Universal Design for Learning (UDL) in Inclusive Preschool Science Classrooms. *Journal of Science Education*.https://scholarworks.rit.edu/cgi/viewcontent.cgi?article=1178&context=jsesd

Lohmann, M.J., Hovey, K.A., & Gauvreau, A.N. (2023) Universal Design for Learning (UDL) in Inclusive Preschool Science Classrooms. *Journal of Science Education*. 10.14448/jsesd.15.0005

Lowrey, K. A., Hollingshead, A., & Howery, K. (2017). A closer look: Examining teachers' language around UDL, inclusive classrooms, and intellectual disability. *Intellectual and Developmental Disabilities*, 55(1), 15–24. 10.1352/1934-9556-55.1.1528181885

Lowrey, K. A., Hollingshead, A., Howery, K., & Bishop, J. B. (2017). More Than One Way: Stories of UDL and Inclusive Classrooms. *Research and Practice for Persons with Severe Disabilities : the Journal of TASH*, 42(4), 225–242. 10.1177/1540796917711668

Lowrey, K., Classen, A., & Sylvest, A. (2019). Exploring Ways to Support Preservice Teachers' Use of UDL in Planning and Instruction. *Journal of Educational Research & Practice*, 9(1), 261–281. 10.5590/JERAP.2019.09.1.19

Lyra, O., Koullapi, K., & Kalogeropoulou, E. (2023). Fears towards disability and their impact on teaching practices in inclusive classrooms: An empirical study with teachers in Greece. *Heliyon*, 9(5), e16332. Advance online publication. 10.1016/j.heliyon.2023.e1633237305505

Lyster, R. (2015). Using form-focused tasks to integrate language across the immersion curriculum. *System*, 54, 4–13. 10.1016/j.system.2014.09.022

Maccessibility. (2011, November 12). Blind faith: A decade of Apple accessibility. *M12Y*. https://maccessibility.net/2011/02/10/blind-faith-a-decade-of-apple-accessibility

MacKay, A. W. (2009). *Connecting Care and Challenge: Tapping our Human Potential – Inclusive Education: A Review of Programming and Services in New Brunswick*.https://www2.gnb.ca/content/dam/gnb/Departments/ed/pdf/K12/mackay/ReportOnInclusiveEducationSummaryDocument.pdf

349

Mackey, M. (2019). Accessing middle school social studies content through Universal Design for Learning. *Journal of Educational Research and Practice*, 9(1), 81–88. 10.5590/JER-AP.2019.09.1.06

Mady, C. (2017). Multilingual immigrants' French and English acquisition in Grade 6 French immersion: Evidence as means to improve access. *Language and Intercultural Communication*, 18(2), 204–224. 10.1080/14708477.2017.1364259

Mady, C. (2018). Teacher Adaptations to Support Students with Special Education Needs in French Immersion: An Observational Study. *Journal of Immersion and Content-Based Language Education*, 6(2), 244–268. 10.1075/jicb.17011.mad

Mady, C., & Arnett, K. (2016). French as a second language teacher candidates' conceptions of allophone students and students with learning difficulties. *Canadian Journal of Applied Linguistics. Canadian Journal of Applied Linguistics*, 18(2), 78–95.

Mady, C., & Masson, M. (2018). Principals' Beliefs About Language Learning and Inclusion of English Language Learners in Canadian Elementary French Immersion Programs. *Canadian Journal of Applied Linguistics. Canadian Journal of Applied Linguistics*, 21(1), 71–93. 10.7202/1050811ar

Mahoney, K., & Harsma, E. (2021). Exploring the Connection Between Universal Design for Learning and Culturally Responsive Teaching: Community, Choice, and Support for Diverse Learners through Different Teaching Modalities. In E. Langran & D. Rutledge (Eds.), *Proceedings of SITE Interactive Conference (pp. 40-43). Online, United States: Association for the Advancement of Computing in Education* (AACE). https://www.learntechlib.org/primary/p/220163/

Marshall, L., & Moys, J.-L. (2020). Readers' experiences of Braille in an evolving technological world. *Visible Language*, 54(1-2).

Mårtensson, P., Fors, U., Wallin, S. B., Zander, U., & Nilsson, G. H. (2016). Evaluating research: A multidisciplinary approach to assessing research practice and quality. *Research Policy, 45*(3), 593-603. https://doi.org/10.1016/j.respol.2015.11.009

Martiniello, N., Barlow, M., & Wittich, W. (2021). Exploring correlates of braille reading performance in adults and older adults with visual impairment: A retrospective study. *Scientific Studies of Reading*. Advance online publication. 10.1080/10888438.2021.1969402

Martiniello, N., Eisenbarth, W., Lehane, C., Johnson, A., & Wittich, W. (2019). Exploring the use of smartphones and tablets among people with visual impairments: Are mainstream devices replacing the use of traditional visual aids? *Assistive Technology*, 1–12. 10.1080/10400435.2019.168208431697612

Martiniello, N., Haririsanati, L., & Wittich, W. (2020). Enablers and barriers encountered by working-age and older adults who pursue braille training. *Disability and Rehabilitation*. Advance online publication. 10.1080/09638288.2020.183325333053313

Compilation of References

Martiniello, N., & Wittich, W. (2019). Employment and visual impairment: Issues in adulthood. In Ravenscraft, J. (Ed.), *Routledge Handbook of Visual Impairment* (pp. 415–437). Routledge. 10.4324/9781315111353-26

Mason, M., Larson, E. J., Desgroseilliers, P., Carr, W., & Lapkin, S. (2020) *Accessing opportunity: A study on challenges in French-as-a-second-language education teacher supply and demand in Canada*. Office of the Commissioner of Official Languages. https://www.clo-ocol.gc.ca/en/publications/studies/2019/accessing-opportunity-fsl

Massouti, A. (2021). Pre-service teachers' perspectives on their preparation for inclusive teaching: Implications for organizational change in teacher education. *The Canadian Journal for the Scholarship of Teaching and Learning*, 12(1). Advance online publication. 10.5206/cjsotlrca-cea.2021.1.10611

Mathewson, T. G. (2020, July 13). Boston schools deny some students with disabilities enrollment into dual-language programs. *Boston Globe*.https://www.bostonglobe.com/2020/07/13/metro/boston-schools-deny-some-disabled-students-enrollment-into-dual-language-programs/

Matteson, S. (2023). Universal Design for Learning in Asynchronous Online Instruction. In E. Langran, P. Christensen & J. Sanson (Eds.), *Proceedings of Society for Information Technology & Teacher Education International Conference* (pp. 2537-2540). New Orleans, LA, United States: Association for the Advancement of Computing in Education (AACE). Retrieved October 9, 2023 from https://www.learntechlib.org/primary/p/222153/

Matthewes, S. H., & Ventura, G. (2022) *On Track to Success? Returns to vocational education against different alternatives*. Discussion Paper 038. Centre for Vocational Educational Research. https://cver.lse.ac.uk/textonly/cver/pubs/cverdp038.pdf

Maurer, M. (2009). The difference the dots make: A personal history with Braille. *Journal of Visual Impairment & Blindness*, 103(4), 196–198. 10.1177/0145482X0910300402

McCarthy, A. M., Maor, D., McConney, A., & Cavanaugh, C. (2023). Digital transformation in education: Critical components for leaders of system change. *Social Sciences & Humanities Open*, 8(1), 1–15. 10.1016/j.ssaho.2023.100479

McCarty, T., & Lee, L. (2014). Critical Culturally Sustaining/Revitalizing Pedagogy and Indigenous Education Sovereignty. *Harvard Educational Review*, 84(1), 101–124. 10.17763/haer.84.1.q83746nl5pj34216

McCord, K., Gruben, A., & Rathgeber, J. (2014). *Accessing music: Enhancing student learning in the general music classroom Using UDL*. Alfred Music.

McDaid, R., & Nowlan, E. (2021). Barriers to recognition for migrant teachers in Ireland'. *European Educational Research Journal*, 21(2), 247–264. 10.1177/14749041211031724

McGuire, J. M., & Scott, S. S. (2006). Universal design for instruction: Extending the universal design paradigm to college instruction. *Journal of Postsecondary Education and Disability*, 19(2), 124–134. https://files.eric.ed.gov/fulltext/EJ844629.pdf

McGuire-Schwartz, M. E., & Arndt, J. S. (2007). Transforming universal design for learning in early childhood teacher education from college classroom to early childhood classroom. *Journal of Early Childhood Teacher Education*, 28(2), 127–139. 10.1080/10901020701366707

McKenna, J. W., Solis, M., Garwood, J., & Parenti, M. (2023). Characteristics of Individualized Education Programs for Students With Learning Disabilities: A Systematic Review. *Learning Disability Quarterly*. Advance online publication. 10.1177/07319487231182697

McKenzie, J., Karisa, A., Kahonde, C., & Tesni, S. (2021) *Review of Universal Design for Learning in Low- and Middle-Income Countries*. Including Disability in Education in Africa (IDEA). https://www.cbm.org/fileadmin/user_upload/UDL_review_report_2021.pdf

McLaughlin, H., & Kenny, M. (2004). *Diversity in Early Years Education North and South— Implications for Teacher Education* [Report for the Centre for Cross Border Studies and the Standing Conference on Teacher Education, North and South].

Mealin, S., & Murphy-Hill, E. (2012). An exploratory study of blind software developers. 2012 IEEE Symposium on Visual Languages and Human-Centric Computing (VL/HCC).

Meegan, J. (2023). Tensions and dilemmas: A narrative inquiry account of a teacher-researcher. *Irish Educational Studies*, 1–16. Advance online publication. 10.1080/03323315.2023.2236592

Meijer, C., & Watkins, A. (2016). Changing Conceptions of Inclusion Underpinning Education Policy. In *Implementing Inclusive Education: Issues in Bridging the Policy-Practice Gap* (Vol. 8, pp. 1–16). Emerald Group Publishing Limited. https://doi.org/10.1108/S1479-363620160000008001

Mental Health Commission of Canada. (2022). *Children and Youth*. https://mentalhealthcommission .ca/what-we-do/children-and-youth/

Meo, G. (2008). Curriculum Planning for All Learners: Applying Universal Design for Learning (UDL) to a High School Reading Comprehension Program. *Preventing School Failure*, 52(2), 21–30. 10.3200/PSFL.52.2.21-30

Merriam, S. B. (1988). *Case study research in education: a qualitative approach*. Jossey-Bass Publishers.

Mertler, C. A. (2021). Action Research as Teacher Inquiry: A Viable Strategy for Resolving Problems of Practice. *Practical Assessment, Research & Evaluation*, 26, 1–12.

Meyer, A., Rose, D. H., & Gordon, D. (2014). *Universal Design for Learning: Theory & Practice*. Wakefield, MA. https://www.cast.org/products-services/resources/2014/universal-design -learning-theory-practice-udl-meyer

Meyer, A., & Rose, D. H. (2002). *Teaching every student in the digital age: universal design for learning*. Association for Supervision & Curriculum Development.

Meyer, A., Rose, D. H., & Gordon, D. (2014). *Universal Design for Learning: Theory and Practice*. CAST Professional Publishing.

Compilation of References

Milian, M., & Erin, J. N. (2001). *Diversity and visual impairment: the influence of race, gender, religion, and ethnicity on the individual.* American Foundation for the Blind.

Miller, D., & Lang, P. (2016). Using the Universal Design for Learning Approach in Science Laboratories To Minimize Student Stress. *Journal of Chemical Education*, 93(11), 1823–1828. 10.1021/acs.jchemed.6b00108

Mills, C. (2008). Reproduction and transformation of inequalities in schooling: The transformative potential of the theoretical constructs of Bourdieu. *British Journal of Sociology of Education*, 29(1), 79–89. 10.1080/01425690701737481

Minhas, R., Jaiswal, A., Chan, S., Trevisan, J., Paramasivam, A., & Spruyt-Rocks, R. (2022). Prevalence of Individuals with Deafblindness and Age-Related Dual-Sensory Loss. *Journal of Visual Impairment & Blindness*, 116(1), 36–47. 10.1177/0145482X211072541

Minkara, M. (2019). *Planes, Trains & Canes.* Retrieved November 12 from https://monaminkara.com/ptc

Misbah, N. H., Mohamad, M., Yunus, M., & Ya'acob, A. (2017). Identifying the Factors Contributing to Students' Difficulties in the English Language Learning. *Creative Education*, 8(13), 1999–2008. 10.4236/ce.2017.813136

Mkandawire, M. T., Mwanjejele, J., Luo, Z., & Ruzagirizad, A. U. (2016). What Mismatch Challenges are there between What Teacher Education Institutions Teach and What is Expected at Work Place? Retrospective Views of Secondary School Teachers from Tanzania and Malawi Studying in China. *American Scientific Research Journal for Engineering, Technology, and Sciences*, 22, 39–49.

Mohamed, Z., Valcke, M., & De Wever, B. (2017). Are they ready to teach? Student teachers' readiness for the job with reference to teacher competence frameworks. *Journal of Education for Teaching*, 43(2), 151–170. 10.1080/02607476.2016.1257509

Molenaar, I. (2022). Towards hybrid human-AI learning technologies. *European Journal of Education*, 57(4), 1–14. 10.1111/ejed.12527

Montanari, S. (2013). A Case Study of Bi-literacy Development among Children Enrolled in an Italian–English Dual Language Program in Southern California. *International Journal of Bilingual Education and Bilingualism*, 17(5), 509–525. 10.1080/13670050.2013.833892

Montero-Mesa, L., Fraga-Varela, F., Vila-Couñago, E., & Rodríguez-Groba, A. (2023). Digital Technology and Teacher Professional Development: Challenges and Contradictions in Compulsory Education. *Education Sciences*, 13(10), 1029. 10.3390/educsci13101029

Montgomery, A., & Smith, A. (2006). Teacher Education in Northern Ireland: Policy Variations Since Devolution. *Scottish Educational Review*, 37(3), 46–58. 10.1163/27730840-03703005

Moore, C., & Nichols Hess, A. (2020) *Universal Design for Learning with (and without) Technology.* Pod Newtwork. https://podnetwork.org/universal-design-for-learning-with-and-without-technology/

Moore, E. J., Smith, F. G., Hollingshead, A., & Wojcik, B. (2018). Voices From the Field: Implementing and Scaling-Up Universal Design for Learning in Teacher Preparation Programs. *Journal of Special Education Technology*, 33(1), 40–53. 10.1177/0162643417732293

Morales, T. (2015). *VoiceOver turns 10*. Retrieved October 31 from https://www.applevis.com/blog/voiceover-turns-10

Moran, A. (2008). Challenges surrounding widening participation and fair access to initial teacher education: Can it be achieved? *Journal of Education for Teaching*, 34(1), 63–77. 10.1080/02607470701773481

Moran, A. (2012). Crises as catalysts for change: Re-energising teacher education in Northern Ireland. *Educational Research*, 54(2), 137–147. 10.1080/00131881.2012.680039

Morgan, P. L., Farkas, G., Hillemeier, M. M., Mattison, R., Maczuga, S., Li, H., & Cook, M. (2015). Minorities are disproportionately underrepresented in special education: Longitudinal evidence across five disability conditions. *Educational Researcher*, 44(5), 278–292. 10.3102/0013189X1559115727445414

Mrachko, A. (2020). Using the Universal Design for Learning Framework to Plan for All Students in the Classroom: Representation and Visual Support. *The Elementary STEM Journal*, 25(1), 22–24.

Mrachko, A., & Vostal, B. (2020). Using the "Universal Design for Learning" Framework to Plan for All Students in the Classroom: Engagement Through Choice. *The Elementary STEM Journal*, 25(2), 29–31.

Muhling, S., & Mady, C. (2017). Inclusion of Students With Special Education Needs in French as a Second Language Programs: A Review of Canadian Policy and Resource Documents. *Canadian Journal of Educational Administration and Policy*, 183, 15–29.

Murawski, W. W., & Scott, K. L. (2019). *What really works with Universal Design for Learning*. Corwin Press.

ΜχΚενζιε, ϑ., & Δαλτον, Ε. (2020). Υνιϖερσαλ δεσιγν φορ λεαρνινγ ιν ινχλυσιϖε εδυχατιον πολιχψ ιν Σουτη Αφριχα. *Αφριχαν ϑουρναλ οφ Δισαβιλιτψ*, 9, 1–8. ηττπσ://δοι.οργ/ΠΜΙΔ:3339206210.4102/αφοδ.ϖ9ι0.776

National Center on Disability and Journalism. (2021). *Disability Language Style Guide*. Walter Cronkite School of Journalism and Mass Communication. Retrieved November 12 from https://ncdj.org/style-guide/

National Council for Curriculum and Assessment (NCCA) & National Association of Boards of Management in Special Education (NAMBSE). (2019). *Level 2 Learning Programmes Guidelines for Teachers*. https://www.curriculumonline.ie/getmedia/38c33cf1-9e58-44f4-ad5b-ffbd9da20a6a/L2LPS-Guidelines-Jan-2019-version.pdf

Compilation of References

National Council for Curriculum and Assessment (NCCA), & Department of Education. (2018). *JuniorCycle_-English_-specification_amended_2018.* https://www.curriculumonline.ie/getmedia/ d14fd46d-5a10-46fc-9002-83df0b4fc2ce/JuniorCycle_-English_-specification_amended_2018 .pdf

National Council for Curriculum and Assessment (NCCA). (1999). *Special Educational Needs: Curriculum Issues Discussion Paper.* https://ncca.ie/media/1834/special_educational_needs _curriculum_issues_-_discussion_paper.pdf

National Council for Special Education (NCSE). (2014). *Delivery for Students with Special Educational Needs A better and more equitable way.* https://ncse.ie/wp-content/uploads/2014/ 09/NCSE_Booklet_webFINAL_10_06_14.pdf

National Council for Special Education (NCSE). (2019). *Policy Advice on Special Schools and Classes - An Inclusive Education for an Inclusive Society?* www.ncse.ie

National Forum. (2020). *INDEx Survey: Final Summary Report.* https://hub.teachingandlearning .ie/wp-content/uploads/2021/06/INDEx-Survey-Final-Report-15-April-2021.pdf

National Inventors Hall of Fame. (2002). *Raymond Kurzweil: Optical character recognition (U.S. Patent No. 6,199,042).* National Inventors Hall of Fame. Retrieved September 30 from https:// www.invent.org/inductees/raymond-kurzweil

Navaitienė, J., & Stasiūnaitienė, E. (2023). The Goal of the Universal Design for Learning: Development of All to Expert Learners. In A. Galkienė, & O, Monkevičienė (Eds). *Improving Inclusive Education through Universal Design for Learning (pp. 23–57).* Springer. https://link .springer.com/content/pdf/10.1007/978-3-030-80658-3.pdf

Navarro, S. B., Zervas, P., Fabregat Gesa, R., & Sampson, D. G. (2016). Developing Teachers' Competences for Designing Inclusive Learning Experiences. *Journal of Educational Technology & Society*, 19(1), 17–27.

Navarro, S. B., Zervas, P., Gesa, R. F., & Sampson, D. G. (2016). Developing teachers' competences for designing inclusive learning experiences. *Journal of Educational Technology & Society*, 19(1), 17–27.

Nelson, L. L. (2021). *Design and deliver: Planning and teaching using Universal Design for Learning.* Paul H. Brookes Publishing Co.

Nelson, L. L., & Posey, A. (2019). *A Tree for all; Your coloring book of UDL principles and Practice.* CAST Professional Publishing.

Neubauer, B. E., Witkop, C. T., & Varpio, L. (2019). How phenomenology can help us learn from the experiences of others. *Perspectives on Medical Education*, 8(2), 90–97. 10.1007/ S40037-019-0509-230953335

New Brunswick Department of Education and Early Childhood Development. (2013). *Inclusive Education* (Policy 322) https://www2.gnb.ca/content/dam/gnb/Departments/ed/pdf/K12/policies -politiques/e/322A.pdf

355

Nguyen, H. T., & Watanabe, M. F. (2013). Using Visual Supports to Teach English Language Learners in Physical Education. *Journal of Physical Education, Recreation & Dance*, 84(8), 46–53. 10.1080/07303084.2013.818432

Nicol, J. (2024 February 28). *About the UDL Project.* The UDL Project. Retrieved from http://theudlproject.com

Nicolay, A.-C., & Poncelet, M. (2015). Cognitive Benefits in Children Enrolled in an Early Bilingual Immersion School: A Follow Up Study. *Bilingualism: Language and Cognition*, 18(4), 789–795. 10.1017/S1366728914000868

Ni, H., & Wu, X. (2023). Research or teaching? That is the problem: A narrative inquiry into a Chinese college English teacher's cognitive development in the teaching-research nexus. *Frontiers in Psychology*, 14, 1018122. https://www.frontiersin.org/articles/10.3389/fpsyg.2023.1018122. 10.3389/fpsyg.2023.101812236818100

Novak, K. (2018, March 9) Why UDL Matters for English Language Learners. Language Magazine. https://www.languagemagazine.com/2018/03/09/why-udl-matters-for-english-language-learners/

Novak, K. (2016). *UDL Now!: A Teacher's Guide to Applying Universal Design for Learning in Today's Classrooms.* Cast Professional Publishing.

Novak, K., & Rose, D. (2016). *UDL Now!: A teacher's guide to applying universal design for learning in today's classrooms.* CAST Professional Publishing.

O'Connor, E., Marcogliese, E., Anis, H., Faye, G., Flynn, A., Hayman, E., & Stambouli, J. (2023). Adapting Experiential Learning in Times of Uncertainty: Challenges, Strategies, and Recommendations Moving Forward. *Engaged Scholar Journal: Community-Engaged Research, Teaching, and Learning*, 8(4), 49–56. 10.15402/esj.v8i4.70793

O'Neill, G., & Maguire, T. (2019). Developing assessment and feedback approaches to empower and engage students: A sectoral approach in Ireland. In *Transforming Higher Education Through Universal Design for Learning.* Routledge. 10.4324/9781351132077-17

OECD. (2009). *Creating effective teaching and learning environments: First results from TALIS.* OECD.

Office of Educational Technology. (2023). *Artificial Intelligence and Future of Teaching and Learning: Insights and Recommendations.* U.S. Department of Education. https://www2.ed.gov/documents/ai-report/ai-report.pdf

Ok, M. W., Rao, K., Bryant, B., & McDougall, D. (2017). Universal Design for Learning in Pre-K to Grade 12 Classrooms: A Systematic Review of Research. *Exceptionality*, 25(2), 116–138. 10.1080/09362835.2016.1196450

Oliver, K., Innvar, S., Lorenc, T., Woodman, J., & Thomas, J. (2014). A systematic review of barriers to and facilitators of the use of evidence by policymakers. *BMC Health Services Research*, 14(1), 2. Advance online publication. 10.1186/1472-6963-14-224383766

Compilation of References

Omodan, B. (2023). Unveiling Epistemic Injustice in Education: A critical analysis of alternative approaches. *Social Sciences & Humanities Open*, 8(1), 100699. Advance online publication. 10.1016/j.ssaho.2023.100699

Ontario Human Rights Commission. (2018) *Policy on accessible education for students with disabilities.* OHRC. https://www.ohrc.on.ca/en/policy-accessible-education-students-disabilities

Optelec. (n.d.). *About Optelec: History.* Optelec. Retrieved November 12 from https://in.optelec .com/about/History

Organization for Economic Cooperation and Development (OECD). (2005). *Teachers matter: Attracting, developing, and retaining effective teachers.* https://www.oecd.org/edu/school/34990905 .pdf ISBN-92-64-01802-6

Owiny, R. L., Brawand, A., & Josephson, J. (2019). UDL and Literacy. *What Really Works With Universal Design for Learning*, 21.

Padilla, A. M., Fan, L., Xu, X., & Silva, D. (2013). A Mandarin/English Two-way Immersion Program: Language Proficiency and Academic Achievement. *Foreign Language Annals*, 46(4), 661–679. 10.1111/flan.12060

Page, D. D. (1980). Securing and Maintaining Qualified Readers for Visually Impaired College Students. *Journal of Visual Impairment & Blindness*, 74(2), 71–75. 10.1177/0145482X8007400206

Pan, C. (2014) *Falling Behind: 2014 Report on the Shortage of Teachers in French Immersion and Core French in British-Columbia and Yukon.* Canadian Parents for French.

Pape, T. L.-B., Kim, J., & Weiner, B. (2002). The shaping of individual meanings assigned to assistive technology: A review of personal factors. *Disability and Rehabilitation*, 24(1-3), 5–20. 10.1080/09638280011006623511827155

Parette, H. P., & Blum, C. (2015). Including all young children in the technology-supported curriculum: A UDL technology integration framework for 21st-century classrooms. *Technology and digital media in the early years: Tools for teaching and learning*, 129-149.

Paseka, A., & Schwab, S. (2020). Parents' attitudes towards inclusive education and their perceptions of inclusive teaching practices and resources. *European Journal of Special Needs Education*, 35(2), 254–272. 10.1080/08856257.2019.1665232

Patel, V., Lindenmeyer, A., Gao, F., & Yeung, J. (2023). A qualitative study exploring the lived experiences of patients living with mild, moderate and severe frailty, following hip fracture surgery and hospitalisation. *PLoS One*, 18(5), e0285980. 10.1371/journal.pone.028598037200345

Patfield, S., Gore, J., & Harris, J. (2023). Shifting the focus of research on effective professional development: Insights from a case study of implementation. *Journal of Educational Change*, 24(2), 345–363. 10.1007/s10833-021-09446-y

Patton Davis, L., & Museus, S. D. (2019). What Is Deficit Thinking? An Analysis of Conceptualizations of Deficit Thinking and Implications for Scholarly Research. *Currents (Ann Arbor)*, 1(1). Advance online publication. 10.3998/currents.17387731.0001.110

Pearson, M. (2015). Modeling Universal Design for Learning Techniques to Support Multicultural Education for Pre-Service Secondary Educators. *Multicultural Education*.

Peng, H., Jager, S., & Lowie, W. (2021). A person-centred approach to L2 learners' informal mobile language learning. *Computer Assisted Language Learning*. Advance online publication. 10.1080/09588221.2020.1868532

Perryman, J., & Calvert, G. (2020). What Motivates People to Teach, and Why Do They Leave? Accountability, Performativity and Teacher Retention. *British Journal of Educational Studies*, 68(1), 3–23. 10.1080/00071005.2019.1589417

Piccolo, G. M. (2022). Pelo direito de aprender: Contibucioes do modelo social da deficiencia a la inclusao escolar. *Educação em Revista*, 38, e36926. 10.1590/0102-4698368536926

Pierce, J., & Telford, J. (2023). From McDonaldization to place-based experience: Revitalizing outdoor education in Ireland. *Journal of Adventure Education and Outdoor Learning*, 1–14. Advance online publication. 10.1080/14729679.2023.2254861

Pine, G. J. (2009). Teacher action research: Building knowledge democracies. *Teacher Action Research: Building Knowledge Democracies*. 10.4135/9781452275079

Poitras, J. (2023, May 8) N.B. reviews gender-identity policy in schools as supporters accuse minister of caving to anti-LGBTQ pressure. *CBC News*. https://www.cbc.ca/news/canada/new-brunswick/nb-education-gender-policy-1.6836059

Polly, D., Burchard, K. P., Castillo, C., Drake, P., Horne, S., Howerton, A., Peake, S., & Schmitt, K. (2020). Examining Action Research and Teacher Inquiry Projects: How Do they Help Future and Current Teachers? *School-University Partnerships*, 12(4), 36–47.

Popova, A., Evans, D. K., Breeding, M. E., & Arancibia, V. (2022). Teacher Professional Development around the World: The Gap between Evidence and Practice. *The World Bank Research Observer*, 37(1), 107–136. 10.1093/wbro/lkab006

Porter, G., & AuCoin, A. (2012). *Strengthening Inclusion, Strengthening Schools.*https://www2.gnb.ca/content/dam/gnb/Departments/ed/pdf/K12/Inclusion/StrengtheningInclusionStrengtheningSchools.pdf

Posey, A. (2018). *Engage the Brain: How to Design for Learning That Taps into the Power of Emotion.* ASCD.

Posey, A., & Novak, K. (2020). *Unlearning: Changing your beliefs and your classroom with UDL.* CAST Professional Publishing.

Compilation of References

Pruss, V. (2017, August 23). Anglophone Schools 'Desperate' for Supply Teachers as Early French Immersion. *CBC News*. https://www.cbc.ca/news/canada/new-brunswick/french-immersion -teacher-shortage-new-brunswick-ingersoll-1.4258892

Purdy, N., Hunter, J., & Totton, L. (2020). Examining the legacy of the Warnock Report in Northern Ireland: A Foucauldian genealogical approach. *British Educational Research Journal*, 46(3), 706–723. 10.1002/berj.3604

PwC. (2018). *Inclusion of People with Disability in VET Cross Sector Project Environmental Scan*. https://www.skillsforaustralia.com/2018/02/02/inclusion-of-people-with-disability-in-vet -environmental-scan-released/

Queen's University Faculty of Education. (2023). CONT691: Universal Design for Learning. *Professional Studies*. https://pros.educ.queensu.ca/courses/CONT691

Quirke, M., & McCarthy, P. (2020) *A Conceptual Framework of Universal Design for Learning (UDL) for the Irish Further Education and Training Sector*. Solas. https://www.solas.ie/f/70398/ x/b1aa8a51b6/a-conceptual-framework-of-universal-design-for-learning-udl-for-the-ir.pdf

Rabelo, A. O. (2022). The Importance of Narrative Inquiry in Education. *The Journal for Critical Education Policy Studies*, 19(3), 112–138. https://eric.ed.gov/?id=EJ1340278

Rani, K., & Tyagi, T. K. (2022). Experiential Learning in School Education: Prospects and Challenges. *International Journal of Advance and Applied Research*, 10(2), 178–183. 10.5281/ zenodo.7652609

Rao, K., & Okolo, C. (n.d.). *Teacher Education and Professional Development on UDL*.

Rao, K. (2015). Universal design for learning and multimedia technology: Supporting culturally and linguistically diverse students. *Journal of Educational Multimedia and Hypermedia*, 24(2), 121–137. https://scholarspace.manoa.hawaii.edu/server/api/core/bitstreams/c273b37c-5b7b-450e -8667-fdd7d15e182a/content

Rao, K., & Meo, G. (2016). Using Universal Design for Learning to Design Standards-Based Lessons. *SAGE Open*, 6(4). Advance online publication. 10.1177/2158244016680688

Rao, K., Ok, M. W., & Bryant, B. R. (2014). A Review of Research on Universal Design Educational Models. *Remedial and Special Education*, 35(3), 153–166. 10.1177/0741932513518980

Rao, K., Ok, M. W., Smith, S. J., Evmenova, A. S., & Edyburn, D. (2019). Validation of the UDL reporting criteria with extant UDL research. *Remedial and Special Education*. Advance online publication. 10.1177/0741932519847755

Rao, K., Smith, S. J., & Lowrey, K. A. (2017). UDL and intellectual disability: What do we know and where do we go? *Intellectual and Developmental Disabilities*, 55(1), 37–47. 10.135 2/1934-9556-55.1.3728181886

Ratcliffe, R. (2013, October 7) Professional development in teaching: the challenges, solutions and status quo. *The Guardian*. https://www.theguardian.com/teacher-network/teacher-blog/2013/oct/07/professional-development-teaching-learning

Régie de l'assurance maladie du Québec. (2018). *Tariff for insured visual aids and related services, CQLR c A-29, r 8.1 (Health Insurance Act)*. http://canlii.ca/t/53hjp

Reinders, H., & Wattana, S. (2014). Can I say something? The effects of digital game play on willingness to communicate. *Language Learning & Technology*, 18, 101–123.

Reinhardt, K. S., Robertson, P. M., & Johnson, R. D. (2021). Connecting inquiry and Universal Design for Learning (UDL) to teacher candidates' emerging practice: Development of a signature pedagogy. *Educational Action Research*, 0(0), 1–18. 10.1080/09650792.2021.1978303

Resch, K., Schrittesser, I., & Knapp, M. (2022). Overcoming the theory-practice divide in teacher education with the 'Partner School Programme'. A conceptual mapping. *European Journal of Teacher Education*. Advance online publication. 10.1080/02619768.2022.2058928

Reynor, E. (2021). From student teachers to educators: Walking the talk with universal design for learning. *A review of inclusive education and employment practices, 2(12)*. https://www.ahead.ie/journal/From-student-teachers-to-Educators-Walking-the-Talk-with-Universal-Design-for-Learning

Reynor, E. (2019). Developing Inclusive Education in Ireland: The case for UDL in Initial Teacher Education. In Gronseth, S. L., & Dalton, E. M. (Eds.), *Universal Access Through Inclusive Instructional Design* (pp. 258–267). Routledge. 10.4324/9780429435515-34

Riley, T., & Hawe, P. (2005). Researching practice: The methodological case for narrative inquiry. *Health Education Research*, 20(2), 226–236. 10.1093/her/cyg12215479707

Roberts, J. (2018). From the Editor: The Possibilities and Limitations of Experiential Learning Research in Higher Education. *Journal of Experiential Education, 41*(1), 3-7. 10.1177/1053825917751457

Rodriguez-Mojica, C., & Briceño, A. (2018). Sentence Stems That Support Reading Comprehension. *The Reading Teacher*, 72(3), 398–402. 10.1002/trtr.1705

Rogers, S. A., & Gronseth, S. L. (2021). Applying UDL to Online Active Learning. *The Journal of Applied Instructional Design*, 10(1). Advance online publication. 10.59668/223.3748

Roisin, D., Heelan, A., & Tobin, T. J. (2020). *AHEAD Ireland FET Project*. Paper presented at the Pathways15. https://www.atend.com.au/resource/119/pathways15-keynote-ahead-ireland-fet-project/

Roman-Lantzy, C. (2019a). *CVI & Autism: Shared Behaviors, Not Diagnoses*. Retrieved July 18 from https://youtu.be/EFPB9r-dIlA

Roman-Lantzy, C. (2019b). *Teaching and Learning in Phase I CVI*. Retrieved Aug. 15 from https://pcvis.vision/educators-and-therapists/phase-i-cvi/

Compilation of References

Roman-Lantzy, C. (2007). *Cortical visual impairment: An approach to assessment and intervention*. American Foundation for the Blind.

Root, J. R., Jimenez, B., & Saunders, A. (2022). Leveraging the UDL Framework to Plan Grade-Aligned Mathematics in Inclusive Settings. *In Practice*, 1(1), 13–22. 10.1177/2732474521990028

Rose, D. H., Hasselbring, T. S., Stahl, S., & Zabala, J. (2005). Assistive technology and universal design for learning: Two sides of the same coin. *Handbook of special education technology research and practice*, 507-518.

Rose, D., & Meyer, A. (2006). *A Practical Reader in Universal Design for Learning*.

Rose, D., Gravel, J. W., & Tucker-Smith, N. (2021). *Cracks in the foundation: Personal reflections on the past and future of the UDL Guidelines*. CAST. Retrieved November 12 from https://www.cast.org/products-services/events/2022/01/cracks-foundation-past-future-udl-guidelines-rose-gravel-tucker-smith

Rose, D. (2001). Universal Design for Learning. *Journal of Special Education Technology*, 16(2), 66–67. 10.1177/016264340101600208

Rose, D. H., Gravel, J. W., & Domings, Y. (2012). Universal design for learning "unplugged": Applications in low-tech settings. In Hall, T. E., Meyer, A., & Rose, D. H. (Eds.), *Universal design for learning in the classroom: Practical applications* (pp. 120–134). Guilford Press. https://eric.ed.gov/?id=ED568861

Rose, D. H., & Meyer, A. (2002). *Teaching every student in the digital age: Universal design for learning*. ERIC.

Rose, D. H., & Meyer, A. (2006). *A practical reader in universal design for learning*. Harvard Education Press. Harvard Education Press.

Rose, D. H., Robinson, K. H., Hall, T. E., Coyne, P., Jackson, R. M., Stahl, W. M., & Wilcauskas, S. L. (2018). Accurate and informative for all: Universal Design for Learning (UDL) and the future of assessment. In *Handbook of accessible instruction and testing practices* (pp. 167–180). Springer. 10.1007/978-3-319-71126-3_11

Rose, D., & Meyer, A. (2002). *Teaching every student in the Digital Age: Universal Design for Learning* (1st ed.). Association for Supervision and Curriculum Development. https://www.cast.org/products-services/resources/2002/universal-design-learning-udl-teaching-every-student-rose

Rosenblum, L. P., & Herzberg, T. S. (2015). Braille and tactile graphics: Youths with visual impairments share their experiences. *Journal of Visual Impairment & Blindness*, 109(3), 173–184. 10.1177/0145482X1510900302

Rosen, L. T. (2021). Mapping out epistemic justice in the clinical space: Using narrative techniques to affirm patients as knowers. *Philosophy, Ethics, and Humanities in Medicine; PEHM*, 16(1), 9. 10.1186/s13010-021-00110-034696799

Roulston, S., Brown, M., Taggart, S., & Eivers, E. (2023). A Century of Growing Apart and Challenges of Coming Together: Education Across the Island of Ireland. *Irish Studies in International Affairs, 34*(2), 78-121. https://doi.org/10.1353/isia.2023.a899832

Rubery, M. (2016). *The untold story of the talking book.* Harvard University Press. 10.4159/9780674974555

Ruble, L. A., McGrew, J. H., Wong, W. H., & Missall, K. N. (2018). Special education teachers' perceptions and intentions toward data collection. *Journal of Early Intervention*, 40(2), 177–191. 10.1177/1053815118771391307742 83

Rundle, A. G., Park, Y., Herbstman, J. B., Kinsey, E. W., & Wang, Y. C. (2020). COVID-19–Related school closings and risk of weight gain among children. *Obesity (Silver Spring, Md.)*, 28(6), 1008–1009. 10.1002/oby.2281332227671

Runyan, N. H., & Carpi, F. (2011). Seeking the 'holy Braille' display: Might electromechanically active polymers be the solution? *Expert Review of Medical Devices*, 8(5), 529–532. 10.1586/erd.11.4722026617

Rusconi, L., & Squillaci, M. (2023). Effects of a Universal Design for Learning (UDL) Training Course on the Development Teachers' Competences: A Systematic Review. *Education Sciences*, 13(5), 466. 10.3390/educsci13050466

Ryles, R. (1996). The impact of braille reading skills on employment, income, education, and reading habits. *Journal of Visual Impairment & Blindness*, 90(3), 219–226. 10.1177/0145482X9609000311

Sadato, N., Okada, T., Honda, M., & Yorekura, Y. (2002). Critical period for cross-modal plasticity in blind humans: A functional MRI study. *NeuroImage*, 16(2), 389–400. 10.1006/nimg.2002.111112030824

Saia, T. (2023). Embracing Disability Culture in Schools. *Language, Speech, and Hearing Services in Schools*, 54(3), 794–798. Advance online publication. 10.1044/2023_LSHSS-22-0014237059085

Salvia, J., Ysseldyke, J. E., & Bolt, S. (2009). *Assessment in Special and Inclusive Education* (11th ed.). Houghton Mifflin Company.

Sandoval Gomez, A., & McKee, A. (2020) When Special Education and Disability Studies Intertwine: Addressing Educational Inequities Through Processes and Programming. *Frontiers in Education, 5.* https://www.frontiersin.org/articles/10.3389/feduc.2020.587045. DOI=10.3389/feduc.2020.587045

Schuck, L., Wall-Emerson, R., Kim, D. S., & Nelson, N. (2019). Predictors Associated with College Attendance and Persistence among Students with Visual Impairments. *Journal of Postsecondary Education and Disability*, 32(4), 339–358.

Schwandt, T. A., & Gates, E. F. (2018). Case study methodology. In Denzin, N. K., & Lincoln, Y. S. (Eds.), *The Sage Handbook of Qualitative Research* (pp. 600–630). Sage Publishers.

Compilation of References

Schwartz, S. (2023, June 21) Where Teachers Say Professional Development Falls Short. *Education Week*. https://www.edweek.org/leadership/where-teachers-say-professional-development-falls-short/2023/06

SCWI. (2021) School College Work Initiative 2021. *Newsletter, 1*(6). https://www.scwi.ca/resources/flipbook/SCWI_Newsletter_Spring_2021_V2/inc/html/4.html?page=1

Sellen, P. (2016, October). *Teacher workload and professional development in England's secondary schools: Insights from TALIS: 10 October 2016*. Education Policy Institute. https://dera.ioe.ac.uk/27930/1/TeacherWorkload_EPI.pdf

Senjam, S. S., Manna, S., & Bascaran, C. (2021). Smartphones-Based Assistive Technology: Accessibility Features and Apps for People with Visual Impairment, and its Usage, Challenges, and Usability Testing. *Clinical Optometry*, 13, 311–322. 10.2147/OPTO.S33636134866955

Seymour, M. (2023). Enhancing the online student experience through the application of Universal Design for Learning (UDL) to research methods learning and teaching. *Education and Information Technologies*. Advance online publication. 10.1007/s10639-023-11948-637361769

Shakespeare, T. (2021). The Social Model of Disability. In L. J. Davis (Ed.), *The disability studies reader*. Routledge (Taylor & Francis Group). 10.4324/9781003082583-3

Shambaugh, N., & Floyd, K. K. (2018). Universal design for learning (UDL) guidelines for mobile devices and technology integration in teacher education. In *Handbook of research on digital content, mobile learning, and technology integration models in teacher education* (pp. 1-21). IGI Global.

Shandana, S., & Mujtaba, B. G. (2016). Use it or lose it: Prudently using case study as a research and educational strategy. *American Journal of Education and Learning*, 1(2), 83–93. 10.20448/804.1.2.83.93

Sharma, U. (2018). *Preparing to Teach in Inclusive Classrooms*. Oxford Research Encyclopedias., 10.1093/acrefore/9780190264093.013.113

Sharma, U., Armstrong, A. C., Merumeru, L., Simi, J., & Yared, H. (2019). Addressing barriers to implementing inclusive education in the Pacific. *International Journal of Inclusive Education*, 23(1), 65–78. 10.1080/13603116.2018.1514751

Sharma, U., Furlonger, B., & Forlin, C. (2019). The Impact of Funding Models on the Education of Students With Autism Spectrum Disorder. *Australasian Journal of Special and Inclusive Education*, 43(1), 1–11. 10.1017/jsi.2019.1

Sharma, U., Loreman, T., & Forlin, C. (2011). Measuring teacher efficacy to implement inclusive practices. *Journal of Research in Special Educational Needs*, 12(1), 12–21. 10.1111/j.1471-3802.2011.01200.x

Sharp, L. A., Bonjour, G. L., & Cox, E. (2019). Implementing the math workshop approach: An examination of perspectives among elementary, middle, and high school teachers. *International Journal of Instruction*, 12(1), 69–82. 10.29333/iji.2019.1215a

Shemshack, A., & Spector, J. M. (2020). A systematic literature review of personalized learning terms. *Smart Learning Environments*, 7(33), 33. Advance online publication. 10.1186/s40561-020-00140-9

Shinohara, K., & Wobbrock, J. O. (2011). In the shadow of misperception: Assistive technology use and social interactions. CHI 2011, Vancouver.

Shores, M. (2021). Using UDL to explore best practices in teaching online statistics: The impact of COVID-19 on academic learning. In *SITE Interactive Conference* (pp. 257-261). Association for the Advancement of Computing in Education (AACE).

Simpson, M., & Anderson, B. (2009). Redesigning Initial Teacher Education. In *Effective Blended Learning Practices: Evidence-Based Perspectives in ICT-Facilitated Education* (pp. 62–78). IGI Global. 10.4018/978-1-60566-296-1.ch004

Sims, S., & Jerrim, J. (2022). *Traditional and progressive orientations to teaching: new empirical evidence on an old debate* (CEPEO Working Paper No. 22-08). Centre for Education Policy and Equalising Opportunities, UCL. https://EconPapers.repec.org/RePEc:ucl:cepeow:22-08

Sims, S., Fletcher-Wood, H., O'Mara-Eves, A., Cottingham, S., Stansfield, C., Van Herwegen, J., & Anders, J. (2021). *What are the Characteristics of Teacher Professional Development that Increase Pupil Achievement? A systematic review and meta-analysis.* Education Endowment Foundation. https://educationendowmentfoundation.org.uk/education-evidence/evidence-reviews/teacherprofessional-development-characteristics

Siu, Y.-T., & Presley, I. (2020). *Access technology for blind and low vision accessibility.* APH Press, American Printing House for the Blind.

Skinner, M. E., & Smith, A. T. (2011). Creating Success for Students with Learning Disabilities in Postsecondary Foreign Language Courses. *International Journal of Special Education*, 26(2), 42–57.

Slee, R. (2001). Social justice and the changing directions in educational research: The case of inclusive education. *International Journal of Inclusive Education*, 5(2–3), 167–177. 10.1080/13603110010035832

Sleeter, C. (2008). An Invitation To Support Diverse Students Through Teacher Education. *Journal of Teacher Education*, 59(3), 212–219. 10.1177/0022487108317019

Smith Canter, L. L., King, L. H., Williams, J. B., Metcalf, D., & Myrick Potts, K. R. (2017). Evaluating Pedagogy and Practice of Universal Design for Learning in Public Schools. *Exceptionality Education International*, 27(1), 1–16. 10.5206/eei.v27i1.7743

Smith, C. (2020). Challenges and opportunities for teaching students with disabilities during the COVID-19 pandemic. *International Journal of Multidisciplinary Perspectives in Higher Education*, 5(1), 167–173. 10.32674/jimphe.v5i1.2619

Compilation of References

Smith, F. G. (2012). Analyzing a College Course that Adheres to the Universal Design for Learning (UDL) Framework. *The Journal of Scholarship of Teaching and Learning*, 12(3), 31–61. https://scholarworks.iu.edu/journals/index.php/josotl/article/view/2151

Smith, S. J., & Harvey, E. E. (2014). K-12 online lesson alignment to the principles of Universal Design for Learning: The khan academy. *Open Learning*, 29(3), 222–242. 10.1080/02680513.2014.992402

Smith, S. J., Rao, K., Lowrey, K. A., Gardner, J. E., Moore, E., Coy, K., Marino, M., & Wojcik, B. (2019). Recommendations for a national research agenda in UDL: Outcomes from the UDL-IRN preconference on research. *Journal of Disability Policy Studies*, 30(3), 174–185. 10.1177/1044207319826219

Smyth, E., Devlin, A., Bergin, A., & McGuinness, S. (2022). *A North-South comparison of education and training systems: Lessons for policy* [Report]. ESRI. 10.26504/rs138

Souto-Manning, M., Rabadi-Raol, A., Robinson, D., & Perez, A. (2019). What stories do my classroom and its materials tell? Preparing early childhood teachers to engage in equitable and inclusive teaching. *Young Exceptional Children*, 22(2), 62–73. 10.1177/1096250618811619

Sowell, J., & Sugisaki, L. (2021). Accommodating Learning Disabilities in the English Language Classroom. *English Teaching Forum*. https://americanenglish.state.gov/files/ae/resource_files/etf_59_1_pg02-11.pdf

Spina, C. (2021). *Creating Inclusive Libraries by Applying Universal Design: a Guide*. Rowman & Littlefield.

Spratt, J., & Florian, L. (2015). Inclusive pedagogy: From learning to action. Supporting each individual in the context of 'everybody.' *Teaching and Teacher Education*, 49, 89–96. 10.1016/j.tate.2015.03.006

Stake, R. E. (1995). The art of case study research. *Sage (Atlanta, Ga.)*.

Steinbrenner, J. R., Hume, K., Odom, S. L., Morin, K. L., Nowell, S. W., Tomaszewski, B., Szendrey, S., McIntyre, N. S., Yücesoy-Özkan, S., & Savage, M. N. (2020). *Evidence-based practices for children, youth, and young adults with Autism*. The University of North Carolina at Chapel Hill, Frank Porter Graham Child Development Institute, National Clearinghouse on Autism Evidence and Practice Review Team.

Stein, L. (2016). Schools Need Leaders – Not Managers: It's Time for a Paradigm Shift. *Journal of Leadership Education*, 15(2), 21–30. Advance online publication. 10.12806/V15/I2/I3

Stephens, M., & Kaiser, M. R. (2018). A comparison of visual and audio scaffolds in L2 English reading. *Indonesian Journal of Applied Linguistics*, 8(2), 380–387. 10.17509/ijal.v8i2.13303

Stolz, S. A. (2023). The practice of phenomenology in educational research. *Educational Philosophy and Theory*, 55(7), 822–834. 10.1080/00131857.2022.2138745

Strangman, N., Meyer, A., Hall, T., & Proctor, C. P. (2014). New technologies and universal design for learning in the foreign language classroom. In *Worlds apart? Disability and foreign language learning* (pp. 164–176). Yale University Press. 10.12987/yale/9780300116304.003.0009

Sullivan, B., Glenn, M., Roche, M., & McDonagh, C. (2016). *Introduction to critical reflection and action for teacher researchers*. Routledge. 10.4324/9781315693033

Suprayogi, M. N., & Valcke, M. (2016). Differentiated Instruction in Primary Schools: Implementation and Challenges in Indonesia. *PONTE International Scientific Research Journal*, 72(6), 2–18. 10.21506/j.ponte.2016.6.1

Swenor, B. K. (2021). Including disability in all health equity efforts: An urgent call to action. *The Lancet. Public Health*, 6(6), e359–e360. 10.1016/S2468-2667(21)00115-834051160

Swenor, B. K., & Meeks, L. M. (2019). Disability inclusion—Moving beyond mission statements. *The New England Journal of Medicine*, 380(22), 2089–2091. 10.1056/NEJMp190034831141629

Tafazoli, D., & Meihami, H. (2023). Narrative inquiry for CALL teacher preparation programs amidst the COVID-19 pandemic: Language teachers' technological needs and suggestions. *Journal of Computers in Education*, 10(1), 163–187. 10.1007/s40692-022-00227-x

Takahashi, A. R., & Araujo, L. (2020). Case study research: Opening up research opportunities. *RAUSP Management Journal*, 56(1), 100–111. 10.1108/RAUSP-05-2019-0109

Tanase, M. F. (2021). Culturally Responsive Teaching in Urban Secondary Schools. *Education and Urban Society*. Advance online publication. 10.1177/00131245211026689

Tangen, D., & Spooner-Lane, R. (2008). Avoiding the deficit model of teaching: Students who have EAL/EAL and learning difficulties. *Australian Journal of Learning Difficulties*, 13(2), 63–71. 10.1080/19404150802380522

Taunton, S. A., Brian, A., & True, L. (2017). Universally designed motor skill intervention for children with and without disabilities. *Journal of Developmental and Physical Disabilities*, 29(6), 941–954. 10.1007/s10882-017-9565-x

Tefera, A. A., Artiles, A. J., Lester, A., & Cuba, M. (2019). Grappling with the paradoxes of inclusive education in the U.S.: Intersectional considerations in policy and practice. In Hartmann, M., Hummel, M., Lichtblau, M., Löser, J., & Thoms, S. (Eds.), *Facetten Inklusiver Bildung* (pp. 117–125). Klinkhardt.

Ten Hoor, G. A., Plasqui, G., Ruiter, R. A., Kremers, S. P., Rutten, G. M., Schols, A. M., & Kok, G. (2016). A new direction in psychology and health: Resistance exercise training for obese children and adolescents. *Psychology & Health*, 31(1), 1–8. 10.1080/08870446.2015.107015826155905

Text of H.R. 4137 (110th): Higher Education Opportunity Act (Passed Congress version)—GovTrack.us. Retrieved June 16, 2023, from https://www.govtrack.us/congress/bills/110/hr4137/text

Compilation of References

The Teaching Council Act—Teaching Council. (2001). https://www.teachingcouncil.ie/en/about
-us1/relevant-legislation/the-teaching-council-act/

Theriault, M. (2014). French Immersion: A Growing Concern with Growing Pains. *The Manitoba
Teacher*, 92, 8–9.

Thoma, R., Farassopoulos, N., & Lousta, C. (2023). Teaching STEAM through universal design
for learning in early years of primary education: Plugged-in and unplugged activities with emphasis on connectivism learning theory. *Teaching and Teacher Education*, 132, 104210. Advance
online publication. 10.1016/j.tate.2023.104210

Thompson, J. (2023). NASA resilience and leadership: Examining the phenomenon of awe. *Frontiers
in Psychology*, 14, 1158437. Advance online publication. 10.3389/fpsyg.2023.115843737359869

Tindall, D., MacDonald, W., Carroll, E., & Moody, B. (2015). Pre-service teachers' attitudes
towards children with disabilities: An Irish perspective. *European Physical Education Review*,
21(2), 206–221. 10.1177/1356336X14556861

TNTP. (2015). The Mirage: Confronting the Hard Truth about Our Quest for Teacher Development. *The New Teacher Project*. https://files.eric.ed.gov/fulltext/ED558206.pdf

Tobin, T. J., & Behling, K. T. (2018). *Reach everyone, teach everyone: Universal Design for
learning in higher education*. West Virginia University Press.

Tomlinson, C. A. (2014). *The Differentiated Classroom: Responding to the Needs of all Learners*. ASCD.

Toro, V., Camacho-Minuche, G., Pinza-Tapis, E., & Paredes, F. (2019). The Use of the Communicative Language Teaching Approach to Improve Students' Oral Skills. *English Language
Teaching*, 12(1), 110. 10.5539/elt.v12n1p110

Truth and Reconciliation Commission of Canada. (2023). *Exhibits*. https://exhibits.library.utoronto
.ca/items/show/2420

Tuttle, D. W., & Tuttle, N. R. (2004). *Self-esteem and adjusting with blindness: The process of
responding to life's demands*. Charles C. Thomas Publisher Ltd.

Tyler, A. E., Ortega, L., Uno, M., & Park, H. I. (2018). *Usage-inspired L2 instruction: Researched
pedagogy*. John Benjamins. 10.1075/lllt.49

Unal, N. U., Karal, M. A., & Tan, S. (2022). Developing Accessible Lesson Plans with Universal
Design for Learning (UDL*).International Journal of Disability Development and Education*,
69(4), 1442–1456. 10.1080/1034912X.2020.1812539

UNESCO. (1994). *The Salamanca Statement and Framework for Action on Special Needs Education*. Retrieved from the United Nations Educational, Scientific, and Cultural Organization
website: https://unesdoc.unesco.org/ark:/48223/pf0000098427

UNESCO. (2017). *A Guide for Ensuring Inclusion and Equity in Education.* Retrieved from the United Nations Educational, Scientific, and Cultural Organization website: https://unesdoc .unesco.org/ark:/48223/pf0000248254

UNESCO. (2020a). *Towards inclusion in education: Status, trends and challenges.* The UNESCO Salamanca Statement 25 years on. Retrieved from the United Nations Educational, Scientific, and Cultural Organization website: https://unesdoc.unesco.org/ark:/48223/pf0000374246

UNESCO. (2020b). *Inclusion and education: all means all.* Global education monitoring *report.* Retrieved from the United Nations Educational, Scientific, and Cultural Organization website: https://unesdoc.unesco.org/ark:/48223/pf0000373718

United Nations Educational Scientific and Cultural Organisation (UNESCO). (1994). The Salamanca Statement and Framework for Action on Special Needs Education. *Adopted by the World Conference on Special Needs Education: Access and Quality. Salamanca, Spain, 7-10 June, 1994.* https://unesdoc.unesco.org/ark:/48223/pf0000098427

United Nations. (2008). *Convention on the Rights of Persons with Disabilities.* https://www.un .org/disabilities/documents/convention/convoptprot-e.pdf

United Nations. (2020a). *Decade of Action. Ten Years to Transform Our World.* Retrieved from the United Nations Educational, Scientific, and Cultural Organization website: https://www.un .org/sustainabledevelopment/decade-of-action

United Nations. (2020b). *The sustainable development goal report—SDG Indicators.* Retrieved from the United Nations Educational, Scientific, and Cultural Organization website: https:// unstats.un.org/sdgs/report/2020/

United Nations. (2023). *The 17 Goals.* https://sdgs.un.org/goals

United States Department of Education [USDofE] (2023) *The State of School Diversity in the United States.* Office of Planning, Evaluation and Policy Development. https://www2.ed.gov/ rschstat/eval/resources/diversity.pdf

University of New Brunswick and Department of Education & Early Childhood Development. (2014) Universal Design for Learning Action Research. Department of Education & Early Childhood Development. https://www2.gnb.ca/content/dam/gnb/Departments/ed/pdf/ UDLActionResearch.pdf

Uyen, B. P., Tong, D. H., & Lien, N. B. (2022). The Effectiveness of Experiential Learning in Teaching Arithmetic and Geometry in Sixth Grade. *Frontiers in Education*, 7, 858631. 10.3389/ feduc.2022.858631

Valencia, R. R. (2010). *Dismantling contemporary deficit thinking.* Routledge., 10.4324/9780203853214

Vanorsdale, C. (2019) Communicative Language Teaching in E-Learning: How Confident are the Instructors? *E-Learn 2017 Proceedings*, 489-493

Compilation of References

Vargas-Hernandez, J. G., Rodríguez-Maillard, C., & Vargas-González, O. C. (2023). Organizational Ecology and Its Implications on Organizational Ecological Innovation. *Journal of Business Ecosystems*, 4(1), 1–16. 10.4018/JBE.320482

Varma, R., Vajaranant, T., & Burkemper, B. (2016). Visual impairment and blindness in adults in the United States: Demographic and geographic variations from 2015 to 2050. *Journal of the American Medical Association: Opthalmology*, 134(7), 802–809.27197072

Vasilez, J. (2023) *Indigenizing Education: Universal Design for Learning and Indigenous Leadership Frameworks.* Ed.D. Dissertations in Practice, 76. University of Washington Tacoma. https://digitalcommons.tacoma.uw.edu/edd_capstones/76

Vasilez, J. (2023). *Indigenizing Education: Universal Design for Learning and Indigenous Leadership Frameworks.* Ed.D. Thesis, Dissertations in Practice. University of Washington Tacoma. https://digitalcommons.tacoma.uw.edu/edd_capstones/76

Vitelli, E. M. (2015). Universal Design for Learning: Are We Teaching It to Preservice General Education Teachers? *Journal of Special Education Technology*, 30(3), 166–178. 10.1177/0162643415618931

Vostal, B. R., & Mrachko, A. A. (2021). Using the "Universal Design for Learning" Framework to Plan for All Students in the Classroom: Encouraging Executive Functions. *The Elementary STEM Journal*, 25(3), 32–36.

Vostal, B. R., Oehrtman, J. P., & Gilfillan, B. (2023). School Counselors Engaging All Students: Universal Design for Learning in Classroom Lesson Planning. *Professional School Counseling*, 27(1). Advance online publication. 10.1177/2156759X231203199

Vygotsky, L. (1962). *Thought and language.* MIT Press. 10.1037/11193-000

Vygotsky, L. S. (1980). *Mind in Society: Development of Higher Psychological Processes* (Cole, M., John-Steiner, V., Scribner, S., & Souberman, E., Eds.). Harvard University Press.

W3C. (2018). *Web Content Accessibility Guidelines (WCAG) 2.1.* Retrieved June 9 from https://www.w3.org/TR/WCAG21/

Waitoller, F. R., & Artiles, A. J. (2013). A decade of professional development research for inclusive education a critical review and notes for a research program. *Review of Educational Research*, 83(3), 319–356. 10.3102/0034654313483905

Waitoller, F. R., & King Thorius, K. A. (2016). Cross-pollinating culturally sustaining pedagogy and universal design for learning: Toward an inclusive pedagogy that accounts for dis/ability. *Harvard Educational Review*, 86(3), 366–389. 10.17763/1943-5045-86.3.366

Warrick, D. D. (2023). Revisiting resistance to change and how to manage it: What has been learned and what organizations need to do. *Business Horizons*, 66(4), 433–441. 10.1016/j.bushor.2022.09.001

Waxman, H.C., Alford, B.L., Brown, D.B., Hattie, J., & Anderman, E.M. (2013). Individualized Instruction. *International Guide to Student Achievement*, 405–407

Webb, A. S., & Welsh, A. J. (2019). Phenomenology As a Methodology for Scholarship of Teaching and Learning Research. *Teaching & Learning Inquiry*, 7(1), 168–181. 10.20343/teachlearninqu.7.1.11

Weiss, C. R., & Johnson-Koenke, R. (2023). Narrative Inquiry as a Caring and Relational Research Approach: Adopting an Evolving Paradigm. *Qualitative Health Research*, 33(5), 388–399. 10.1177/10497323231158619368032 13

Wertz, F. J. (2023). Phenomenological methodology, methods, and procedures for research in psychology. In Cooper, H., Coutanche, M. N., McMullen, L. M., Panter, A. T., Rindskopf, D., & Sher, K. J. (Eds.), *APA handbook of research methods in psychology: Research designs: Quantitative, qualitative, neuropsychological, and biological* (pp. 83–105). American Psychological Association. 10.1037/0000319-005

White, J. (2015, May 27) Teachers frustrated with inclusive classrooms, NLTA says. *CBC News.* https://www.cbc.ca/news/canada/newfoundland-labrador/teachers-frustrated-with-inclusive-classrooms-nlta-says-1.3088326

Whitehead, I. A. (2019). *The Transformation of Initial Teacher Education: The Changing Nature of Teacher Training*. Routledge. 10.4324/9780429424564

Wight, M. C. S. (2015). Students with Learning Disabilities in the Foreign Language Learning Environment and the Practice of Exemption. *Foreign Language Annals*, 48(1), 39–55. 10.1111/flan.12122

Wilkins, C., & Lall, R. (2011). 'You've got to be tough and I'm trying': Black and minority ethnic student teachers' experiences of initial teacher education. *Race, Ethnicity and Education*, 14(3), 365–386. 10.1080/13613324.2010.543390

Wilson, M., & Mackie, K. (2018) Design. In *Learning by Doing: Postsecondary Experiential Education*. Open Library. https://ecampusontario.pressbooks.pub/adultedpseee/chapter/developing-ee-design-phase/

Winzer, M. A. (2007). Confronting difference: An excursion through the history of special education. In Florian, L. (Ed.), *The SAGE Handbook of Special Education* (pp. 20–30). Sage Publications. 10.4135/9781848607989.n3

Wise, N. (2012). Access to Special Education for Exceptional Pupils in French Immersion Program: An Equity Issue. In *Proceedings of the Canadian Parents for French Roundtable on Academically Challenged Students in French Second Language Programs* (pp. 34-38). Canadian Parents for French.

Wolbring, G., & Nguyen, A. (2023). Equity/Equality, Diversity and Inclusion, and Other EDI Phrases and EDI Policy Frameworks: A Scoping Review. *Trends in Higher Education*, 2(1), 168–237. 10.3390/higheredu2010011

Compilation of References

Woll, B., & Wei, L. (2019). *Cognitive Benefits of Language Learning: Broadening our perspectives*. Final Report to the British Academy, British Academy. https://www.thebritishacademy.ac .uk/sites/default/files/Cognitive-Benefits-LanguageLearning-Final-Report.pdf

Woodcock, S., Gibbs, K., Hitches, E., & Regan, C. (2023). Investigating Teachers' Beliefs in Inclusive Education and Their Levels of Teacher Self-Efficacy: Are Teachers Constrained in Their Capacity to Implement Inclusive Teaching Practices? *Education Sciences*, 13(3), 280. 10.3390/educsci13030280

World Health Organization. (2022). *Global report on assistive technology*. https://apps.who.int/ iris/bitstream/handle/10665/354357/9789240049451-eng.pdf

Wormsley, D. P., & D'Andrea, F. M. (1997). *Instructional Strategies for Braille Literacy*. American Foundation for the Blind.

Wulandari, D., Shandy Narmaditya, B., Hadi Utomo, S., & Hilmi Prayi, P. (2019). Teachers' Perception on Classroom Action Research. *KnE Social Sciences*, 3(11), 313. 10.18502/kss.v3i11.4015

Wu, Y.-H., Martiniello, N., & Swenor, B. K. (2021). Building a More Accessible Conference for Researchers With Vision Impairment. *JAMA Ophthalmology*. Advance online publication. 10.1001/jamaophthalmol.2021.561334967843

Xin, W., Liu, C., Zhang, Z., & Yao, X. (2023). A person-centred examination of inclusive teachers' beliefs about teaching students with intellectual and developmental disabilities: Profiles and relations to teacher efficacy. *International Journal of Developmental Disabilities*, 1–13. Advance online publication. 10.1080/20473869.2023.2196470

Yazan, B. (2015). Three approaches to case study methods in education: Yin, Merriam and Stake. *The Qualitative Report*, 20(2), 134–152. 10.46743/2160-3715/2015.2102

Ydo, Y. (2020). Inclusive education: Global priority, collective responsibility. *Prospects*, 49(3), 97–101. 10.1007/s11125-020-09520-y

Yildiz, K. (2022). Experiential learning from the perspective of outdoor education leaders. *Journal of Hospitality, Leisure, Sport and Tourism Education*, 30, 100343. Advance online publication. 10.1016/j.jhlste.2021.100343

Yin, R. (2014). *Case study research: design and methods* (5th ed.). Sage Publication.

Yin, R. K. (2018). *Case study research - design and methods* (6th ed.). Sage Publications.

Young, S. (2014). *I'm not your inspiration, thank you very much*. TEDx. https://www.ted.com/ talks/stella_young_i_m_not_your_inspiration_thank_you_very_much?language=en

Zaic, B. (2021) A Personalized Learning Approach to Educating Students Identified with Special Education Needs. Project in MSc in Special Education, *Culminating Projects in Special Education, 98*. https://repository.stcloudstate.edu/sped_etds/98

Zhang, X. (2020). A bibliometric analysis of second language acquisition between 1997 and 2018. *Studies in Second Language Acquisition*, 42(1), 199–222. 10.1017/S0272263119000573

Zhao, L., Hwang, W. Y., & Shih, T. K. (2021). Investigation of the physical learning environment of distance learning under COVID-19 and its influence on students' health and learning satisfaction. *International Journal of Distance Education Technologies*, 19(2), 77–98. 10.4018/IJDET.20210401.oa4

Zulu, P. M. (2019). Teachers' Understanding and Attitudes towards Communicative Language Teaching Method in ESL Classrooms of Zambia. *International Journal of Humanities Social Sciences and Education*, 6(6), 1–13.

About the Contributors

Frederic Fovet is an Associate Professor within the School of Education and Technology at Royal Roads University in Canada. He has previously been an Assistant Professor in the Faculty of Education at the University of Prince Edward Island. Frederic has also been Director of the Office for Students with Disabilities at McGill University for a period of 4 years, over the duration of his PhD. He was responsible in this role for the campus wide development of UDL. Frederic acts as a consultant on UDL, both domestically and internationally, in the K-12 and post-secondary sectors. Frederic was the instigator and Program Chair for the three first Pan-Canadian Conferences on UDL which were held in 2015, 2017 and 2019, in Montreal, Charlottetown, and Victoria respectively. He has been a member of the editorial board of the International Journal of Disability and Social Justice (IJDSJ) since its launch in 2020.

* * *

Karen Buckley is an Assistant Professor in the School of Inclusive and Special Education at the Institute of Education at DCU. As a qualified post-primary teacher and experienced lecturer in teacher education, Karen has enjoyed working across a range of educational settings in second level, further education and higher education. With particular research interest in inclusive pedagogy, Karen is an advocate for inclusive practice to improve and optimise teaching, learning and assessment in higher education. Karen holds a Bachelor of Arts Degree in English and Sociology, a Master of Arts Degree in Sociology and Post Graduate Diploma in Education. She is currently a Doctoral candidate in Maynooth University where she is exploring Teacher Education, Identity and Professional Development practices.

Sarah Dunne is an English and Religious Education teacher in Kingswood Community College. She completes her undergraduate degree in Mater Dei Institute of Education- a college of DCU and her Professional Masters of Education in Trinity College Dublin.

Margaret Flood is an Assistant Professor in Inclusive Education at Maynooth University Ireland. Her experience in inclusive and special education includes teaching, teacher professional learning design and delivery, policy development and curriculum design. As a Fulbright Scholar, in 2021 Margaret worked with Lynch School of Education and Humanities at Boston College and CAST to explore equity, diversity, inclusion, and social justice through the lens of UDL. She was also a member for the UDL Guidelines 3.0 Collaborative from working on the review of Guidelines 2.2 to design the new 3.0 Guidelines. Margaret is the creator and host of #UDLchatIE and of the Podcast 'Talking about all things Inclusion'.

About the Contributors

Tracy Galvin is a Lecturer in Higher Education Academic Practice at the Center for Curriculum Enhancement and Approval. Tracy's key areas of expertise are initial teacher education, academic practice, and professional development in inclusive, equitable, and accessible curriculum design. Her research and professional practice are underpinned by Universal Design for Learning (UDL) principles and Equality, Diversity, and Inclusion (EDI). Tracy has led institutional projects and change across several universities to inform inclusive pedagogies to better support learner outcomes and experiences. She holds SFHEA and SFSEDA, where she also acts as a mentor and assessor to support learning and teachig in HE. She co-leads the professional development team with INCLUDE (International Collaboratory for Leadership in Universally Designed Education), an international community of practice network for UDL.

Pam Gurney is an Assistant Teaching Professor at Thompson Rivers University. She currently teaches in the Bachelor of Education and Graduate Programs. Pam has served as an educator for over 25 years spanning roles such as elementary teacher, high school teacher, Learning Support Teacher, Assistive Technology Resource Teacher, ELL Resource Teacher, and District Coordinator of Inclusive Education Services. Her interests involve neurodiversities, assistive technology, and inclusion.

Kathy Howery is an educational consultant and has been a sessional lecturer at several Universities in Alberta. Kathy has published in the area of Universal Design for Learning and students with significant intellectual disabilities, and the lived experience of students who use Speech Generating Devices to communicate. In addition, Kathy has co-authored several book chapters focusing best practices in providing supports and services to students with complex needs.Kathy provides ongoing consultation to several Alberta school jurisdictions.

Alisa Lowrey is a professor in the School of Education at the University of Southern Mississippi. Alisa's work centers around efforts to prepare teachers to serve individuals with the most significant support needs in inclusive settings in both K-12 and postsecondary settings. This has taken her down her current path of examining the implementation of UDL and EBPs in inclusive educational systems.

Natalina Martiniello received a B.A. in English Literature and Educational Studies from McGill University and a M.Sc and Ph.D. in Vision Science (Vision Impairment and Rehabilitation) from Université de Montréal. She is an Assistant Professor at the School of Optometry, Université de Montréal, where her research focuses on braille, accessibility and inclusive technology for individuals who are blind or who have low vision. She previously worked as a Certified Vision Rehabilitation Therapist, providing braille and assistive technology instruction to individuals with visual impairments of all ages. As a researcher, practitioner and person with lived experience, she regularly writes and presents on inclusion, diversity, equity and accessibility for individuals with visual impairments, especially as this relates to digital accessibility, access to information and braille literacy. She is the Past-President of Braille Literacy Canada.

Louise O'Reilly is an Education Officer with the National Council for Curriculum and Assessment with responsibility for English, Senior Cycle programmes, and, Drama, Theatre and Film Studies. Louise's research interests include curriculum development, assessment, critical literacy and partnership in policy development. Louise has just completed her doctoral thesis, Perspectives on Partnership, with the School of Education in UCD.

Jennifer Roberts is a lecturer in Education at the School of Social Sciences, Education and Social Work at Queen's University Belfast. Jennifer is a trained teacher and has worked in Initial Teacher Education in Northern Ireland since 2016. She is currently the pathway convenor for PGCE English at QUB and her expertise is in developing ways to make learning accessible to all pupils in the classroom. Of particular interest are those who are at risk of academic underachievement. Her research interests are around pedagogy in the classroom, including initial teacher education and how best to equip candidates for the profession. Jennifer has led projects on inclusive practice, literacy, reading and program evaluation.

About the Contributors

Leonard Troughton is a special educator with 20+ years of experience working with individuals with emotional and behavioral disabilities. His teaching and research include (a) use of cognitive-behavioral and social skills interventions for students with EBD, (b) supporting educational transitions for students with EBD, (c) providing classroom and behavioral management strategies for general and special education teachers, and (d) preparing future special education teachers to work with students with disabilities, particularly those students with EBD. Dr. Troughton currently is an Assistant Professor in the Special Education Program at the University of Southern Mississippi.

Lauren Tucker is an associate professor in the special education department. She has a dual certification in special and regular education with over 10 years in the field. Dr. Tucker has expertise in assistive technology, universal design for learning, online learning, and technology implementation. She conducts assistive technology evaluations, consultations, and trainings around the state of Connecticut. Dr. Tucker passionately promotes universal design for learning to enhance learning for all individuals. Her research focuses on technology integration, teacher learning, assistive technology for accommodations, and implementing communication and visual supports.

Haley Whitelaw is a Professor and program coordinator at the Norton Wolf School of Aviation and Aerospace Technology at Fanshawe College (Ontario, Canada) since 2022. Prior to Aviation, Haley developed curriculum and taught at Fanshawe's School of Tourism, Hospitality & Culinary Arts since 2013. Haley is a graduate of the Master of Arts in Interdisciplinary Studies program at Royal Roads University (British Columbia, Canada).

Index

A

academic achievement 29, 31, 32, 183
Action Research 3, 29, 36, 46, 50, 61, 62, 82, 102, 130, 131, 132, 133, 134, 136, 154, 155, 156, 157, 158, 281, 320
Alternate Secondary Pathways 108, 118

B

Bilingual Classroom 160, 161, 162, 163, 164
bilingual education 161, 162, 163, 164, 166, 177, 178, 179, 181, 183

C

Childhood Development 29, 36, 46, 52, 281
childhood education 188, 189, 191, 192, 203, 210, 218, 291
Children's Mental and Physical Health 192, 193, 202, 211
civil rights 220, 230
classroom observation 84, 87, 88, 90, 96, 105
Classroom Practice 309
coaching logs 87, 88, 92, 93, 96, 97, 98
Communicative Methods 161, 162, 164, 165, 166, 167, 172, 174, 175, 186
competency frameworks 285, 286, 288, 295, 296, 304, 309, 311
COVID-19 Pandemic 109, 135, 188, 191, 193, 196, 198, 205, 206, 207, 208, 211, 214, 216, 217, 247, 276, 280
curriculum outcomes 29, 39, 43, 44

D

data collection 10, 62, 86, 106, 112, 136, 140, 146, 149
deficit model 4, 5, 9, 16, 23, 27, 160, 161, 165, 173, 185, 255, 256, 260, 267, 268, 309

Design Learning 31
digital revolution 220
disabling barriers 220, 221, 222
Diverse Learners 4, 5, 6, 9, 15, 23, 62, 107, 108, 119, 120, 155, 160, 163, 164, 165, 171, 173, 175, 178, 191, 195, 207, 255, 256, 269, 277, 281, 282, 287, 307, 310, 312, 314
Diversity 4, 5, 7, 17, 62, 68, 74, 107, 110, 118, 121, 122, 129, 166, 167, 172, 174, 176, 186, 187, 203, 219, 220, 221, 223, 224, 225, 226, 227, 233, 236, 237, 238, 241, 242, 243, 244, 249, 254, 255, 256, 257, 274, 280, 281, 282, 285, 287, 292, 293, 294, 306, 307, 308, 309, 310, 311, 316, 317, 318

E

Early Childhood 21, 29, 36, 39, 46, 50, 52, 54, 156, 177, 188, 189, 191, 192, 203, 210, 214, 215, 216, 218, 251, 275, 281, 291
Early Childhood Education 188, 189, 191, 192, 203, 210, 218, 291
educational technologies 192, 220, 221, 233, 241, 243, 244
Elementary Education 11, 35, 36
Evidence-Based Practices 35, 80, 81, 84, 85, 89, 90, 94, 99, 106, 134

F

French Immersion 162, 163, 164, 173, 177, 178, 181, 182, 183, 184, 185
Further Education 107, 108, 109, 111, 120, 121, 123, 126, 286, 291, 306, 316

G

Global Perspective 112
grade-level curriculum 29, 39

H

Hybrid Course 131

I

inclusive education 19, 21, 23, 25, 26, 35, 36, 51, 52, 55, 56, 57, 75, 77, 78, 89, 102, 106, 122, 124, 155, 156, 176, 214, 222, 266, 273, 274, 275, 279, 285, 286, 287, 289, 294, 297, 303, 307, 308, 310, 311, 312, 314, 315, 317, 318, 319, 320, 322

Inclusive Practices 54, 55, 57, 63, 75, 80, 81, 83, 84, 89, 94, 99, 101, 102, 103, 106, 121, 154, 179, 258

incremental improvements 193, 211

Initial Teacher Education 75, 78, 285, 286, 291, 293, 294, 298, 300, 302, 304, 311, 313, 315, 316, 317, 319, 320, 322

In-Service Teachers 8, 14, 130, 132, 153, 154, 163, 173, 174, 239, 267

Interactive Multi-Sensory Physical Movements 188, 189, 191, 193, 211

J

Junior Cycle 53, 54, 56, 57, 60, 61, 63, 66, 67, 68, 71, 72, 75, 76, 77, 286

K

K-12 Education 10, 111, 160

K-12 Schools 81, 111, 174, 219

K-12 Sector 1, 2, 5, 6, 10, 11, 13, 19, 107, 108, 110, 111, 112, 118, 120, 160, 164, 167, 168, 173, 174, 253, 254, 255, 256, 262, 266, 269, 270, 271, 272, 281, 282

L

language teacher 160, 167, 169, 172, 176, 182

learning environment 30, 31, 32, 33, 34, 35, 36, 37, 38, 39, 40, 41, 42, 45, 57, 61, 62, 66, 69, 139, 142, 184, 185, 191, 192, 193, 194, 206, 213, 218, 222, 238, 254, 285, 299, 300

learning needs 62, 83, 194, 201, 218, 226, 306, 309

learning opportunities 45, 56, 60, 75, 82, 117, 140, 192, 223, 235, 236, 286, 287, 288, 289, 293, 306, 311

Learning Programmes 56, 63, 75, 78

Lesson Plans 48, 62, 68, 128, 138, 194, 196, 198, 203, 204, 206, 207, 211, 241, 264

lived experiences 10, 24, 55, 167, 225, 242, 256

M

Management of Change 2, 10, 12, 15, 19, 27, 267, 269, 271

middle class 3, 18

Model Practices 4, 9, 19, 27, 160, 256, 260, 261, 267

Multi-Sensory Environment 193, 194, 196, 218

P

PD package 83, 87, 94

phenomenological analysis 167

physical movements 138, 188, 189, 191, 193, 202, 211, 218

power dynamics 3, 9, 164, 172, 186

pre-service teacher 5, 8, 9, 14, 160, 163, 173, 180, 267, 268, 285

primary education 53, 54, 55, 65, 280, 286, 291, 292

Professional development 4, 8, 13, 20, 25, 51, 75, 80, 81, 90, 94, 96, 105, 106, 153, 155, 160, 163, 174, 178, 179, 180, 204, 256, 259, 261, 262, 263, 265, 267, 268, 273, 276, 278, 279, 280, 291, 292, 294, 295, 296, 298, 306, 307, 308, 311, 313, 314, 320, 322

professional learning 20, 36, 45, 49, 50, 56, 75, 82, 86, 302, 311

professional standard 296, 310, 311

public education 29, 30, 35, 36, 39, 41, 45, 50

Q

qualitative data 112, 196, 199

S

school-based teams 36, 50
second language 7, 11, 160, 161, 162, 164, 165, 166, 167, 168, 169, 170, 171, 172, 174, 175, 176, 177, 178, 180, 181, 182, 183, 185, 186
Second Language Instruction 160, 164, 180, 186
simple solution 193, 211
special education 22, 26, 55, 77, 78, 91, 106, 126, 130, 135, 138, 141, 143, 145, 146, 149, 150, 153, 154, 157, 177, 182, 183, 184, 185, 186, 189, 194, 206, 214, 250, 268, 273, 274, 275, 279, 288, 311, 313, 316, 320, 321
special educator 83, 90
Students With Disabilities 31, 35, 36, 102, 118, 125, 133, 150, 161, 163, 164, 166, 168, 170, 171, 173, 175, 178, 179, 183, 213, 217, 220, 221, 238, 247, 255, 275, 278, 292, 307, 310, 311
Student Teachers 285, 286, 293, 294, 295, 297, 298, 300, 301, 302, 305, 306, 307, 308, 309, 310, 312, 313, 318, 320, 322

T

Teacher Competencies 284, 285, 296, 299, 304, 310
team-based approach 195, 202, 205, 210, 211
text-to-speech software 220, 223, 224, 226, 228, 230, 232, 233, 234, 235, 237, 239, 240
Theory and Practice 78, 176, 253, 254, 266, 269, 272
Three UDL Principles 119, 129, 166, 169, 186, 204, 256, 282
Tour Guides 107, 109, 113
Traditional classrooms 188, 196
training sessions 96, 98, 197, 198, 202, 204, 206, 207, 208, 211

U

UDL Implementation 1, 2, 3, 6, 9, 10, 11, 12, 13, 14, 15, 16, 17, 18, 19, 22, 27, 29, 35, 36, 37, 42, 47, 50, 62, 63, 75, 83, 87, 105, 111, 112, 117, 119, 120, 121, 131, 133, 134, 135, 141, 172, 175, 180, 188, 189, 218, 220, 222, 244, 253, 254, 257, 258, 260, 262, 265, 266, 269, 270, 271, 272, 275, 282, 307, 308, 315
Universal Design 1, 4, 20, 21, 22, 23, 24, 25, 26, 27, 29, 30, 31, 51, 52, 53, 54, 56, 57, 77, 78, 80, 81, 105, 106, 107, 108, 110, 122, 123, 124, 125, 126, 127, 128, 129, 130, 131, 132, 146, 155, 156, 157, 160, 161, 165, 169, 176, 177, 178, 179, 180, 181, 183, 184, 185, 187, 188, 189, 191, 213, 214, 215, 216, 217, 219, 220, 221, 222, 233, 235, 236, 243, 247, 250, 253, 255, 267, 268, 273, 274, 275, 276, 277, 278, 279, 280, 281, 282, 285, 296, 310, 312, 313, 314, 315, 316, 317, 318, 319, 320, 321
Universal Design for Learning (UDL) 1, 4, 20, 21, 22, 23, 24, 25, 26, 27, 29, 30, 31, 51, 52, 53, 54, 57, 77, 78, 80, 81, 105, 106, 107, 108, 110, 122, 123, 124, 125, 126, 127, 128, 129, 130, 131, 146, 155, 156, 157, 160, 161, 165, 169, 176, 177, 178, 179, 180, 181, 183, 184, 185, 187, 188, 189, 191, 213, 214, 216, 217, 247, 250, 253, 255, 267, 268, 273, 274, 275, 276, 277, 278, 279, 280, 281, 282, 285, 296, 312, 313, 314, 315, 316, 317, 318, 319, 320, 321

V

Virtual Tour 107, 109, 113, 114, 116
Visual Impairment 222, 223, 224, 225, 227, 245, 246, 247, 248, 249, 250, 251, 252
Vocational Education 120, 121, 123, 124, 125

W

writing instruction 85, 86, 88, 95

Publishing Tomorrow's Research Today

Uncover Current Insights and Future Trends in Education

with IGI Global's Cutting-Edge Recommended Books

Print Only, E-Book Only, or Print + E-Book.
Order direct through IGI Global's Online Bookstore at www.igi-global.com or through your preferred provider.

ISBN: 9781668493007
© 2023; 234 pp.
List Price: US$ 215

ISBN: 9798369300749
© 2024; 383 pp.
List Price: US$ 230

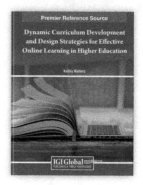

ISBN: 9781668486467
© 2023; 471 pp.
List Price: US$ 215

ISBN: 9781668465387
© 2024; 389 pp.
List Price: US$ 215

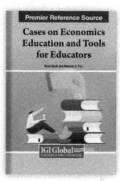

ISBN: 9781668475836
© 2024; 359 pp.
List Price: US$ 215

ISBN: 9781668444238
© 2023; 334 pp.
List Price: US$ 240

Do you want to stay current on the latest research trends, product announcements, news, and special offers? Join IGI Global's mailing list to receive customized recommendations, exclusive discounts, and more.
Sign up at: www.igi-global.com/newsletters.

Scan the QR Code here to view more related titles in Education.

www.igi-global.com | Sign up at www.igi-global.com/newsletters | facebook.com/igiglobal | twitter.com/igiglobal | linkedin.com/igiglobal

Ensure Quality Research is Introduced to the Academic Community

Become a Reviewer for IGI Global Authored Book Projects

  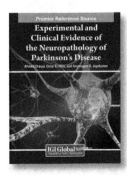 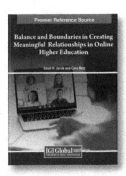

The overall success of an authored book project is dependent on quality and timely manuscript evaluations.

Applications and Inquiries may be sent to:
development@igi-global.com

Applicants must have a doctorate (or equivalent degree) as well as publishing, research, and reviewing experience. Authored Book Evaluators are appointed for one-year terms and are expected to complete at least three evaluations per term. Upon successful completion of this term, evaluators can be considered for an additional term.

If you have a colleague that may be interested in this opportunity, we encourage you to share this information with them.

Publishing Tomorrow's Research Today
IGI Global
e-Book Collection

Including Essential Reference Books Within Three Fundamental Academic Areas

Business & Management
Scientific, Technical, & Medical (STM)
Education

- Acquisition options include Perpetual, Subscription, and Read & Publish
- No Additional Charge for Multi-User Licensing
- No Maintenance, Hosting, or Archiving Fees
- Continually Enhanced Accessibility Compliance Features (WCAG)

| Over **150,000+** Chapters | Contributions From **200,000+** Scholars Worldwide | More Than **1,000,000+** Citations | Majority of e-Books Indexed in Web of Science & Scopus | Consists of Tomorrow's Research Available Today! |

Recommended Titles from our e-Book Collection

Innovation Capabilities and Entrepreneurial Opportunities of Smart Working
ISBN: 9781799887973

Advanced Applications of Generative AI and Natural Language Processing Models
ISBN: 9798369305027

Using Influencer Marketing as a Digital Business Strategy
ISBN: 9798369305515

Human-Centered Approaches in Industry 5.0
ISBN: 9798369326473

Modeling and Monitoring Extreme Hydrometeorological Events
ISBN: 9781668487716

Data-Driven Intelligent Business Sustainability
ISBN: 9798369300497

Information Logistics for Organizational Empowerment and Effective Supply Chain Management
ISBN: 9798369301593

Data Envelopment Analysis (DEA) Methods for Maximizing Efficiency
ISBN: 9798369302552

Request More Information, or Recommend the IGI Global e-Book Collection to Your Institution's Librarian

For More Information or to Request a Free Trial, Contact IGI Global's e-Collections Team: eresources@igi-global.com | 1-866-342-6657 ext. 100 | 717-533-8845 ext. 100

Printed in the USA
CPSIA information can be obtained
at www.ICGtesting.com
LVHW081756041124
795688LV00005B/604

9 781668 447505